# UNDERSTANDING DATABASES

UNDERSTANDING DATA TYPES

# UNDERSTANDING DATABASES

## CONCEPTS AND PRACTICE

**Suzanne W. Dietrich**
*Arizona State University*

| SENIOR VP | Smita Bakshi |
| SENIOR DIRECTOR | Don Fowley |
| EDITORIAL ASSISTANT | Molly Geisinger |
| SENIOR MANAGING EDITOR | Judy Howarth |
| SENIOR PRODUCTION EDITOR | Loganathan Kandan |
| COVER PHOTO CREDIT | © photographs/Getty Images |

This book was set in 9.5/12.5 pt Source Sans Pro by Straive™.

Founded in 1807, John Wiley & Sons, Inc. has been a valued source of knowledge and understanding for more than 200 years, helping people around the world meet their needs and fulfill their aspirations. Our company is built on a foundation of principles that include responsibility to the communities we serve and where we live and work. In 2008, we launched a Corporate Citizenship Initiative, a global effort to address the environmental, social, economic, and ethical challenges we face in our business. Among the issues we are addressing are carbon impact, paper specifications and procurement, ethical conduct within our business and among our vendors, and community and charitable support. For more information, please visit our website: www.wiley.com/go/citizenship.

Evaluation copies are provided to qualified academics and professionals for review purposes only, for use in their courses during the next academic year. These copies are licensed and may not be sold or transferred to a third party. Upon completion of the review period, please return the evaluation copy to Wiley. Return instructions and a free of charge return shipping label are available at: www.wiley.com/go/returnlabel. If you have chosen to adopt this textbook for use in your course, please accept this book as your complimentary desk copy. Outside of the United States, please contact your local sales representative.

ISBN: 978-1-119-58064-5 (PBK)
ISBN: 978-1-119-82800-6 (EVALC)

### Library of Congress Cataloging-in-Publication Data

Names: Dietrich, Suzanne Wagner, author.
Title: Understanding databases : concepts and practice / Suzanne W.
   Dietrich, Arizona State University.
Description: Hoboken, NJ : Wiley, [2021] | Includes bibliographical
   references and index.
Identifiers: LCCN 2021015796 (print) | LCCN 2021015797 (ebook) | ISBN
   9781119580645 (paperback) | ISBN 9781119827948 (adobe pdf) | ISBN
   9781119580669 (epub)
Subjects: LCSH: Relational databases.
Classification: LCC QA76.9.D32 D535 2021 (print) | LCC QA76.9.D32 (ebook)
   | DDC 005.75/6—dc23
LC record available at https://lccn.loc.gov/2021015796
LC ebook record available at https://lccn.loc.gov/2021015797

The inside back cover will contain printing identification and country of origin if omitted from this page. In addition, if the ISBN on the back cover differs from the ISBN on this page, the one on the back cover is correct.

SKY10027880_070121

*To my Jerry,*

*Whose perseverance and ingenuity*
*shine as guiding stars in my universe*

*With Love,*
*Suzanne*

# CONTENTS

LIST OF FIGURES      XV
LIST OF TABLES      XIX
PREFACE      XXIII

**1 INTRODUCTION TO DATABASES AND THE RELATIONAL DATA MODEL**      1

   **1.1**    Databases Are a Tool,    1
   **1.2**    Overview of Data and Models,    3
   **1.3**    The Relational Data Model,    7
       **1.3.1**    Definition,    7
       **1.3.2**    Uniqueness,    8
       **1.3.3**    Referential Integrity,    9
         ■ Special Topic 1.1: Primary Key and Referential
           Integrity,    13
       **1.3.4**    Additional Constraints,    13
   Chapter Notes Summary,    14
   Chapter Reminders,    15
   Practice,    16
       Practice Problems: MLS,    16
       Practice Problems: COURSE SCHEDULE,    16
   End of Chapter Exercises,    17
   Answers to Self-Check Questions,    18
   Answers to Practice Problems: MLS,    18
   Answers to Practice Problems: COURSE SCHEDULE,    19
   Bibliographic Notes,    20
   More to Explore,    20

**2 CONCEPTUAL DESIGN**      21

   **2.1**    Gathering Requirements,    21
   **2.2**    Entity-Relationship Diagrams,    22
         ■ How to 2.1: Design an ER Diagram,    24
         ■ Special Topic 2.2: (**Min, Max**) Pairs,    26
         ■ Special Topic 2.3: Recursive Relationships and Role
           Names,    26
         ■ Special Topic 2.4: Ternary Relationships,    27
         ■ Special Topic 2.5: EER for Modeling Inheritance,    27
   **2.3**    Mapping ER Diagrams to Tables,    29
         ■ How to 2.6: Map an ER Diagram to Relations,    31

**2.4**    Other Graphical Approaches,    33
Chapter Notes Summary,    35
Chapter Reminders,    36
Practice,    36
    Practice Problems: INVESTMENT PORTFOLIO,    36
    Practice Problems: NEW HOME,    37
    Practice Problems: WEB PAGE,    38
End of Chapter Exercises,    38
Answers to Self-Check Questions,    40
Answers to Practice Problems: INVESTMENT PORTFOLIO,    41
Answers to Practice Problems: NEW HOME,    42
Answers to Practice Problems: WEB PAGE,    47
Bibliographic Notes,    50
More to Explore,    50

**3    RELATIONAL ALGEBRA    51**

**3.1**    Query Design,    51
    ■ How to 3.1: Query Design,    51
**3.2**    Algebra Operators,    55
    ■ Note 3.2: Overview of Relational Algebra,    55
**3.2.1**    Filtering,    55
**3.2.2**    Sets,    57
**3.2.3**    Joins,    59
**3.2.4**    Division,    60
**3.3**    Relational Completeness,    62
    Aggregation and Grouping,    63
**3.4**    Query Optimization,    64
    ■ How to 3.3: Heuristic Query Optimization,    65
Chapter Notes Summary,    68
Chapter Reminders,    68
Practice,    68
    Practice Problems: INVESTMENT PORTFOLIO,    69
    Practice Problems: NEW HOME,    70
    Practice Problems: WEB PAGE,    70
End of Chapter Exercises,    71
Answers to Self-Check Questions,    73
Answers to Practice Problems: INVESTMENT PORTFOLIO,    74
Answers to Practice Problems: NEW HOME,    75
Answers to Practice Problems: WEB PAGE,    76
Bibliographic Notes,    77
More to Explore,    77

**4    RELATIONAL CALCULUS    78**

**4.1**    Logical Foundations,    78
    ■ Note 4.1: Overview of Relational Calculus
        Languages,    79

**4.2**   Tuple Relational Calculus,   80
   **4.2.1**   Fundamental Query Expressions,   80
      ■ How to 4.2: Writing a Fundamental Query in TRC,   80
   **4.2.2**   Quantification of Variables,   81
   **4.2.3**   Atoms and Formula,   84
   **4.2.4**   Relational Completeness,   85
      Aggregation and Grouping,   87
**4.3**   Domain Relational Calculus,   88
   **4.3.1**   Fundamental Query Expressions,   88
      ■ How to 4.3: Writing a Fundamental Query in DRC,   88
   **4.3.2**   Quantification of Variables,   90
   **4.3.3**   Atoms and Formula,   93
   **4.3.4**   Relational Completeness,   94
      Aggregation and Grouping,   96
**4.4**   Safety,   97
Chapter Notes Summary,   97
Chapter Reminders,   98
Practice,   98
   Practice Problems: INVESTMENT PORTFOLIO,   98
   Practice Problems: NEW HOME,   99
   Practice Problems: WEB PAGE,   100
End of Chapter Exercises,   100
Answers to Self-Check Questions,   102
Answers to Practice Problems: INVESTMENT PORTFOLIO,   104
Answers to Practice Problems: NEW HOME,   107
Answers to Practice Problems: WEB PAGE,   110
Bibliographic Notes,   111
More to Explore,   112

**5   SQL: AN INTRODUCTION TO QUERYING     113**

**5.1**   Foundations,   113
      ■ Note 5.1: SQL Syntax,   113
      ■ Syntax 5.2: Basic SQL Query,   115
**5.2**   Fundamental Query Expressions,   116
      ■ How to 5.3: Writing a Fundamental
         Query in SQL,   116
   **5.2.1**   Queries Involving One Table,   116
   **5.2.2**   Queries Involving Multiple Tables,   119
      ■ How to 5.4: Writing a Reflection Query,   121
**5.3**   Nested Queries,   122
      ■ Special Topic 5.5: A Glimpse at Query Optimization,   123
      ■ Special Topic 5.6: Views and Inline Views,   124
**5.4**   Set Operators,   124
**5.5**   Aggregation and Grouping,   126
      ■ Special Topic 5.7: Arithmetic Expressions,   128
**5.6**   Querying with null Values,   129

**5.7**  Relational Completeness,  131

    **5.7.1**  Fundamental Operators,  131

    **5.7.2**  Additional Operators,  132

    Safety,  134

Chapter Notes Summary,  134

Chapter Reminders,  135

Practice,  136

    Practice Problems: INVESTMENT PORTFOLIO,  136

    Practice Problems: NEW HOME,  137

    Practice Problems: WEB PAGE,  138

End of Chapter Exercises,  138

Answers to Self-Check Questions,  141

Answers to Practice Problems: INVESTMENT PORTFOLIO,  143

Answers to Practice Problems: NEW HOME,  145

Answers to Practice Problems: WEB PAGE,  148

Bibliographic Notes,  149

More to Explore,  150

## 6  SQL: BEYOND THE QUERY LANGUAGE  151

**6.1**  Data Definition,  151

    ■ Syntax 6.1: **Create Table** Statement,  152

    ■ Syntax 6.2: **Drop Table** Statement,  154

    ■ Syntax 6.3: **Alter Table** Statement,  155

    ■ Special Topic 6.4: **Create Index**,  155

    ■ Syntax 6.5: **Create View** Statement,  156

**6.2**  Data Manipulation,  156

    Insert,  157

    ■ Syntax 6.6: **Insert into** Statement,  157

    ■ Special Topic 6.7: Database Population,  158

    Update,  158

    ■ Syntax 6.8: **Update** Statement,  158

    Delete,  159

    ■ Syntax 6.9: **Delete** Statement,  159

**6.3**  Database User Privileges,  160

    ■ Syntax 6.10: **Grant** Statement,  161

    ■ Syntax 6.11: **Revoke** Statement,  161

Chapter Notes Summary,  162

Chapter Reminders,  163

Practice,  163

    Practice Problems: INVESTMENT PORTFOLIO,  163

    Practice Problems: NEW HOME,  165

    Practice Problems: WEB PAGE,  165

End of Chapter Exercises,  166

Answers to Self-Check Questions,  167

Answers to Practice Problems: INVESTMENT PORTFOLIO,  168

Answers to Practice Problems: NEW HOME,    168
Answers to Practice Problems: WEB PAGE,    168
Bibliographic Notes,    169
More to Explore,    169

**7**    DATABASE PROGRAMMING    170

**7.1**    Persistent Stored Modules,    170
     ■ Syntax 7.1: **Create Procedure** Statement,    171
     ■ Syntax 7.2: **Create Function** Statement,    172
**7.2**    Call-Level Interface,    173
**7.3**    Java and JDBC,    174
**7.4**    Python and DB-API,    178
Chapter Notes Summary,    180
Chapter Reminders,    181
Practice,    181
     Practice Problems: INVESTMENT PORTFOLIO,    182
     Practice Problems: NEW HOME,    182
     Practice Problems: WEB PAGE,    183
End of Chapter Exercises,    184
Answers to Self-Check Questions,    186
Answers to Practice Problems: INVESTMENT PORTFOLIO,    187
Answers to Practice Problems: NEW HOME,    189
Answers to Practice Problems: WEB PAGE,    192
Bibliographic Notes,    194
More to Explore,    195

**8**    XML AND DATABASES    196

**8.1**    Overview of XML,    196
**8.2**    DTD,    199
     ■ Syntax 8.1: DTD Overview,    199
DTDs and Relational Databases,    202
**8.3**    XML Schema,    203
     ■ Syntax 8.2: XSD Overview of Element and Attribute
       Declarations,    204
Simple Types,    204
Complex Types,    206
     ■ Syntax 8.3: XSD Attribute Declarations: use, default,
       fixed,    208
XSDs and Relational Databases,    210
**8.4**    Structuring XML for Data Exchange,    211
Chapter Notes Summary,    213
Chapter Reminders,    214
Practice,    216
     Practice Problems,    216

End of Chapter Exercises,    216
Answers to Self-Check Questions,    219
Answers to Practice Problems,    220
Bibliographic Notes,    224
More to Explore,    224

**9    TRANSACTION MANAGEMENT    225**

**9.1**    ACID Properties of a Transaction,    225
**9.2**    Recovery Control,    228
          ■ How to 9.1: Recovery Control: **UNDO** and **REDO**,    229
**9.3**    Concurrency Control,    230
    **9.3.1**    Serializability,    231
                  ■ How to 9.2: Create a Precedence Graph,    232
    **9.3.2**    Locking,    233
                  Well-Formed,    234
                  Two-Phase Locking (2PL),    235
                  Isolation,    235
                  Deadlock and Livelock,    237
    **9.3.3**    Timestamps,    238
                  ■ Algorithm 9.3: Basic Timestamp Protocol,    238
Chapter Notes Summary,    241
Chapter Reminders,    242
Practice,    243
          Practice Problems,    243
End of Chapter Exercises,    243
Answers to Self-Check Questions,    245
Answers to Practice Problems,    247
Bibliographic Notes,    248
More to Explore,    248

**10    MORE ON DATABASE DESIGN    249**

**10.1**    Database Design Goals,    249
**10.2**    Functional Dependencies,    250
                  ■ Algorithm 10.1: Attribute Closure,    252
                  ■ Special Topic 10.2: Minimal Set of Functional
                      Dependencies,    253
                  ■ How to 10.3: Heuristic Determination of a
                      Candidate Key,    253
**10.3**    Decomposition,    255
                  ■ How to 10.4: Determine Breakdown of **F** for a
                      Decomposition,    256
                  ■ How to 10.5: Determine Lossless Pairwise
                      Decomposition,    257
                  ■ Algorithm 10.6: Lossless-Join Property for Database
                      Schema,    259

**10.4** Normal Forms, 261
  ■ How to 10.7: Determine the Normal Form of a
    Relation, 262
  ■ Algorithm 10.8: BCNF Decomposition Algorithm, 263
Reflections: EMPLOYEE TRAINING, 265
Chapter Notes Summary, 266
Chapter Reminders, 266
Practice, 267
  Practice Problems: INVESTMENT PORTFOLIO, 267
  Practice Problems: NEW HOME, 267
  Practice Problems: WEB PAGE, 268
End of Chapter Exercises, 268
Answers to Self-Check Questions, 269
Answers to Practice Problems: INVESTMENT PORTFOLIO, 270
Answers to Practice Problems: NEW HOME, 271
Answers to Practice Problems: WEB PAGE, 272
Bibliographic Notes, 273
More to Explore, 273

**A** WinRDBI A-1

**A.1** Overview, A-1
**A.2** Query Languages, A-1
  Intermediate Tables and Renaming of Attributes, A-2
  Relational Algebra, A-2
  Relational Calculus, A-3
  SQL, A-4
**A.3** Implementation Overview, A-5
**A.4** Summary, A-5

BIBLIOGRAPHY B-1

INDEX I-1

# List of Figures

| | | |
|---|---|---:|
| 1.1 | Data abstraction diagram. | 2 |
| 1.2 | Network, hierarchical, and relational data models: employees working in departments. | 3 |
| 1.3 | Entity-Relationship diagram: employees working in departments. | 4 |
| 1.4 | Object-oriented data model: employees working in departments. | 5 |
| 1.5 | Abstract representation of a call-level interface. | 5 |
| 1.6 | XML and JSON: employee representation. | 6 |
| 1.7 | employee table: sample instance. | 8 |
| 1.8 | Visualization of the no duplicate tuples constraint on a relation. | 8 |
| 1.9 | Referential integrity constraint: abstract and example. | 10 |
| 1.10 | Visual schema: employee-title example. | 11 |
| 1.11 | Visual schema: abstraction of ONLINE RETAILER example. | 12 |
| 1.12 | ONLINE RETAILER abstract instance for item, supplier, and item_supplier. | 13 |
| 1.13 | Abstract visual schema. | 15 |
| 2.1 | Abstract ER diagram illustrating entity and attributes. | 23 |
| 2.2 | Example relationships for 1:1, 1:N, and M:N cardinality ratios. | 23 |
| 2.3 | Abstract ER diagram illustrating weak entity. | 24 |
| 2.4 | EMPLOYEE TRAINING ER diagram. | 25 |
| 2.5 | EMPLOYEE TRAINING ER diagram with (min, max) pairs. | 27 |
| 2.6 | Recursive parent–child relationship. | 27 |
| 2.7 | Ternary relationship and its corresponding representation using binary relationships. | 28 |
| 2.8 | Mapping entities to tables. | 29 |
| 2.9 | Mapping relationships to tables. | 30 |
| 2.10 | Relational database schema for EMPLOYEE TRAINING enterprise. | 32 |

| | | |
|---|---|---|
| 2.11 | EMPLOYEE TRAINING visual relational schema. | 33 |
| 2.12 | UML conceptual class diagram for EMPLOYEE TRAINING. | 34 |
| 2.13 | Crow's Foot diagram for EMPLOYEE TRAINING. | 35 |
| 2.14 | WAREHOUSE ER diagram. | 39 |
| 2.15 | GRADEBOOK ER diagram. | 40 |
| 2.16 | INVESTMENT PORTFOLIO ER diagram. | 42 |
| 2.17 | INVESTMENT PORTFOLIO relational schema. | 43 |
| 2.18 | INVESTMENT PORTFOLIO visual relational schema. | 44 |
| 2.19 | NEW HOME ER diagram. | 45 |
| 2.20 | NEW HOME relational schema. | 46 |
| 2.21 | NEW HOME visual relational schema. | 47 |
| 2.22 | WEB PAGE ER diagram. | 48 |
| 2.23 | WEB PAGE relational schema. | 49 |
| 2.24 | WEB PAGE visual relational schema. | 49 |
| 3.1 | Query design: What is the title of 'DB01'? | 52 |
| 3.2 | Query design: What are the names of employees who took 'DB01'? | 53 |
| 3.3 | Query design: Which employees took 'Database' courses? | 54 |
| 3.4 | Selection. | 56 |
| 3.5 | Projection. | 56 |
| 3.6 | Division abstract example. | 61 |
| 3.7 | Query trees: Who took 'DB01'? | 65 |
| 3.8 | Abstract examples of query trees for commutative and associative operators. | 66 |
| 3.9 | Introduce projections in query tree: Who took 'DB01'? | 67 |
| 5.1 | Abstraction of results for *sql_SalariesByTitle*. | 127 |
| 6.1 | SQL column and table constraints syntax summary. | 153 |
| 6.2 | Script for creating the EMPLOYEE TRAINING database. | 154 |
| 6.3 | Syntax summary: DDL, DML, and user access privileges. | 164 |
| 7.1 | Abstraction of architecture for database application programming. | 174 |
| 8.1 | XML employees sample. | 197 |

| | | |
|---|---|---|
| 8.2 | Tree structure of XML. | 198 |
| 8.3 | DTD for employees XML document. | 200 |
| 8.4 | DTD for a table-based mapping to an XML document. | 202 |
| 8.5 | Sample data for a table-based mapping to XML. | 202 |
| 8.6 | XML schema outline. | 203 |
| 8.7 | XSD example of a custom simple type. | 204 |
| 8.8 | Additional examples of restrictions in XSD. | 205 |
| 8.9 | Examples of complex types based on sequence and choice. | 206 |
| 8.10 | XSD example of sequence complex type with occurrence constraints. | 207 |
| 8.11 | XSD example of sequence complex type with element references. | 207 |
| 8.12 | XSD examples of complex types with simple and complex content. | 208 |
| 8.13 | XSD examples of empty element type definitions. | 209 |
| 8.14 | XSD examples of definitions using ID, IDREF, and IDREFS. | 209 |
| 8.15 | XSD for employee XML document. | 210 |
| 8.16 | XSD for table-based mapping. | 211 |
| 8.17 | ONLINE RETAILER XML structure. | 212 |
| 9.1 | Precedence graph for Schedule A. | 232 |
| 9.2 | Precedence graph for Schedule D. | 233 |
| 9.3 | Precedence graph for Schedule G. | 236 |
| 9.4 | System log for Practice Problems. | 243 |
| 9.5 | System log for End of Chapter Exercises. | 244 |
| 9.6 | Precedence graph for Schedule E. | 245 |
| 9.7 | Precedence graph for Schedule F. | 246 |
| 9.8 | Precedence graph for Schedule P. | 247 |
| 10.1 | supplier candidate key determination example. | 254 |
| 10.2 | empdept candidate key determination example. | 254 |
| 10.3 | department candidate key determination example. | 255 |
| 10.4 | supplier dependency preserving decomposition example. | 256 |
| 10.5 | empdept dependency preserving decomposition example. | 256 |

10.6    supplier lossless-join pairwise decomposition example.                           258

10.7    empdept lossless-join pairwise decomposition example.                           258

10.8    empaddr lossless-join pairwise decomposition counterexample.                    258

10.9    supplier lossless-join decomposition algorithm trace.                           259

10.10   empdept lossless-join decomposition algorithm trace.                            260

10.11   empaddr lossless-join decomposition algorithm trace.                            260

10.12   workson BCNF decomposition example.                                             264

10.13   hoursworked BCNF decomposition example.                                         264

10.14   EMPLOYEE TRAINING database schema with functional dependencies.                 265

10.15   EMPLOYEE TRAINING lossless-join determination.                                  265

10.16   INVESTMENT PORTFOLIO database schema with functional dependencies.              270

10.17   INVESTMENT PORTFOLIO lossless-join determination.                               270

10.18   NEW HOME database schema with functional dependencies.                          271

10.19   NEW HOME lossless-join determination.                                           271

10.20   WEB PAGE database schema with functional dependencies.                          272

10.21   WEB PAGE lossless-join determination.                                           272

A.1     WinRDBI User Interface. Source: WinRDBI.                                         A-2

# LIST OF TABLES

| | | |
|---|---|---|
| 1.1 | Summary of Terminology Correspondence for the Relational Data Model | 7 |
| 1.2 | Key Definition Summary with Examples | 9 |
| 1.3 | Summary of Referential Integrity in the ONLINE RETAILER Schema | 12 |
| 1.4 | Summary of Relational Schema Notation | 15 |
| 2.1 | Summary of Keys in EMPLOYEE TRAINING Schema | 32 |
| 2.2 | Summary of Mapping Heuristics | 36 |
| 2.3 | INVESTMENT PORTFOLIO Entity Summary | 43 |
| 2.4 | INVESTMENT PORTFOLIO Relationship Summary | 43 |
| 2.5 | NEW HOME Entity Summary | 45 |
| 2.6 | NEW HOME Relationship Summary | 46 |
| 2.7 | WEB PAGE Entity Summary | 48 |
| 2.8 | WEB PAGE Relationship Summary | 49 |
| 3.1 | Query Design Examples | 52 |
| 3.2 | Summary of Filtering Operators | 56 |
| 3.3 | Relational Algebra Sample Filtering Queries | 57 |
| 3.4 | Summary of Set Operators | 58 |
| 3.5 | Relational Algebra Sample Set Queries | 58 |
| 3.6 | Summary of Fundamental Relational Algebra Operators | 62 |
| 3.7 | Relational Algebra Summary of Fundamental EMPLOYEE TRAINING Queries | 62 |
| 3.8 | Summary of Additional Relational Algebra Operators | 62 |
| 3.9 | Relational Summary of Additional EMPLOYEE TRAINING Queries | 63 |
| 3.10 | Summary of Pushing Selections Down | 66 |
| 3.11 | Chapter Summary of Relational Algebra Operators | 69 |
| 4.1 | Truth Tables for and, or, not | 79 |

| 4.2 | Truth Tables for De Morgan's Laws | 79 |
| 4.3 | TRC Sample Filtering Queries | 80 |
| 4.4 | TRC Sample Set Queries | 82 |
| 4.5 | TRC Division – Universal Truth Table | 83 |
| 4.6 | TRC Division – Existential Truth Table | 83 |
| 4.7 | TRC Summary of Fundamental Relational Algebra Operators | 86 |
| 4.8 | TRC Summary of Fundamental EMPLOYEE TRAINING Queries | 86 |
| 4.9 | TRC Summary of Additional EMPLOYEE TRAINING Queries | 87 |
| 4.10 | DRC Sample Filtering Queries | 89 |
| 4.11 | DRC Sample Set Queries | 91 |
| 4.12 | DRC Division – Universal Truth Tables | 92 |
| 4.13 | DRC Division – Existential Truth Table | 92 |
| 4.14 | DRC Summary of Fundamental Relational Algebra Operators | 95 |
| 4.15 | DRC Summary of Fundamental EMPLOYEE TRAINING Queries | 95 |
| 4.16 | DRC Summary of Additional EMPLOYEE TRAINING Queries | 95 |
| 4.17 | TRC and DRC Summary of Fundamental Relational Algebra Operators | 98 |
| 5.1 | SQL Sample Queries with One Table | 117 |
| 5.2 | SQL Reflection Queries with One Table | 118 |
| 5.3 | SQL Sample Queries with Two Tables | 119 |
| 5.4 | SQL Reflection Queries with Two Tables | 120 |
| 5.5 | SQL: Which employees have taken a training course? | 122 |
| 5.6 | SQL: Which employees have *not* taken a training course? | 123 |
| 5.7 | Example SQL Queries for Set Operators | 125 |
| 5.8 | Alternative Example SQL Queries for Set Operators | 125 |
| 5.9 | SQL Summary of Fundamental Relational Algebra Operators | 131 |
| 5.10 | SQL Summary of Fundamental EMPLOYEE TRAINING Queries | 131 |
| 5.11 | SQL Summary of Additional EMPLOYEE TRAINING Queries | 132 |
| 5.12 | SQL Division Truth Table | 134 |
| 6.1 | Table Privileges | 161 |

| | | |
|---|---|---|
| 7.1 | Abbreviated JDBC API | 177 |
| 7.2 | JDBC Abstraction | 181 |
| 7.3 | MySQLdb Abstraction | 181 |
| 8.1 | Occurrence Constraints in DTDs versus XSDs | 214 |
| 8.2 | DTD and XSD Example Attribute Declaration Constraints | 215 |
| 8.3 | Summary of XSD Simple Type Restrictions | 215 |
| 8.4 | Summary of XSD Complex Type Definitions | 215 |
| 8.5 | Data for XML Document | 218 |
| 9.1 | Pseudocode for Example Banking Transactions | 226 |
| 9.2 | Concurrent Transactions Illustrating Consistency Violation | 227 |
| 9.3 | Concurrent Transactions Illustrating Isolation Violation | 227 |
| 9.4 | Concurrent Transactions for Durability Discussion | 228 |
| 9.5 | Format of System Log Entries | 228 |
| 9.6 | Abstraction of Example Banking Transactions | 230 |
| 9.7 | Well-formed Transactions Releasing Locks When Done with Data Item | 234 |
| 9.8 | Two-Phase Locked Transactions | 235 |
| 9.9 | Two-Phase Locked with Isolation | 236 |
| 9.10 | Deadlock Illustration | 237 |
| 9.11 | Trace of Basic Timestamp Protocol on Schedule D | 239 |
| 9.12 | Trace of Basic Timestamp Protocol on Schedule E | 239 |
| 9.13 | Trace of Basic Timestamp Protocol on Schedule I | 240 |
| 9.14 | Two-Phase Locking Protocol on Schedule I | 240 |
| 9.15 | Two-Phase Locking Protocol on Schedule J | 240 |
| 9.16 | Trace of Basic Timestamp Protocol on Schedule J | 241 |
| 9.17 | Locking Operations on a Data Item D | 242 |
| 9.18 | Bookkeeping for Timestamps on a Data Item D | 242 |
| 9.19 | Two-Phase Locking Schedule SC | 246 |
| 9.20 | Trace of Basic Timestamp Protocol for Schedule A | 246 |
| 9.21 | Trace of Basic Timestamp Protocol for Schedule SC | 247 |

9.22    Two-Phase Locking Protocol on Schedule P                              248

9.23    Trace of Basic Timestamp Protocol for Schedule P                      248

10.1    Sample Spreadsheet Data                                              250

10.2    Functional Dependency Inference Rules                                251

10.3    Trace of Attribute Closure Algorithm                                 253

10.4    Summary: Determination of Database Design Goals                      267

A.1     WinRDBI Summary of Fundamental Relational Algebra Operators          A-3

A.2     WinRDBI Summary of Additional Relational Algebra Operators           A-3

# Preface

The goal of this book is to provide an introduction to databases to a diverse audience, incorporating fundamental concepts and essential practice. The succinct presentation of the underlying formalism forms a strong foundation for its application to solving problems. Visual components are integrated throughout the text, including the use of a visual relational schema linking primary and foreign keys to highlight referential integrity. Summary figures and tables provide an overview of essential information. Practice is an integral component of the text with a variety of solved real-world problems at the end of each chapter. Formative self-assessment is also incorporated through self-check questions at the end of each section.

## Chapter Features

- *Learning Objectives*: Listed at the beginning of each chapter describing learner goals.
- *Margin Notes*: Notes in the margin highlight important aspects in the textual description.
- *Self-Check Questions*: Formative self-assessment questions in each section for students to test their understanding as they read with answers included at the end of the chapter.
- *Interactivities (eBook only)*: Multiple-choice questions integrated in the eBook for additional formative self-assessment opportunities.
- *Boxed Content*: Special Topic, Algorithm, How To, Syntax, and Note boxes interspersed to emphasize valuable knowledge.
- *Chapter Notes Summary*: Margin notes revisited at the end of the chapter, reviewing its storyline.
- *Chapter Reminders*: Summary figures and tables that highlight fundamental chapter knowledge.
- *Practice Problems*: Essential practice of problem-solving applied to a variety of real-world scenarios.
- *End of Chapter Exercises*: Exercises that instructors can assign students to apply their knowledge.
- *Bibliographic Notes*: Relevant foundational references for the chapter knowledge.
- *More to Explore*: Hints to students on additional topics to explore, going beyond the chapter's presentation.

## Organization

The book is intended for a one-semester introductory course on databases for both database fluency courses and the traditional database course. The chapters covering fundamental concepts for all are shown on the left and the advanced topics designed for computer science majors to the right. The braces indicate possible alternatives for chapter sequence based on the instructor's emphasis and assignment structure.

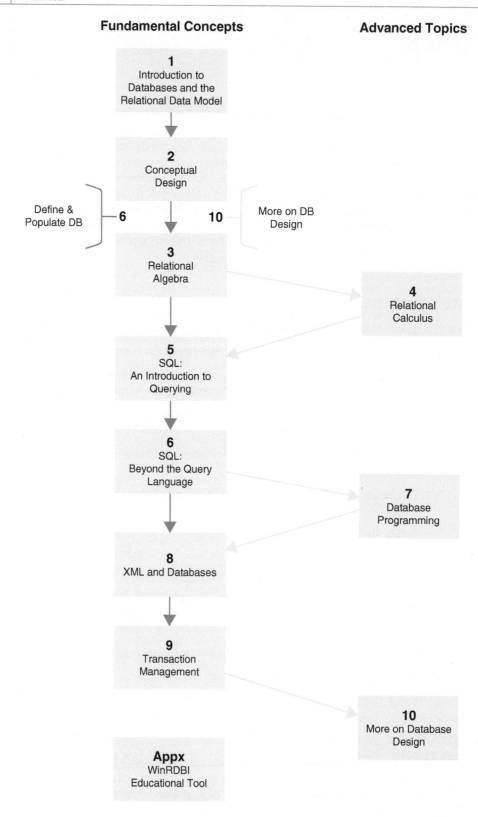

The appendix describes the WinRDBI educational tool (winrdbi.asu.edu) that provides a hands-on approach to understanding query languages, including relational algebra, relational calculus, and SQL. The syntax of the relational algebra and calculus languages presented in this book use the WinRDBI languages with the data and queries for the chapter and practice scenarios provided on the book's companion website.

## Web Resources

An online companion site supplements the book by providing many resources for instructors and students: www.wiley.com/go/dietrich/databases1e

Supporting material based on computational aspects of the book include the following:

- Data and queries for the EMPLOYEE TRAINING in-chapter scenario as well as all three practice scenarios: INVESTMENT PORTFOLIO, NEW HOME, and WEB PAGE. SQL database scripts verified in MySQL

- Java and Python source code for the database programming chapter, which covers Java/JDBC and Python DB-API as the MySQLdb implementation

- XML, DTD, and XSD for the ONLINE RETAILER practice scenario in the XML and Databases chapter

## Acknowledgments

There are many people who are involved in the process of writing and publishing a book. I appreciate the thoughtful guidance provided by the reviewers: Chia L. Chen, Tuskegee University; Ruben Gamboa, University of Wyoming; Carson K. Leung, University of Manitoba; Dennis Roebuck, Delta College; Traian Marius Truta, Northern Kentucky University; Li Yang, Western Michigan University; and Sen Zhang, State University of New York at Oneonta. My thanks to those at John Wiley & Sons over the years from proposal to production: Don Fowley, Judy Howarth, Joanna Dingle, Jennifer Yee, Jennifer Brady, and Beth Golub. I also appreciate the assistance of Amy Hendrickson at texnology.com who provided LaTeX assistance on the book.

I would also like to thank Don Goelman from Villanova who inspired me to break databases out of the computer science box. Our work together on the Databases for Many Majors project combined our expertise on teaching database concepts into a suite of visualizations that introduce this critical knowledge to a wider audience, providing motivation for the writing of this book.

The task of writing a book requires a long-term commitment of time and energy. I want to express my sincere gratitude to my family and friends for their encouragement and understanding.

S. W. DIETRICH

*Phoenix, Arizona*
*June 2021*

# Introduction to Databases and the Relational Data Model

**1**

## LEARNING OBJECTIVES

- To explain fundamental features of a database
- To learn about different types of databases
- To understand the fundamental concepts of a relation
- To describe and identify primary and foreign keys

Databases are a tool that provide many features beyond the definition, population, and retrieval of data, including support for concurrent access by multiple users, recovering from failures, and managing user access privileges. This chapter provides a brief history of various data models and then introduces the relational data model, which is the focus of this text. Relational databases provide the conceptual simplicity of modeling data using tables yet provide the power to handle numerous types of applications. The relational data model supports the specification of various constraints to manage the integrity of the data.

## 1.1 Databases Are a Tool

Data are everywhere. Data are stored in many different formats in various shapes and sizes. Smaller data sets may be stored in files as just textual data, such as in a comma-separated value (csv) file. In a csv file, each line represents *related* data values separated by commas. Spreadsheets are another common method of storing data, but spreadsheets must be interpreted by a specific program. A csv file can also be interpreted by spreadsheet programs or programs specifically written to analyze the data.

Many may be familiar with the use of a simple spreadsheet that uses basic formulas for maintaining information. For certain data, a spreadsheet works quite well, e.g. student grades for classes. However, for other data, it is difficult to determine how to represent it correctly in a blank canvas of rows and columns in a spreadsheet. What if there are multiple kinds of relationships between the data? Does one use multiple worksheets with references between them? The complexity of the data representation quickly escalates. What about analyzing the data that requires more than a simple formula? Data are typically copied to a new worksheet and functions applied, perhaps with further manipulation to determine the answer. When examining the data for various properties, there would be numerous copies of the data with different views of the data in each worksheet. What if the spreadsheet is shared with another user who needs other views of the data? Now there are many different copies of the data across various users. How would the data in these many copies get updated to be consistent in the presence of updates?

Data are typically shared by many constituents who need access to the data at the same time. What if multiple users are trying to update the data simultaneously? Also, each user should only have access to the parts of the related data that they need. Restricting access to pieces of data is difficult to accomplish with shared csv files or spreadsheets because typically the operating system of the computer on which the data are stored handles the security access to the entire file. Backups of the data are also handled at the level of the operating system by the system administrator. If the system should go down, how is the information recovered from this system failure?

> **Databases provide efficient shared access to persistent data, with inherent support for concurrent users, recovering from failures, and managing user access privileges.**

Databases are a tool that should be in everyone's toolbox. Databases provide efficient shared access to persistent data. Databases describe the structure of the data to be stored, including additional constraints that must hold on the data. Databases support the insertion, modification, deletion, and analysis of data. A question asked of the database is called a *query*. Thus, the *query language* provides various operations for analyzing the data and the relationships between the data, without having to make additional copies of the information. Databases also inherently support multiple users, called *concurrency control*, and manage system failures, called *recovery control*. The *data security* component of the database system specifies user access privileges to control the amount or type of data that the user is allowed to see.

The various features incorporated into databases evolved over time based on issues identified by the use of file systems. Historically, persistent data was stored in file systems on disk, and programs were written to manipulate the data. An initial program was written to create the file. Another program was written to read the file and process any additions, deletions, or modifications of the data. The analysis of the data required writing programs to read the file and process the data programmatically to answer the questions. What if the data gathered over time needed to be changed? This would require writing a program to convert the existing file structure into the new one and *every* program that accessed the old data format would need to be changed! Since security was handled by the operating system, typically, a read and/or write password was associated with the file. Multiple programs could read the file at the same time, but when a program was writing the file, no other program could be reading the same file. Thus, concurrent access to data was severely limited. Recovery of data was based on a backup schedule of the files by the operating system, which dictated the amount of information loss in the presence of failures.

> **The goals of a database include specifying views for different users of the data, which are unaffected by adding new data or by changing access mechanisms to improve performance.**

There is a well-known *data abstraction* diagram that highlights the data goals of a database as shown in Figure 1.1. At the highest level, the database provides various views of its data. The logical level represents what data are stored and the relationships between the data. The physical level represents how the data are stored. The idea is to create an independence between the levels, when possible. The term *logical data independence* refers to the ability to add data to the database without affecting the current views defined over the data, whereas *physical data independence* references the capability to add indexes or other mechanisms to improve the performance of the database system without requiring a change to the logical level.

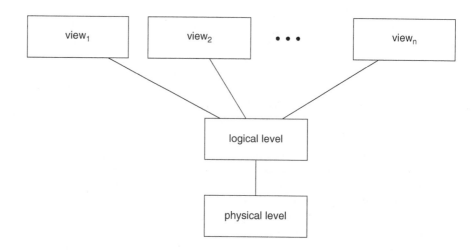

**FIGURE 1.1**
Data abstraction diagram.

## Self Check

1. What is the language called that supports the analysis of data in a database system?
2. What is the name of the database mechanism that handles the correctness of the data in the presence of multiple users?
3. What does the term *logical data independence* mean?

## 1.2 Overview of Data and Models

The spreadsheets that are commonplace today on microcomputers only came into existence in the late 1970s. Before that, persistent data was either stored in files on disks or in early databases. For disk files, programs needed to be written to process the persistent data. For the early databases in the 1960s, commands were embedded into the programming language, where the data model consisted of a network of graphs interconnecting the data. In the late 1960s, hierarchical databases were introduced that simplified the complex networks to a hierarchical tree structure, which was more efficient for data that was inherently hierarchical but problematic for other structured data. In the 1970s, the relational data model was introduced based on a simpler concept of tables with rows and columns, yet fundamentally was based on a mathematical foundation. This data model became quite popular, and is still popular today, providing a conceptually simpler data model that can handle a large range of application domains.

Figure 1.2 represents a sample scenario of employees working in departments in each of these data models. A department has many employees working in it, and an employee only works in one department. In the network database representation, di represents the characteristics describing the department. Similarly, each eij indicates the descriptive properties of an employee working in

**Network Set**

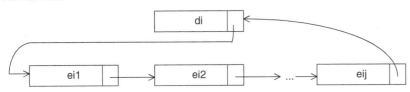

**Hierarchy**

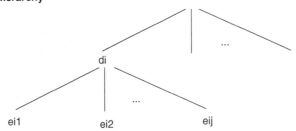

**Relations**

| employee | | | | | | department | |
|---|---|---|---|---|---|---|---|
| eID | eLast | eFirst | eTitle | eSalary | worksin | dID | dName |
| ei1 | | | | | di | di | |
| ei2 | | | | | di | ... | |
| ... | | | | | | | |
| eij | | | | | di | | |
| ... | | | | | | | |

**FIGURE 1.2**
Network, hierarchical, and relational data models: employees working in departments.

> **Network and hierarchical databases inherently represented one-to-many associations with database commands embedded within a programming language.**

department di. The link is a conceptual representation of the record's participation in a network set, representing a one-to-many relationship. The department di is the *owner* of the set and the employees working in that department are its members. There would be a logical link for each network set in which a record type participated. For a many-to-many relationship, where one record of a type is related to many of the other and similarly in the other direction, then a new record type could be introduced that was the owner of two network sets. Hierarchical databases used one-to-many parent–child relationships in a tree structure, where di is the parent of the collection of eij employees working in that department. Data that did not inherently fit the tree structure with a child having a single parent became problematic.

In a relational database, there is a relation representing the departments and another relation representing the employees. The names of the columns of a relation are called *attributes* and a row in a table is called a *tuple*. In the illustrated mapping of the relations, each department is described by a unique id and its name (dID and dName) and each employee is described by the attributes eID, eLast, eFirst, eTitle, eSalary as well as the worksin attribute, having the value of the dID that designates the department in which the employee works.

> **Relational databases use tables to represent concepts that are linked by attribute values.**

In the mid-1970s, research presented conceptual data models, designed to represent the concepts in the database and the associations between them. Chapter 2 introduces a conceptual data model known as the Entity-Relationship (ER) Model that uses ER diagrams for representing the entities in the data and their relationships. Figure 1.3 shows an ER diagram for employees working in departments. An ER diagram uses rectangles to represent entities and diamonds for relationships between entities. An oval indicates an attribute that describes the object to which it is linked. An employee works in one department and a department has many (N) employees working in it. Chapter 2 also briefly describes two other conceptual data models that are also used for representing the conceptual design of a database: UML (Unified Modeling Language) class diagrams and Crow's Foot notation. From these graphical data models, mappings define how to store the conceptual model into a physical model, such as relations.

> **Conceptual data models typically use graphical representations to illustrate the concepts in the database and the associations between them.**

In the 1980s–1990s, object-oriented programming languages (OOPLs) were introduced in computer science and researchers sought to make objects within these languages persistent as part of an object-oriented database system. This direction was interesting because it was again embedding database commands (through the use of language bindings) within programming languages, which is somewhat counterintuitive in that it appeared as if the field was taking a step backward. However, certain applications that inherently support the concept of an object benefited from the storage of object properties on disk physically near each other. This storage benefit resulted in performance gains over the relational model for this niche. Also, the use of immutable object identifiers (oids) to uniquely identify an object and to define the associations between these objects with oids seemed quite natural. There was also a movement to incorporate object-oriented concepts into relational database systems, creating an object-relational hybrid. These systems provided a

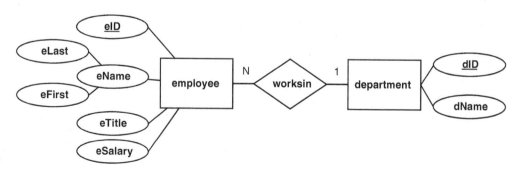

**FIGURE 1.3**
Entity-Relationship
diagram: employees
working in departments.

methodology to generate an identifier for a tuple and to explicitly maintain relationships in the database using these identifiers.

Figure 1.4 depicts a department object and an employee object with properties, including references using the inherent object identifier. The department object instance for di has a unique oid of oid_di, which is the value of the worksin relationship in the sample employee object. Similarly, the relationship named employees in the department di uses the oids of the employee objects. This is in contrast to relational databases, which use the value of attributes to link related information. The value of a property described by an attribute may change over time, which means it is mutable, whereas the assigned object identifier on the creation of an object will never change over time. The values of the object's properties can change without having any effect on the immutable oid.

> **Object-oriented databases are integrated within object-oriented programming languages, using the value of an immutable object identifier to relate persistent objects.**

oid_di

| Department |
|---|
| dID: di
dName: ...
employees: { oid_ei1, oid_ei2, ..., oid_eij } |

oid_ei1

| Employee |
|---|
| eID: ei1
eName: ( ..., ...)
eTitle: ...
eSalary: ...
worksin: oid_di |

**FIGURE 1.4**
Object-oriented data model: employees working in departments.

Another benefit of object databases was the integration of the programming language and database, where the data were persistent objects manipulated by the programming language. This is in contrast to what is called an *impedance mismatch* between programming languages and relational database systems. A relational database returns a collection of tuples as the answer to a query, and a programming language must look at each of these tuples one at a time. There are *call-level interfaces* (CLIs) defined for most languages that provide a methodology for a programmer to query a relational database, which returns its result as a collection over which the program iterates. An abstract representation of a call-level interface is visually depicted in Figure 1.5. Some systems have abstracted this to frameworks that use the OOPL to automatically wrap the access to the relational database. These object relational wrappers are popular in that they abstract the details of the database access away from the lower level programming and provide a view of the data that is integrated with the programming language.

> **Programming languages use a call-level interface for querying a relational database, which results in an *impedance mismatch* between the set of answers returned by the database and the program examining the answers one-at-a-time by iterating over that set.**

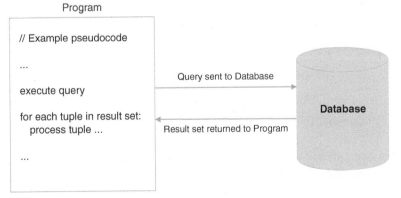

**FIGURE 1.5**
Abstract representation of a call-level interface.

Today, there are many notations, tools, and systems for dealing with data in its many shapes and sizes. For example, there are specialized databases and systems for handling geographical information systems and computer-aided design. There are also widely used alternatives to csv files for handling and exchanging data in human readable form, such as the eXtensible Markup Language (XML) and JavaScript Object Notation (JSON). You may have heard of these acronyms. Just as programs can read csv files, there are libraries in various programming languages for handling XML and JSON. Although the file is just text and can be read by humans, it is meant to be processed by programs. XML is somewhat similar to the HyperText Markup Language (HTML) recognized by Web browsers in that it is a markup language with tags and content; however, the tags are user-defined and provide a way to document the data contained in the file. XML is a standard and there are many data exchange standards for various application domains that use XML. JSON is a simple text representation based on key-value pairs that tends to have less overhead for processing than XML. Many database systems and frameworks provide support for XML and JSON data formats. Figure 1.6 provides a representation of an employee in both XML and JSON.

> **XML and JSON are textual representations for exchanging data that are supported by most database systems and programming languages.**

**XML**
```
<employee>
    <eID>111</eID>
    <eName>
        <eLast>Last111</eLast>
        <eFirst>First111</eFirst>
    </eName>
    <eTitle>Database Administrator</eTitle>
    <eSalary>75111</eSalary>
</employee>
```

**JSON**
```
{"eID": "111",
 "eName": {
     "eLast": "Last111",
     "eFirst": "First111"
     }
 "eTitle": "Database Administrator",
 "eSalary": 75111
 }
```

**FIGURE 1.6**
XML and JSON:
employee
representation.

Today, there are vast amount of data in myriad formats. The features provided by a relational database are useful for many applications, providing structure to the data with inherent integrity constraints, concurrency, and recovery control as well as data security. In real life, data is messy and integrity constraints are costly. What about applications that do not need the cost associated with the strict guidelines of concurrency and recovery control? A lot of data are represented as streams of information. How are such data processed? The term *Big Data* is a popular phrase that indicates a significant *volume* of data in a *variety* of formats that are generated at high *velocity*. A good example is the data generated by various social media sites. How can one gain insight from these data? Big Data is outside the scope of this introductory text. However, the concepts covered in this text will help you understand various facets of data and its analysis through querying.

This text focuses on understanding the relational data model through a balanced mix of theory and practice. Theory is necessary so that a depth of knowledge can be learned and applied to solve another problem. Practice is necessary to reinforce the learning in an active way to create the necessary mental models of how to utilize the theory in real life.

## Self Check

4. What is the name of the type of data model that graphically represents the concepts and their relationships?

5. Which data model uses an immutable identifier to create associations between concepts?

6. Name a textual representation, other than csv, that is commonly used in data exchange and supported by database systems.

# 1.3 The Relational Data Model

Relational databases are a valuable tool for providing solutions to mission-critical applications in industry, especially those involving e-commerce. Relational databases provide the conceptual simplicity of modeling information using tables yet provide the power to handle many different types of application domains.

## 1.3.1 Definition

The relational data model is widely accepted because of its conceptual simplicity and its theoretical foundations. The conceptual simplicity of a relation is based on concepts with which most of us are familiar, such as a table data structure having rows and columns or a file having records and fields. Table 1.1 provides a summary of the terminology correspondence. A *relation* corresponds to the concept of a table or a file. The rows of a table or records of a file are called the *tuples* of a relation. The names of the columns or fields are *attributes*. The *degree* or *arity* of a relation corresponds to its number of columns. The term *cardinality* refers to the number of tuples or rows in the table.

**Table 1.1  Summary of Terminology Correspondence for the Relational Data Model**

| Relation | Table | File |
| --- | --- | --- |
| tuple | row | record |
| attribute | column name | field |
| degree or arity | number of columns | number of fields |
| cardinality | number of rows | number of records |

A relation is described by its *schema* or intension. For example, r(a1, a2, ..., an) describes a relation named r having n attributes named a1, a2, ..., an, respectively. Each attribute ai has an associated domain of basic or atomic values. An atomic value is one that is not divisible into smaller components. In this foundational definition of the relational data model, the atomic-valued domain is an underlying assumption. Over time, there have been some extensions to the SQL standard to handle object-relational features, XML, or JSON, but these are advanced features that are outside the scope of this introductory text. Therefore, this presentation assumes that the values of attributes must be simple. Thus, a complex attribute must be stored as its simpler components, such as an address, which is broken down into street address, city, state, and zip. To represent multiple values, a table must be introduced with multiple tuples representing those values.

> A *schema* of a relation refers to its description with its name and attributes. An *instance* of a relation is a *set* of tuples – unordered without duplicates.

Formally, an *instance* or extension of a relation r having schema r(a1, a2, ..., an) is a set of n-tuples. Each n-tuple is an ordered list of n-values where the ith value corresponds to the value of the ith attribute ai, which is an element from the domain associated with ai or a null value. A null value designates that the value of that attribute in the tuple is unknown. Figure 1.7 shows part of a sample instance of an employee relation having schema employee(eID, eLast, eFirst, eTitle, eSalary).

> A null value designates that the value of that attribute in the tuple is unknown.

Since a relation extension is a set of tuples and a mathematical set is defined as an unordered collection with no duplicate elements, there is no implied ordering between the tuples in a relation and there can be no duplicate tuples. Two tuples are duplicates if they have the same value for all of their attributes. For the employee table, the *no duplicate tuples* constraint indicates that

| employee | | | | |
|---|---|---|---|---|
| **eID** | **eLast** | **eFirst** | **eTitle** | **eSalary** |
| 222 | Last222 | First222 | Software Engineer | 51722 |
| 321 | Last321 | Fiirst321 | Database Administrator | 68321 |
| 666 | Last666 | Fiirst666 | Project Lead | 66666 |
| 999 | Last999 | First999 | Manager | 100999 |
| ... | ... | ... | ... | ... |

**FIGURE 1.7**
employee **table: sample instance.**

no two tuples can have the same value for all of their attributes: eID, eLast, eFirst, eTitle, and eSalary. However, for the employee schema, the eID attribute is assumed to be a unique employee identifier such that no two employee tuples can have the same value for the eID attribute. For a relation, a uniqueness constraint can be defined based on some of the attributes in the relation's schema.

## 1.3.2 Uniqueness

Up to this point, a relation schema is described by a tupling of the relation's attributes, which is typically denoted by parentheses, e.g. r(a1, a2, ..., an). When only the names of the attributes of a relation are of interest and not the ordering of the attributes within the tuple of the relation, a relation's schema can also be described using set notation to refer to the set of attributes in the schema. Typically, curly braces { and } surround the elements of a set. By convention, let R represent the set of attributes for a relation r. Therefore, R = { a1, a2, ..., an } for the relation schema r(a1, a2, ..., an). For the employee table, EMPLOYEE = { eID, eLast, eFirst, eTitle, eSalary }.

> **Dot notation t.a accesses the value of an attribute a of a tuple t. Dot notation also references multiple attributes:**
> t.(ai, ..., aj) = (t.ai, ..., t.aj).

Dot notation accesses the value of an attribute of a tuple. For example, given a tuple t over a relation having schema r(a1, a2, ..., an), t.ai references the value of attribute ai of the tuple t. Consider extending this dot notation to reference the value of multiple attributes resulting in a tuple of attribute values. Let t be a tuple over a relation having schema r(a1, a2, ..., an), then t.(ai, ..., aj) = (t.ai, ..., t.aj) where { ai, ..., aj } ⊆ R. If { ai, ..., aj } ⊂ R, then t.(ai, ..., aj) references some of the attributes of the tuple t. If { ai, ..., aj } = R, then t.(ai, ..., aj) references the entire tuple.

The *no duplicate tuples* constraint built into the definition of a relation as a set of tuples can be restated as: Let t1 and t2 be distinct tuples over a relation having schema r(a1, a2, ..., an), then t1.(a1, a2, ..., an) ≠ t2.(a1, a2, ..., an). Thus, the *no duplicate tuples* constraint is a default uniqueness constraint for a relation. Figure 1.8 visualizes this constraint definition by illustrating that when t1 and t2 are referencing distinct tuples over the relation r, i.e. t1 ≠ t2, then the values associated with the tuples cannot be equal: t1.(a1, a2, ..., an) ≠ t2.(a1, a2, ..., an).

**FIGURE 1.8**
**Visualization of the no duplicate tuples constraint on a relation.**

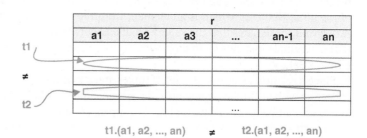

A *superkey* for a relation having schema r(a1, a2, ..., an) is defined to be any set of attributes { ai, ..., aj } satisfying { ai, ..., aj } ⊆ R such that for any two distinct tuples t1 and t2, t1.(ai, ..., aj) ≠ t2.(ai, ..., aj). A superkey defines a uniqueness constraint for a relation, but a superkey may contain more attributes than necessary to uniquely identify a tuple. For example, EMPLOYEE is a superkey of employee(eID, eLast, eFirst, eTitle, eSalary), but eID by itself uniquely identifies an employee tuple. A minimal superkey, a superkey for which no subset forms a superkey, is called a *candidate key*. Therefore, eID is a candidate key of employee, whereas EMPLOYEE is not a candidate key since { eID } ⊆ EMPLOYEE and eID is a superkey.

> **A *superkey* is a set of attributes that uniquely identify a tuple in the table. A *candidate key* is a superkey for which no subset forms a superkey.**

Candidate keys are designated on a relation schema using an underline, e.g.

employee(<u>eID</u>, eLast, eFirst, eTitle, eSalary)

A relation may have several candidate keys. For example, if it can be assumed that the combination of the eLast and eFirst attributes uniquely identifies an employee, then { eLast, eFirst } and { eID } are each a candidate key. Typically, all candidate keys are underlined to visually illustrate the uniqueness constraints on the relation.

employee(<u>eID</u>, <u>eLast, eFirst</u>, eTitle, eSalary)

The primary candidate key used to uniquely identify tuples in a table definition is called the *primary key*. In addition to specifying a uniqueness constraint, a primary key implies that the value of the attributes forming the primary key cannot be null. For the employee table, the { eID } candidate key is much smaller than the combination of the { eLast, eFirst } attributes. Thus, { eID } is chosen as the primary key for employee.

> **A *primary key* is the candidate key chosen to uniquely identify tuples in a table definition. The value of the primary key attributes cannot be null.**

Based on the above discussion, it is noteworthy to realize that a primary key is a candidate key and a candidate key is a superkey. Therefore, a primary key is a superkey. Table 1.2 summarizes the definitions and relationships between superkeys, candidate keys, and primary keys. Note that there are many superkeys for the employee table, which are only indicated in the table as an ellipsis (...). Any subset of attributes of employee that contain eID or the combination of eLast, eFirst is a superkey. These similarities and differences between the key definitions are important when declaring the database structure and when evaluating the properties of a given database design, which will be covered in Chapter 10.

**Table 1.2  Key Definition Summary with Examples**

| Key | Definition | employee **Example** |
|---|---|---|
| superkey | a set of attributes such that the values of these attributes are unique for any two distinct tuples (t1 ≠ t2) | { eID, eLast, eFirst, eTitle, eSalary } ... |
| candidate key | a minimal superkey – a superkey for which no subset is a superkey | { eID }, { eLast, eFirst } |
| primary key | candidate key chosen as primary | { eID } |

## 1.3.3 Referential Integrity

A relational database does not consist of a single relation but a collection of relations that are logically related. Therefore, the schema of a relational database is a set of relation schemas, along with constraints that define the relationships between the relations. Each relation name must be unique within a relational database schema. An attribute name is unique within a relation schema.

The most common logical relationship between relations in a relational database schema is given by a *referential integrity constraint*, where the attribute value in one table references

> A *foreign key* in a table references the primary key in *another* table, defining a *referential integrity constraint.*

an attribute value in another table. For example, consider a relational database consisting of the employee relation and a title relation, where the relation schema title(tTitle, tMinSalary, tMaxSalary) denotes the possible titles (tTitle) for employees and the minimum and maximum salaries for the given title (tMinSalary and tMaxSalary). Let the value of the eTitle attribute of the employee table reference the primary key tTitle of the title table, indicating that the value of eTitle is either null or appears as the value of the tTitle attribute for some tuple in the title table. The eTitle attribute is called a *foreign key.*

An attribute or set of attributes is a *foreign key* of a referencing table r1 if it references the primary key of the referenced table r2. Thus, the foreign key of r1 and the primary key of r2 must have the same domain. The referential integrity constraint requires that if the value of the foreign key attributes in r1 is not null, then it is equal to the value of the primary key attributes of some tuple in r2. In the context of a single attribute as a foreign key, let f denote the foreign key attribute of r1 and p denote the primary key attribute of r2, then for a tuple t1 ranging over r1 either t1.f = null or there exists a tuple t2 in r2 such that t1.f = t2.p. Figure 1.9 provides a pictorial representation of this referential integrity constraint for both the abstract example and the employee/title example at the instance level. For the abstract example, the figure indicates that the non-null value for the foreign key attribute f in r1 must appear as a value for the primary key attribute p in r2. For the employee/title example, the value Database Administrator for the eTitle foreign key attribute in the employee relation must appear as the value of the tTitle primary key attribute for some row in the title relation.

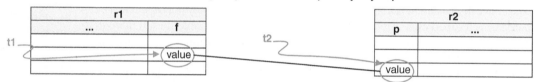

**FIGURE 1.9**    Referential integrity constraint: abstract and example.

The referential integrity constraint is enforcing an instance-level constraint. However, how can this constraint be represented at the schema level? The schema of the tables in the example are

employee(<u>eID</u>, eLast, eFirst, eTitle, eSalary)
title(<u>tTitle</u>, tMinSalary, tMaxSalary)

This textual representation of the schema indicates the primary key, but it does not indicate the foreign keys with the referenced table. Different books use various techniques for representing the primary–foreign key relationship. Textually, the industry-standard SQL uses a referential integrity clause to define this relationship (see Chapter 6). This text uses a visual schema with different color and shaped keys positioned next to attributes that are part of a primary or foreign key, and a line linking the primary and foreign keys. A primary key attribute has a gold key positioned to its left; a foreign key attribute has an orange key positioned to its right. Figure 1.10 illustrates the relational schema, primary and foreign keys, and referential integrity constraint visually for the employee-title example.

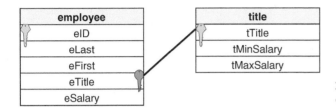

**FIGURE 1.10**   **Visual schema:** employee-title **example.**

The definition of a primary key, and therefore, a referencing foreign key, may have multiple attributes. A key that has multiple attributes is called a *composite* key. Composite keys occur frequently in practice. Consider an abstraction of an ONLINE RETAILER that sells items by multiple suppliers. The quantity available for an item differs by supplier. The price of the item on a customer's order depends on the supplier. An item on an order is typically called a lineitem with a purchased quantity. An order can have multiple lineitems identified within the order by a linenumber. An order is associated with exactly one customer. Here is a textual schema indicating primary keys and only some descriptive attributes for brevity.

> A *composite* **primary or foreign key consists of more than one attribute.**

```
customer(cust_id, cust_name ... )
order(order_id, cust_id, order_date, order_total, ... )
item(item_id, item_name, ...)
supplier(supp_id, supp_name, ...)
item_supplier(item_id, supp_id, qty_available, supp_price, ...)
lineitem(order_id, linenumber, item_id, supp_id, price, quantity, ...)
```

Figure 1.11 visually depicts the schema with both primary and foreign keys. The table item_supplier has a composite primary key consisting of item_id and supp_id, which is shown by a gold edge linking the primary key symbols. Since an item is supplied by many suppliers and a supplier supplies many items, it is the combination of the item and supplier that determines the available quantity of the item by that supplier. In the lineitem table, there are both a composite primary key and a composite foreign key. A lineitem is uniquely identified by the order number and the linenumber since an order can include many items. The purchase is for an item supplied by a supplier. Therefore, the composite foreign key is the combination of the item_id and supp_id, which is shown by an orange edge linking the foreign key symbols. This composite foreign key is linked to its referenced primary key in item_supplier. The order_id is also a foreign key in lineitem.

This ONLINE RETAILER schema is much more complicated than the simpler example schema shown with employees and titles. Thus, more interesting observations can be made regarding the referential integrity and the implications on the relationship between the sets of values in the primary and foreign keys. Recall that when defining relations, the term *cardinality* was introduced to refer to the number of tuples in a relation. Mathematically, cardinality means the number of elements in a set, which makes sense since a relation is a set of tuples. The cardinality of a set is denoted by enclosing the set or its name within vertical bars. Therefore, $| r |$ denotes the cardinality

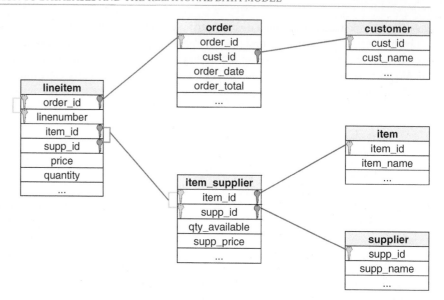

**FIGURE 1.11**
Visual schema: abstraction of ONLINE
RETAILER example.

of a relation r. Although cardinality appears to be a straightforward concept, there are important observations worth noting with respect to uniqueness and referential integrity constraints in databases.

Earlier, dot notation was introduced on a tuple to access that value of an attribute and then extended to a tupling of values when given a tuple of attribute names. Consider a further extension of dot notation as it applies to a relation name. Given a relation r having schema r(a1, a2, ..., an), let r.ai reference the set of (distinct) values for attribute ai in the instance of r. Thus, |r.ai| denotes the cardinality or the number of distinct set of values for ai. More formally, let r.ai = { t.ai | t ∈ r }. Extending this definition to a tupling of attribute names yields r.(ai, ..., aj) = { (t.ai, ..., t.aj) | t ∈ r }. The definition of referential integrity indicates that a non-null foreign key value must appear as a primary key value in its referencing table. Therefore, the set of distinct values for a foreign key must be a subset (may be equal) of the set of distinct values for its corresponding primary key. In the abstract scenario appearing earlier, r1.f ⊆ r2.p and |r1.f| ≤ |r2.p|. Table 1.3 summarizes the referential integrity constraints defined in the ONLINE RETAILER schema with respect to the set of values. The relationship between cardinalities of the sets is based on the set of values.

Table 1.3    **Summary of Referential Integrity in the**
**ONLINE RETAILER Schema**

| Foreign key | ⊆ | Primary key |
|---|---|---|
| item_supplier.item_id | ⊆ | item.item_id |
| item_supplier.supp_id | ⊆ | supplier.supp_id |
| order.cust_id | ⊆ | customer.cust_id |
| lineitem.order_id | ⊆ | order.order_id |
| lineitem.(item_id, supp_id) | ⊆ | item_supplier.(item_id, supp_id) |

Based on the referential integrity constraints in the ONLINE RETAILER schema, what can be concluded about lineitem.item_id? The ⊆ operator is transitive, so lineitem.item_id ⊆ item.item_id. Similarly, lineitem.supp_id ⊆ supplier.supp_id. However, the combination of the item_id and supp_id in lineitem must appear in that same combination in item_supplier, as indicated by the composite foreign key referencing the composite primary key. For example, consider an abstract instance of the item, supplier, and item_supplier tables shown in Figure 1.12. This figure shows two items and two suppliers with two item_supplier tuples where item i1 is supplied by sa and item i2 is supplied by sb. If a lineitem tuple was to be inserted having item i1 being supplied by supplier sb, this would violate referential integrity and not be allowed because there is no corresponding (i1, sb, ...) tuple in the item_supplier table although i1 is a valid item_id and sb is a valid supp_id.

| item | | |
|---|---|---|
| item_id | item_name | ... |
| i1 | item1 | |
| ... | | |
| i2 | item2 | |

| supplier | | |
|---|---|---|
| supp_id | supp_name | ... |
| sa | suppliera | |
| ... | | |
| sb | supplierb | |

| item_supplier | | |
|---|---|---|
| item_id | supp_id | ... |
| i1 | sa | |
| ... | | |
| i2 | sb | |

**FIGURE 1.12**
ONLINE RETAILER **abstract instance for item, supplier, and** item_supplier.

## SPECIAL TOPIC 1.1   Primary Key and Referential Integrity

Referential integrity designates an association between the concepts represented by the primary and foreign keys. The *subset of* relation between the foreign and primary key instances provides insight into the participation of the primary key in this association. As discussed earlier, if f is a foreign key in r1 referencing the primary key p of r2, then r1.f ⊆ r2.p. There are two scenarios to consider:

- r1.f ⊂ r2.p: There exists a primary key value pi that is not participating in the association.

- r1.f = r2.p: Every primary key value pi is participating in the association.

Consider an example for the ONLINE RETAILER where item_supplier.item_id ⊂ item.item_id. In this case, there exists an item that is not currently supplied by any supplier. In other words, there exists an item that is not participating in the "supplied by" association. Similarly, if lineitem.(item_id, supplier_id)=item_supplier.(item_id, supplier_id), then every supplied item has been ordered, because the primary key appears as a foreign key value in the lineitem table.

## 1.3.4 Additional Constraints

The ability to define constraints that must hold on the data is a powerful feature of databases. It is the responsibility of the database system to enforce these constraints. For example, when modifications (insert, update, delete) are attempted on the data, the database system must check that the change will not violate the defined constraints. For example, when adding a tuple to a table, will the values of the primary key attribute(s) be unique in the table instance? If the value of an attribute changes, is the attribute part of a primary key or foreign key? Both the primary key and referential integrity constraint must be verified before allowing the change to occur. As another example, consider the deletion of a tuple. If the tuple is involved as a referenced primary key, the database system must check that there does not exist a foreign key value referencing that tuple. Otherwise, the deletion of the tuple would result in a referential integrity constraint violation.

There are additional constraints that can be defined on the data besides primary and foreign keys. Various constraints and their syntax in the SQL industry-standard language will be covered in Chapter 6. However, some of these constraints will be motivated here as an integral component of a relational database.

> **Use a *not null* constraint when an attribute must have a value.**

Recall that the primary key constraint means that the value of the primary key attributes cannot be null and must form a unique tuple in the table. Both of these simpler constraints can be defined on an attribute or a combination of attributes. For example, on the employee table, you may want to require that each of the non-primary key attributes cannot be null because employees in the database must have a value for last name, first name, title, and salary.

> **Use a *unique* constraint to define multiple candidate keys.**

There are also other situations besides primary keys where a uniqueness constraint must hold. One scenario was already alluded to in the definition of a primary key. If there are multiple candidate keys for a table, a unique constraint can be added to enforce the other candidate keys. Another example is enforcing a constraint on the cardinality of a relationship. For example, consider extending the sample dept table to include an attribute called mgrId, which if not null must be a valid eID value in the employee table. If an employee can be the manager of only one department, then a unique constraint on mgrId can be defined to enforce this requirement.

> **Use a *check* constraint to define simple constraints on the values of attributes.**

There may be attributes in the database that have a fixed, small number of possible values. For example, the sex of a newborn child added to an employee's corresponding health insurance record must be male or female. A check constraint can define the list of valid values, e.g. 'M' or 'F'.

The primary key, referential integrity, not null, unique, and check constraints are the most common specified constraints besides the textual or numeric types of the attributes. The details for specifying these constraints in SQL along with additional features of SQL are covered in Chapter 6.

## Self Check

7.  What terminology refers to an attribute value that is unknown?
8.  Describe the relationship between a superkey, candidate key, and primary key?
9.  What is the name of the constraint defined between a foreign and primary key?

## Chapter Notes Summary

### Databases Are a Tool

- Databases provide efficient shared access to persistent data, with inherent support for concurrent users, recovering from failures, and managing user access privileges.
- The goals of a database include specifying views for different users of the data, which are unaffected by adding new data or by changing access mechanisms to improve performance.

### Overview of Data and Models

- Network and hierarchical databases inherently represented one-to-many associations with database commands embedded within a programming language.
- Relational databases use tables to represent concepts that are linked by attribute values.
- Conceptual data models typically use graphical representations to illustrate the concepts in the database and the associations between them.
- Object-oriented databases are integrated within object-oriented programming languages, using the value of an immutable object identifier to relate persistent objects.

- Programming languages use a call-level interface for querying a relational database, which results in an *impedance mismatch* between the set of answers returned by the database and the program examining the answers one-at-a-time by iterating over that set.
- XML and JSON are textual representations for exchanging data that are supported by most database systems and programming languages.

## The Relational Data Model

- A *schema* of a relation refers to its description with its name and attributes. An *instance* of a relation is a *set* of tuples – unordered without duplicates.
- A null value designates that the value of that attribute in the tuple is unknown.
- Dot notation t.a accesses the value of an attribute a of a tuple t. Dot notation also references multiple attributes: t.(ai, ..., aj) = (t.ai, ..., t.aj).
- A *superkey* is a set of attributes that uniquely identify a tuple in the table. A *candidate key* is a superkey for which no subset forms a superkey.
- A *primary key* is the candidate key chosen to uniquely identify tuples in a table definition. The value of the primary key attributes cannot be null.
- A *foreign key* in a table references the primary key in *another* table, defining a *referential integrity constraint*.
- A *composite* primary or foreign key consists of more than one attribute.
- Use a *not null* constraint when an attribute must have a value.
- Use a *unique* constraint to define multiple candidate keys.
- Use a *check* constraint to define simple constraints on the values of attributes.

# Chapter Reminders

The chapter introduced two different notations for indicating the schema of a relation: textual and visual. The textual summary as an ordered tuple with candidate keys underlined is shown in Table 1.4. The visual notation for a relational schema places gold keys to the left of the attribute names that form the primary key. Composite keys include lines that link the attributes together, illustrating the composite nature of the key. A foreign key places an orange key to the right of the attribute names. Links between the foreign key and the primary key that it references indicate the referential integrity constraint. Figure 1.13 represents a visual schema for the abstract example of relation r1 having an attribute f that is a foreign key referencing the primary key attribute p of relation r2. Within the chapter, Figure 1.10 illustrates a simple visual schema for the employee-title example, whereas Figure 1.11 presents a visual schema for the ONLINE RETAILER example that has composite primary and foreign keys.

**Table 1.4  Summary of Relational Schema Notation**

| Concept | Abstract | Example |
|---|---|---|
| Relation name | r | employee |
| Ordered tuple | r(a1, a2, ..., an) | employee(elD, eLast, eFirst, eTitle, eSalary) |
| Set of attributes | R = { a1, a2, ..., an } | EMPLOYEE = { elD, eLast, eFirst, eTitle, eSalary } |

**FIGURE 1.13**  Abstract visual schema.

# Practice

Use the scenarios below to practice your understanding of the relational data model by identifying constraints and comparing cardinalities. There are sample answers provided at the end of the chapter after the solutions to the self-check questions.

## Practice Problems: MLS

Consider a scenario of selling houses. There is a multiple listing service (MLS) that provides information about homes for sale. A unique MLS number is assigned to the listing, along with the date and price of the listing. Other required properties to post the listing include the address (street, city, state, zip) and the listing agent with realty.

1.  What is the schema of the relation mls that describes a listing? Indicate the primary key in your answer.

2.  Comment on other constraints, if any, that are associated with the relation: not null, unique, check.

The MLS must also maintain a history of price changes, which is displayed on the Web page with the date and price on that date.

3.  What is the schema of the relation pricehistory that describes a history of the price changes to the listing? Indicate the primary key in your answer.

4.  Comment on other constraints, if any, that are associated with the relation: not null, unique, check.

Consider the schema for the mls and pricehistory tables from the answers above.

5.  Does mls have any foreign keys? If so, identify with the referenced table.

6.  Does pricehistory have any foreign keys? If so, identify with the referenced table.

Write an expression to answer the following questions using dot notation and either the set relationships ($\subseteq, \subset, \supseteq, \supset$) or the comparison operators ($\leq, <, >, \geq$). State any assumptions.

7.  Compare the cardinality of the unique MLS number in the mls relation to its cardinality in the pricehistory relations.

8.  Compare the set of distinct values of the unique MLS number in the pricehistory relation to the mls relation.

9.  Compare the cardinality of the mls relation to the cardinality of the pricehistory relation.

10. Compare the cardinality of the address in the mls relation to the cardinality of the unique MLS number in the mls relation.

## Practice Problems: COURSE SCHEDULE

Consider a scenario of university courses that are described in a course catalog with a unique course id, a title, a catalog description, and the number of credits.

1.  What is the schema of the relation catalog that describes a course? Indicate the primary key in your answer.

2.  Comment on other constraints, if any, that are associated with the relation: not null, unique, check.

The schedule for course registration provides a unique line number for a course offering, the course id for the course, the date and time that the course is offered, along with the classroom and the instructor of record.

3.  What is the schema of the relation schedule that describes the course offerings for registration? Indicate the primary key in your answer.

4.  Comment on other constraints, if any, that are associated with the relation: not null, unique, check.

Consider the schema for the catalog and schedule tables from the answers above.

5. Does catalog have any foreign keys? If so, identify with the referenced table.

6. Does schedule have any foreign keys? If so, identify with the referenced table.

Write an expression to answer the following questions using dot notation and either the set relationships ($\subseteq, \subset, \supseteq, \supset$) or the comparison operators ($\leq, <, >, \geq$). State any assumptions.

7. Compare the cardinality of the unique course number in the catalog relation to its cardinality in the schedule relations.

8. Compare the set of distinct values of the course number in the schedule relation to the catalog relation.

9. Compare the cardinality of the catalog relation to the cardinality of the schedule relation.

10. Compare the cardinality of the classroom in the schedule relation to the cardinality of the unique schedule line number in the schedule relation.

# End of Chapter Exercises

Consider the course management system (CMS) that your university uses to facilitate course communication and grade recording. There is a database behind this CMS to maintain information regarding courses, students, students enrolled in courses, graded items, and scores on graded items.

A course is uniquely identified by a course id and has descriptive attributes of title, semester, and year.

1. What is the schema of the relation course that describes a course? Indicate the primary key in your answer.

2. Comment on other constraints, if any, that are associated with the relation: not null, unique, check.

A student is uniquely identified by the student id and is further described by a last name, first name, and university email address.

3. What is the schema of the relation student that describes a student? Indicate the primary key in your answer.

4. Comment on other constraints, if any, that are associated with the relation: not null, unique, check.

The enrollment information of a student in a course associates the student id with a course id.

5. What is the schema of the relation enrolled that describes the enrollment of a student in the course? Indicate the primary key in your answer.

6. Comment on other constraints, if any, that are associated with the relation: not null, unique, check.

A graded item has a unique id, a name, its weight, the total number of possible points, and the unique course id associated with the graded item.

7. What is the schema of the relation gradeditem that describes a graded item in the CMS? Indicate the primary key in your answer.

8. Comment on other constraints, if any, that are associated with the relation: not null, unique, check.

The score on an item associates a grade by a student enrolled in a course for the graded item.

9. What is the schema of the relation score that records the score of a graded item? Indicate the primary key in your answer.

10. Comment on other constraints, if any, that are associated with the relation: not null, unique, check.

Consider the collection of tables representing the CMS scenario that you defined: course, student, enrolled, gradeditem, score.

11. Draw a visual schema that clearly indicates the primary and foreign keys, including links indicating referential integrity.

Write an expression to answer the following questions using dot notation and either the set relationships ($\subseteq$, $\subset$, $\supseteq$, $\supset$) or the comparison operators ($\leq$, $<$, $>$, $\geq$). State any assumptions.

12. Compare the cardinality of the unique course id in the course relation to its cardinality in the enrolled relation.

13. Compare the set of distinct values of the course id in the enrolled relation to the course relation.

14. Compare the cardinality of the course table with the cardinality of the enrolled relation.

15. Compare the cardinality of the combination of the course id and student id in the score relation with the combination of these attributes in the enrolled relation.

16. Compare the set of distinct values of the course id in the gradeditem relation to the course relation.

## Answers to Self-Check Questions

1. query language

2. concurrency control

3. The ability of the database to add data without affecting the views of the data already defined.

4. Entity-Relationship diagrams

5. Object-Oriented

6. XML or JSON

7. A null value designates that the value of that attribute in the tuple is unknown.

8. A superkey is a set of attributes that uniquely identify a tuple in a relation. A candidate key is a superkey for which no subset forms a superkey. A primary key is the candidate key chosen to uniquely identify tuples in the table's definition.

9. referential integrity constraint

## Answers to Practice Problems: MLS

1. mls(<u>mlsnum</u>, listprice, listdate, street, city, state, zip, listagent, listrealty)

2. Constraints:
   **candidate keys:** mlsnum is the primary key.
   **not null:** all fields are required to have a value.
   **unique:** no additional unique constraints besides primary key.
   **check:** listprice must be positive.

3. pricehistory(<u>mlsnum, pricedate</u>, amount)

4. Constraints:

**candidate keys:** The primary key is composite: the combination of mlsnum and pricedate is required to uniquely identify a tuple. This primary key limits a price change to once per day, which is reasonable for the enterprise.

**not null:** all fields are required to have a value.

**unique:** no additional unique constraints besides primary key.

**check:** amount must be positive.

5. The mls relation does not have any foreign keys.

6. The mlsnum in the pricehistory relation is a foreign key, referencing the primary key of the mls relation.

7. $|mls.mlsnum| \geq |pricehistory.mlsnum|$

8. $pricehistory.mlsnum \subseteq mls.mlsnum$

9. $|mls| \leq |pricehistory|$, assuming that there is at least one price change per mls listing.

10. $|mls.(street, city, state, zip)| \leq |mls.mlsnum|$, since a particular property may be sold multiple times.

# Answers to Practice Problems: Course Schedule

1. catalog(<u>courseid</u>, title, description, credits)

2. Constraints:

**candidate keys:** courseid is the primary key.

**not null:** all fields are required to have a value.

**unique:** no additional unique constraints besides primary key; e.g. two different colleges may offer a course titled 'Databases'.

**check:** credits must be positive.

3. schedule(<u>linenumber</u>, courseid, classdatetime, classroom, instructor)

4. Constraints:

**candidate keys:** The primary key is the schedule linenumber. A course may have several offerings in the schedule.

**not null:** courseid and classdatetime must not be null; primary keys have an implicit not null and unique constraint; the classroom or instructor may be null if they have not yet been assigned.

**unique:** no additional unique constraints besides primary key.

**check:** none

5. The catalog relation does not have any foreign keys.

6. The courseid in the schedule relation is a foreign key, referencing the primary key of the catalog relation.

7. $|catalog.courseid| \geq |schedule.courseid|$

8. $schedule.courseid \subseteq catalog.courseid$

9. |catalog| ≤ |schedule|, assuming that there is at least one course offering for a class; in reality, this relationship is much more complicated because a course is not offered every semester.

10. |schedule.classroom| ≤ |schedule.linenumber|, since a classroom is used for multiple course offerings throughout the day.

## Bibliographic Notes

The foundation of the relational data model was introduced in 1970 [Codd, 1970]. The Object Data Standard [Cattell and Barry, 2000] provides a description of an object model, the specification of a schema using language bindings, and an object query language (OQL). There are many Web resources available on XML and JSON data.

## More to Explore

The Databases for Many Majors project (databasesmanymajors.faculty.asu.edu) introduces fundamental database concepts to students in many disciplines using visualizations. The Introduction to Relational Databases visualization highlights some issues with using spreadsheets and illustrates how relational databases, as a collection of tables, use the association between primary and foreign keys to link tables together to answer a query. There are 20 self-assessment questions at the end of the visualization to check your understanding.

# Conceptual Design

2

**LEARNING OBJECTIVES**

- To recognize the importance of gathering requirements for the conceptual design
- To model the gathered requirements using an Entity-Relationship diagram
- To apply the specified approach for mapping Entity-Relationship diagrams to a collection of relations
- To become familiar with alternative graphical approaches for database design

The first phase of building a database is to plan its design using a conceptual model. The requirements of the database must be gathered from the user and then represented using the conceptual data model. The Entity-Relationship (ER) data model is popular for describing the entity types or concepts to be represented in the database and the types of relationships or associations between these concepts. The ER data model includes constraints to model the number of times that an entity can be associated by a relationship and whether an instance of the entity must participate in the relationship. There is a visual component of the ER data model, known as ER diagrams, that graphically illustrate the conceptual model. This chapter presents ER diagrams for the representation of the database design and a methodology for mapping ER diagrams to a collection of relations for storing the data in the enterprise. Two other graphical conceptual models that are widely used are presented to illustrate their similarities: Unified Modeling Language (UML) conceptual class diagrams and Crow's Foot notation. UML conceptual class diagrams developed for modeling object-oriented programs can also be used for designing databases. The Crow's Foot notation is another conceptual data model for designing databases that developed about the same time as ER diagrams.

## 2.1 Gathering Requirements

The process of designing a relational database schema can be quite complex. One of the first steps in the design process is to gather the requirements of the enterprise. A conceptual data model acts as a bridge between the requirements document and the implementation. Consider the following brief requirements of an enterprise on employee training:

A company wants to maintain a database on the training courses that it provides to its employees. Each training course is offered to fit within a technology area deemed important by the company for its strategic directions. Each technology area has an employee identified as its lead, who has the responsibility to maintain a Web page on the company's intranet to provide its employees with the current state of this technology area. The employees that took a training course on a given date are maintained in the database.

Does this description provide enough information to design the database? Probably not, but it does provide a good starting point. You should be thinking of questions to ask your users:

- What characteristics do you want the database to maintain about employees, training courses, and technology areas?

- Must a technology area have an employee lead? Can an employee lead more than one technology area?

- Does a training course have to be classified in one of the technology areas? Can it be classified in more than one technology area?

- Can an employee take the same training course more than once?

The answers that your users provide regarding how their company works will guide the database design. In this scenario, assume the following:

- The characteristics of an employee include a unique employee identification number, a last name, a first name, a title, and a salary. An employee can be the lead of at most one technology area. An employee can take many training courses but can take a given training course at most once.

- The characteristics of a training course include a unique course identity, a title, and the length of the course in hours. A training course must be classified within exactly one of the identified technology areas. Many employees can take a training course and the date that an employee takes a training course must be maintained.

- The characteristics of a technology area include a unique area identity, a title, and the URL of the Web page for the technology area. A technology area must have exactly one employee lead but can have many associated training courses.

> **Gather the requirements of the enterprise and use the conceptual data model to represent those constraints at a higher level of abstraction.**

Once the requirements of the enterprise are gathered, the next step is to model a conceptual design. During the conceptual design process, requirements may have to be refined in an iterative process. The goal of a conceptual data model is to capture the constraints of the enterprise at a higher level of abstraction than the level of implementation. ER diagrams are a tool for representing a database design.

## 2.2 Entity-Relationship Diagrams

The Entity-Relationship conceptual data model uses a graphical notation to represent this abstraction through Entity-Relationship (ER) diagrams. The fundamental components of ER diagrams are entities and relationships. An entity represents the type of an object of interest in the enterprise. In an ER diagram, a rectangular box denotes an entity with the name of the entity given within the rectangle. An entity is described by its characteristics, which are called attributes. Attribute names are enclosed within ovals that are linked by edges to the entity it is describing. An attribute is assumed to have a single value unless it is denoted by a double oval, indicating that the attribute can have multiple values. Some attributes are *composite* attributes, which are made up of simpler components. A composite attribute is linked to its simpler attributes via edges. Canonical examples of composite attributes are full name, which is composed of first and last name, and address, which is made up of the street, city, state, and zip. An attribute whose value uniquely identifies an entity instance is a *key* attribute, which is indicated by underlining its name. The term key attribute here refers to a candidate key, which was introduced in Chapter 1 for the relational data model. Figure 2.1 shows an ER diagram of an abstract entity e with descriptive attributes, summarizing the different types of attributes (single-valued, multivalued, composite, key).

> **Rectangles denote entities and ovals represent attributes.**

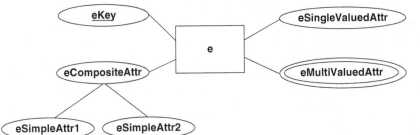

**FIGURE 2.1**
Abstract ER diagram illustrating entity and attributes.

A relationship is an association between entities. The name of a relationship is displayed within a diamond that is linked to the entities involved in the relationship. Binary relationships, which involve two entities, are the most common type of relationship encountered in the conceptual database design process. The edges linking entities to relationships are annotated to describe the cardinality ratio of the relationship. A cardinality ratio, such as 1:1 (one-to-one), 1:N (one-to-many)/N:1 (many-to-one), M:N (many-to-many), indicates a constraint on the number of times that the entities may be involved in the relationship. Figure 2.2 illustrates the representation of cardinality ratios in an ER diagram. The relationship ab is 1:1; an instance of entity a is related to at most one instance of entity b, and an instance of entity b is related to at most one instance of entity a. The relationship cd is 1:N; an instance of entity c is related to at most one instance of entity d, and an instance of entity d is related to possibly many instances of entity c. The relationship ef is M:N; an instance of entity e is related to possibly many instances of entity f, and an instance of entity f is related to possibly many instances of entity e.

> **Diamonds indicate relationships between entities.**

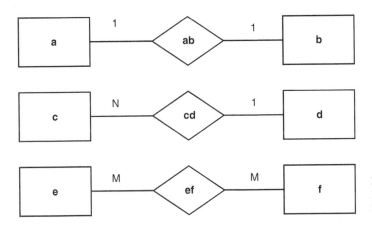

**FIGURE 2.2**
Example relationships for 1:1, 1:N, and M:N cardinality ratios.

ER diagrams also provide for the specification of a *participation constraint*, indicating whether a given instance of an entity is required to participate in an instance of the relationship. The participation constraint is denoted by the edge linking the entity to the relationship. A single edge denotes a *partial participation* constraint of the entity in the relationship. A given instance of an entity may participate in the relationship but it is not required to participate. A double edge denotes a *total participation* of the entity in the relationship. A given instance of an entity must participate in the relationship.

Up to this point, there has been an implicit assumption that each entity contains attributes that uniquely identify that entity across the entire enterprise. However, this may not be the case for all entities. The canonical example in an extended employee database is the dependents of an

> **Cardinality ratios and participation constraints indicate important information about a relationship.**

employee. Descriptive attributes for a dependent typically include first name, birth date, and sex. None of these attributes or combination thereof can uniquely identify a dependent in the enterprise since it is possible that there are two dependents in the database for two different employees that have the same first name, birth date, and sex. However, the first name and birth date should uniquely identify a dependent for a given employee. The **dependent** entity is called a *weak* entity and can be identified by its *partial key* given by first name and birth date for a given employee. An entity that has attributes that uniquely identify an instance of the entity across the entire enterprise is called a *strong* entity.

The abstract ER diagram of Figure 2.3 illustrates a weak entity w, which is denoted by a double rectangle on the ER diagram. The weak entity has a *partial key* or *discriminator*, called wPartialKey, which is an attribute or a combination of attributes that uniquely identifies the entity within its *identifying owner*. ER diagrams indicate the partial key by underlining the attribute name by a dashed line. The *identifying owner* is designated by its participation with the weak entity in an *identifying relationship*, which is denoted by a double diamond on the ER diagram. In Figure 2.3, the identifying relationship i associates the weak entity w with its identifying owner o. A weak entity has total participation, indicated by the double edge, in its identifying relationship since it must participate in this relationship to be uniquely identified in the enterprise. The cardinality ratios indicate that the identifying relationship is a 1:N relationship. An instance of the weak entity w is associated with exactly one instance of the identifying owner class. An instance of entity o may be associated with several weak entity instances.

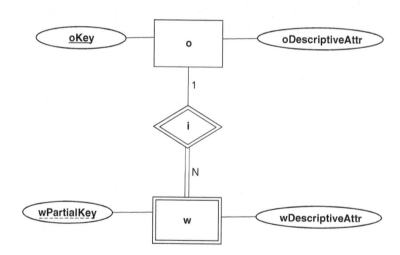

**FIGURE 2.3**
Abstract ER diagram illustrating weak entity.

## HOW TO 2.1   Design an ER Diagram

Using the gathered requirements, identify the important concepts in the enterprise and the associations between these concepts. Entities are typically denoted by the nouns in the gathered requirements and the attributes as adjectives that describe the concept. Relationships are the associations between the entities, which are typically found as verbs in the requirements description.

**Strong entity:** For each strong entity, draw a rectangle and label the inside of the rectangle with the name of the entity.

**Entity attributes:** Add descriptive attributes for the entity by drawing an oval for each attribute and labeling the inside of the oval with the name of the characteristic for that entity. Identify the key of the entity by underlining the attribute name. If the characteristic can have multiple values, use a double oval for the attribute. Note that a key attribute must be single-valued. Also, an attribute must describe the entity to which it is linked.

**Relationship:** For each association between two entities, draw a diamond and label it with the name of the relationship. Then draw lines from the diamond to the rectangles representing the associated entities.

**Relationship attributes:** Examine the requirements to determine whether the relationship has characteristics that only describe the association. If so, add attribute(s) to the relationship.

**Cardinality ratio:** For each entity, determine the maximum number of times (1 or N) that the entity is related to the other entity by the relationship under consideration. If entity a can be related to at most one b, place a 1 on the line linking the relationship to b; otherwise, place the letter N, denoting that an instance of entity a can be related to many instances of entity b. If a can be related to many

b's and a b can be related to many a's, then the letters M and N are used to denote a many-to-many relationship.

**Participation constraint:** For each entity, determine the minimum number of times that the entity is related to the other entity. If an entity must participate in the relationship, then draw a double line between the entity and the relationship's diamond.

**Weak entity:** For each weak entity, draw a double rectangle and label the inside of the rectangle with the name of the entity. Link its partial key, underlined with dashes, and any descriptive attributes of the entity. Draw a double line to a double diamond that represents the identifying relationship, which is linked by a single line to the identifying owner entity. Note that the weak entity has one identifying owner instance, so the edge between the identifying relationship and identifying owner is labeled with a 1. The double line indicating the total participation of the weak entity in the identifying relationship is labeled with an N because an identifying owner may be related to multiple weak entity instances, which are uniquely identified within that owner by the partial key.

Figure 2.4 gives an ER diagram for the Employee Training enterprise. In the working example, the entities are employee, training course, and technology area. The employee entity has attributes eID, eName, eTitle, and eSalary. The attributes eID, eTitle, and eSalary are simple attributes. The attribute eName is a composite attribute, which consists of the simple attributes eLast and eFirst. Although not included in this example, a multivalued eSkills attribute could

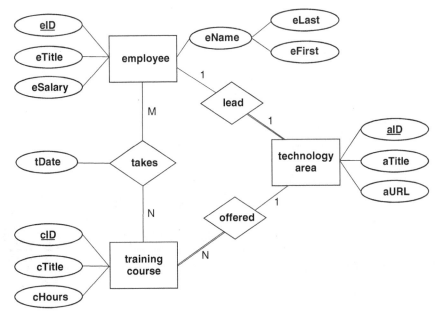

**FIGURE 2.4**
Employee Training ER diagram.

be defined that represents the skill set of an employee. In the EMPLOYEE TRAINING enterprise, each entity has a key attribute corresponding to the unique identity for that entity.

The EMPLOYEE TRAINING ER has three relationships: lead, offered, and takes. The lead relationship has a 1:1 cardinality ratio because an employee can lead at most one technology area and a technology area is led by one employee. The offered relationship has a 1:N cardinality ratio since a training course is classified within one of the identified technology areas and a technology area can have many associated training courses. The takes relationship has an M:N cardinality ratio because an employee can take many training courses and many employees take a training course.

Figure 2.4 includes the participation constraints on the relationships for the EMPLOYEE TRAINING enterprise. The participation of an employee in the role of a lead in a technology area is partial since an employee may or may not lead a technology area, whereas the participation of a technology area in the lead relationship is total since a technology area must have an employee lead. For the offered relationship, a training course must be classified within one of the identified technology areas. Note that a technology area does not have to offer training courses. This may seem counterintuitive. However, both entities involved in a relationship cannot have total participation. A technology area needs to be created first, so that when a training course is added, the course can be classified within a technology area. Similarly, for the M:N takes relationship, a training course must exist before an employee takes the course, so training course has partial participation in takes. Since an employee may not take a training course, the employee entity's participation in takes is partial.

## SPECIAL TOPIC 2.2    (Min, Max) Pairs

There is an alternative method available for specifying the cardinality and participation constraints on an ER diagram. Specifically, the edge between the entity and the relationship is labeled with a (min, max) pair, representing the minimum and maximum number of times that an entity participates in the relationship. The use of (min, max) pairs has the potential to provide more detailed information than the combination of cardinality and participation constraints, which only uses 0, 1 and M or N. The min and max can specify a given number that represents a constraint from the enterprise being modeled. A minimum of 0 represents partial participation, whereas a minimum of 1 or greater represents total participation. The double line for total participation is only used in conjunction with (min, max) pairs in the presence of a weak entity, linking the weak entity to its identifying relationship. Figure 2.5 illustrates the EMPLOYEE TRAINING ER diagram with the use of (min, max) pairs instead of the combination of cardinality ratios and participation constraints shown in Figure 2.4.

## SPECIAL TOPIC 2.3    Recursive Relationships and Role Names

A relationship that defines an association between the same entity is called a *recursive* relationship. There are many examples of recursive relationships in real life, such as employee supervision or a parent–child relationship. Role names are added to the edge linking the entity and relationship to distinguish between the two roles of the entity involved in the binary relationship. Figure 2.6 denotes a recursive relationship. A person can have at most two parents, as indicated by the (0, 2) on the edge labeled with the parent role. A person does not have to have children and can have possibly many children, designated by the (0, n) on the edge labeled with the role of children.

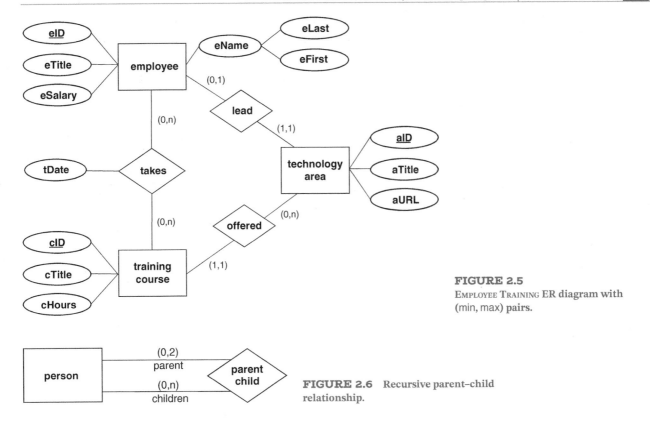

**FIGURE 2.5**
EMPLOYEE TRAINING ER diagram with (min, max) pairs.

**FIGURE 2.6** Recursive parent–child relationship.

## SPECIAL TOPIC 2.4  Ternary Relationships

The most common relationships involve two entities and are called *binary* relationships. However, there are relationships that relate more than two entities. For example, a *ternary* relationship relates three entities. A canonical example of a ternary relationship is in a university enterprise where a course is offered in a particular semester by an instructor of record. Typically, the university assigns a schedule number for each course offering. This ternary relationship can be represented with four entities and three binary relationships, as shown in Figure 2.7. The new offering entity with a schedule number is related to the original entities (course, semester, instructor) with three 1:N binary relationships. The offering entity is indicating the one course, semester, and instructor that it represents.

## SPECIAL TOPIC 2.5  EER for Modeling Inheritance

The EER conceptual data model extends the ER model with inherent support for modeling data organized as class hierarchies through features that provide the specification of the inheritance of properties and the associated constraints of the specialization. Interested readers should refer to the bibliographic notes of this chapter for references on exploring this advanced feature of conceptual modeling.

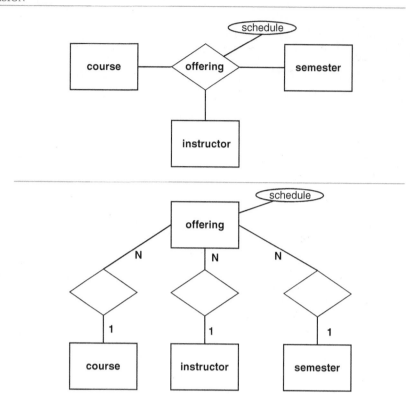

**FIGURE 2.7**

Ternary relationship and its corresponding representation using binary relationships.

There is still a constraint of the EMPLOYEE TRAINING enterprise that has not been discussed in the context of the ER diagram of Figure 2.4. "An employee can take many training courses but can take a given training course at most once." The cardinality of the takes relationship must be M:N since an employee can take many training courses and a training course is taken by many employees. The takes relationship has an attribute tDate, representing the date that the employee takes the training course. The single-valued characteristic of the tDate attribute of the takes relationship implies the constraint limiting an employee to take a specific course once. Otherwise, the tDate attribute should be multivalued, representing the dates that an employee took the training course.

There are, however, instance-level constraints that cannot be easily captured at the level of abstraction provided by ER diagrams, including domain constraints and some explicit constraints of the enterprise. Domain constraints limit the value of an attribute to a specific domain. Consider a domain constraint on eTitle, which would limit the title of an employee to be only those employee titles within the company. Some explicit constraints of an enterprise can only be enforced by the application code at the implementation level. As an example of such an explicit constraint, consider adding a constraint to the EMPLOYEE TRAINING enterprise that would require an employee lead to have taken at least one training course in the technology area that they lead. Although the ER diagram cannot represent all constraints, there are other constraints that can be captured by ER diagrams and their enhancements for object-oriented modeling that are beyond the scope of this book.

> **ER diagrams capture most constraints at a conceptual level. All constraints must be considered at the implementation level.**

Using ER diagrams, the Entity-Relationship conceptual data model provides, at a glance, a graphical representation of most of the constraints of an enterprise that would otherwise be hidden in the textual description of the requirements of the enterprise. The next section covers a heuristic algorithm for mapping ER diagrams to the relational data model that results in a correct representation of the enterprise at the implementation level.

# Self Check

1. What shape in an ER diagram denotes a descriptive characteristic of an entity or relationship?
2. If an entity must participate in the relationship, what type of line is drawn between the entity's rectangle and the relationship's diamond?
3. What term describes an attribute that consists of multiple components?

## 2.3  Mapping ER Diagrams to Tables

Once the conceptual design of the enterprise is complete, the next step is the design of the enterprise within the implementation data model. The mapping of the ER diagram to relational tables is guided by a set of rules. These rules are first illustrated using the abstract entities and relationships of Figures 2.1, 2.3, and 2.9. Then the rules are applied to the EMPLOYEE TRAINING ER diagram of Figure 2.4.

Figure 2.1 contains a strong entity e having a key attribute eKey, a composite attribute eCompositeAttr consisting of the simple attributes eSimple1 and eSimple2, a single-valued attribute eSingleValuedAttr and a multivalued attribute eMultiValuedAttr. The entity e is mapped to a table with the same name where the key attribute, the single-valued attribute, and the simple attributes of the composite attribute are included as attributes of the table:

> **Map an entity to a table, including its key attributes, single-valued attributes, and simple components of any composite attributes.**

e(eKey, eSingleValuedAttr, eSimple1, eSimple2)

Since the eKey attribute uniquely identifies an instance of the entity e, the attribute eKey also forms the key of the table e.

Since the domain of attributes in a relational table must be atomic-valued, a multivalued attribute of an entity cannot be directly included in the table for the entity. A separate table is created for each multivalued attribute having as attributes the key of the entity and the multivalued attribute. The table eMulti is created for the multivalued attribute eMultiValuedAttr of the entity e:

eMulti(eKey, eMultiValuedAttr)

Since each entity instance can have multiple values of eMultiValuedAttr, the key for the table eMulti is a composite key consisting of eKey and eMultiValuedAttr.

Figure 2.3 illustrates a weak entity. A weak entity w is mapped to its own table of the same name, containing its partial key and descriptive attributes as well as the key attribute of its identifying owner:

w(oKey, wPartialKey, wDescriptiveAttr)

The key of the table w is formed by the combination of the key of its identifying owner oKey and the partial key of the weak entity wPartialKey.

Figure 2.8 summarizes the mapping of the abstract ER diagram of Figures 2.1 and 2.3, illustrating both strong and weak entities along with composite and multivalued attributes.

e(eKey, eSingleValuedAttr, eSimple1, eSimple2)

eMulti(eKey, eMultiValuedAttr)

w(oKey, wPartialKey, wDescriptiveAttr)

**FIGURE 2.8**
Mapping entities to tables.

Figure 2.9(a) contains an abstract ER diagram denoting a binary relationship r between two abstract entities e1 and e2. The general approach for mapping relationships creates a table r for

**Map a relationship to a table, including the primary key attributes of the associated entities and any descriptive attributes of the relationship.**

each relationship r. The key attributes of the entities involved in the relationship and the descriptive attributes of the relationship, if any, are included as the attributes of the corresponding table.

$$r(e1Key, e2Key, rAttr)$$

Note that the key attributes of e1 and e2 are foreign keys in the table for the relationship r. The key of the table r depends on the cardinality ratio of the relationship. Figure 2.9(a) indicates the cardinality ratios as an abstract specification of $x$ and $y$ on the edges associating the relationship r to its entities e1 and e2. Figure 2.9(b) uses the cardinality ratios in the table to summarize the mapping alternatives, which are elaborated in the accompanying textual description. Note that if the entities e1 and e2 have multiple candidate key attributes, then only the primary one should be included in the mapping of the relationship.

(a)

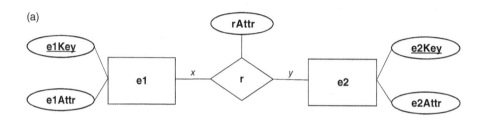

(b)

| Cardinality ratio $x:y$ | Heuristic design | Alternative design |
|---|---|---|
| 1:1 | e1(e1Key, e1Attr) | e1(e1Key, e1Attr) |
| | e2(e2Key, e2Attr) | e2(e2Key, e2Attr, e1Key, rAttr)* |
| | r(e1Key, e2Key, rAttr) | * assumes e2 has total participation in r |
| 1:N | e1(e1Key, e1Attr) | e1(e1Key, e1Attr) |
| | e2(e2Key, e2Attr) | e2(e2Key, e2Attr, e1Key, rAttr) |
| | r(e1Key, e2Key, rAttr) | |
| M:N | e1(e1Key, e1Attr) | |
| | e2(e2Key, e2Attr) | |
| | r(e1Key, e2Key, rAttr) | |

**FIGURE 2.9**
Mapping relationships to tables.

**The key of a table representing a relationship depends on its cardinality ratio.**

A cardinality ratio of 1:1 indicates that an entity instance of e1 is related to at most one instance of entity e2 and an entity instance of e2 is related to at most one instance of entity e1. Therefore, either attribute e1Key or e2Key uniquely identifies an instance of the relationship, which is given by the table r. Since each attribute forms a key of table r, each attribute is underlined separately.

$$r(e1Key, e2Key, rAttr)$$

There is an alternative approach for the mapping of a relationship having a 1:1 cardinality ratio. Instead of creating a separate table for r, the key attributes of one side of the relationship r with the descriptive attributes of r are included in a table corresponding to one of the entities involved in the relationship. The decision of which table to modify depends on the participation constraint of the entity in the relationship. In Figure 2.9, let entity e2 have total participation in the relationship r. The alternative design includes the e1Key and rAttr attributes in the table for e2:

$$e2(\underline{e2Key}, e2Attr, e1Key, rAttr)$$

Since entity e2 has total participation in the relationship r, an instance of e2 must be related to exactly one instance of entity e1. If both entities have partial participation in the relationship, the database designer must make an informed choice between the general approach with a separate table for r versus the alternative approach with null values.

A cardinality ratio of 1:N indicates that an entity instance of e1 is related to possibly many instances of entity e2 and an entity instance of e2 is related to at most one instance of entity e1. Therefore, the value of the attribute e2Key uniquely identifies a tuple in the table r and is the key of r:

$$r(e1Key, \underline{e2Key}, rAttr)$$

There is also an alternative design for mapping a relationship having a 1:N cardinality ratio. Instead of creating a table for r, include the attributes of the 1-side of the relationship in the table for the entity on the N-side of the relationship. In Figure 2.9, the table e2 is modified to include the e1Key and rAttr attributes:

$$e2(\underline{e2Key}, e2Attr, e1Key, rAttr)$$

Note that there is a symmetrical case for a cardinality ratio of N:1, which is not detailed here.

A cardinality ratio of M:N indicates that an entity instance of e1 is related to possibly many instances of entity e2 and an entity instance of e2 is related to possibly many instances of entity e1. Therefore, neither e1Key nor e2Key can uniquely identify a tuple in the table r. However, together e1Key and e2Key form a composite key of the table r:

$$r(\underline{e1Key, e2Key}, rAttr)$$

although the actual key for r must be ultimately determined in the context of the semantics and constraints of the enterprise being modeled. There is no alternative approach for mapping a relationship having an M:N cardinality ratio. Since each entity instance involved in the relationship is potentially related to many instances of the other entity, a separate table for the relationship r must be defined.

> **Alternative mapping strategies for 1:1 and 1:N relationships include the relationship information in one of the associated entity tables.**

## HOW TO 2.6   Map an ER Diagram to Relations

**Strong entity:** For each strong entity, create a relation with the same name as the entity and include all simple components of any composite attributes and single-valued attributes. The key of the entity is the key of the table.

**Weak entity:** A weak entity requires its own table. The attributes of this table include the key of the identifying owner along with the simple components of any composite attributes and single-valued attributes. The key of the table is the combination of the key of the identifying owner and the partial key of the weak entity.

**Relationship:** For each non-identifying relationship, create a table with the primary key attributes of both related entities and any descriptive attributes of the relationship. Determine the key(s) of the table using the cardinality ratio of the relationship. Note that there are alternative design heuristics for mapping relationships with 1:1 and 1:N cardinality ratios.

**Multivalued attributes:** A multivalued attribute requires its own table because the relational model has simple types. Include the attribute(s) that form the key of the entity that the attribute is describing. The key of the resulting table is a composite key consisting of the key attribute(s) of the entity in combination with the multivalued attribute.

A relational mapping of the EMPLOYEE TRAINING ER diagram of Figure 2.4 is shown in Figure 2.10, where primary keys are underlined. Table 2.1 summarizes the primary and foreign keys that appear in the EMPLOYEE TRAINING relational database schema. The employee table contains the single-valued attributes eID, eTitle, and eSalary and the simple attributes eLast and eFirst of the composite attribute eName with key eID. The technologyArea table includes the mapping of both the technology area entity and the lead relationship. Since a technology area must be related to an employee lead, the key attribute eID for employee is included as a foreign key in the technologyArea table as the attribute aLeadID. Similarly, the trainingCourse table maps both the training course entity and the offered relationship. Since a training course must be offered within exactly one technology area, the key attribute aID of technology area is included as a foreign key in the trainingCourse table as the attribute areaID. Since the takes relationship has an M:N cardinality ratio, a separate table takes is created having the key attributes of the employee and training course entities and the descriptive attribute tDate. The composite key (eID, cID) of takes uniquely identifies the date the employee took the course. If an employee could take the same training course more than once, then all attributes of the table would form a composite key.

**FIGURE 2.10**
Relational database
schema for EMPLOYEE
TRAINING enterprise.

employee(eID, eLast, eFirst, eTitle, eSalary)
technologyArea(aID, aTitle, aURL, aLeadID)
trainingCourse(cID, cTitle, cHours, areaID)
takes(eID, cID, tDate)

Table 2.1   **Summary of Keys in EMPLOYEE TRAINING Schema**

| Table | Primary key | Foreign key | References |
|---|---|---|---|
| employee | eID | – | – |
| technologyArea | aID | aLeadID | employee.eID |
| trainingCourse | cID | areaID | technologyArea.aID |
| takes | eID,cID | eID | employee.eID |
|  |  | cID | trainingCourse.cID |

Table 2.1 provides a summary of the primary and foreign keys in the table. The textual schema of the mapping given in Figure 2.10 indicates the primary key by underlining the attributes but the foreign keys are not necessarily obvious. Those attributes having the same name across tables are probably foreign keys. However, there are no requirements to name primary and foreign keys the same. For example, areaID in trainingCourse is a foreign key referencing the primary key aID of technologyArea. Similarly, aLeadID in technologyArea is a foreign key referencing the eID of employee. Different books use various techniques for representing the primary–foreign key relationship. Textually, the industry-standard SQL uses a referential integrity clause to define this relationship (see Chapter 6). This text uses a visual schema with different color and shaped keys positioned next to attributes that are part of a primary or foreign key, and a line linking the primary and foreign key. A primary key attribute has a gold key positioned to its left; a foreign key attribute has an orange key positioned to its right.

Figure 2.11 illustrates a visual schema for the EMPLOYEE TRAINING enterprise. Each primary key has a yellow gold key on its left. Since the primary key of takes consists of the combination of the eID and cID attributes, these keys are linked together, indicating that the primary key is composite. Each foreign key has an orange key to its right. The diagram links the orange foreign key to its corresponding gold primary key. Based on physical drawing constraints, sometimes the

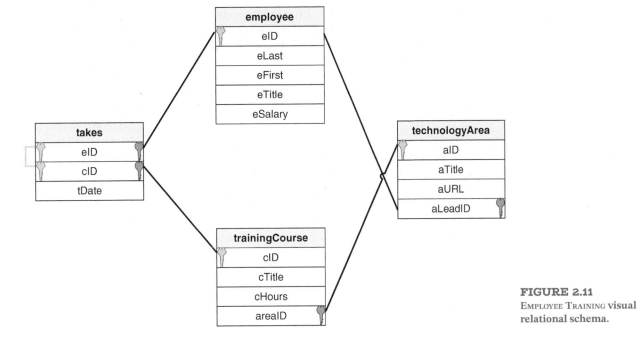

**FIGURE 2.11**

Employee Training **visual relational schema.**

link is not directly attached to the key symbol but rather links the attributes. For example, the aLeadID foreign key attribute of technologyArea is linked to its corresponding eID primary key attribute in employee.

## Self Check

4. The given mapping of the Employee Training ER diagram uses the alternative approach for its 1:1 lead relationship. What would change in the relational schema if lead was mapped to its own table? Include the schema changes and indicate the primary and foreign keys.

5. The given mapping of the Employee Training ER diagram uses the alternative approach for its 1:N offered relationship. What would change in the relational schema if offered was mapped to its own table? Include the schema changes and indicate the primary and foreign keys.

6. The user wants to add an eSkills multivalued attribute to describe an employee. How would this be mapped to the relational model?

## 2.4 Other Graphical Approaches

There are other widely used conceptual data models for designing databases. Although the models differ in syntax, all of the models represent concepts with their characteristics and associations between these concepts. There are also mechanisms for indicating how many times an instance of a concept can be related by the association, and whether an instance of the concept must participate in the association. The conceptual class diagrams of the Unified Modeling Language (UML), originally developed for modeling object-oriented programs, can also be used for database design. Another notation that developed in parallel with ER diagrams is known as Crow's Foot notation, based on one of the components of these diagrams. A brief overview of each of these models illustrates their similarities.

> **Conceptual data models represent similar information using syntax required by the specific model.**

UML class diagrams typically have three components in a rectangle, from top to bottom: class name, state of the class (properties), and its behavior (methods). For designing a relational database, only the first two components are needed for the name of the concept and its characteristics. An association between classes is represented as a line that directly links the two classes, and the line is labeled with the association name. UML class diagrams use *multiplicities* to represent the min and max number of times that the concept is associated with the other in the association. A multiplicity is formatted as min..max, which is quite similar to the (min, max) pairs of ER diagrams (see Special Topic 2.2). Figure 2.12 represents a UML conceptual class diagram for the EMPLOYEE TRAINING enterprise. Note that the multiplicities are labeled across the line near the associated class. For example, the 0..1 multiplicity of an employee leading a technologyArea appears next to the technologyArea class, representing that an employee is not required to lead a technologyArea but an employee can lead at most one technologyArea. In UML diagrams, an association that has descriptive attributes is represented by an *association class* with the name of the association and its properties, having a dashed line linking the association class to the association link. This is illustrated in Figure 2.12 for the takes association class between employee and trainingCourse.

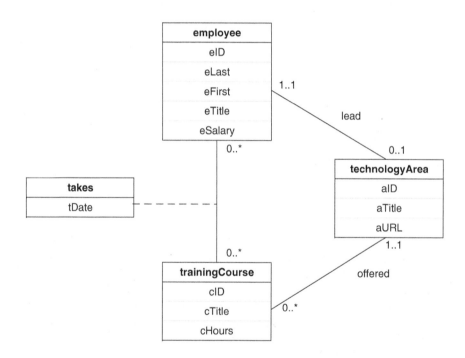

**FIGURE 2.12**
UML conceptual class diagram for
EMPLOYEE TRAINING.

The Crow's Foot notation is similar to UML diagrams in that a rectangle represents the concept and its attributes, along with a labeled line that links the two concepts. The notation for cardinality and participation constraints differ. Specifically, a symbol resembling a crow's foot represents that a concept can be associated to possibly many of the related concept, whereas a single line represents a concept being associated with at most one of the related concept. The participation constraint uses a circle to indicate a minimum participation of 0, and a single line indicates total participation. Associations cannot have characteristics, so a new concept is introduced for an association that has descriptive attributes. Associations must then be introduced to relate the new concept to the concepts in the original association. Figure 2.13 provides a Crow's Foot diagram for the EMPLOYEE TRAINING enterprise, which illustrates the cardinality and participation constraints as well as the introduction of takes that is related to the employee and trainingCourse entities. Note that this representation of an association with attributes is similar to the approach used to model ternary relationships in an ER diagram using only binary relationships by introducing a new entity (see Special Topic 2.4).

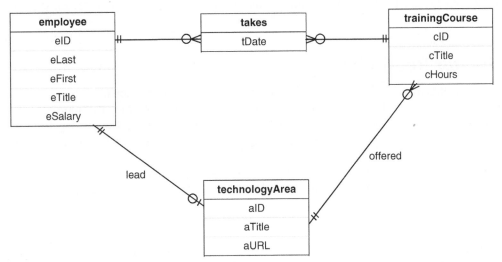

**FIGURE 2.13**
Crow's Foot diagram for
EMPLOYEE TRAINING.

## Self Check

7.  How does UML denote cardinality ratio and participation constraints?
8.  What does a Crow's Foot represent in the diagram?
9.  What does a circle represent in a Crow's Foot diagram?

## Chapter Notes Summary

### Gathering Requirements

- Gather the requirements of the enterprise and use the conceptual data model to represent those constraints at a higher level of abstraction.

### Entity-Relationship Diagrams

- Rectangles denote entities and ovals represent attributes.
- Diamonds indicate relationships between entities.
- Cardinality ratios and participation constraints indicate important information about a relationship.
- ER diagrams capture most constraints at a conceptual level. All constraints must be considered at the implementation level.

### Mapping ER Diagrams to Tables

- Map an entity to a table, including its key attributes, single-valued attributes, and simple components of any composite attributes.
- Map a relationship to a table, including the primary key attributes of the associated entities and any descriptive attributes of the relationship.
- The key of a table representing a relationship depends on its cardinality ratio.

- Alternative mapping strategies for 1:1 and 1:N relationships include the relationship information in one of the associated entity tables.

**Other Graphical Approaches**

- Conceptual data models represent similar information using syntax required by the specific model.

# Chapter Reminders

Table 2.2 summarizes the heuristics for mapping an ER diagram to a relational database schema. Fortunately, a relational database schema developed from scratch following the approach outlined in this chapter tends to result in a good design. However, often there is an existing database that needs to be updated based on changes in requirements over time. How does one represent these constraints and reason about the characteristics of the database? Chapter 10 provides an overview of database design by examining the use of functional dependencies for the representation of the database constraints. Functional dependencies provide the basis for inspecting the quality of the database design.

**Table 2.2   Summary of Mapping Heuristics**

| ER component | Diagram | Table | Attributes | Key |
|---|---|---|---|---|
| strong entity e | e | e | simple attributes of e | key of e |
| weak entity w | w | w | primary key of identifying owner o and simple attributes of w | primary key of o in combination with partial key of w |
| relationship r | r | r | primary key of each entity involved in the relationship and descriptive attributes of r | depends on cardinality ratio of r and semantics of enterprise |
| multivalued attribute m | m | m | primary key of component c it is describing and the attribute m | primary key of c in combination with m |

# Practice

Three scenarios given below provide practice for drawing ER diagrams and the subsequent mapping to a relational database schema. There are sample answers provided at the end of the chapter after the solutions to the self-check questions.

# Practice Problems: INVESTMENT PORTFOLIO

This simplified INVESTMENT PORTFOLIO case study maintains information regarding clients that invest in stocks and mutual funds. Each client has a unique taxpayer identification number, a name, and an address. A client may invest in stocks and/or mutual funds.

A stock is uniquely identified by its ticker, which is its identifying symbol on the stock exchange. The name of issue for a stock is the name of the company. A stock has a rating, which is an assessment of the stock. The principal business of a stock denotes the primary business from which the company obtains its revenue. There are several prices associated with a stock. Besides the current price of a stock, the high and low price ranges are recorded for the calendar year. The return value for a stock, which is the price appreciation, is recorded for the prior year and five-year period.

A mutual fund is also uniquely identified by a ticker symbol and has a fund name. The principal objective of the fund is also recorded, e.g. 'G' – growth, 'I' – income, and 'S' – stability. Similar to stocks, mutual funds record a current offering price and a high and low price range. A percent yield from investment income is also maintained. A mutual fund may be associated with at most one fund family.

A fund family has a unique identification number and the company's name and address. A fund family, as its name implies, can have many associated mutual funds but must have at least one mutual fund. Based on the high-level introduction to the Investment Portfolio enterprise, assume the following:

- The characteristics of a client include a unique taxpayer identification number, a name, and an address. A client can invest in many stocks and in many mutual funds. The number of shares that a client has of a stock or mutual fund in their investment portfolio is also recorded.
- The characteristics of a stock include the stock's unique ticker on the stock exchange and additional descriptive properties that include name of issue, rating, principal business, high and low price range, current price, and return values for the prior year and five-year period.
- The characteristics of a mutual fund include the mutual fund's unique ticker and additional descriptive properties that include the name of the fund, principal objective, high and low price range, the current offering price, and the fund's yield. A mutual fund may be associated with at most one fund family.
- The characteristics of a fund family include a unique identification, a name and address. A fund family may have many mutual funds and must be associated with at least one mutual fund.

1. Given the above requirements, create an ER diagram that captures the Investment Portfolio design.

2. Map the ER diagram to a relational schema.

## Practice Problems: New Home

The New Home case study maintains information regarding new homebuilders and the models that they offer at various subdivisions. A homebuilder may offer the same model at more than one subdivision, and the price that they offer a model may be different at each subdivision. Each subdivision has lots that are identified by a lot number. Each lot has an associated street address, size in square feet, and possibly an additional premium for that lot. A premium is usually assessed if the lot is larger than the average lot or is on a cul de sac or corner within the subdivision. When a lot is sold, there is a homebuilder's model associated with the sale. The status of the sale is also recorded.

Assume the following based on the high-level introduction to the New Home enterprise:

- The characteristics of a homebuilder include a unique identification number, a name, and an address and phone number for the headquarters of that homebuilder. An address is further broken down into the street address, city, and zip code. The state is not recorded in this enterprise since the state is assumed. A homebuilder offers several models.
- The characteristics of a model include an identification number for the model that is unique for its homebuilder. A model also has a name and square footage. Whether the model is a single-story or two-story home is also recorded. A model may be offered at various subdivisions. The price that a model is offered at a given subdivision is recorded.
- The characteristics of a subdivision include its name, which is assumed to be unique, and the city and zip code where the subdivision is located. The state is assumed to be local to the enterprise.

- The characteristics of a lot include a lot number that is only unique for its subdivision. Each lot has an associated street address, size in square footage, and a possible premium. A sold lot has a particular homebuilder's model associated with it. The status of the sale indicates whether the house construction is pending or completed.

1. Given the above requirements, create an ER diagram that captures the NEW HOME design.

2. Map the ER diagram to a relational schema.

## Practice Problems: WEB PAGE

A company wants to keep track of its digital assets on its website, including graphics and documents. In addition, they want to know what pages link to which external sites so that the links can be verified periodically. Based on the high-level introduction to the WEB PAGE enterprise, assume the following:

- The characteristics of a Web page include a unique identification number, a title, its Uniform Resource Locator (URL), which gives the address of the Web page, and the number of times that the Web page has been accessed, or its hits.
- A Web page may link to an internal Web page or an external site, using an href. A Web page links to many internal and external sites. A Web page also displays many graphics and may provide links to company-related documents.
- The properties of an external website include a unique site identifier, its title, and its URL. The number of times that the link has been followed from each site within the company is recorded.
- A graphic displayed on a Web page has a unique identifier, a name, its type (e.g. tif, gif, jpg, bmp), the source (src) specification, and an alternative description for accessibility. A graphic may be displayed on many sites within the company's website, especially the company logo.
- A document has a unique identifier, its name, its type (e.g. pdf, rtf, csv), a description, its date, and the number of times it has been downloaded. A given document can be accessed from only one Web page within the company. Many Web pages can link to documents.

1. Given the above requirements, create an ER diagram that captures the WEB PAGE design.

2. Map the ER diagram to a relational schema.

## End of Chapter Exercises

Consider the following requirements for maintaining meta-data about the schema of a relational database: When the schema of a database is defined, either graphically or through the use a data definition language, the database must maintain the definition of the database schema for validation purposes. A named database schema consists of several relations. The name of the schema must be unique, and the names of relations are only unique within the database schema. The database also records the degree of the relation. A relation consists of probably several attributes, and attribute names are unique within a relation. Other information recorded about an attribute includes its type and its position. A relation must have a primary key, which consists of one or more of its attributes. A relation may have one or more foreign keys. A foreign key must consist of one or more attributes of the relation in which it appears as a foreign key. A foreign key references the relation in which it appears as a primary key.

1. Draw an ER diagram for the enterprise. State any assumptions that you needed to make in your conceptual model. State any semantics of the enterprise that cannot be captured by the conceptual design.

Consider the following requirements for an online store:
Customers have typical information such as name (last name, first name, and middle initial), address (street, city, state, postal code, country), phone number, and email. To place an order, customers must be registered users having a unique login name and password.

The customer shops the online store by category, where a category has a unique code and description. Each type of item in the online store belongs to exactly one category. An item is described by a unique item number, name, description, and price and has an associated graphic for display on the Web page. Since items may come in different colors and sizes, a customer selects a specific item by also specifying its color and size, which is represented in the database by a code that is unique within the item number. The database also records the current quantity in stock of that item for a given color and size.

The customer places selected items in a shopping cart, specifying the quantity of that item being placed in the cart. There is a unique number associated with the cart along with the date and total price. A shopping cart is associated with exactly one customer, and a customer has exactly one shopping cart. The contents of the shopping cart can be updated until the customer confirms the cart contents by placing an order. The shopping cart is then classified as an order and the unique identification of the cart is replaced by an order number. Note that a customer can have many orders, but an order is associated with exactly one customer.

2. Draw an ER diagram for the enterprise. *(Hint: Consider a design that views a shopping cart and an order as the same type of entity, which has an additional type attribute to distinguish a cart from an order.)* State any assumptions that you need to make in your conceptual model. State any semantics of the enterprise that cannot be captured by the conceptual design.

Consider the WAREHOUSE ER diagram given in Figure 2.14:

3. Provide a textual description of the enterprise being represented by the ER diagram.

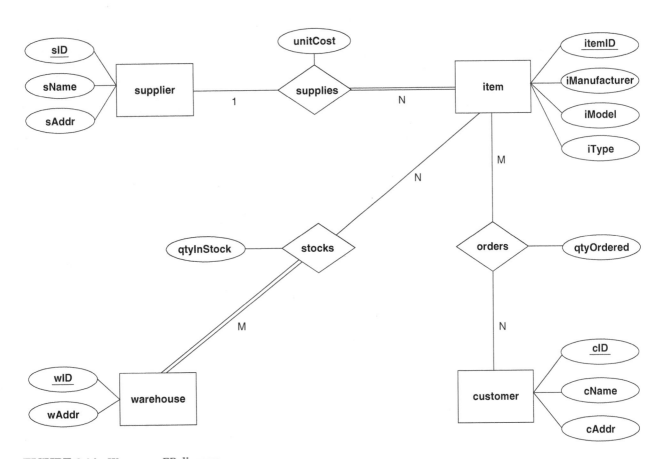

**FIGURE 2.14**  WAREHOUSE ER diagram.

4. Map the ER diagram to the relational data model, indicating the primary and foreign keys in the database schema. State any assumptions.

Consider the GRADEBOOK ER diagram given in Figure 2.15:

5. Provide a textual description of the enterprise being represented by the ER diagram.

6. Map the ER diagram to the relational data model, indicating the primary and foreign keys in the database schema. State any assumptions.

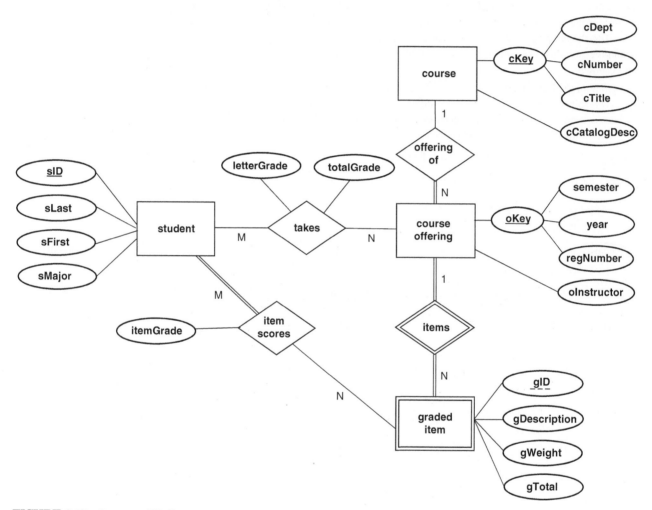

**FIGURE 2.15**   GRADEBOOK ER diagram.

# Answers to Self-Check Questions

1. oval

2. double line

3. composite

4. Revise the technologyArea table by removing the aLeadID attribute, and add a new table lead(aID, aLeadID), where aID is a foreign key referencing the aID key attribute of technologyArea and aLeadID is a foreign key referencing the eID attribute of employee.

5. Revise the trainingCourse table by removing the areaID attribute, and add a new table offered(cID, areaID), where cID is a foreign key referencing the cID key attribute of trainingCourse and areaID is a foreign key referencing the aID attribute of technologyArea.

6. Multivalued attributes require the addition of a table to the schema that includes the key attributes of the entity that it is describing. In this case, add the table eSkills(eID, eSkill) to the relational schema for EMPLOYEE TRAINING.

7. A UML diagram uses multiplicities in the format of min..max to represent the minimum and maximum number of times that an instance of a class participates in the association.

8. A Crow's Foot denotes that an entity instance can be related to possibly many instances of the associated entity.

9. A circle indicates that an instance of an entity has partial participation in the relationship, i.e. it is not required to participate in the relationship.

# Answers to Practice Problems: INVESTMENT PORTFOLIO

1. **ER diagram**

   Figure 2.16 provides an ER diagram corresponding to the conceptual design of the INVESTMENT PORTFOLIO enterprise. Tables 2.3 and 2.4 summarize the entities and relationships in the ER diagram, including the type of an attribute, which is either a character string (C) or a numeric (N). The entities client, stock, mutualFund, and fundFamily are strong entities having unique identifiers across the entire database. The relationships stockPortfolio and mutualFundPortfolio have a many-to-many cardinality ratio since a client can invest in many stocks/mutual funds and a stock or mutual fund can be part of many portfolios. There is a descriptive attribute on these M:N relationships, indicating the number of shares of the investment that the client's portfolio contains. The hasFundFamily relationship has a one-to-many cardinality ratio since a fund family can have many mutual funds, but a mutual fund may be associated with at most one fund family. The total participation of the fundFamily entity in the hasFundFamily relationship indicates that a fund family must have at least one mutual fund.

2. **Relational schema**

   Figure 2.17 provides the textual relational schema corresponding to the conceptual design of the INVESTMENT PORTFOLIO enterprise shown in Figure 2.16. The schema includes a table for each entity (client, stock, mutualFund, and fundFamily). The many-to-many portfolio relationships between a client and the stocks and mutual funds that they own are mapped as the tables stockPortfolio and mutualFundPortfolio, respectively. The one-to-many relationship hasFundFamily, relating a fund family to its associated mutual fund, is mapped as the familyID attribute of the mutualFund table since a mutual fund belongs to exactly one fund family. The corresponding visual relational schema in Figure 2.18 highlights the primary and foreign keys, including the referential integrity constraints.

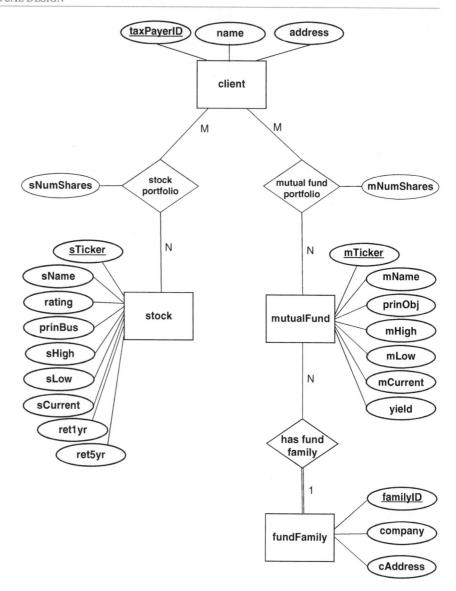

**FIGURE 2.16**
INVESTMENT PORTFOLIO ER diagram.

## Answers to Practice Problems: NEW HOME

1. **ER diagram**

   Figure 2.19 provides an ER diagram capturing the conceptual design of the NEW HOME enterprise. Tables 2.5 and 2.6 summarize the entities and relationships in the ER diagram, including the type of an attribute, which is either a character string (C) or a numeric (N). The entities homebuilder and subdivision are strong entities since each has an identification number or name that is unique across the database. The entities model and lot are weak entities and cannot exist in the database without being associated to a homebuilder and subdivision, respectively. This existence dependence is modeled in the ER diagram by the total participation of the weak entity in its identifying relationship. Since weak entities cannot be uniquely identified in the database without their associated identifying owner, a model is uniquely identified by a combination of the homebuilder ID and model ID (hID, mID),

**Table 2.3   Investment Portfolio Entity Summary**

| Entity | Attribute | Type | Description |
|---|---|---|---|
| client | taxPayerID | C | The unique taxpayer ID that identifies a client |
| | name | C | The name of the client |
| | address | C | The address of the client |
| stock | sTicker | C | The unique id to identify a stock |
| | sName | C | The name of the company to which the stock belongs |
| | rating | C | The rating of the stock with values limited to 'NR' (no-rating), 'C' (nonpaying issue), or 'A' (backed) |
| | prinBus | C | The principal business in which the company engages |
| | sHigh | N | The highest rate of the stock |
| | sLow | N | The lowest rate of the stock |
| | sCurrent | N | The current rate of the stock |
| | ret1Yr | N | The returns made by the stock over one year |
| | ret5Yr | N | The returns made by the stock over five years |
| mutualFund | mTicker | C | The unique id to identify a mutual fund |
| | mName | C | The name of the mutual fund |
| | prinObj | C | The principal objective of the fund with values limited to 'G' (growth), 'I' (income), and 'S' (stability) |
| | mHigh | N | The highest rate of the mutual fund |
| | mLow | N | The lowest rate of the mutual fund |
| | mCurrent | N | The current rate of the mutual fund |
| | yield | N | The yield made by the mutual fund |
| fundFamily | familyID | C | The unique id to identify the fund family |
| | company | C | The name of the fund family |
| | cAddress | C | The address of the fund family |

**Table 2.4   Investment Portfolio Relationship Summary**

| Relationship | Description |
|---|---|
| stockPortfolio | An M:N relationship between a stock and a client. A client can have many shares of a stock and a stock has many shareholders. The **sNumShares** attribute, which is a numeric type, represents the number of shares of a stock that a client has. |
| mutualFundPortfolio | An M:N relationship between a mutual fund and a client. An client can have many shares of a mutual fund and a mutual fund has many shareholders. The **mNumShares** attribute, which is a numeric type, represents the number of shares of a mutual fund that a client has. |
| hasFundFamily | A 1:N relationship between a mutual fund and fund family. A fund family may have many mutual funds and must be associated with at least one mutual fund. A mutual fund is associated with exactly one fund family. |

client(taxPayerID, name, address)
stock(sTicker, sName, rating, prinBus, sHigh, sLow, sCurrent, ret1Yr, ret5Yr)
mutualFund(mTicker, mName, prinObj, mHigh, mLow, mCurrent, yield, familyID)
fundFamily(familyID, company, cAddress)
stockPortfolio(taxPayerID, sTicker, sNumShares)
mutualFundPortfolio(taxPayerID, mTicker, mNumShares)

**FIGURE 2.17**
Investment Portfolio
relational schema.

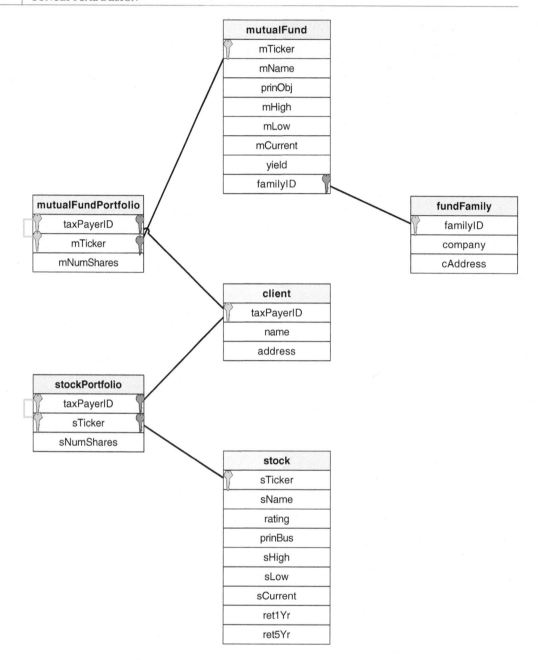

**FIGURE 2.18**
INVESTMENT PORTFOLIO
**visual relational
schema.**

and a lot is uniquely identified by a combination of the subdivision name and the lot number (sName, lotNum). The price that a model is offered at a subdivision is represented as an attribute of the M:N relationship offered between model and subdivision. The status of a sold lot is an attribute of the 1:N sold relationship between lot and model. Note that the participation constraint of a lot in the sold relationship is partial since a lot may not be sold.

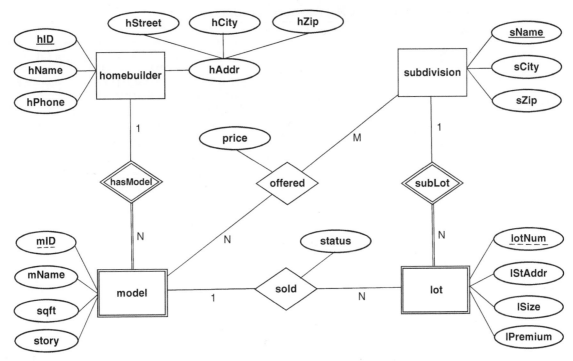

**FIGURE 2.19** New Home ER diagram.

Table 2.5    New Home **Entity Summary**

| Entity | Attribute | Type | Description |
|---|---|---|---|
| homebuilder | hID | C | The unique ID that identifies a homebuilder |
| | hName | C | The name of the homebuilder |
| | hPhone | C | The phone number of the homebuilder |
| | hStreet | C | The street address of the homebuilder |
| | hCity | C | The city of the homebuilder |
| | hZip | C | The zip code of the homebuilder |
| model | mID | C | The unique id to identify a model for a homebuilder |
| | mName | C | The name of the model |
| | sqft | N | The square footage of the model |
| | story | N | A 1 or a 2 indicating the number of stories in the model |
| subdivision | sName | C | The unique name of the subdivision |
| | sCity | C | The city of the subdivision |
| | sZip | C | The zip code of the subdivision |
| lot | lotNum | N | The unique number to identify a lot within a subdivision |
| | lStAddr | C | The street address of the lot |
| | lSize | N | The size of the lot in square feet |
| | lPremium | N | The additional cost associated with the lot |

**Table 2.6**    **NEW HOME Relationship Summary**

| Relationship | Description |
|---|---|
| offered | An M:N relationship between subdivisions and a model. One subdivision can offer many models and a model may be offered at many subdivisions. The **price** attribute, which is a numeric type, represents the price that a homebuilder's model is offered at that subdivision. |
| hasModel | A 1:N relationship between a homebuilder and a model. A homebuilder has many models, but a model is associated with one homebuilder. |
| subLot | A 1:N relationship between a model and a lot. A lot has at most one model that can be on that lot and a model can be on several lots. |
| sold | A 1:N relationship between a model and a lot. The **status** attribute is of type character string. The status can be either 'P' (Pending) or 'C' (Closed). A sold lot has a home being built on it of the associated model. 'P' means the house is in the process of being built. 'C' means the house is now completed. |

**FIGURE 2.20**
NEW HOME relational schema.

homebuilder(<u>hID</u>, hName, hStreet, hCity, hZip, hPhone)
model(<u>hID, mID</u>, mName, sqft, story)
subdivision(<u>sName</u>, sCity, sZip)
offered(<u>sName, hID, mID</u>, price)
lot(<u>sName, lotNum</u>, lStAddr, lSize, lPremium)
sold(<u>sName, lotNum</u>, hID, mID, status)

2. **Relational schema**

   Figure 2.20 provides the textual relational schema corresponding to the conceptual design of the NEW HOME enterprise given by Figure 2.19. There is a table for each strong entity (homebuilder and subdivision). There is also a table for each weak entity (model and lot), which includes the primary key of its identifying owner. Note that identifying relationships for weak entities are not explicitly mapped to a separate table but are used to indicate the identifying owner of the weak entity. The remaining relationships (offered and sold) in the ER diagram are each mapped to a table. The offered M:N relationship must be mapped to a separate table based on the many-to-many characteristics of the relationship. However, the sold 1:N relationship may be mapped either as a separate table or as part of the lot table. If mapped as part of the lot table, then the attributes identifying the model (hID and mID) and the descriptive attribute status would be null for a lot that is available. Since the participation of the lot entity in the sold relationship is partial, the mapping approach of providing a separate table for the sold relationship is appropriate. There is a tuple in the sold table only if the lot is sold. Therefore, a lot is considered available if there is no corresponding tuple in the sold table. The corresponding visual relational schema in Figure 2.21 highlights the primary and foreign keys, including the referential integrity constraints.

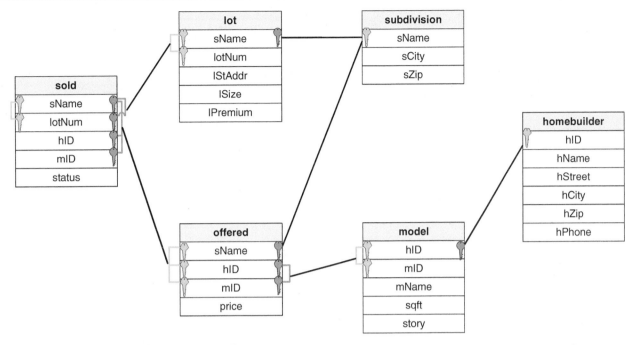

**FIGURE 2.21** NEW HOME visual relational schema.

## Answers to Practice Problems: WEB PAGE

1. **ER diagram**

   The conceptual design for the WEB PAGE enterprise is given by the ER diagram of Figure 2.22. Tables 2.7 and 2.8 summarize the entities and relationships in the ER diagram, including the type of an attribute, which is either a character string (C) or a numeric (N). The ER diagram has four strong entities, corresponding to webpage, site, graphic, and document. The ER diagram contains a recursive relationship (internal link). Role names on the edges linking the relationship to the entity indicate the role that the entity plays with respect to the cardinality ratio of the relationship. For example, a Web page can be the source and target of many internal links. The ER diagram also contains two many-to-many relationships for displaying graphics (displays) and linking to external sites (external link). The document link relationship is one-to-many since a Web page can link to multiple documents, but a given document is only accessible from one Web page.

2. **Relational schema**

   Figure 2.23 provides the textual relational schema corresponding to the conceptual design of the WEB PAGE enterprise given by Figure 2.22. There is a table for each entity (webpage, site, graphic, document) and for each M:N relationship (internal, external, displays) in the ER diagram. The one 1:N relationship document link is mapped as the wID attribute of the document table since a document is linked on exactly one Web page. In the internal table, the role names on the edges of the corresponding relationship form the attribute names sourceID and targetID. The corresponding visual relational schema in Figure 2.24 highlights the primary and foreign keys, including the referential integrity constraints.

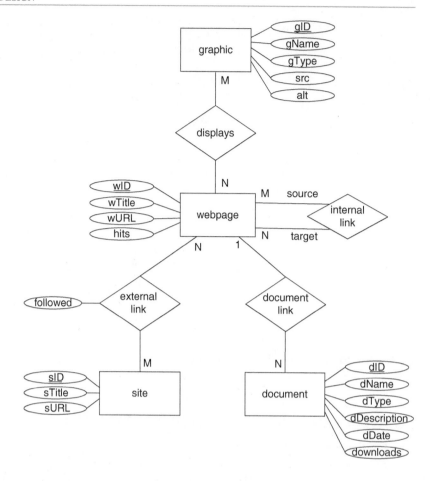

**FIGURE 2.22**
WEB PAGE ER diagram.

Table 2.7    WEB PAGE **Entity Summary**

| Entity | Attribute | Type | Description |
|---|---|---|---|
| webpage | webID | C | The unique ID that identifies a Web page |
| | webTitle | C | The title of the Web page |
| | url | C | The URL of the Web page |
| | hits | N | The number of hits to the Web page. This must be a nonnegative integer |
| site | sID | C | An ID that uniquely identifies the external site |
| | sTitle | C | The title of the external page |
| | sURL | C | The URL of the external page |
| graphic | gID | C | An ID that uniquely identifies a graphic |
| | gName | C | The name of the graphic file – not including the extension |
| | gType | C | The extension of the graphic file, which determines its type, i.e. tif, jpg, gif, bmp |
| | src | C | The src specification on the img tag of the html |
| | alt | C | An alternative description of the image for accessibility |
| document | dID | C | An ID that uniquely identifies a document |
| | dName | C | The name of the document – not including the extension |
| | dType | C | The extension of the document file, which determines its type, i.e. pdf, rtf, csv |
| | dDescription | C | A description of the document |
| | dDate | C | The date of the document stored as a string in the format yyyy-mm-dd |
| | downloads | N | The number of times that the document has been downloaded. This must be a nonnegative integer |

Table 2.8    WEB PAGE **Relationship Summary**

| Relationship | Description |
|---|---|
| internal link | A Web page may be the source or target of multiple internal pages. |
| external link | A Web page may link to many external websites and an external website may link to many internal pages. The **followed** numeric attribute represents the number of times that the external link has been followed from the Web page. This must be a nonnegative integer. |
| document link | A document should be accessible by only one page in the company's website for configuration management. However, a Web page may provide links to multiple documents. |
| displays | A graphic may be displayed on many Web pages and a Web page may display many graphics. |

webpage (<u>wID</u>, wTitle, wURL, hits)
site (<u>sID</u>, sTitle, sURL)
graphic (<u>gID</u>, gName, gType, src, alt)
document (<u>dID</u>, dName, dType, dDescription, dDate, downloads, wID)
internal (<u>sourceID, targetID</u>)
external (<u>wID, sID</u>, followed)
displays (<u>wID, gID</u>)

**FIGURE 2.23**
WEB PAGE **relational schema.**

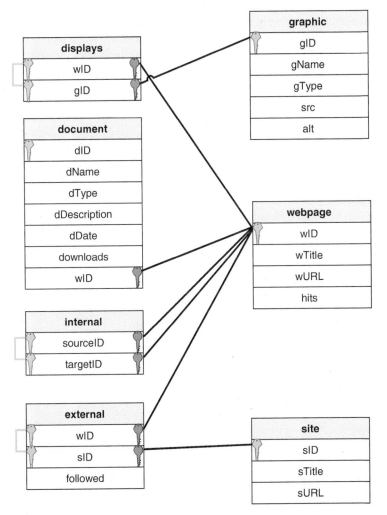

**FIGURE 2.24**
WEB PAGE **visual relational schema.**

# Bibliographic Notes

There are many papers on conceptual modeling for databases. Peter Chen [1976] proposed the Entity-Relationship Conceptual Model in 1976, and its use in database design was formalized in 1981 by Ng [1981]. Teorey et al. [1986] provided a design methodology for developing an ER model, which is then translated to the relational model. Although the ER conceptual data model is well established in the database community, the Unified Modeling Language (UML) standard (see Rumbaugh, Jacobson, and Booch [2004]) developed for the design of software can also be used for database design [Dietrich and Urban, 2010]. There is a high degree of similarity between conceptual modeling with ER diagrams and the conceptual class diagrams of UML. The book [Dietrich and Urban, 2010] provides side-by-side diagrams of ER and UML diagrams, including the enhanced Entity-Relationship diagrams that include inheritance. The conceptual models are mapped to various implementation data models, including relational, object-relational, and object-oriented. The notation known informally as *Crow's Foot*, which is used in the popular MySQL Workbench product [Oracle, 2019], originated from a 1976 article by Gordon Everest [1976] who introduced the notation as using *inverted arrows*.

# More to Explore

The Databases for Many Majors project (databasesmanymajors.faculty.asu.edu) provides visualizations to introduce fundamental database concepts to a diverse audience of students. The Conceptual Database Design animation visualizes the concepts presented in this chapter, introducing the components of Entity-Relationship diagrams and presenting the heuristic approach for mapping ER diagrams to relations. The visualization also includes 20 formative self-assessment questions that help the viewers check their understanding.

# Relational Algebra

3

**LEARNING OBJECTIVES**

- To identify the tables needed in the design of a query

- To apply relational algebra operators to answer a query

- To express a relational algebra query as a tree and to apply optimization techniques

Relational algebra is a procedural query language having specific operators to apply to a relation or relations for retrieving data. An understanding of this formal language is essential for learning any query language, especially the SQL standard described in Chapter 5. Although the language is formal, it is this formalism of relations as sets of tuples that makes relational databases conceptually simpler to understand. The first step in answering any query is to consider its design, which essentially consists of determining the tables needed to answer that question and how to combine them. The relational algebra operators are introduced incrementally and illustrated using example queries over the EMPLOYEE TRAINING relational database schema. Relational completeness reflects on the expressiveness of the relational algebra operators and discusses how limited forms of aggregation and grouping of results can be supported in relational algebra. Since there are multiple ways to write a relational algebra expression to correctly answer a query, query optimization explores which of the several correct approaches provides a more efficient evaluation.

## 3.1 Query Design

Before exploring the various operations of the relational algebra query language, let's first look at the design of a query. Given an English description of a question, it is important to examine the relational schema and identify which tables are needed to answer that question. An important component of the identification of tables is knowing the information that the user needs as the answer to the question. This knowledge impacts the tables needed to provide the query answer.

> **Identify the tables needed to answer the query and return the specified result.**

### HOW TO 3.1   Query Design

Designing a query starts by examining the schema of the database, either the visual or textual schema. The data is only needed to execute the query to find the answer. Include only the tables in the query design that are needed to answer the query. Adding unnecessary tables is inefficient. Include the following tables in the query design:

- The tables that must be filtered to answer the query

- The tables that contain the desired output of the query

- The tables that provide the required linking on the primary–foreign key relationships

Consider sample queries summarized in Table 3.1 with the attributes representing the schema of the result listed beneath the English query description. There is a corresponding figure for each query, providing an annotated query design as shown in Figure 3.1, Figure 3.2, and Figure 3.3, respectively. In the figures, the ? box restates the query and the exclamation mark (!) summarizes the identified tables needed to answer the query. The numbers indicate the order of the tables with annotations indicating the attributes of interest and the arrows showing the direction of the traversal of the primary–foreign key relationships.

Table 3.1    **Query Design Examples**

| Query description and desired attributes | Tables needed to answer the query |
| --- | --- |
| What is the title of the course with unique id 'DB01'? <br><br> (cTitle) | trainingCourse |
| Which employees took the course with unique id 'DB01'? <br><br> (eLast, eFirst) | takes <br><br> employee |
| What are the ids of the employees who took courses in the technology area having the title 'Database'? <br><br> (eID) | technologyArea <br> trainingCourse <br><br> takes |

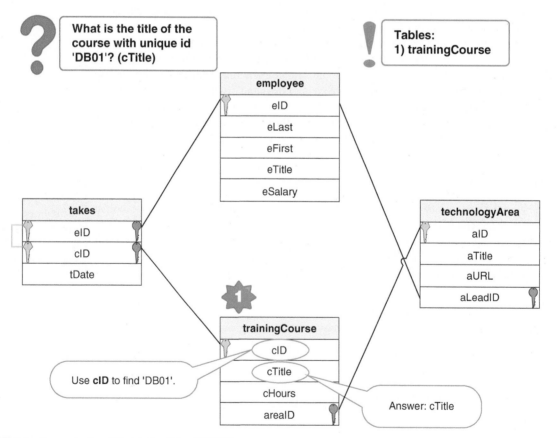

**FIGURE 3.1**   Query design: What is the title of 'DB01'?

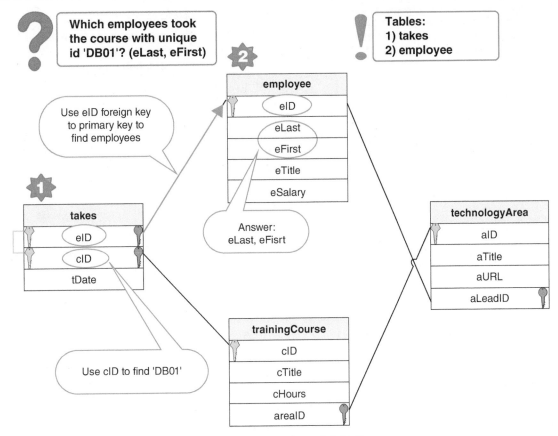

**FIGURE 3.2** Query design: What are the names of employees who took 'DB01'?

Figure 3.1 illustrates the first query that is asking for the title of the course with a specific unique course id of 'DB01'. There are two tables that contain the cID attribute, representing the unique course id: trainingCourse and takes. The query asks for the title of that course and not who took the course. Therefore, trainingCourse is a necessary table, containing both the cID attribute as the primary key of the table and the cTitle attribute, which is needed to answer the query. Therefore, only the table trainingCourse is needed.

The second query, illustrated in Figure 3.2, asks for the names of the employees who took 'DB01'. Therefore, the takes table is a good starting point for the query, providing the information on which employees took a course given by the attribute cID. Note that the query requests the first and last names of these employees, which is not part of the takes table. Only the employee id is in takes. Therefore, the query requires the employee table to retrieve the names. Since the eID attribute appears in employee as a primary key and takes as a foreign key, these two tables can be combined on this relationship to find the answer to the query. Thus, both takes and employee are identified as needed tables.

Figure 3.3 describes the design of the third query, requesting the ids of the employees who took courses in the technology area that has the title 'Database'. The first table needed for this query is the technologyArea table, which contains the aTitle attribute. To find the training courses in this technology area, include the trainingCourse table by using the primary–foreign key relationship between the aID primary key of technologyArea and the areaID foreign key of trainingCourse. Then, use the takes table to find the employees who took these training

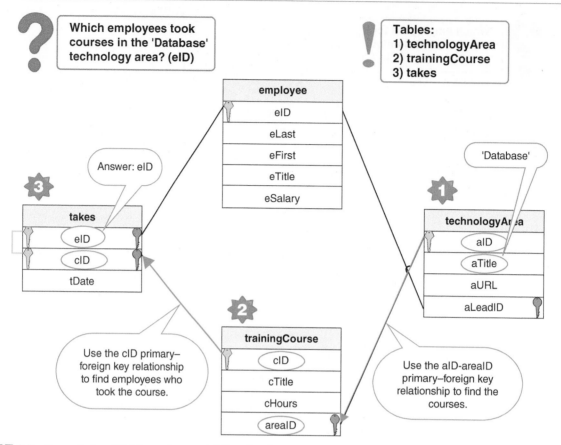

**FIGURE 3.3**   Query design: Which employees took 'Database' courses?

courses, relating the primary key cID attribute of trainingCourse with the foreign key cID attribute of takes. Therefore, the identified tables for this query include technologyArea, trainingCourse, and takes.

The design of a query is an important first step. Note that the above examples illustrate that the relationship between primary and foreign keys can be used from primary to foreign key or from foreign to primary key to combine tables for answering a query. Once the tables are identified that are needed to answer the query, the next step is using the relational algebra operators to filter and combine the tables to find the correct answer.

## Self Check

Identify the tables needed to answer the following questions, where the attributes for the result are listed below the query specification.

1.    Which employees earn more than $75,000?
(eID, eLast, eFirst, eTitle, eSalary)

2.    Which employees took the 'Big Data' course and on what date?
(eID, tDate)

3.    What are the names of the employees who took the 'Big Data' course?
(eLast, eFirst)

# 3.2 Algebra Operators

Relational algebra is a procedural language. Each operator takes operand relations and some-times additional criteria to produce a result. The schema of the result is derived from a cor-rect relational algebra expression. The operators are introduced incrementally with illustrative examples using the EMPLOYEE TRAINING enterprise. Filtering operators filter the relations either horizontally or vertically. Horizontal filtering returns only some of the rows based on criteria, and vertical filtering returns only some of the columns based on a list of attributes. The set oper-ators combine relations, which are sets of tuples, using union, intersection, and difference. The result of a set operator has the same schema as its operand relations but differs in the amount of tuples in the resulting relation. The join operators provide the capability to return a relation with more attributes by combining its operand tables. The division operator is a more complex operator that assists in answering queries that want to know what values are related to *all* values in another table.

## NOTE 3.2  Overview of Relational Algebra

**Syntax:**

This chapter introduces the syntax of relational algebra using its formal symbols. However, practicing queries is an important component of learning. There is an educational tool, called WinRDBI (see Appendix A), that recognizes relational algebra where the formal mathematical sym-bols have been replaced with keywords. The companion website for the book provides WinRDBI relational alge-bra query files for those queries appearing in the chapter and practice exercises. The queries in the text that can be checked with the educational tool are preceded by a checkmark ($\sqrt{}$). WinRDBI uses identifiers starting with a lowercase letter to denote relation and attribute names. Identifiers that begin with an uppercase letter denote variables. Constants are either single-quoted strings or numeric constants.

**Intermediate Tables:**

The result of a relational algebra query is a relation. Sometimes it is useful to break down queries into logical parts with descriptive names. WinRDBI uses named tables to store the result of a query expression.

intermediateTable := queryExpression;

assigns the result of the **queryExpression** to the named **intermediateTable**. The attribute names for the schema of **intermediateTable** are derived from the **queryExpression**. How-ever, if renaming of attributes is desired, then the syntax

intermediateTable(attr1, ..., attrn) := queryExpression;

provides for the renaming of the output schema of **queryExpression** to the schema given by the attribute list attr1, ..., attrn.

## 3.2.1  Filtering

The two most common relational algebra operators are operators that filter a relation, either hor-izontally or vertically. Since these filtering operators apply to one relation, they are called unary operators. The horizontal filtering operator that returns a subset of tuples that satisfy a given condition is known as the *selection* operator and is denoted by the symbol $\sigma$. The vertical filtering operator that returns a subset of specified attributes is called the *projection* operator and is denoted by the symbol $\pi$. Recall that Chapter 1 introduced the notation that a relation is referenced in low-ercase and its schema with the same name but in uppercase, where the schema represents the set of attributes for that table. Table 3.2 provides an overview of the filtering operators, including its definition, schema, and upperbound on the resulting cardinality. For each relational algebra operator, it is important to understand the schema and the expected cardinality of the result.

The selection operation $\sigma_\theta(r)$ retrieves some of the tuples from the operand relation r that sat-isfy the selection condition $\theta$, visually shown in Figure 3.4. Typically, the selection condition $\theta$ is a Boolean combination of comparison terms, which means using and, or, and not to combine

> *Selection* horizontally filters a relation, whereas *projection* vertically filters a relation.

**Table 3.2    Summary of Filtering Operators**

| Operator expression | Definition | Schema | Cardinality (upperbound) |
|---|---|---|---|
| $\sigma_\theta(r)$ | $\{\, t \mid t \in r \ and \ \theta \,\}$ | R | $\lvert r \rvert$ |
| $\pi_A(r)$ | $\{\, t.a_1, ...t.a_j \mid t \in r \ and \ a_i \in A \,\}$ | A | $\lvert r \rvert$ |

comparisons that use relational operators, such as $=, <, >$. The schema of the resulting selection is identical to the operand relation since the entire tuple is retrieved. The cardinality of the resulting relation ranges from 0, when no tuples of the operand relation satisfy the selection condition, to the cardinality of the operand relation, when all tuples of the operand relation satisfy the selection condition. In Figure 3.4, the cardinality of r is shown to have $k$ tuples, and the selection contains only two tuples: $r_2$ and $r_{k-1}$. Note that in general the resulting selection $\sigma_\theta(r)$ contains a subset, not necessarily proper, of the tuples in the original table r.

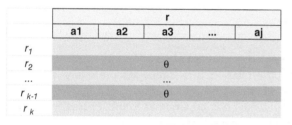

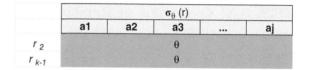

**FIGURE 3.4**    Selection.

The projection operation $\pi_A(r)$ retrieves some of the attributes of a relation as specified by the list of attributes given by the subscript A, pictorially illustrated in Figure 3.5. For $\pi_A(r)$ to be a valid expression, the set of attributes appearing in A must be a subset of R ($A \subseteq R$). The schema of the resulting relation is determined by the projection operation itself. The maximum cardinality of the resulting relation is the same cardinality as the operand relation, which occurs when the primary key is projected in the resulting attribute list. If the primary key (or any other unique attribute) of the operand relation is not included in the projection, then there is the potential for duplicate tuples, which are automatically removed from the resulting relation based on the definition of a relation as a set of tuples. Figure 3.5 shows that three attributes have been included in the projection (a1, a2, aj) with the cardinality of r and $\pi_A(r)$ being the same. Thus, one of the attributes in the projection is unique.

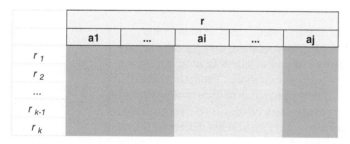

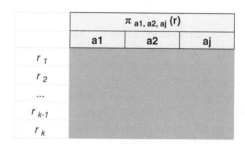

**FIGURE 3.5**    Projection.

Table 3.3 provides sample queries that illustrate the filtering operations over the EMPLOYEE TRAINING enterprise. Each query has a label so that it can be referred to within the text, along with its English description. The table also shows the corresponding formal relational algebra expression that provides the answer to the query. Note that the selection sample query *alg_Managers* must have the same schema as the employee table, which is (eID, eLast, eFirst, eTitle, eSalary), and the number of tuples in the result is the number of employees who are managers. The projection sample query *alg_Titles* has the schema given by the list of attributes in the projection, which is just eTitle, and the number of tuples in the result are the number of different titles in the table.

**Table 3.3  Relational Algebra Sample Filtering Queries**

| Query label and description | √Relational algebra |
|---|---|
| *alg_Managers*:<br>    Which employees are managers, i.e. have the title 'Manager'? | $\sigma_{eTitle='Manager'}$(employee) |
| *alg_Titles*:<br>    What employee titles appear in the database? | $\pi_{eTitle}$(employee) |

The application of a filtering operation itself returns a relation. Therefore, filtering operations can be combined in succession to return the desired result. Consider as an example the query that returns the last and first names of employees who are managers.

*alg_ManagerNames*:

$$\sqrt{} \qquad \pi_{eLast,\ eFirst}\left(\sigma_{eTitle='Manager'}(\text{employee})\right)$$

The parentheses indicate the precedence of the operations. The selection for manager occurs first, and the projection is applied to the selection result.

## Self Check

Write the following filtering queries in relational algebra:

4. Which employees earn more than $75,000?
   (eID, eLast, eFirst, eTitle, eSalary)
5. Which technology area titles are in the database?
   (aTitle)
6. What are the titles of courses offered in the technology area with id 'DB'?
   (cTitle)

## 3.2.2 Sets

Recall from Chapter 1 that relations are sets of tuples, which is essentially a collection of rows without duplicates. Therefore, the set operators of union (∪), difference (−), and intersection (∩) play a role in relational algebra. These operators take two relations as arguments or operands and are, therefore, called binary operators. There are some assumptions that must hold on the schemas of the operand relations for the valid application of these operators. Specifically, the operand relations must be compatible. The simplest assumption for compatibility is that the operand relations have identical sets of attribute names and domains although a more general definition for compatibility can be specified based on attribute position and domain. This book uses the simpler compatibility assumption.

> Use union, difference, and intersection to combine compatible operand relations.

The set operators combine the two compatible operand tables in specific ways. Table 3.4 provides an overview of the set operators, including its definition, schema, and upperbound on the resulting cardinality. Due to the simple compatibility assumption, the schema of the operand tables and the result must be the same. The union combines the tuples from both operand relations, eliminating duplicates. Thus, the upperbound on the cardinality is the sum of the cardinalities of the operand relations. The difference returns the tuples from the first operand relation that are not in the second operand relation. The upperbound of the result cardinality is the cardinality of the first table if there are no common tuples in the second operand. The intersection returns the tuples that are in both operand relations. Therefore, the intersection cardinality upperbound is the minimum cardinality of the operand relations when one table is a subset of the other.

**Table 3.4    Summary of Set Operators**

| Operator expression | Definition | Schema | Cardinality (upperbound) |
|---|---|---|---|
| $r \cup s$ | $\{ t \mid t \in r \text{ or } t \in s \}$ | $R = S$ | $\mid r \mid + \mid s \mid$ |
| $r - s$ | $\{ t \mid t \in r \text{ and } t \notin s \}$ | $R$ | $\mid r \mid$ |
| $r \cap s$ | $\{ t \mid t \in r \text{ and } t \in s \}$ | $R = S$ | $\min(\mid r \mid, \mid s \mid)$ |

Table 3.5 provides sample queries that illustrate the set operations over the EMPLOYEE TRAINING enterprise. Each query has a label, its English description, and corresponding answer in relational algebra. Note that all queries are based on the eID attribute, requiring the introduction of a projection operation to provide compatible operand relations. Query *alg_ManagerOrProjectLead* unions the employees who are managers with the employees who are project leads. Query *alg_ManagersNoCourses* uses set difference to find the employees who are managers and have not taken a training course. Query *alg_ManagersTookCourses* illustrates intersection by finding the managers who have taken a training course.

**Table 3.5    Relational Algebra Sample Set Queries**

| Query label and description | √Relational algebra |
|---|---|
| *alg_ManagerOrProjectLead*: | |
| Which employees are managers or project leads? | $\pi_{eID}(\sigma_{eTitle='Manager'}(employee)) \cup \pi_{eID}(\sigma_{eTitle='Project\ Lead'}(employee))$ |
| *alg_ManagersNoCourses*: | |
| Which managers have not taken any courses? | $\pi_{eID}(\sigma_{eTitle='Manager'}(employee)) - \pi_{eID}(takes)$ |
| *alg_ManagersTookCourses*: | |
| Which managers have taken a training course? | $\pi_{eID}(\sigma_{eTitle='Manager'}(employee)) \cap \pi_{eID}(takes)$ |

# Self Check

Write the following set queries in relational algebra, simply returning a collection of employee identifiers:

7.  Which Database Administrators took the 'DB01' course?
8.  Which employees are Database Administrators or took the 'DB01' course?
9.  Which Database Administrators did not take the 'DB01' course?

## 3.2.3 Joins

The relational algebra operators introduced thus far are either horizontally or vertically filtering an existing relation or adding/removing tuples from compatible relations. This section covers the operations required to combine two tables based on the primary and foreign keys between them. This concept is known as a *join*. A join is fundamentally a Cartesian product operation followed by a selection.

> **Use *joins* to combine relations on the primary–foreign key relationship.**

The binary Cartesian product operator ($\times$) retrieves all possible combinations of the tuples from the operand relations.

$$p \times q = \{\, t_p t_q \mid t_p \in p \text{ } and \text{ } t_q \in q \,\}$$

A simplifying assumption for the product operator is that the operand relations do not have any attribute names in common, i.e. $P \cap Q = \emptyset$. Otherwise, the relation resulting from the product would have duplicate attribute names. The schema of $p \times q$ represented as a set of attributes is $P \cup Q$. The degree of the resulting relation is the sum of the degree of the operand relations, i.e. $degree(p) + degree(q)$. The cardinality of $p \times q$, denoted $\mid p \times q \mid$, is the result of multiplying the cardinality of the operand relations, i.e. $\mid p \mid * \mid q \mid$.

For an example over the EMPLOYEE TRAINING enterprise, it is somewhat difficult to determine a realistic query that is just a Cartesian product because it generates all possible combinations. However, one likely scenario for a Cartesian product is the determination of all combinations of employee ids with the training courses offered by the company:

*alg_employeeTrainingCoursePossibilities*:

$\sqrt{}\qquad \pi_{\text{eID}}(\text{employee}) \times \pi_{\text{cID}}(\text{trainingCourse})$

Taking the difference of these possibilities with the actual instance of which employee took which training course ($\pi_{\text{eID, cID}}(\text{takes})$) results in finding the employees with the courses that they have not taken.

The join operator ($\bowtie_\theta$) is defined as a Cartesian product of the operand relations followed by a selection using the $\theta$ condition.

$$p \bowtie_\theta q = \sigma_\theta(p \times q)$$

Consider the following query over the EMPLOYEE TRAINING enterprise that retrieves the employees who lead technology areas:

*alg_employeeLeads*:

$\sqrt{}\qquad \text{employee} \bowtie_{\text{eID=aLeadID}} \text{technologyArea}$

This query represents the join of the employee and technologyArea tables such that the employee identification number (eID) is equal to the identification number of the area lead (aLeadID), joining the foreign key in technologyArea with its corresponding primary key in employee. The schema of the resulting join contains all the attributes of the employee (eID, eLast, eFirst, eTitle, eSalary) and technologyArea (aID, aTitle, aURL, aLeadID) tables. Thus, the degree of the join is nine. If only some of the attributes are desired, a projection operation can be introduced. The cardinality of the join is the same as the cardinality of technologyArea since there is exactly one eID value that matches the value of the aLeadID foreign key attribute.

A natural join ($\bowtie$) is a shorthand notation for a join that occurs quite frequently in practice. The join condition is assumed to be a conjunction of equality comparisons such that the value of attributes with the same name in both operand relations is equal. A projection is automatically introduced to include only one copy of the duplicate attributes. A natural join is formally defined as follows where the common attributes in both operand relations are denoted by $P \cap Q = \{ ai, \ldots, aj \}$.

$$p \bowtie q = \pi_{P \cup Q}(\sigma_{p.ai=q.ai \text{ and } \ldots \text{ and } p.aj=q.aj}(p \times q))$$

Consider an example query over the EMPLOYEE TRAINING enterprise that retrieves the course title and offerings of each training course:

*alg_CourseTitleOfferings*:

√      $\pi_{\text{cTitle, tDate}}(\text{trainingCourse} \bowtie \text{takes})$

The natural join in the query *alg_CourseTitleOfferings* joins the trainingCourse and takes tables such that the cID attributes in both tables are equal. The resulting schema for the natural join contains only one copy of the cID attribute. The projection returns the desired attributes for the result of the query.

## Self Check

Write the following queries in relational algebra:

10. Which employees took the 'Big Data' course and on what date?
    (eID, tDate)

11. Which employees took the course with unique id 'DB01'?
    (eLast, eFirst)

12. What are the ids of the employees who took courses in the technology area having the title 'Database'?
    (eID)

## 3.2.4 Division

> **The division operator finds those values in the first operand relation that are related to *all* of the values in the second operand relation.**

The division operator ($\div$) is one of the most complicated relational algebra operators. The types of queries that use the division operator typically find those values in the first operand relation that are related to *all* of the values in the second operand relation. Therefore, for the division operation $p \div q$ to be a valid expression, $Q \subseteq P$. The schema of the division result $p \div q$ is $P - Q$. A tuple $t$ is in $p \div q$ if for all tuples $t_q \in q$, there exists a tuple $t_p \in p$ such that $t_p.(Q) = t_q$ and $t_p.(P - Q) = t$. Consider the definition of the division operator defined based on previous relational algebra operators:

$$p \div q = \pi_{P-Q}(p) - \pi_{P-Q}((\pi_{P-Q}(p) \times q) - p)$$

Let's consider the details of this equivalence using a motivational, abstract example and breaking down this large complicated query into a sequence of intermediate relations. The sample query asks for the values of a from the abTable that are related to *all* of the b values appearing in the bTable. The operand relations are abTable(a,b) and bTable(b), and the answer to the query is abTable $\div$ bTable. Figure 3.6 shows a sample instance for the operand tables and the resulting answer table. The value a2 is not in the result since a2 is not related to both b1 and b2. Note that a3 is included in the result because it is related to both b1 and b2, as well as b3.

Consider the definition of division in the context of the abstract example:

√      $\pi_a(\text{abTable}) - \pi_a((\pi_a(\text{abTable}) \times \text{bTable}) - \text{abTable})$

| abTable | |
| --- | --- |
| a | b |
| a1 | b1 |
| a1 | b2 |
| a2 | b2 |
| a3 | b1 |
| a3 | b2 |
| a3 | b3 |

| bTable |
| --- |
| b |
| b1 |
| b2 |

| abTable ÷ bTable |
| --- |
| a |
| a1 |
| a3 |

**FIGURE 3.6**   Division abstract example.

Let's break down this division definition into more manageable parts. Since the result of a correct relational algebra expression is a relation, each simpler component of the complicated definition can be broken down into a named relation, using the syntax := to assign the result of the relational algebra expression to a name.

The left operand of the outermost difference defines a table containing the a's that appear in the abTable, which is named aTable:

√   $aTable := \pi_a(abTable);$

> Use := as an assignment operator to assign the result of a relational algebra expression to a name.

The Cartesian product to be named allaWithAllb, which is the left operand of the innermost difference, specifies all possible combinations of a's appearing in the abTable (reusing aTable) with b's appearing in the bTable:

√   $allaWithAllb := aTable \times bTable;$

The innermost difference finds the a's that are not related to some b by taking all possibilities and subtracting the actual relationships given by the abTable, and then projecting on attribute a:

√   $aNotRelatedToSomeb := \pi_a(allaWithAllb - abTable);$

The outermost difference returns the a's related to *all* b's by taking all possible a's and subtracting those a's that are not related to some b:

√   $aRelatedToAllb := aTable - aNotRelatedToSomeb;$

The division operator looks complicated but when broken down as shown above is cleverly combining the data to find a nontrivial answer.

Consider a query over the EMPLOYEE TRAINING enterprise to illustrate a database query that involves division, finding the id of those employees who took *all* of the training courses offered by the company.

$$\pi_{eID, cID}(takes) \div \pi_{cID}(trainingCourse)$$

# Self Check

Consider the given query to find the employees who took *all* of the training courses offered by the company: $\pi_{eID, cID}(takes) \div \pi_{cID}(trainingCourse)$

13.  What is the schema of the result?
14.  Write out this division query in terms of its fundamental relational algebra operators using named tables.
15.  Write a relational algebra expression to find the ids of employees who did not take *all* of the training courses offered by the company.

## 3.3 Relational Completeness

**Query languages that are at least as expressive as relational algebra are *relationally complete*.**

Thus far, the chapter introduced filtering, set, join, and division operations for retrieving information from a relational database. Technically, five of these operators are fundamental relational algebra operators that characterize a complete set of operators: $\sigma, \pi, \cup, -, \times$. Table 3.6 summarizes these fundamental relational algebra operators, including its schema, degree, and cardinality upperbound, and Table 3.7 provides examples of the these fundamental operators using queries over the EMPLOYEE TRAINING enterprise. Some of the introduced operations are additional operators that are defined in terms of the fundamental operators: $\cap, \bowtie_\theta, \bowtie$. Table 3.8 summarizes the additional operators in terms of their definition using fundamental operators. The introducing discussion of the join, natural join, and division operators in Section 3.2 already described these operators in terms of the fundamental relational algebra operators. Table 3.9 provides a summary of the examples for the additional operators over the EMPLOYEE TRAINING enterprise. Relational query languages that provide the capabilities of relational algebra are called *complete*. Chapter 4 introduces declarative relational calculus query languages, which are relationally complete. SQL, introduced in Chapter 5, is also relationally complete and introduces additional capabilities beyond relational algebra expressiveness, such as aggregation and grouping.

**Table 3.6　Summary of Fundamental Relational Algebra Operators**

| Relational algebra expression | Schema | Degree | Cardinality (upperbound) |
|---|---|---|---|
| $\sigma_\theta(r)$ | R | degree(r) | $|r|$ |
| $\pi_A(r)$ | $A \subseteq R$ | degree(A) | $|r|$ |
| $r \cup s$ | $R = S$ | degree(r) = degree(s) | $|r| + |s|$ |
| $r - s$ | R | degree(r) | $|r|$ |
| $p \times q$ | $P \cup Q$ | degree(p) + degree(q) | $|p| * |q|$ |

**Table 3.7　Relational Algebra Summary of Fundamental EMPLOYEE TRAINING Queries**

| Query | √Relational algebra |
|---|---|
| $Q_\sigma$ | $\sigma_{eTitle='Manager'}(employee)$ |
| $Q_\pi$ | $\pi_{eTitle}(employee)$ |
| $Q_\cup$ | $\pi_{eID}(\sigma_{eTitle='Manager'}(employee)) \cup \pi_{eID}(\sigma_{eTitle='Project\,Lead'}(employee))$ |
| $Q_-$ | $\pi_{eID}(\sigma_{eTitle='Manager'}(employee)) - \pi_{eID}(takes)$ |
| $Q_\times$ | $\pi_{eID}(employee) \times \pi_{cID}(trainingCourse)$ |

**Table 3.8　Summary of Additional Relational Algebra Operators**

| Expression | Definition in terms of fundamental operators |
|---|---|
| $r \cap s$ | $r - (r - s)$ |
| $p \bowtie_\theta q$ | $\sigma_\theta (p \times q)$ |
| $p \bowtie q$ | $\pi_{P \cup Q}(\sigma_{p.ai=q.ai\,and\,...\,and\,p.aj=q.aj}(p \times q))\,where\,P \cap Q = \{\,ai, ..., aj\,\}$ |
| $p \div q$ | $\pi_{P-Q}(p) - \pi_{P-Q}((\pi_{P-Q}(p) \times q) - p)$ |

Table 3.9 **Relational Summary of Additional EMPLOYEE TRAINING Queries**

| Query | √Relational algebra |
|-------|---------------------|
| $Q_\cap$ | $\pi_{eID}(\sigma_{eTitle='Manager'}(employee)) \cap \pi_{eID}(takes)$ |
| $Q_{\bowtie_\theta}$ | $employee \bowtie_{eID=aLeadID} technologyArea$ |
| $Q_\bowtie$ | $\pi_{cTitle,tDate}(trainingCourse \bowtie takes)$ |
| $Q_\div$ | $\pi_{eID,cID}(takes) \div \pi_{cID}(trainingCourse)$ |

## Aggregation and Grouping

Some text coverage of relational algebra includes a detailed discussion of formal operators for aggregation and grouping within the context of this formal language. Aggregation refers to providing a single, aggregate result by examining data, such as minimum, maximum, average, sum, count. A typical example query of aggregation is counting, such as finding the number of employees in the database. Grouping is usually applied with an aggregation to determine an aggregate result for the group, such as how many employees of each title are in the database. Rather than focus on operators for aggregation and grouping in the context of the formal languages, this coverage illustrates how to use the fundamental relational algebra operators to find a minimum/maximum or a limited form of counting. The details of aggregation and grouping in the context of SQL appear in Section 5.5.

> Although there is no inherent support for aggregation and grouping in fundamental relational algebra, some queries involving minimum/maximum and only one/more than one can be answered.

For an aggregation example over the EMPLOYEE TRAINING enterprise, consider finding the employees who have the minimum salary, returning the entire employee tuple:

√ empSal := $\pi_{eSalary}(employee)$;
    empSalCopy(eSalaryCopy) := empSal;
    empSalNotMin := $\pi_{eSalary}(empSal \bowtie_{eSalary>eSalaryCopy} empSalCopy)$;
    empSalMin := empSal − empSalNotMin;
    employeesMinSalary := employee $\bowtie$ empSalMin;

The named tables empSal and empSalCopy each contain a single attribute consisting of employee salaries but having different attribute names. The named table empSalNotMin finds those employee salaries that are *not* minimum by joining the employee salary tables and selecting those salaries that are greater than another salary. The minimum salary is obtained by subtracting the salaries that are not minimum from all employee salaries. The named table empSalMin is joined with employee to find the employee(s) having the minimum salary.

> To rename attributes in a named table, list the new attribute names within parentheses during the assignment.

To introduce the concept of grouping, consider a variation of the above query to find the minimum salary for each title in the database.

√ empSalTitle := $\pi_{eTitle, eSalary}(employee)$;
    empSalTitleCopy(eTitleCopy, eSalaryCopy) := empSalTitle;
    empSalTitleNotMin := $\pi_{eTitle, eSalary}$
        $(empSalTitle \bowtie_{eTitle=eTitleCopy \text{ and } eSalary>eSalaryCopy} empSalTitleCopy)$;
    empSalTitleMin := empSalTitle − empSalTitleNotMin;

Essentially, the intermediate results of the named tables must contain both the title and the salary attributes so that the comparisons are based on the titles being the same with different salaries.

A combination of the relational algebra operators also supports a limited form of counting. Consider as a motivational example over the EMPLOYEE TRAINING enterprise, a query that finds the ids of employees who took courses in *more than one* technology area.

$\checkmark$  elDalDs(elD, aID) := $\pi_{elD,\ arealD}$(takes $\bowtie$ trainingCourse);
  elDalDsCopy(elDCopy, aIDCopy) := elDalDs;
  elDsMoreThanOne := $\pi_{elD}$(elDalDs $\bowtie_{elD=elDCopy\ and\ aID<>aIDCopy}$ elDalDsCopy);

The named table **elDalDs** contains the identifiers of employees along with the area identifier of the training courses that the employees have taken. The named table **elDalDsCopy** is a copy of the **elDalDs** table with the attributes renamed. By joining **elDalDs** with its copy such that the employee identifiers are the same and the area identifiers are different gives the employees who have taken courses in more than one technology area. Note that this query is actually illustrating grouping in combination with the limited counting since it is finding those employees who took courses in more than one technology area.

## Self Check

16. Which of the following relational algebra operators is not a fundamental operator? Identify all that apply.

    $\cup, \bowtie, \times, \cap$

17. Using a sequence of named tables, write a relational algebra query to find the minimum manager salary.

    (eSalary)

18. Write a relational algebra query to find the employees who have taken courses in only one technology area.

    (elD)

    *Hint: You may use named tables in the section coverage to simplify your answer.*

## 3.4 Query Optimization

There are multiple ways to write a relational algebra expression to correctly answer a query. When you compared your answer to the self-check answer provided at the end of the chapter, you may have noticed that you have a similar but not exactly the same answer. Consider the self-check question that asks for the names of the employees who took the course with the unique id 'DB01'. The provided answer is

*alg_db01_version1*

$\checkmark$      $\pi_{eLast,\ eFirst}(\sigma_{cID='DB01'}$(takes) $\bowtie$ employee)

Another correct answer is

*alg_db01_version2*

$\checkmark$      $\pi_{eLast,\ eFirst}(\sigma_{cID='DB01'}$(takes $\bowtie$ employee))

The first version finds the **takes** tuples filtered for 'DB01' and joins the filtered tuples with **employee** to find the names of the employees who took the course. The second version joins all of the **takes** table with the **employee** table, combining the takes and employee information and then filtering to find 'DB01' in this combination. Which is more efficient? The general heuristic that is typically applied for determining which query is more efficient is based on minimizing the number of tuples in the intermediate expressions within a query. The first approach that joins the filtered **takes** tuples finding the needed employee names is probably more efficient than the second approach that finds the names of all employees and then filters that result based on the unique course identifier.

In examining the textual representation of the relational algebra versions of these two answers, they only differ by the position of one right parenthesis, but the run-time meaning of the versions is quite different. The formalism of relational algebra expressions as query trees facilitates the visualization of the query and provides a foundation for introducing query optimization techniques. Figure 3.7 illustrates the pictorial representation of a query tree for the queries *alg_db01_version1* and *alg_db01_version2*.

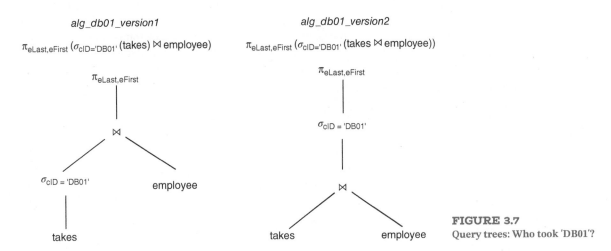

FIGURE 3.7
Query trees: Who took 'DB01'?

A query tree represents parent–child relationships for the algebraic operations in the expression between a relational algebra operator and its associated operands. Unary relational algebra operators, such as $\sigma$ and $\pi$, will have only one child, whereas binary relational algebra operators will have two children. Nodes that represent stored tables in the database do not have children nodes. Note that every node in the tree represents a relation. A leaf node is a stored table, such as takes and employee. An internal node is an intermediate relation, representing the instance associated with the relational algebra expression. The associated execution of the query given by the tree starts at the leaves and then proceeds up the tree to the final result given by the node at the top, which is called the *root* node.

The goal of query optimization is to find an equivalent query that executes more efficiently. So the first question is how to find such an alternative. These alternatives are based on the theoretical properties of the relational algebra operators, which will be explored in more depth. An exhaustive search of the alternatives for evaluating a query can cost more than the evaluation of the query as given. Therefore, as mentioned earlier, a heuristic approach is generally taken to minimize the number of tuples in the intermediate expressions within the query. Typically, the query optimization heuristic performs selections as early as possible to reduce the size of the internal nodes and then examines the join ordering based on the earlier selections. A final step introduces projections to reduce the amount of data by eliminating unnecessary attributes.

> **Query optimization finds an equivalent query that should execute more efficiently.**

## HOW TO 3.3   Heuristic Query Optimization

**Step 1: Pushing Selections Down the Tree**
Push the selections down the tree nearest to the table (stored or intermediate) that it is filtering.

**Step 2: Reordering Joins**
Reorder joins using the commutative and associative properties of these operators based on the filtered expressions from Step 1. If possible,

combine a Cartesian project followed by a selection into a theta-join.

**Step 3: Introducing Projections**
Assuming that data reside at different sites, introduce projections to decrease communication time and to increase security.

Table 3.10 summarizes the applicability of pushing a selection ($\sigma$) down the tree through an operator node. The table indicates when the given expression can be rewritten to the expression resulting from pushing the selection down through the operator node. The applicability column indicates when that transformation is applicable, where a checkmark (✓) shows that the transformation is applicable based on the properties of the operators and a question mark (?) shows that the transformation is only applicable under certain conditions, which are indicated in the comments column. For example, the given expression of $\sigma_\theta(r \times s)$ can be transformed to $\sigma_\theta(r) \times s$ when $\theta$ involves only attributes of r or $r \times \sigma_\theta(s)$ when $\theta$ involves only attributes of s.

**Table 3.10  Summary of Pushing Selections Down**

| Given expression | Push $\sigma$ | Applicability | Comments |
|---|---|---|---|
| $\sigma_\theta(\pi_A(r))$ | $\pi_A(\sigma_\theta(r))$ | ✓ | $\theta$ involves attributes in A and $A \subset R$ |
| $\sigma_{\theta_1}(\sigma_{\theta_2}(r))$ | $\sigma_{\theta_2}(\sigma_{\theta_1}(r))$ | ✓ | successive $\sigma$s are commutative |
| $\sigma_\theta(r \cup s)$ | $\sigma_\theta(r) \cup \sigma_\theta(s)$ | ✓ | r and s are compatible, so $\theta$ applies to both r and s |
| $\sigma_\theta(r \times s)$ | $\sigma_\theta(r) \times s$ | ? | if $\theta$ involves attributes of R |
| $\sigma_\theta(r \times s)$ | $r \times \sigma_\theta(s)$ | ? | if $\theta$ involves attributes of S |
| $\sigma_\theta(r \cap s)$ | $\sigma_\theta(r) \cap \sigma_\theta(s)$ | ✓ | r and s are compatible, so $\theta$ applies to both r and s |
| $\sigma_\theta(r \bowtie s)$ | $\sigma_\theta(r) \bowtie s$ | ? | if $\theta$ involves attributes of R |
| $\sigma_\theta(r \bowtie s)$ | $r \bowtie \sigma_\theta(s)$ | ? | if $\theta$ involves attributes of S |

The reordering of joins is possible due to the commutativity and associativity properties of joins. In fact, most of the binary relational algebra operators are commutative and associative: $\times, \cup, \cap, \bowtie, \bowtie_\theta$. Commutativity refers to the ordering of the operands, e.g. r op s $\equiv$ s op r. Associativity refers to the grouping of the expressions without changing their order, e.g. (r op s) op t $\equiv$ r op (s op t). The combination of the commutative and associative properties allows reordering of the query tree to support smaller intermediate relations. Figure 3.8 shows abstract query trees that illustrate the commutativity and associativity properties of such operators. Note that the binary operators that involve difference, including division, are not commutative nor associative.

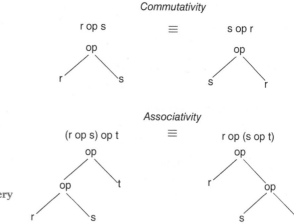

**FIGURE 3.8**  Abstract examples of query trees for commutative and associative operators.

Introducing projections in the execution plan of a query may reduce communication time and increase security. Data involved in answering a query may be stored at various sites. Rather than send all the data from an intermediate expression to the requesting site to execute the query, the amount of data can be reduced by introducing projections to vertically filter the data to the attributes necessary to answer the query. There is a cost associated with a projection for eliminating potentially duplicate tuples. Therefore, there is a trade-off in the time to vertically filter versus the communication costs of unnecessary data. In this coverage of query optimization, projections are introduced for each intermediate expression. This provides an additional benefit for checking one's understanding of relational algebra operators and expressions. As an example, consider the query tree for the *alg_db01_version* of the query that finds the names of the employees who took 'DB01'. Figure 3.9 shows the projections introduced for query optimization. After the horizontal filtering of takes for 'DB01', only the eID attribute is necessary for the natural join. Only some of the employee attributes are required: eID for the natural join and eLast, eFirst for the query result. The resulting inline textual representation of the query is

*alg_db01_version1_projections*

$\sqrt{}$  $\pi_{eLast,\ eFirst}(\pi_{eID}(\sigma_{cID='DB01'}(\text{takes})) \bowtie \pi_{eID,eLast,eFirst}(\text{employee}))$

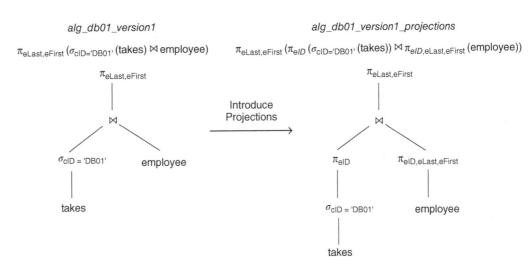

**FIGURE 3.9**  Introduce projections in query tree: Who took 'DB01'?

The automation of query optimization is complex and requires knowledge of the various statistics on the tables in the database, including

- the number of tuples in each table;
- the number of unique values of each attribute in the table; and
- the physical storage characteristics of the table and associated index structures.

These statistics are costly to maintain for each insertion, deletion, or modification to the database. Typically, these statistics are gathered using a separate utility program for the database that the database administrator schedules to run periodically when the database is not heavily utilized.

## Self Check

19. Which binary relational algebra operators are commutative and associative?
20. Should the query optimization step of introducing projections always be applied?
21. What properties of the natural join operator allow for the reordering of the query tree to support smaller intermediate tables?

## Chapter Notes Summary

### Query Design

- Identify the tables needed to answer the query and return the specified result.

### Algebra Operators

- Selection horizontally filters a relation, whereas projection vertically filters a relation.
- Use union, difference, and intersection to combine compatible operand relations.
- Use joins to combine relations on the primary–foreign key relationship.
- The division operator finds those values in the first operand relation that are related to *all* of the values in the second operand relation.
- Use := as an assignment operator to assign the result of a relational algebra expression to a name.

### Relational Completeness

- Query languages that are at least as expressive as relational algebra are *relationally complete.*
- Although there is no inherent support for aggregation and grouping in fundamental relational algebra, some queries involving minimum/maximum and only one/more than one can be answered.
- To rename attributes in a named table, list the new attribute names within parentheses during the assignment.

### Query Optimization

- Query optimization finds an equivalent query that should execute more efficiently.

## Chapter Reminders

Table 3.11 summarizes the relational algebra operators introduced in this chapter.

## Practice

There are practice problems for each of the enterprises introduced earlier in the text: Investment Portfolio, New Home, and Web Page. The book's companion website has the data for the enterprises in WinRDBI so that you can execute the practice questions. There are sample answers provided at the end of the chapter after the solutions to the self-check questions.

**Table 3.11**  **Chapter Summary of Relational Algebra Operators**

| Operator | Name | Definition | Schema | Notes |
|---|---|---|---|---|
| $\sigma_\theta(r)$ | selection | $\{\, t \mid t \in r \; and \; \theta \,\}$ | R | $\theta$ is a Boolean combination of conditions |
| $\pi_A(r)$ | projection | $\{\, t.a_1, ..., t.a_j \mid$ $t \in r \; and \; a_i \in A \,\}$ | A | $A \subseteq R$ |
| $r \cup s$ | union | $\{\, t \mid t \in r \; or \; t \in s \,\}$ | R = S | r and s must have compatible (i.e. same) schema |
| $r - s$ | difference | $\{\, t \mid t \in r \; and \; t \notin s \,\}$ | R | r and s must have compatible (i.e. same) schema |
| $r \times s$ | Cartesian product | $\{\, t \mid t_r t_s \; where$ $t_r \in r \; and \; t_s \in s \,\}$ | R ∪ S | r and s must NOT have any attributes in common |
| $r \cap s$ | intersection | $r - (r - s)$ | R = S | r and s must have compatible (i.e. same) schema |
| $r \bowtie_\theta s$ | theta join | $\sigma_\theta(r \times s)$ | R ∪ S | Theoretically, common attribute names referenced using dot notation (r.A1 = s.A1) |
| $r \bowtie s$ | natural join | $\pi_{R \cup S}(\sigma_\theta(r \times s))$ $where \; \theta \; equijoins$ $R \cap S$ | R ∪ S | Theoretically, results in Cartesian product if no attribute names in common |
| $r \div s$ | division | $\pi_{R-S}(r) - \pi_{R-S}$ $((\pi_{R-S}(r) \times s) - r)$ | R − S | $S \subseteq R$ |

# Practice Problems: INVESTMENT PORTFOLIO

Answer the following practice queries in relational algebra over the INVESTMENT PORTFOLIO schema (see Figure 2.18 for the visual relational schema and Figure 2.16 for its conceptual design as an ER diagram):

client(taxPayerID, name, address)
stock(sTicker, sName, rating, prinBus, sHigh, sLow, sCurrent, ret1Yr, ret5Yr)
mutualFund(mTicker, mName, prinObj, mHigh, mLow, mCurrent, yield, familyID)
fundFamily(familyID, company, cAddress)
stockPortfolio(taxPayerID, sTicker, sNumShares)
mutualFundPortfolio(taxPayerID, mTicker, mNumShares)

1. What clients have invested in which 'A' rated stocks?
   (taxPayerID, name, sTicker, sName)

2. Which clients have invested in both stocks whose principal business is 'Technology' and mutual funds having growth ('G') as a principal objective?
   (taxPayerID, name)

3. What clients have not invested in mutual funds with income ('I') as a principal objective?
   (taxPayerID, name)

4. Which clients have invested in stocks but not in mutual funds?
   (taxPayerID, name)

5. Which clients have more than one no-rating ('NR') stock?
   (taxPayerID, name)

6. Which clients have invested in only one mutual fund with stability ('S') as a principal objective?
(taxPayerID, name)

7. Which mutual funds have the minimum current rate?
(mTicker, mName, mCurrent)

8. What clients have invested in all of the mutual funds within the 'Fictitious' fund family?
(taxPayerID, name)

## Practice Problems: NEW HOME

Answer the following practice queries in relational algebra over the NEW HOME schema (see Figure 2.21 for the visual relational schema and Figure 2.19 for its conceptual design as an ER diagram):

homebuilder(hID, hName, hStreet, hCity, hZip, hPhone)
model(hID, mID, mName, sqft, story)
subdivision(sName, sCity, sZip)
offered(sName, hID, mID, price)
lot(sName, lotNum, lStAddr, lSize, lPremium)
sold(sName, lotNum, hID, mID, status)

1. Are there subdivisions that only offer single-story homes?
(sName, sCity, sZip)

2. List all the homebuilders who offer single-story models with at least 2000 square feet in subdivisions located in 'Tempe'.
(hName, hPhone)

3. Which lots in the 'Terraces' subdivision are available, i.e. not sold?
(lotNum, lStAddr, lSize, lPremium)

4. Which models are not currently offered in any subdivision?
(hName, mName)

5. Which subdivisions offer models from more than one homebuilder?
(sName, sCity, sZip)

6. Which models are offered in only one subdivision?
(hName, mName)

7. Which models offered in the 'Foothills' subdivision have the maximum square footage?
(hName, mName, sqft)

8. Which subdivision offers all the models by the homebuilder 'Homer'?
(sName, sCity, sZip)

## Practice Problems: WEB PAGE

Answer the following practice queries in relational algebra over the WEB PAGE schema (see Figure 2.24 for the visual relational schema and Figure 2.22 for its conceptual design as an ER diagram):

webpage (wID, wTitle, wURL, hits)
site (sID, sTitle, sURL)
graphic (gID, gName, gType, src, alt)
document (dID, dName, dType, dDescription, dDate, downloads, wID)
internal (sourceID, targetID)
external (wID, sID, followed)
displays (wID, gID)

1. Which pages contain a link to SQL ('sql') documents?
   (wID, wTitle)

2. Which pages display graphics having the name 'understandingbook'?
   (wID, wTitle)

3. Which pages do not display any graphics?
   (wID, wTitle)

4. Which pages display 'jpg' graphics but not 'gif' graphics?
   (wID, wTitle)

5. Which pages contain more than one document?
   (wID, wTitle)

6. Which pages contain only one link to an external Web page?
   (wID, wTitle)

7. Which pages have the most hits?
   (wID, wTitle, wURL, hits)

8. Which pages display graphics of all graphic types currently stored in the database?
   (wID, wTitle)

# End of Chapter Exercises

Answer the following queries in relational algebra over the EMPLOYEE TRAINING schema:

```
employee(eID, eLast, eFirst, eTitle, eSalary)
technologyArea(aID, aTitle, aURL, aLeadID)
trainingCourse(cID, cTitle, cHours, areaID)
takes(eID, cID, tDate)
```

1. What are the titles of employees who lead technology areas?
   (eTitle)

2. Which employees have not taken any training courses in the 'Database' technology area?
   (eID, eLast, eFirst, eTitle)

3. Which employees took courses in *only one* technology area?
   (eID, eLast, eFirst, eTitle)
   *Hint: This type of query is not inherently supported by relational algebra. However, this can be expressed in relational algebra by finding those employees who took a course in one technology area and did not take courses in more than one technology area.*

4. What is the maximum salary of employees who lead technology areas?
   (eSalary)

5. Which employees have taken at least one training course in *all* of the technology areas offered by the company?
   (eID, eLast, eFirst, eTitle)

Answer the following queries in relational algebra over the INVESTMENT PORTFOLIO schema:

```
client(taxPayerID, name, address)
stock(sTicker, sName, rating, prinBus, sHigh, sLow, sCurrent, ret1Yr, ret5Yr)
mutualFund(mTicker, mName, prinObj, mHigh, mLow, mCurrent, yield, familyID)
fundFamily(familyID, company, cAddress)
stockPortfolio(taxPayerID, sTicker, sNumShares)
mutualFundPortfolio(taxPayerID, mTicker, mNumShares)
```

6. What clients own more than 200 shares of which stocks?
   (taxPayerID, name, sTicker, sName, sNumShares)

7. Which stock's one-year return has outperformed its five-year return?
   (sTicker, sName, prinBus, ret1Yr, ret5Yr)

8. What clients have not invested in stocks with 'Technology' as its principal business?
   (taxPayerID, name)

9. Which clients have invested in mutual funds but not in individual stocks?
   (taxPayerID, name)

10. Which clients have invested in more than one mutual fund with growth ('G') as its principal objective?
    (taxPayerID, name)

11. Which fund families have only one mutual fund?
    (familyID, company, cAddress)

12. Which stocks have the maximum one-year return?
    (sTicker, sName, prinBus, ret1Yr)

13. Which clients have invested in *all* stocks having a one-year return greater than its five-year return?
    (taxPayerID, name)

Answer the following queries in relational algebra over the NEW HOME schema:

    homebuilder(hID, hName, hStreet, hCity, hZip, hPhone)
    model(hID, mID, mName, sqft, story)
    subdivision(sName, sCity, sZip)
    offered(sName, hID, mID, price)
    lot(sName, lotNum, lStAddr, lSize, lPremium)
    sold(sName, lotNum, hID, mID, status)

14. Which subdivisions offer models with more than 3000 square feet?
    (sName, sCity, sZip)

15. Which lots in the 'Foothills' subdivision are pending ('P')?
    (lotNum, lStAddr, lSize, lPremium)

16. Which subdivisions do not offer any models?
    (sName, sCity, sZip)

17. Which subdivisions do not have any completed ('C') lots?
    (sName, sCity, sZip)

18. Which models are offered in more than one subdivision?
    (hName, mName)

19. Which homebuilders have only one two-story model?
    (hName)

20. Which models in the 'Terraces' subdivision have the lowest price?
    (hName, mName, minPrice)

21. Is there a subdivision that offers at least one model from all the homebuilders in the database?
    (sName, sCity, sZip)

Answer the following queries in relational algebra over the WEB PAGE schema:

    webpage (<u>wID</u>, wTitle, wURL, hits)
    site (<u>sID</u>, sTitle, sURL)
    graphic (<u>gID</u>, gName, gType, src, alt)
    document (<u>dID</u>, dName, dType, dDescription, dDate, downloads, wID)
    internal (<u>sourceID</u>, <u>targetID</u>)
    external (<u>wID</u>, <u>sID</u>, followed)
    displays (<u>wID</u>, <u>gID</u>)

22. Which pages contain links to documents named 'emptraining'?
    (wID, wTitle)

23. Which graphics in the database are stored as the type Portable Network Graphics ('png')?
    (gID, gName, alt)

24. Which pages do not contain any links to documents?
    (wID, wTitle)

25. Which pages contain links to external sites?
    (wID, wTitle, sID, sTitle, followed)

26. Which pages display more than one 'gif' graphic?
    (wID, wTitle)

27. Which pages display only one 'jpg' graphic?
    (wID, wTitle)

28. Which document has the fewest downloads?
    (dID, dName, dType, dDescription, downloads)

29. Which pages contain links to all SQL ('sql') documents currently contained in the database?
    (wID, wTitle)

# Answers to Self-Check Questions

1. employee

2. trainingCourse, takes

3. trainingCourse, takes, employee

4. $\sigma_{eSalary>75000}(\text{employee})$

5. $\pi_{aTitle}(\text{technologyArea})$

6. $\pi_{cTitle}(\sigma_{areaID='DB'}(\text{trainingCourse}))$

7. $\pi_{eID}(\sigma_{eTitle='Database\ Administrator'}(\text{employee})) \cap \pi_{eID}(\sigma_{cID='DB01'}(\text{takes}))$

8. $\pi_{eID}(\sigma_{eTitle='Database\ Administrator'}(\text{employee})) \cup \pi_{eID}(\sigma_{cID='DB01'}(\text{takes}))$

9. $\pi_{eID}(\sigma_{eTitle='Database\ Administrator'}(\text{employee})) - \pi_{eID}(\sigma_{cID='DB01'}(\text{takes}))$

10. $\pi_{eID,\ tDate}(\sigma_{cTitle='BigData'}(\text{trainingCourse}) \bowtie \text{takes})$

11. $\pi_{eLast, eFirst}(\sigma_{cID='DB01'}(\text{takes}) \bowtie \text{employee})$

12. $\pi_{eID}((\sigma_{aTitle='Database'}(\text{technologyArea}) \bowtie_{areaID=aID} (\text{trainingCourse})) \bowtie \text{takes})$

13. (eID)

14. empsTookCourses := $\pi_{eID}(\text{takes})$;
    empsWithAllCourses := empsTookCourses $\times$ $\pi_{cID}(\text{trainingCourse})$;
    empsNotAllCourses := $\pi_{eID}(\text{empsWithAllCourses} - \pi_{eID, cID}(\text{takes})$;
    empsTookAllCourses := empsTookCourses $-$ empsNotAllCourses;

15. $\pi_{eID}(\text{employee}) - (\pi_{eID, cID}(\text{takes}) \div \pi_{cID}(\text{trainingCourse}))$

16. $\bowtie$ and $\cap$ are not fundamental relational algebra operators.

17. empSalMgr := $\pi_{eSalary}(\sigma_{eTitle='Manager'}(\text{employee}))$;
    empSalMgrCopy(eSalaryCopy) := empSalMgr;
    empSalMgrNotMin := $\pi_{eSalary}(\text{empSalMgr} \bowtie_{eSalary>eSalaryCopy}$
        empSalMgrCopy);
    empSalMgrMin := empSalMgr $-$ empSalMgrNotMin;

18. $\pi_{eID}(\text{employee}) - \text{eIDsMoreThanOne}$

19. union, intersection, Cartesian product, joins

20. No. If the data reside at the same site, introducing projections is extra work and therefore, less efficient. However, if the data reside at different sites, then introducing projections can significantly reduce the amount of information that needs to be communicated over the network.

21. The natural join operator is commutative and associative and, thus, allows for the reordering of the query tree.

## Answers to Practice Problems: INVESTMENT PORTFOLIO

1. $\pi_{taxPayerID, name, sTicker, sName}$ ( $((\sigma_{rating='A'}(\text{stock})) \bowtie \text{stockPortfolio}) \bowtie \text{client}$ );

2. technologyClients := $\pi_{taxPayerID}$ ( $((\sigma_{prinBus='Technology'}(\text{stock})) \bowtie \text{stockPortfolio}$ );
   growthClients := $\pi_{taxPayerID}$ ( $((\sigma_{prinObj='G'}(\text{mutualFund})) \bowtie \text{mutualFundPortfolio}$ );
   $\pi_{taxPayerID, name}$ ( (technologyClients $\cap$ growthClients) $\bowtie$ client );

3. investI := $\pi_{taxPayerID}$ ( $((\sigma_{prinObj='I'}(\text{mutualFund})) \bowtie \text{mutualFundPortfolio}$ );
   notInvestI := $(\pi_{taxPayerID}(\text{client})) - \text{investI}$;
   $\pi_{taxPayerID, name}(\text{client} \bowtie \text{notInvestI})$;

4. stocksNotMutualFunds :=
        $(\pi_{taxPayerID}(\text{stockPortfolio})) - (\pi_{taxPayerID}(\text{mutualFundPortfolio}))$;
   $\pi_{taxPayerID, name}(\text{client} \bowtie \text{stocksNotMutualFunds})$;

5. investNR := $\pi_{taxPayerID, sTicker}$ ( $(\sigma_{rating='NR'}(\text{stock})) \bowtie \text{stockPortfolio}$);
   investNRCopy(taxPayerIDCopy, sTickerCopy) := investNR;
   moreThanOneNR := $\pi_{taxPayerID}$ ($\sigma_{taxPayerID=taxPayerIDCopy \text{ and } sTicker<>sTickerCopy}$
        (investNR product investNRCopy));
   $\pi_{taxPayerID, name}(\text{client} \bowtie \text{moreThanOneNR})$;

6. investS := $\pi_{\text{taxPayerID, mTicker}}$ ( $(\sigma_{\text{prinObj='S'}}(\text{mutualFund})) \bowtie$
   mutualFundPortfolio);
   investSCopy(taxPayerIDCopy, mTickerCopy) := investS;
   moreThanOneS :=
   $\quad \pi_{\text{taxPayerID}} (\sigma_{\text{taxPayerID=taxPayerIDCopy and mTicker <> mTickerCopy}}$
   $\qquad$ (investS product investSCopy));
   onlyOneS := ($\pi_{\text{taxPayerID}}(\text{investS})$) − moreThanOneS;
   $\pi_{\text{taxPayerID, name}}(\text{client} \bowtie \text{onlyOneS})$;

7. currentRate := $\pi_{\text{mCurrent}}(\text{mutualFund})$;
   currentRateCopy(mCurrentCopy) := currentRate;
   notMinimumRate :=
   $\quad \pi_{\text{mCurrent}}(\sigma_{\text{mCurrent > mCurrentCopy}}$ (currentRate product currentRateCopy) );
   minimumRate := currentRate − notMinimumRate;
   $\pi_{\text{mTicker, mName, mCurrent}}(\text{mutualFund} \bowtie \text{minimumRate})$;

8. fictitiousFunds := $\pi_{\text{mTicker}}($ $(\sigma_{\text{company='Fictitious'}}$ (fundFamily)) $\bowtie$ mutualFund );
   clientsTickersAtLeastOneFund :=
   $\quad \pi_{\text{taxPayerID, mTicker}}(\text{fictitiousFunds} \bowtie \text{mutualFundPortfolio})$;
   clientsAtLeastOneFund := $\pi_{\text{taxPayerID}}(\text{clientsTickersAtLeastOneFund})$;
   allClientsWithAllFunds := clientsAtLeastOneFund product fictitiousFunds;
   clientsNotAllFunds :=
   $\quad \pi_{\text{taxPayerID}}$ (allClientsWithAllFunds − clientsTickersAtLeastOneFund);
   clientsAllFunds := clientsAtLeastOneFund − clientsNotAllFunds;
   $\pi_{\text{taxPayerID, name}}(\text{client} \bowtie \text{clientsAllFunds})$;

## Answers to Practice Problems: New Home

1. subdivisionsOfferSingle := $\pi_{\text{sName}}(\text{offered} \bowtie (\sigma_{\text{story=1}}(\text{model}) ) )$;
   subdivisionsOfferOther := $\pi_{\text{sName}}(\text{offered} \bowtie (\sigma_{\text{story<>1}}(\text{model}) ) )$;
   subdivision $\bowtie$ (subdivisionsOfferSingle − subdivisionsOfferOther);

2. homebuildersOffering := $\pi_{\text{hID, sName}}((\sigma_{\text{story=1 and sqft>2000}}(\text{model})) \bowtie \text{offered})$;
   tempeSubdivisions := $\pi_{\text{sName}}(\sigma_{\text{sCity='Tempe'}}(\text{subdivision}))$;
   $\pi_{\text{hName, hPhone}}(\text{homebuilder} \bowtie (\text{homebuildersOffering} \bowtie \text{tempeSubdivisions}) )$;

3. allTerracesLots := $\pi_{\text{sName,lotNum}}(\sigma_{\text{sName='Terraces'}}(\text{lot}))$;
   soldTerracesLots := $\pi_{\text{sName,lotNum}}(\sigma_{\text{sName='Terraces'}}(\text{sold}))$;
   availableTerracesLots := allTerracesLots − soldTerracesLots;
   $\pi_{\text{lotNum, lStAddr, lSize, lPremium}}$ (availableTerracesLots $\bowtie$ lot);

4. allModels := $\pi_{\text{hID, mID}}(\text{model})$;
   offeredModels := $\pi_{\text{hID, mID}}(\text{offered})$;
   $\pi_{\text{hName, mName}}$ (((allModels − offeredModels) $\bowtie$ model) $\bowtie$ homebuilder);

5. offersBuilder := $\pi_{\text{sName, hID}}(\text{offered})$;
   offersBuilderCopy(sNameCopy, hIDCopy) := offersBuilder;
   offersMoreThanOneBuilder := $\pi_{\text{sName}}(\sigma_{\text{sName=sNameCopy and hID<>hIDCopy}}$
   $\quad$ (offersBuilder product offersBuilderCopy));
   offersMoreThanOneBuilder $\bowtie$ subdivision;

6. offersModel := $\pi_{hID, mID, sName}$(offered);
   offersModelCopy(hIDCopy, mIDCopy, sNameCopy) := offersModel;
   offeredMoreThanOneSubdivision :=

   $\quad\quad \pi_{hID, mID}$ ($\sigma_{hID=hIDCopy \text{ and } mID=mIDCopy \text{ and } sName<>sNameCopy}$
   $\quad\quad\quad$ (offersModel product offersModelCopy));
   offeredOnlyOneSubdivision :=
   $\quad\quad$ ($\pi_{hID, mID}$(offersModel)) − offeredMoreThanOneSubdivision;
   $\pi_{hName, mName}$((offeredOnlyOneSubdivision ⋈ model) ⋈ homebuilder);

7. foothillsModels := $\pi_{hID, hName, mID, mName, sqft}$
   $\quad\quad$ ((($\sigma_{sName='Foothills'}$(offered)) ⋈ model) ⋈ homebuilder);
   foothillsSqft := $\pi_{sqft}$(foothillsModels);
   foothillsSqftCopy(sqftCopy) := foothillsSqft;
   notMaxFoothillsSqft := $\pi_{sqft}$($\sigma_{sqft<sqftCopy}$(foothillsSqft product
   $\quad\quad$ foothillsSqftCopy));
   maxFoothillsSqft := foothillsSqft − notMaxFoothillsSqft;
   $\pi_{hName, mName, sqft}$ (maxFoothillsSqft ⋈ foothillsModels);

8. homerHID := $\pi_{hID}$($\sigma_{hName='Homer'}$(homebuilder));
   homerModels := $\pi_{hID,mID}$(homerHID ⋈ model);
   offersHomerModels := $\pi_{sName, hID, mID}$(homerModels ⋈ offered);
   allsNameWithAllHModels := ($\pi_{sName}$(offersHomerModels)) product
   homerModels;
   sNameNotSomeHModel := $\pi_{sName}$(allsNameWithAllHModels −
   $\quad\quad$ offersHomerModels);
   subdivision ⋈ (($\pi_{sName}$(offersHomerModels)) − sNameNotSomeHModel);

## Answers to Practice Problems: WEB PAGE

1. $\pi_{wID, wTitle}$(($\sigma_{dType='sql'}$(document)) ⋈ webpage);

2. $\pi_{wID, wTitle}$((($\sigma_{gName='understandingbook'}$(graphic)) ⋈ displays) ⋈ webpage);

3. $\pi_{wID, wTitle}$((($\pi_{wID}$(webpage)) − ($\pi_{wID}$(displays))) ⋈ webpage);

4. jpgGraphics := $\pi_{wID}$(($\sigma_{gType='jpg'}$(graphic)) ⋈ displays);
   gifGraphics := $\pi_{wID}$(($\sigma_{gType='gif'}$(graphic)) ⋈ displays);
   $\pi_{wID, wTitle}$(webpage ⋈ (jpgGraphics − gifGraphics));

5. docCopy(dIDcopy, wIDcopy) := $\pi_{dID, wID}$(document);
   moreThanOneDoc := $\pi_{wID}$($\sigma_{wID=wIDcopy \text{ and } dID <> dIDcopy}$
   $\quad\quad$ (document product docCopy));
   $\pi_{wID, wTitle}$(webpage ⋈ moreThanOneDoc);

6. externalCopy(wIDcopy, sIDcopy) := $\pi_{wID, sID}$(external);
   moreThanOneExternal :=
   $\quad\quad \pi_{wID}$($\sigma_{wID=wIDcopy \text{ and } sID <> sIDcopy}$(external product externalCopy));
   onlyOneExternal := ($\pi_{wID}$(external)) − moreThanOneExternal;
   $\pi_{wID, wTitle}$(webpage ⋈ onlyOneExternal);

7. wIDsHits(wIDCopy, hitsCopy) := $\pi_{\text{wID, hits}}$(webpage);
   wIDsNotMax := $\pi_{\text{wID}}(\sigma_{\text{hits < hitsCopy}}$(wIDsHits product webpage));
   wIDsMaxHits := ($\pi_{\text{wID}}$(webpage)) − wIDsNotMax;
   wIDsMaxHits ⋈ webpage;

8. graphicTypes := $\pi_{\text{gType}}$(graphic);
   atLeastOneGraphicType := $\pi_{\text{wID}}$(displays);
   allPagesAllTypes := (atLeastOneGraphicType product graphicTypes);
   notAllGraphicTypes := $\pi_{\text{wID}}$(allPagesAllTypes − ($\pi_{\text{wID, gType}}$(graphic ⋈ displays)));
   $\pi_{\text{wID, wTitle}}$(webpage ⋈ (atLeastOneGraphicType − notAllGraphicTypes));

## Bibliographic Notes

Codd [1970] introduced the relational data model in 1970. In this article, he also introduced relational algebra. The other query languages discussed later in this text were developed in the years that followed: tuple relational calculus in 1972, domain relational calculus in 1977, and SEQUEL (on which SQL is based) in 1974–1976 timeframe. For a definitive reference on the theory of relational databases, see Maier's book [Maier, 1983].

## More to Explore

The Databases for Many Majors project (databasesmanymajors.faculty.asu.edu) provides visualizations to introduce fundamental database concepts to a diverse audience of students. The Introduction to Querying visualization provides an overview of querying starting from design and queries specified in relational algebra, and ending with a brief introduction to the industry standard query language SQL. The coverage of relational algebra includes visualizations of each of the relational algebra operations (except division).

The WinRDBI educational tool (winrdbi.asu.edu) is an interpreter for relational query languages, including relational algebra. The syntax has been modified to use keywords rather than mathematical symbols. This book's companion website provides the relational algebra examples from the chapter and self-checks for practicing the query language.

# 4 Relational Calculus

- To understand the fundamentals of logic used to express queries in a declarative language
- To understand the relationship between relational algebra and relational calculus
- To write statements in relational calculus to answer a query
- To become familiar with the concept of safety in a declarative query language

Relational calculus is a declarative query language, indicating the properties of the data to be retrieved instead of the procedural paradigm of relational algebra that specifies the operations required to retrieve the data. There are two types of relational calculus query languages: tuple and domain. The differences are based on the use of variables. In tuple relational calculus (TRC), variables range over the tuples of the relation. In domain relational calculus (DRC), variables range over the domain or attributes of a relation. The TRC language is essentially the foundation of the basic query expression in the SQL industry-standard query language. The DRC language is strongly related to the use of declarative languages for the integration of database and artificial intelligence technologies, and is reminiscent of the Prolog programming language. Although the declarative expressions of these languages differ from the procedural operators of relational algebra, the relational calculus languages are *relationally complete*. A query expressible in relational algebra can be expressed in either TRC or DRC as illustrated by example using the fundamental and additional operators of relational algebra in TRC and DRC.

## 4.1 Logical Foundations

Declarative languages use logical foundations to filter and combine tables. Thus, a fundamental understanding of some logic concepts is important to writing correct calculus query expressions. Logical connectives, such as and, or, not, combine references to tables and comparisons of attribute values to other values, such as attributes or literals. The declarative language specifies the properties of the data to retrieve, instead of procedurally combining data using specific operators.

> Relational calculus languages use logic to declaratively specify the properties of the data to be retrieved.

Both relational calculus languages have building blocks, called atoms, that either reference a relation or provide a comparison of attribute values to other attribute values or constants. Atoms that reference a relation bind variables to values forming a tuple in the relation. The comparisons of attribute values typically represent horizontal filtering of a table or the joining of tables. The comparison operators are the relational comparisons: =, <, >, <=, >=, <>. (Note that <> denotes "not equal".) These building blocks are then combined using the Boolean operators: and, or, not.

Table 4.1 reviews the truth tables for these three operators, using $\alpha$ and $\beta$ to refer to a Boolean condition and T represents TRUE and F represents FALSE. Table 4.2 is a companion truth table illustrating De Morgan's laws, which shows that the negation of an and/or is logically equivalent to the or/and with negated operands:

- not $(\alpha$ and $\beta) \equiv$ not $\alpha$ or not $\beta$

- not $(\alpha$ or $\beta) \equiv$ not $\alpha$ and not $\beta$

Combinations of Boolean conditions are essential to the specification of queries in declarative languages, and De Morgan's laws are quite useful for simplifying a Boolean combination.

**Table 4.1    Truth Tables for and, or, not**

| $\alpha$ | $\beta$ | $\alpha$ and $\beta$ | $\alpha$ or $\beta$ | not $\alpha$ | not $\beta$ |
|---|---|---|---|---|---|
| T | T | T | T | F | F |
| T | F | F | T | F | T |
| F | T | F | T | T | F |
| F | F | F | F | T | T |

**Table 4.2    Truth Tables for De Morgan's Laws**

| $\alpha$ | $\beta$ | not $(\alpha$ and $\beta)$ | not $\alpha$ or not $\beta$ | not $(\alpha$ or $\beta)$ | not $\alpha$ and not $\beta$ |
|---|---|---|---|---|---|
| T | T | F | F | F | F |
| T | F | T | T | F | F |
| F | T | T | T | F | F |
| F | F | T | T | T | T |

## NOTE 4.1    Overview of Relational Calculus Languages

**Syntax:**

There are variations in syntax over dialects of the relational calculus languages. Some use formal mathematical symbols. This text uses the syntax of the relational calculus languages recognized by the WinRDBI educational tool (see Appendix A) so that the sample queries are executable. The queries in the chapter that can be checked with the educational tool are preceded by a checkmark ($\sqrt{}$). WinRDBI uses identifiers starting with a lowercase letter to denote relation and attribute names. Identifiers that begin with an uppercase letter denote variables. Constants are either single-quoted strings or numeric constants. Operators used by WinRDBI are keywords rather than formal mathematical symbols.

**Intermediate Tables:**

The result of a relational calculus query is a relation. Sometimes it is useful to break down queries into logical parts with descriptive names. WinRDBI uses named tables to store the result of a query expression.

    intermediateTable := queryExpression;

assigns the result of the queryExpression to the named intermediateTable. The attribute names for the schema of intermediateTable are derived from the queryExpression. However, if renaming of attributes is desired, then the syntax

    intermediateTable(attr1, ..., attrn) := queryExpression;

provides for the renaming of the output schema of queryExpression to the schema given by the attribute list attr1, ..., attrn.

## 4.2 Tuple Relational Calculus

> **In TRC, variables range over tuples of a relation. Use dot notation to reference an attribute.**

Tuple relational calculus (TRC) is important to understand because the heart of the industry-standard query language SQL is a syntactic variation of TRC. Variables in TRC range over tuples or rows of the table. Dot notation references an attribute of the tuple. For example, T.a refers to the attribute a of the tuple variable T.

### 4.2.1 Fundamental Query Expressions

A fundamental TRC expression is of the form

$$\{ \text{T1, T2, } \ldots \text{, Tn} \mid \text{r1(T1) and r2(T2) and } \ldots \text{ and rn(Tn) and } \theta \}$$

where ri(Ti) binds the tuple variable Ti to tuples in its corresponding relation ri and $\theta$ is a Boolean combination of conditions that describe the properties that are to hold true on the data to be retrieved. The output schema is given by the attributes associated with the tuple variables T1, T2, ... , Tn. If only some of the attributes associated with a tuple variable are desired in the query result, then dot notation vertically filters the tuple variable, e.g. T.a.

## HOW TO 4.2   Writing a Fundamental Query in TRC

**Step 1:** First determine the tables that have the required data. Which tables have the attributes that need to be returned in the result? How do you relate the tables to answer the question? Only include the tables that are needed; do not include extra tables. Include these tables in the fundamental query expression to the right of the vertical bar. Include the introduced tuple variables that range over the table in the list of variables to the left of the vertical bar.

**Step 2:** Then filter the tuples based on the query in the condition part of the query specification. These conditions can be filtering based on criteria specified in the question being asked and/or using the primary–foreign key relationships of the relational schema. Note that only constants appearing in the query can be used to filter the results.

**Step 3:** Last, if only some of the attributes from a tuple variable are needed in the result of the query, use dot notation to vertically filter for the required attributes.

Table 4.3 illustrates three sample queries over the EMPLOYEE TRAINING enterprise that illustrate a horizontal filtering (*trc_Managers*), a vertical filtering (*trc_Titles*), and a combination of horizontal and vertical filtering (*trc_SalariesLT60K*). Note that in the examples, E denotes the tuple variable for the **employee** relation, providing a mnemonic association between the tuple variable name and the table name.

**Table 4.3   TRC Sample Filtering Queries**

| Query label and description | √Tuple relational calculus |
| --- | --- |
| *trc_Managers:* | |
| Which employees are managers? | { E \| employee(E) and E.eTitle = 'Manager' } |
| *trc_Titles:* | |
| What employee titles appear in the database? | { E.eTitle \| employee(E) } |
| *trc_SalariesLT60K:* | |
| What are the names and salaries of employees earning less than $60,000? | { E.eLast, E.eFirst, E.eSalary \| employee(E) and E.eSalary < 60000 } |

Besides horizontal filtering, the condition of a fundamental TRC query expression can state the join condition between two tables. Consider the following query over the EMPLOYEE TRAINING enterprise that retrieves the employees who lead technology areas:

> **Use conditions to horizontally filter or join tables.**

*trc_employeeLeads*:

√       { E, A | employee(E) and technologyArea(A) and E.eID = A.aLeadID }

This query represents the join of the employee and technologyArea tables such that the employee identification number (eID) is equal to the identification number of the area lead (aLeadID), joining the foreign key in technologyArea with its corresponding primary key in employee. The schema of the resulting join contains all the attributes of the employee (eID, eLast, eFirst, eTitle, eSalary) and technologyArea (aID, aTitle, aURL, aLeadID) tables. Unlike the procedural relational algebra language that provides a shortcut for the natural join operator (⋈), TRC must specify the equality of the attributes. Consider the example natural join query over the EMPLOYEE TRAINING enterprise that retrieves the course title and offerings of each training course by joining on the common cID attributes and vertically filtering (i.e. projecting) on the cTitle and tDate attributes:

*trc_CourseTitleOfferings*:

√       { C.cTitle, T.tDate | trainingCourse(C) and takes(T) and C.cID = T.cID }

Note that a Cartesian product in TRC is a query that does not specify any join conditions.

## Self Check

Write the following queries in TRC:

1. Which employees earn more than $75,000?
   (eID, eLast, eFirst, eTitle, eSalary)
2. What are the titles of courses offered in the technology area with id 'DB'?
   (cTitle)
3. What are the course offering dates for the 'Big Data' class?
   (cID, tDate)

## 4.2.2 Quantification of Variables

The fundamental TRC query expression discussed up to this point assumes that all of the TRC variables bound immediately to the right of the vertical bar are included in the result of the query expression to the left of the vertical bar. One way of looking at this format of the fundamental query expression is that the tuple variables appearing in the result are bound by their appearance in the relation reference that binds the tuple variable. Tuple variables that are not being returned in the query result must be declared via quantification to define the scope of the variables. Example queries using the set operators and the division operator illustrate how to quantify variables.

> **All variables that are not being returned in the query result must be declared via quantification, defining the scope of the variables.**

### Set Operators

Table 4.4 provides example queries over the EMPLOYEE TRAINING enterprise that correspond to the sample set operator queries from relational algebra. Recall that in the relational algebra examples, compatible relations consisting of just eID values illustrated the union, difference, and intersection operators. In TRC, if these relations already existed, then a union would be or, a difference would be and not, and an intersection would be and (see Section 4.2.4, "Relational Completeness"). To answer these queries in TRC using the EMPLOYEE TRAINING tables as given involves using Boolean conditions and introducing the binding of tuple variables using exists. In *trc_ManagerOrProjectLead*, the or condition represents the union. In *trc_ManagersNoCourses*, and not represents the difference. The variable E represents a tuple in the employee table filtered to be a manager and it is not the case that there exists a tuple in the takes table for that employee. Similarly, there is an existential binding of takes for the intersection query *trc_ManagersTookCourses*, finding the employees who are managers such that there exists a takes tuple for that manager.

**Table 4.4    TRC Sample Set Queries**

| Query label and description | √Tuple relational calculus |
| --- | --- |
| *trc_ManagerOrProjectLead*: | |
| Which employees are managers or project leads? | { E \| employee(E) and (E.eTitle = 'Manager' or E.eTitle = 'Project Lead') } |
| *trc_ManagersNoCourses*: | |
| Which managers have not taken any courses? | { E \| employee(E) and E.eTitle = 'Manager' and not (exists T) (takes(T) and T.eID = E.eID) } |
| *trc_ManagersTookCourses*: | |
| Which managers have taken a training course? | { E \| employee(E) and E.eTitle = 'Manager' and (exists T) (takes(T) and T.eID = E.eID) } |

All variables must be bound to a relation reference before its attribute values can be compared. If a variable is not bound as a result of being returned in the query result, then it will typically be bound by an exists. There is also a forall binding that is useful for division queries.

### Division

Recall that division is a complex binary relational algebra operator that finds those values in the first operand relation that are related to *all* of the values in the second operand relation. For the abstract division example, the schemas of the operand relations are abTable(a,b) and bTable(b) with the specification (abTable ÷ bTable) including an a value in the result of the division provided that the a value is in the abTable and for all possible B values, if B is a tuple in the bTable then the a and b values are related by the abTable.

{ T.a \| abTable(T) and (forall B) (bTable(B) implies
        (exists AB) (abTable(AB) and AB.a=T.a and AB.b=B.b) ) }

Since the implies operator is not formally defined in this version of TRC, the logically equivalent specification using not p or q instead of p implies q is

√    { T.a \| abTable(T) and (forall B) (not bTable(B) or
        (exists AB) (abTable(AB) and AB.a=T.a and AB.b=B.b ) }

Table 4.5 shows the corresponding truth table. The forall formula must be true for all values of the variable B, including those B values that do not form a tuple in the bTable.

Consider a logically equivalent specification of division that uses only existential quantification. An a value is included in the result of the division provided that the a value is in the abTable and it is not the case that there exists a b value that is in the bTable and is *not* related to the a value by the abTable.

**Table 4.5    TRC Division – Universal Truth Table**

| a | b | not bTable(B) | (exists AB) | not bTable(B) or (exists AB) | forall B |
|---|---|---|---|---|---|
| a1 | b1 | F | T | T | |
| | b2 | F | T | T | T |
| | b3 | T | F | T | |
| a2 | b1 | F | F | F | |
| | b2 | F | T | T | F |
| | b3 | T | F | T | |
| a3 | b1 | F | T | T | |
| | b2 | F | T | T | T |
| | b3 | T | T | T | |

√    { T.a | abTable(T) and not (exists B) (bTable(B) and
         not (exists AB) (abTable(AB) and AB.a=T.a and AB.b=B.b ) ) }

This logically equivalent existential specification can be derived from the universal specification using the following logical equivalences:

- Given the universal specification:

  √    { T.a | abTable(T) and (forall B) (not bTable(B) or
         (exists AB) (abTable(AB) and AB.a=T.a and AB.b=B.b) ) }

- Apply the logical equivalence: (forall D) $\mathcal{F}$(D) ≡ not (exists D) not $\mathcal{F}$(D)

  √    { T.a | abTable(T) and not (exists B) not (not bTable(B) or
         (exists AB) (abTable(AB) and AB.a=T.a and AB.b=B.b) ) }

- Apply De Morgan's law: not (p or q) ≡ not p and not q

  √    { T.a | abTable(T) and not (exists B) (bTable(B) and
         not (exists AB) (abTable(AB) and AB.a=T.a and AB.b=B.b) ) }

Table 4.6 shows the corresponding truth table.

**Table 4.6    TRC Division – Existential Truth Table**

| a | b | bTable(B) | not (exists AB) | bTable(B) and not (exists AB) | not (exists B) |
|---|---|---|---|---|---|
| a1 | b1 | T | F | F | |
| | b2 | T | F | F | T |
| | b3 | F | T | F | |
| a2 | b1 | T | T | T | |
| | b2 | T | F | F | F |
| | b3 | F | T | F | |
| a3 | b1 | T | F | F | |
| | b2 | T | F | F | T |
| | b3 | F | F | F | |

In the EMPLOYEE TRAINING enterprise, the division query is asking for employees that have taken *all* of the training courses offered by the company. In relational algebra, the solution divides the projection of the employee and course ids from takes with all of the course ids: $\pi_{eID, cID}$(takes) ÷ $\pi_{cID}$(trainingCourse). The division operator in relational algebra has restrictions imposed on the schemas of the operand relations, such that the schema of the second operand relation must be a subset of the first operand relation. TRC uses logic to find those employees who took all of the training courses. Consider the following versions of the division query that illustrate the use of universal and existential quantification:

*trc_divUniversal*:

√ { E.eID | employee(E) and (forall C) (not trainingCourse(C) or
         (exists T) (takes(T) and T.eID=E.eID and T.cID=C.cID) ) }

*trc_divExistential*:

√ { E.eID | employee(E) and not (exists C) (trainingCourse(C) and
         not (exists T) (takes(T) and T.eID = E.eID and T.cID = C.cID) ) }

As described above, these versions are logically equivalent by the application of De Morgan's law. However, there are subtle differences between the TRC query and the relational algebra query. Technically, if there are no training courses, the TRC query would include all employees, whereas the relational algebra query is specifically looking at employee ids for those who have taken a course. The above TRC queries can be modified to include this restriction by adding an existential expression requiring that the employee took a course.

## Self Check

Write the following queries in TRC:

4.  Which employees took the 'Big Data' course and on what date?
    (eID, tDate)
5.  Which employees did not take the 'Big Data' course?
    (eID)
6.  Which employees took both the 'Big Data' and 'Data Science' courses?
    (eID, eLast, eFirst, eTitle, eSalary)

## 4.2.3 Atoms and Formula

This section provides a more formal look at the general TRC expressions. Consistent with the previous coverage, the TRC expressions use identifiers starting with a lowercase letter to denote relation and attribute names, identifiers that begin with an uppercase letter denote variables (in this case, tuple variables), and constants are either single-quoted strings or numeric constants. To refer to the name of an attribute associated with a tuple variable, dot notation is used. For example, T.a refers to the attribute a of the tuple variable T. The identifiers not, and, or, exists, and forall are used instead of the mathematical symbols denoting negation ($\neg$), conjunction ($\wedge$), disjunction ($\vee$), existential quantification ($\exists$), and universal quantification ($\forall$), respectively.

A general TRC expression is of the form

$$\{ T1, T2, \ldots, Tn \mid \mathcal{F}(T1, T2, \ldots, Tn) \}$$

where $\mathcal{F}$ is a TRC formula, describing the properties that are to hold true on the data to be retrieved. The output schema of $\mathcal{F}$ is given by the attributes associated with the tuple variables T1, T2, ..., Tn.

The building block of a TRC formula is an atom, consisting of a reference to a relation or a comparison of an attribute of a tuple variable to an attribute of another tuple variable or a domain constant. An atom forms the basis of a formula, which is built up from atoms using logical connectives (not, and, or) and quantification (exists, forall).

Let

  r be a relation of degree n
  T and Ti represent tuple variables
  ai represent an attribute
  c be a domain constant
  $\theta$ be a comparison operator ($<, <=, =, >, >=, <>$) and assume that its operands are comparable by $\theta$

An atom is of the form

- r(T)
  TRUE when T is assigned a value forming a tuple in r
- Ti.am $\theta$ Tj.an
  TRUE when Ti.am $\theta$ Tj.an is TRUE; otherwise, FALSE
- T.ai $\theta$ c
  TRUE when T.ai $\theta$ c is TRUE; otherwise, FALSE

A formula is composed of atoms using the following rules:

1. An atom is a formula.
   Its meaning is given by the truth value of the atom.
2. Let $\mathcal{F}$, $\mathcal{F}1$ and $\mathcal{F}2$ be formulas, then the following are formulas:

   - $(\mathcal{F})$
     TRUE when $\mathcal{F}$ is TRUE; otherwise, FALSE
   - not $\mathcal{F}$
     TRUE when $\mathcal{F}$ is FALSE; otherwise, FALSE
   - $\mathcal{F}1$ and $\mathcal{F}2$
     TRUE when both $\mathcal{F}1$ and $\mathcal{F}2$ are TRUE; otherwise, FALSE
   - $\mathcal{F}1$ or $\mathcal{F}2$
     TRUE when either $\mathcal{F}1$ or $\mathcal{F}2$ is TRUE; otherwise, FALSE

3. Let $\mathcal{F}(T)$ be a formula in which the variable T appears free. A variable is free if it is not quantified by an existential or universal quantifier. Then the following are formulas:

   - (exists T)$\mathcal{F}(T)$
     TRUE if there exists a value assigned to T that makes $\mathcal{F}(T)$ TRUE; otherwise, FALSE
   - (forall T)$\mathcal{F}(T)$
     TRUE if any value that is assigned to T makes $\mathcal{F}(T)$ TRUE; otherwise, FALSE

A valid TRC expression { T1, T2, ..., Tn | $\mathcal{F}$(T1, T2, ..., Tn) } has only the tuple variables T1, T2, ..., Tn free in $\mathcal{F}$. Free variables are global variables with respect to the TRC expression $\mathcal{F}$. Any other variable appearing in $\mathcal{F}$ is a local variable, bound by its quantified declaration. The scope of the local variable is the quantified formula.

## 4.2.4 Relational Completeness

The TRC language is relationally complete. Table 4.7 summarizes the TRC expressions for operations involving the fundamental relational algebra operators, which identify the required operations for effective retrieval of information from a relational database.

> An atom, consisting of a reference to a relation or a comparison involving tuple variables, forms the basis of a formula, which is built up from atoms using logical connectives and quantification.

> TRC is relationally complete.

**Table 4.7**    **TRC Summary of Fundamental Relational Algebra Operators**

| Algebra | TRC |
|---------|-----|
| $\sigma_\theta(r)$ | { R \| r(R) and $\theta$ } |
| $\pi_A(r)$ | { R.ai … R.aj \| r(R) } |
| r ∪ s | { T \| r(T) or s(T) } |
| r − s | { T \| r(T) and not s(T) } |
| q × r | { Q, R \| q(Q) and r(R) } |

Table 4.8 illustrates the fundamental operators using queries over the EMPLOYEE TRAINING enterprise. In the examples, the names of the tuple variables are usually abbreviated to one or two characters based on a mnemonic association with the table over which the tuple variable ranges. The EMPLOYEE TRAINING enterprise examples use the following tuple variable naming conventions:

- E refers to the employee relation.

- T refers to the takes relation.

- A refers to the technologyArea relation.

- C refers to the trainingCourse relation.

Although more descriptive tuple variable names are possible, this mnemonic naming convention for tuple variables provides concise yet readable examples. The TRC examples for the set operators ∪ and − are structured to be more similar to the corresponding relational algebra queries. Recall that Section 4.2.2 discussed other formulations of these TRC queries that involved the quantification of variables.

**Table 4.8**    **TRC Summary of Fundamental EMPLOYEE TRAINING Queries**

| Query | √TRC |
|-------|------|
| $Q_\sigma$ | { E \| employee(E) and E.eSalary > 100000 }; |
| $Q_\pi$ | { E.eLast, E.eFirst, E.eTitle \| employee(E) }; |
| $Q_\cup$ | managers := { E.eID \| employee(E) and E.eTitle='Manager' };<br>projectLeads := { E.eID \| employee(E) and E.eTitle='Project Lead' };<br>{ T \| managers(T) or projectLeads(T) }; |
| $Q_-$ | managers := { E.eID \| employee(E) and E.eTitle='Manager' };<br>takenCourse := { T.eID \| takes(T) };<br>{ T \| managers(T) and not takenCourse(T) }; |
| $Q_\times$ | { E.eID, C.cID \| employee(E) and trainingCourse(C) }; |

Table 4.9 summarizes the illustrative example queries over the EMPLOYEE TRAINING enterprise using the additional binary operators of relational algebra (∩, ⋈$_\theta$, ⋈, ÷), which are frequently used combinations of the fundamental operators. The TRC example for ∩ is structured to be similar to its corresponding relational algebra query. The TRC example of division (÷) uses the existential version of the division query discussed in Section 4.2.2.

**Table 4.9    TRC Summary of Additional EMPLOYEE TRAINING Queries**

| Query | √TRC |
|---|---|
| $Q_\cap$ | managers := { E.eID \| employee(E) and E.eTitle='Manager' };<br>takenCourse := { T.eID \| takes(T) };<br>{ T \| managers(T) and takenCourse(T) }; |
| $Q_{\bowtie_\theta}$ | { E, A \| employee(E) and technologyArea(A) and E.eID=A.aLeadID }; |
| $Q_\bowtie$ | { C.cTitle, T.tDate \|<br>     trainingCourse(C) and takes(T) and C.cID=T.cID }; |
| $Q_\div$ | { E.eID \| employee(E) and not (exists C) (trainingCourse(C) and<br>     not (exists T) (takes(T) and T.eID = E.eID and T.cID = C.cID)) }; |

## Aggregation and Grouping

The aggregation and grouping of results are important features in database query languages. Aggregation provides a single, aggregate result through the examination of data, such as a minimum, maximum, average, sum, or count. Grouping typically applies an aggregation to a grouping of data, such as finding the average salaries of employees by title. The details of how the SQL industry-standard query language supports aggregation and grouping appears in Section 5.5. For relational algebra, Section 3.3 described how the formal relational algebra query language supports some forms of aggregation and grouping. This section illustrates how TRC is relationally complete by providing a summary table of the fundamental relational algebra operators and how they are expressed in TRC. Thus, TRC also supports some forms of aggregation and grouping using logic, such as minimum/maximum and a limited form of counting.

> TRC also supports some forms of aggregation and grouping using logic, such as minimum/maximum and a limited form of counting.

Consider the following example queries over the EMPLOYEE TRAINING enterprise that illustrate queries similar to those described in Section 3.3. For example, the employees who have the minimum salary are those employees such that there does not exist another employee who has a lower salary.

*trc_employeeMinSalary*:

√ { E \| employee(E) and not (exists EMP)(employee(EMP) and EMP.eSalary < E.eSalary) }

To group the aggregate result by title, modify the query to find those employees such that there does not exist another employee with the same title who has a lower salary.

*trc_employeeTitleMinSalary*:

√ { E \| employee(E) and
    not (exists EMP)(employee(EMP) and EMP.eTitle = E.eTitle and
        EMP.eSalary < E.eSalary) }

A limited form of counting, such as more than one or only one, is also supported by TRC. To find the employees who took courses in more than one technology area, find the employees who took courses in two different technology areas.

*trc_moreThanOneTechArea*:

√ { E \| employee(E) and (exists T1, C1, T2, C2)
    (takes(T1) and T1.eID = E.eID and trainingCourse(C1) and T1.cID = C1.cID and
    takes(T2) and T2.eID = E.eID and trainingCourse(C2) and T2.cID = C2.cID and
    C1.areaID <> C2.areaID) }

## Self Check

Write the following queries in TRC:

7. What is the maximum manager salary?
   (eSalary)

8. Which employees took more than one course?
   (eID)

9. Which employees have taken courses in only one technology area?
   (eID)
   *Hint: Use named tables, specifically trc_moreThanOneTechArea, to formulate this answer to find those employees who took a course and did not take courses in more than one technology area.*

# 4.3 Domain Relational Calculus

> **In DRC, variables range over the domain of attributes.**

Domain relational calculus (DRC) is a declarative language that states the properties of the data to be retrieved, similarly to TRC. However, in DRC, variables range over the domains or attributes of the relations instead of their tuples. Note that DRC variables are bound by the position of the variable in the relation reference. Thus, DRC is said to have a *positional* syntax, whereas TRC uses dot notation to reference attributes *by name*.

## 4.3.1 Fundamental Query Expressions

A fundamental DRC query expression is of the form

$$\{ D1, D2, \ldots, Dn \mid r1(D1, \ldots, Di) \text{ and } \ldots \text{ and } rk(Dj, \ldots, Dn) \text{ and } \theta \}$$

> **Use an underscore (_) to denote an anonymous variable.**

where the output schema is given by the Di domain variables to the left of the vertical bar, which are bound by the references to their appearance in a relation, and $\theta$ is a Boolean combination of conditions that describe the properties that are to hold true on the retrieved data.

DRC has a positional syntax. If an attribute is not needed to answer the query, a named domain variable does not have to be introduced. Use an anonymous variable, denoted by an underscore, as a placeholder for the attribute.

## HOW TO 4.3   Writing a Fundamental Query in DRC

**Step 1:** First determine the tables that have the required data. Which tables have the attributes that need to be returned in the result? How do you relate the tables to answer the question? Only include the tables that are needed; do not include extra tables. Include these tables in the fundamental query expression to the right of the vertical bar. Include all the domain variables from the relation references in the list of variables to the left of the vertical bar.

**Step 2:** Then filter the results based on the query in the condition part of the query specification. These conditions can be filtering based on criteria specified in the question being asked and/or using the primary–foreign key relationships of the relational schema. Note that only constants appearing in the query can be used to filter the results.

**Step 3:** Last, if only some of the attributes from a list of domain variables are needed to answer the query, use an anonymous variable, denoted by an underscore (_), to vertically filter for the desired attributes. Note that all named variables must appear in the query result for a fundamental query expression.

Table 4.10 illustrates three sample queries over the EMPLOYEE TRAINING enterprise that illustrate a horizontal filtering (*drc_Managers*), a vertical filtering (*drc_Titles*), and a combination of horizontal and vertical filtering (*drc_SalariesLT60K*). Note that in the examples, I, L, F, T, S denote the domain variables for the employee relation, providing a mnemonic association between the domain variable name and its associated attribute name: eID, eLast, eFirst, eTitle, eSalary. Note that more descriptive variable names can be used, e.g. EID, ELast, EFirst, ETitle, ESalary to be self-documenting and is recommended in practice. Both the descriptive and mnemonic variables will be used in the text, with the mnemonic association chosen when needed for its brevity of presentation.

**Table 4.10    DRC Sample Filtering Queries**

| Query label and description | √Domain relational calculus |
|---|---|
| *drc_Managers*: | |
| Which employees are managers? | { I, L, F, T, S \| employee(I, L, F, T, S) and T = 'Manager' } |
| *drc_Titles*: | |
| What employee titles appear in the database? | { T \| employee(_, _, _, T, _) } |
| *drc_SalariesLT60K*: | |
| What are the names and salaries of employees earning less than $60,000? | { L, F, S \| employee(_, L, F, _, S) and S < 60000 } |

The conditions of fundamental DRC query expressions are also used to join relations on primary and foreign key relationships. Consider the query *drc_employeeLeads* over the EMPLOYEE TRAINING enterprise that finds the employees who are leads along with the technology area information that they lead. The condition EID = ALeadID results in a join of the tables on the primary and foreign keys.

*drc_employeeLeads*:

√      { EID, ELast, EFirst, ETitle, ESalary, AID, ATitle, AURL, ALeadID |
        employee(EID, ELast, EFirst, ETitle, ESalary) and
        technologyArea(AID, ATitle, AURL, ALeadID) and EID = ALeadID }

The positional syntax of DRC offers a shortcut for the specification of joins. Rather than introduce a variable ALeadID just to check that it is equal to the variable EID, the variable EID can be used. Only data that matches will be retrieved. Note that the two versions of the query have different result schema since the first includes the ALeadID variable and the second does not.

> Use the same variable name to join attributes via equality.

√       { EID, ELast, EFirst, ETitle, ESalary, AID, ATitle, AURL |
        employee(EID, ELast, EFirst, ETitle, ESalary) and
        technologyArea(AID, ATitle, AURL, EID) }

DRC's positional syntax also offers a shortcut for equality constraints involving constants. Consider the earlier horizontal filtering example *drc_Managers* that checks whether the employee title variable is equal to 'Manager'. Instead of introducing a variable that must be equal to a constant, the constant itself can be used to filter the data. Again, the schema of the results are different due to the number of variables returned.

> Use a constant in the relation reference for a horizontal filtering based on equality.

√ { EID, ELast, EFirst, ESalary | employee(EID, ELast, EFirst, 'Manager', ESalary) }

Similar to TRC, the initial simplifying assumption on a fundamental DRC query expression requires that named variables to the right of the vertical bar must appear in the result. This restriction can be lifted by declaring quantified variables.

## Self Check

Write the following queries using fundamental query expressions in DRC:

10. Which employees earn more than $75,000?
    (eID, eLast, eFirst, eTitle, eSalary)

11. What are the titles of courses offered in the technology area with id 'DB'?
    (cTitle)

12. What are the course offering dates for the 'Big Data' class?
    (cID, tDate)

### 4.3.2  Quantification of Variables

> **Variables that are needed to answer the query but are not part of the result must be declared by quantification to define the scope of the variables.**

The variables appearing in the result schema are bound by the appearance of those variables in a relation reference so that the value can be returned as part of the result. Variables that are needed to answer the query but are not part of the result must be declared by an existential (exists) or universal (forall) quantification that also provides the scope of the variables. The most common quantification is existential–does there exist a value for the variable such that the expression is true? In TRC, queries using the set operators (e.g. difference and intersection) illustrated existential quantification. Universal quantification was demonstrated in the application of the division operator, which finds values for the first operand that are related to *all* of the values in the second operand relation. Thus, example queries using the set and division operators will be included in this discussion.

Note that DRC typically has many more variables in its query expressions than TRC does, since there can be a variable for each attribute instead of a variable for each relation. (The use of anonymous variables for attribute values that are not needed to answer the query reduces the necessity for a variable for each attribute.) Thus, there tends to be more uses of quantification of variables in DRC than TRC. For example, any query that needs to introduce a variable to join on a primary–foreign key relationship where that variable is not included in the result schema will need to declare the join variable. In TRC, the query *trc_CourseTitleOfferings* returned the course title along with the dates that it was offered by joining on the cID attribute that is common in both trainingCourse and takes. The DRC solution takes the same approach but since the variables range over the attributes, a variable for the cID attribute, named CID, must be introduced for the join.

*drc_CourseTitleOfferings*:

√       { CTitle, TDate | (exists CID)
              (trainingCourse(CID, CTitle, _, _) and takes(_, CID, TDate)) }

### Set Operators

If the set operators are applied to intermediate tables that have the same schema, then the union, difference, and intersection operators are represented declaratively using or, and not, and and, respectively (see Section 4.3.4). Table 4.11 provides the same queries from Table 4.4, finding managers or project leads, managers that have not taken any courses, and managers that have taken a training course. The query *drc_ManagerOrProjectLead* is quite similar to its counterpart in TRC, using an or to check for the value of the employee's title. However, the formulation of the queries *drc_ManagersNoCourses* and *drc_ManagersTookCourses* do not require the use of quantification.

Anonymous variables are used as placeholders for attribute values that are not needed in the query and the variable I is bound by its appearance in employee before checking whether that employee has taken a course or not.

**Table 4.11    DRC Sample Set Queries**

| Query label and description | √Domain relational calculus |
|---|---|
| *drc_ManagerOrProjectLead*: | |
| Which employees are managers or project leads? | { I, L, F, T, S | employee(I, L, F, T, S) and (T = 'Manager' or T = 'Project Lead') } |
| *drc_ManagersNoCourses*: | |
| Which managers have not taken any courses? | { I, L, F, T, S | employee(I, L, F, T, S) and T = 'Manager' and not takes(I, _, _) } |
| *drc_ManagersTookCourses*: | |
| Which managers have taken a training course? | { I, L, F, T, S | employee(I, L, F, T, S) and T = 'Manager' and takes(I, _, _) } |

These simpler examples did not require the quantification of variables. Expanding these queries to ask for the managers that have taken a course in the technology area with the id 'DB' illustrates the use of quantification. The queries *drc_ManagersNoDBCourses* and *drc_ManagersDBCourses* must declare the variable CID to use in the join of the takes and trainingCourse tables. The value of the CID variable is not needed in the result because the queries are asking whether the manager has taken a 'DB' course or not.

*drc_ManagersNoDBCourses*:

√       { I, L, F, T, S | employee(I, L, F, T, S) and T = 'Manager' and
               not (exists CID)(takes(I, CID, _) and trainingCourse(CID, _, _, 'DB') ) }

*drc_ManagersDBCourses*:

√       { I, L, F, T, S | employee(I, L, F, T, S) and T = 'Manager' and
               (exists CID)(takes(I, CID, _) and trainingCourse(CID, _, _, 'DB') ) }

## Division

The division operator (÷) is one of the most complicated relational algebra operators. The types of queries that use the division operator typically find those values in the first operand relation that are related to *all* of the values in the second operand relation.

Recall the following abstract example to illustrate the division operation abTable ÷ bTable where the schemas of the operand relations are abTable(a,b) and bTable(b). In DRC, the abstract division example can be stated as: a value of attribute a is included in the result of the division provided that this value is in the abTable and for all possible values of b, if this value of b is in the bTable, then the values of a and b are related by the abTable.

       { A | abTable(A, _) and (forall B) (bTable(B) implies abTable(A,B) ) }

The implies operator has not been formally defined in this variation of the DRC language. However, p implies q is logically equivalent to not p or q. Therefore, the division example restated is

       √{ A | abTable(A, _) and (forall B) (not bTable(B) or abTable(A,B) ) }

Table 4.12 shows the corresponding truth table. The forall formula must be true for all values of the variable B, including those B values that are not in the bTable.

**Table 4.12   DRC Division – Universal Truth Tables**

| A | B | bTable(B) | abTable(A,B) | not bTable(B) | not bTable(B) or abTable(A,B) | forall B |
|---|---|-----------|--------------|---------------|-------------------------------|----------|
| a1 | b1 | T | T | F | T | |
| | b2 | T | T | F | T | T |
| | b3 | F | F | T | T | |
| a2 | b1 | T | F | F | F | |
| | b2 | T | T | F | T | F |
| | b3 | F | F | T | T | |
| a3 | b1 | T | T | F | T | |
| | b2 | T | T | F | T | T |
| | b3 | F | T | T | T | |

There is another logically equivalent specification of division that uses only existential quantification. An A value is included in the result of the division provided that the A value is in the abTable and it is not the case that there exists a B value that is in the bTable and is *not* related to the A value by the abTable.

$$\sqrt{}\{ \text{A} \mid \text{abTable(A, \_) and not (exists B) (bTable(B) and not abTable(A,B)) }\}$$

This logically equivalent existential specification can be derived from the universal specification using the following logical equivalences:

- Given the universal specification:

  $\sqrt{}$   { A | abTable(A, \_) and (forall B) (not bTable(B) or abTable(A,B) ) }

- Apply the logical equivalence: (forall D) $\mathcal{F}$(D) ≡ not (exists D) not $\mathcal{F}$(D)

  $\sqrt{}$   { A | abTable(A, \_) and not (exists B) not (not bTable(B) or abTable(A,B) ) }

- Apply De Morgan's law: not (p or q) ≡ not p and not q

  $\sqrt{}$   { A | abTable(A, \_) and not (exists B) (bTable(B) and not abTable(A,B)) }

Table 4.13 shows the truth table for the resulting existential specification of the division abstract example.

**Table 4.13   DRC Division – Existential Truth Table**

| A | B | bTable(B) | not abTable(A,B) | bTable(B) and not abTable(A,B) | exists B | not exists B |
|---|---|-----------|------------------|--------------------------------|----------|--------------|
| a1 | b1 | T | F | F | | |
| | b2 | T | F | F | F | T |
| | b3 | F | T | F | | |
| a2 | b1 | T | T | T | | |
| | b2 | T | F | F | T | F |
| | b3 | F | T | F | | |
| a3 | b1 | T | F | F | | |
| | b2 | T | F | F | F | T |
| | b3 | F | F | F | | |

In the EMPLOYEE TRAINING example, the division query is asking for the employees that have taken *all* of the offered training courses. The query *drc_divUniversal* illustrates the use of the forall quantifier, requiring that if CID is the primary key of a training course, then the employee has taken that course. Using the application of the logical equivalences as shown above for the abstract division example, the query *drc_divExistential* uses the exists quantifier to find the employees such that it is not the case that there is a training course that the employee has not taken.

*drc_divUniversal*:

√ { EID | employee(EID, _, _, _, _) and
            (forall CID) (not trainingCourse(CID, _, _, _) or takes(EID, CID, _) ) }

*drc_divExistential*:

√ { EID | employee(EID, _, _, _, _) and
            not (exists CID) (trainingCourse(CID, _, _, _) and not takes(EID, CID, _) ) }

# Self Check

Write the following queries in DRC:

13. Which employees took the 'Big Data' course and on what date?
    (eID, tDate)
14. Which employees did not take the 'Big Data' course?
    (eID)
15. Which employees took both the 'Big Data' and 'Data Science' courses?
    (eID, eLast, eFirst, eTitle, eSalary)

## 4.3.3  Atoms and Formula

A general DRC expression is of the form

$$\{ D1, D2, \dots, Dn \mid \mathcal{F}(D1, D2, \dots, Dn) \}$$

where $\mathcal{F}$ is a DRC formula, describing the properties that are to hold true on the data to be retrieved. The output schema of $\mathcal{F}$ is given by the domain variables D1, D2, …, Dn. The result of the DRC expression is the set of all tuples (d1, d2, …, dn) such that when di is substituted for Di $(1 \le i \le n)$, the formula $\mathcal{F}$ is true.

The building block of a DRC formula is an atom, consisting of a reference to a relation or a comparison of a domain variable to another domain variable or domain constant. An atom forms the basis of a formula, which is built up from atoms using logical connectives (not, and, or) and quantification (exists, forall).

> An atom, consisting of a reference to a relation or a comparison involving domain variables, forms the basis of a formula, which is built up from atoms using logical connectives and quantification.

Let

  r be a relation of degree n
  Di be a domain variable
  c be a domain constant
  $\theta$ be a comparison operator $(<, <=, =, >, >=, <>)$ and assume that its operands are comparable by $\theta$

An atom is of the form

- r(D1, D2, …, Dn)
  TRUE when D1, D2, …, Dn are assigned values forming a tuple in r
- Di $\theta$ Dj
  TRUE when Di $\theta$ Dj is TRUE; otherwise, FALSE

- Di $\theta$ c

  TRUE when Di $\theta$ c is TRUE; otherwise, FALSE

A formula is composed of atoms using the following rules:

1. An atom is a formula.

   Its meaning is given by the truth value of the atom.

2. Let $\mathcal{F}$, $\mathcal{F}1$, and $\mathcal{F}2$ be formulas, then the following are formulas:

   - $(\mathcal{F})$

     TRUE when $\mathcal{F}$ is TRUE; otherwise, FALSE
   - not $\mathcal{F}$

     TRUE when $\mathcal{F}$ is FALSE; otherwise, FALSE
   - $\mathcal{F}1$ and $\mathcal{F}2$

     TRUE when both $\mathcal{F}1$ and $\mathcal{F}2$ are TRUE; otherwise, FALSE
   - $\mathcal{F}1$ or $\mathcal{F}2$

     TRUE when either $\mathcal{F}1$ or $\mathcal{F}2$ is TRUE; otherwise, FALSE

3. Let $\mathcal{F}(D)$ be a formula in which the variable D appears free. A variable is free if it is not quantified by an existential or universal quantifier. Then the following are formulas:

   - (exists D)$\mathcal{F}(D)$

     TRUE if there exists a value assigned to D that makes $\mathcal{F}(D)$ TRUE; otherwise, FALSE
   - (forall D)$\mathcal{F}(D)$

     TRUE if any value that is assigned to D makes $\mathcal{F}(D)$ TRUE; otherwise, FALSE

A valid DRC expression { D1, D2, ... , Dn | $\mathcal{F}$(D1, D2, ... , Dn) } has only the domain variables D1, D2, ... , Dn free in $\mathcal{F}$. A free variable in a DRC expression is analogous to a global variable in a programming language. Any other variable appearing in $\mathcal{F}$ must be a bound variable, which is similar to a local variable, and is declared through quantification. The scope of the bound variable is the quantified formula. The most commonly used quantifier is exists although the forall quantifier is used for division-type queries.

### 4.3.4 Relational Completeness

**DRC is a relationally complete language.**

The DRC language is *relationally complete*, indicating that any query expressible in relational algebra is expressible in DRC. Example queries over the EMPLOYEE TRAINING enterprise illustrate both the expressive power of DRC and the features of the language. In the examples, the names of the domain variables are based on the identifier of the variable's associated attribute. In most cases, the initial letter of the attribute name is capitalized to form the identifier of the domain variable. Although abbreviated domain variable names are possible, this domain variable naming convention results in self-documenting examples.

The fundamental relational algebra operators characterize the required operations for effectively retrieving information from a relational database. Table 4.14 summarizes the DRC expressions for operations involving the fundamental relational algebra operators.

Table 4.15 provides the DRC queries that correspond to the illustrative examples over the EMPLOYEE TRAINING enterprise using the fundamental operators. Note that the examples for the set operators ($\cup$ and $-$) are structured using intermediate tables to illustrate the direct correspondence between the relational algebra and calculus queries. Alternative formulations of these queries were discussed in Section 4.3.2.

Table 4.16 summarizes the examples for the additional binary operators ($\cap, \bowtie_\theta, \bowtie, \div$) that are convenient shorthand notation for frequently used combinations of the fundamental operators of relational algebra. Similarly, the example for the set operator $\cap$ uses intermediate tables to

**Table 4.14  DRC Summary of Fundamental Relational Algebra Operators**

| Algebra | DRC |
|---|---|
| $\sigma_\theta(r)$ | { R1, ... Rn \| r(R1, ... , Rn) and $\theta$ } |
| $\pi_A(r)$ | { Ri, ... Rj \| r(R1, ... , Ri, ... , Rj, ... , Rn) } |
| r ∪ s | { D1, ... Dn \| r(D1, ... , Dn) or s(D1, ... , Dn) } |
| r − s | { D1, ... Dn \| r(D1, ... , Dn) and not s(D1, ... , Dn) } |
| q × r | { Q1, ... Qm, R1, ... Rn \| q(Q1, ... , Qm) and r(R1, ... , Rn) } |

**Table 4.15  DRC Summary of Fundamental EMPLOYEE TRAINING Queries**

| Query | √DRC |
|---|---|
| $Q_\sigma$ | { EID, ELast, EFirst, ETitle, ESalary \|<br>        employee(EID, ELast, EFirst, ETitle, ESalary) and<br>        ESalary > 100000 }; |
| $Q_\pi$ | { ELast, EFirst, ETitle \| employee(_, ELast, EFirst, ETitle, _) }; |
| $Q_\cup$ | managers := { EID \| employee(EID, _, _, 'Manager', _) };<br>projectLeads := { EID \| employee(EID, _, _, 'Project Lead', _) };<br>{ EID \| managers(EID) or projectLeads(EID) }; |
| $Q_-$ | managers := { EID \| employee(EID, _, _, 'Manager', _) };<br>takenCourse := { EID \| takes(EID, _, _) };<br>{ EID \| managers(EID) and not takenCourse(EID) }; |
| $Q_\times$ | { EID, CID \| employee(EID, _, _, _, _) and<br>        trainingCourse(CID, _, _, _) }; |

**Table 4.16  DRC Summary of Additional EMPLOYEE TRAINING Queries**

| Query | √DRC |
|---|---|
| $Q_\cap$ | managers := { EID \| employee(EID, _, _, 'Manager', _) };<br>takenCourse := { EID \| takes(EID, _, _) };<br>{ EID \| managers(EID) and takenCourse(EID) }; |
| $Q_{\bowtie_\theta}$ | { EID, ELast, EFirst, ETitle, ESalary, AID, ATitle, AURL, ALeadID \|<br>        employee(EID, ELast, EFirst, ETitle, ESalary) and<br>        technologyArea(AID, ATitle, AURL, ALeadID) and EID=ALeadID }; |
| $Q_\bowtie$ | { CTitle, TDate \| (exists CID)<br>        (trainingCourse(CID, CTitle, _, _) and<br>        takes(_, CID, TDate)) }; |
| $Q_\div$ | { EID \| employee(EID, _, _, _, _) and<br>        not (exists CID) (trainingCourse(CID, _, _, _) and not takes(EID, CID, _) ) }; |

more closely resemble its relational algebra formulation. The division example uses the existential version of the query discussed in Section 4.3.2.

## Aggregation and Grouping

> **DRC supports limited forms of aggregation and grouping using logic, such as minimum/ maximum and a limited form of counting.**

DRC is relationally complete and, therefore, supports limited forms of aggregation and grouping using logic, such as minimum/maximum and a limited form of counting. Recall that Section 3.3 described how the formal relational algebra query language supports some forms of aggregation and grouping, and Section 4.2.4 illustrated the same examples in TRC. These queries over the EMPLOYEE TRAINING enterprise are illustrated here in DRC. For example, the employees who have the minimum salary are those employees such that there does not exist another employee who has a lower salary.

*drc_employeeMinSalary*:

√ { EID, ELast, EFirst, ETitle, ESalary | employee(EID, ELast, EFirst, ETitle, ESalary)
       and not (exists Salary)(employee(_, _, _, _, Salary) and Salary < ESalary) }

To group the aggregate result by title, modify the query to find those employees such that there does not exist another employee with the same title who has a lower salary.

*drc_employeeTitleMinSalary*:

√ { EID, ELast, EFirst, ETitle, ESalary | employee(EID, ELast, EFirst, ETitle, ESalary)
       and not (exists Salary)(employee(_, _, _, ETitle, Salary) and Salary < ESalary) }

DRC also supports a limited form of counting, such as more than one and only one. The query *drc_moreThanOneTechArea* finds employees who took courses in two different technology areas to satisfy the query.

*drc_moreThanOneTechArea*:

√ { EID, ELast, EFirst, ETitle, ESalary | employee(EID, ELast, EFirst, ETitle, ESalary)
       and (exists CID1, CID2, AID1, AID2)(takes(EID, CID1, _) and
       trainingCourse(CID1, _, _, AID1) and takes(EID, CID2, _) and
       trainingCourse(CID2, _, _, AID2) and AID1 <> AID2) }

## Self Check

Write the following queries in DRC:

16. What is the maximum manager salary?
    (eSalary)

17. Which employees took more than one course?
    (eID)

18. Which employees have taken courses in only one technology area?
    (eID)
    *Hint: Use named tables, specifically drc_moreThanOneTechArea, to formulate this answer to find those employees who took a course and did not take courses in more than one technology area.*

## 4.4 Safety

By illustrating how the operators of relational algebra can be expressed in the relational calculus languages, the previous examples have demonstrated the relational completeness of TRC and DRC. Although the result of a relational algebra expression is finite, not all relational expressions produce a finite result. Consider the companion TRC and DRC expressions that attempt to find employees who do not lead a technology area, assuming there exists an intermediate table trc_employeeLeads containing the ids of the employees that lead technology areas:

$$\{ E \mid not\ trc\_employeeLeads(E) \}$$
$$\{ EID \mid not\ technologyArea(\_, \_, \_, EID) \}$$

There are infinitely many values that are not area leads. To find those employees who do not lead a technology area, first limit the variables to values of the employee table and then check whether the employee id value appears in the trc_employeeLeads or technologyArea tables:

√   { E.eID | employee(E) and not (exists L) (trc_employeeLeads(L) and L.eID=E.eID) }
√   { EID | employee(EID, _, _, _, _) and not technologyArea(_, _, _, EID) }

A *safe* relational calculus expression guarantees a finite result, by limiting (either directly or indirectly) the values of a variable by its appearance in a positive atom. The Employee Training examples illustrating the relational completeness of the TRC and DRC languages are safe. Only *safe* relational algebra expressions can be realized in relational algebra. Therefore, relational algebra and safe TRC and safe DRC are equivalent in expressive power.

> A *safe* relational calculus expression guarantees a finite result, by limiting the values of a variable by its appearance in a positive atom.

## Chapter Notes Summary

### Logical Foundations

- Relational calculus languages use logic to declaratively specify the properties of the data to be retrieved.

### Tuple Relational Calculus

- In TRC, variables range over tuples of a relation. Use dot notation to reference an attribute.
- Use conditions to horizontally filter or join tables.
- All variables that are not being returned in the query result must be declared via quantification, defining the scope of the variables.
- An atom, consisting of a reference to a relation or a comparison involving tuple variables, forms the basis of a formula, which is built up from atoms using logical connectives and quantification.
- TRC is relationally complete.
- TRC also supports some forms of aggregation and grouping using logic, such as minimum/ maximum and a limited form of counting.

### Domain Relational Calculus

- In DRC, variables range over the domain of attributes.
- Use an underscore (_) to denote an anonymous variable.
- Use the same variable name to join attributes via equality.
- Use a constant in the relation reference for a horizontal filtering based on equality.
- Variables that are needed to answer the query but are not part of the result must be declared by quantification to define the scope of the variables.

- An atom, consisting of a reference to a relation or a comparison involving domain variables, forms the basis of a formula, which is built up from atoms using logical connectives and quantification.
- DRC is a relationally complete language.
- DRC supports limited forms of aggregation and grouping using logic, such as minimum/maximum and a limited form of counting.

**Safety**

- A *safe* relational calculus expression guarantees a finite result, by limiting the values of a variable by its appearance in a positive atom.

# Chapter Reminders

Table 4.17 summarizes the TRC and DRC syntax for each of the fundamental relational algebra operators, illustrating that safe TRC and safe DRC have the same expressive power as relational algebra.

**Table 4.17**    **TRC and DRC Summary of Fundamental Relational Algebra Operators**

| Algebra | TRC | DRC |
|---------|-----|-----|
| $\sigma_\theta(r)$ | { R \| r(R) and $\theta$ } | { R1, ... Rn \| r(R1, ... , Rn) and $\theta$ } |
| $\pi_A(r)$ | { R.ai ... R.aj \| r(R) } | { Ri, ... Rj \| r(R1, ... , Ri, ... , Rj, ... , Rn) } |
| r ∪ s | { T \| r(T) or s(T) } | { D1, ... Dn \| r(D1, ... , Dn) or s(D1, ... , Dn) } |
| r − s | { T \| r(T) and not s(T) } | { D1, ... Dn \| r(D1, ... , Dn) and not s(D1, ... , Dn) } |
| q × r | { Q, R \| q(Q) and r(R) } | { Q1, ... Qm, R1, ... Rn \| q(Q1, ... , Qm) and r(R1, ... , Rn) } |

# Practice

There are practice problems for each of the enterprises introduced earlier in the text: INVESTMENT PORTFOLIO, NEW HOME, and WEB PAGE. The book's companion website has the data for the enterprises in WinRDBI so that you can execute the practice problems. There are sample answers provided at the end of the chapter after the solutions to the self-check questions.

# Practice Problems: INVESTMENT PORTFOLIO

Answer the following practice problems in relational calculus (TRC and DRC) over the INVESTMENT PORTFOLIO schema (see Figure 2.18 for the visual relational schema and Figure 2.16 for its conceptual design as an ER diagram):

    client(taxPayerID, name, address)
    stock(sTicker, sName, rating, prinBus, sHigh, sLow, sCurrent, ret1Yr, ret5Yr)
    mutualFund(mTicker, mName, prinObj, mHigh, mLow, mCurrent, yield, familyID)
    fundFamily(familyID, company, cAddress)
    stockPortfolio(taxPayerID, sTicker, sNumShares)
    mutualFundPortfolio(taxPayerID, mTicker, mNumShares)

1. What clients have invested in which 'A' rated stocks?
   (taxPayerID, name, sTicker, sName)

2. Which clients have invested in both stocks whose principal business is 'Technology' and mutual funds having growth ('G') as a principal objective?
   (taxPayerID, name)

3. What clients have not invested in mutual funds with income ('I') as a principal objective?
   (taxPayerID, name)

4. Which clients have invested in stocks but not in mutual funds?
   (taxPayerID, name)

5. Which clients have more than one no-rating ('NR') stock?
   (taxPayerID, name)

6. Which clients have invested in only one mutual fund with stability ('S') as a principal objective?
   (taxPayerID, name)

7. Which mutual funds have the minimum current rate?
   (mTicker, mName, mCurrent)

8. What clients have invested in all of the mutual funds within the 'Fictitious' fund family?
   (taxPayerID, name)

# Practice Problems: NEW HOME

Answer the following practice problems in relational calculus (TRC and DRC) over the NEW HOME schema (see Figure 2.21 for the visual relational schema and Figure 2.19 for its conceptual design as an ER diagram):

    homebuilder(hID, hName, hStreet, hCity, hZip, hPhone)
    model(hID, mID, mName, sqft, story)
    subdivision(sName, sCity, sZip)
    offered(sName, hID, mID, price)
    lot(sName, lotNum, lStAddr, lSize, lPremium)
    sold(sName, lotNum, hID, mID, status)

1. Are there subdivisions that only offer single-story homes?
   (sName, sCity, sZip)

2. List all the homebuilders who offer single-story models with at least 2000 square feet in subdivisions located in 'Tempe'.
   (hName, hPhone)

3. Which lots in the 'Terraces' subdivision are available, i.e. not sold?
   (lotNum, lStAddr, lSize, lPremium)

4. Which models are not currently offered in any subdivision?
   (hName, mName)

5. Which subdivisions offer models from more than one homebuilder?
   (sName, sCity, sZip)

6. Which models are offered in only one subdivision?
   (hName, mName)

7. Which models offered in the 'Foothills' subdivision have the maximum square footage?
   (hName, mName, sqft)

8. Which subdivision offers all the models by the homebuilder 'Homer'?
   (sName, sCity, sZip)

# Practice Problems: WEB PAGE

Answer the following practice problems in relational calculus (TRC and DRC) over the WEB PAGE schema (see Figure 2.24 for the visual relational schema and Figure 2.22 for its conceptual design as an ER diagram):

> webpage (wID, wTitle, wURL, hits)
> site (sID, sTitle, sURL)
> graphic (gID, gName, gType, src, alt)
> document (dID, dName, dType, dDescription, dDate, downloads, wID)
> internal (sourceID, targetID)
> external (wID, sID, followed)
> displays (wID, gID)

1. Which pages contain a link to SQL ('sql') documents?
   (wID, wTitle)

2. Which pages display graphics having the name 'understandingbook'?
   (wID, wTitle)

3. Which pages do not display any graphics?
   (wID, wTitle)

4. Which pages display 'jpg' graphics but not 'gif' graphics?
   (wID, wTitle)

5. Which pages contain more than one document?
   (wID, wTitle)

6. Which pages contain only one link to an external Web page?
   (wID, wTitle)

7. Which pages have the most hits?
   (wID, wTitle, wURL, hits)

8. Which pages display graphics of all graphic types currently stored in the database?
   (wID, wTitle)

# End of Chapter Exercises

Answer the following exercises in TRC and DRC over the EMPLOYEE TRAINING schema:

> employee(eID, eLast, eFirst, eTitle, eSalary)
> technologyArea(aID, aTitle, aURL, aLeadID)
> trainingCourse(cID, cTitle, cHours, areaID)
> takes(eID, cID, tDate)

1. Which employees have taken both the 'Introduction to Databases' and the 'Query Languages' training courses?
   (eID, eLast, eFirst, eTitle)

2. Which employees have not taken all of the training courses in the 'Database' technology area?
   (eID, eLast, eFirst, eTitle)

3. Which employee leads have taken more than one training course in the technology area that they lead?
   (eID, eLast, eFirst, eTitle)

4. Which training courses in the 'Database' technology area have the maximum number of hours?
   (cID, cTitle, cHours)

5. Which employees have taken *all* training courses offered in the year 2017?
   (eID, eLast, eFirst, eTitle)

Answer the following queries in TRC and DRC over the INVESTMENT PORTFOLIO schema:

    client(taxPayerID, name, address)
    stock(sTicker, sName, rating, prinBus, sHigh, sLow, sCurrent, ret1Yr, ret5Yr)
    mutualFund(mTicker, mName, prinObj, mHigh, mLow, mCurrent, yield, familyID)
    fundFamily(familyID, company, cAddress)
    stockPortfolio(taxPayerID, sTicker, sNumShares)
    mutualFundPortfolio(taxPayerID, mTicker, mNumShares)

6. What clients own more than 200 shares of which stocks?
   (taxPayerID, name, sTicker, sName, sNumShares)

7. Which stock's one-year return has outperformed its five-year return?
   (sTicker, sName, prinBus, ret1Yr, ret5Yr)

8. What clients have not invested in stocks with 'Technology' as its principal business?
   (taxPayerID, name)

9. Which clients have invested in mutual funds but not in individual stocks?
   (taxPayerID, name)

10. Which clients have invested in more than one mutual fund with growth ('G') as its principal objective?
    (taxPayerID, name)

11. Which fund families have only one mutual fund?
    (familyID, company, cAddress)

12. Which stocks have the maximum one-year return?
    (sTicker, sName, prinBus, ret1Yr)

13. Which clients have invested in *all* stocks having a one-year return greater than its five-year return?
    (taxPayerID, name)

Answer the following queries in TRC and DRC over the NEW HOME schema:

    homebuilder(hID, hName, hStreet, hCity, hZip, hPhone)
    model(hID, mID, mName, sqft, story)
    subdivision(sName, sCity, sZip)
    offered(sName, hID, mID, price)
    lot(sName, lotNum, lStAddr, lSize, lPremium)
    sold(sName, lotNum, hID, mID, status)

14. Which subdivisions offer models with more than 3000 square feet?
    (sName, sCity, sZip)

15. Which lots in the 'Foothills' subdivision are pending ('P')?
    (lotNum, lStAddr, lSize, lPremium)

16. Which subdivisions do not offer any models?
    (sName, sCity, sZip)

17. Which subdivisions do not have any completed ('C') lots?
    (sName, sCity, sZip)

18. Which models are offered in more than one subdivision?
    (hName, mName)

19. Which homebuilders have only one two-story model?
    (hName)

20. Which models in the 'Terraces' subdivision have the lowest price?
    (hName, mName, minPrice)

21. Is there a subdivision that offers at least one model from all the homebuilders in the database?
    (sName, sCity, sZip)

Answer the following queries in TRC and DRC over the WEB PAGE schema:

    webpage (<u>wID</u>, wTitle, wURL, hits)
    site (<u>sID</u>, sTitle, sURL)
    graphic (<u>gID</u>, gName, gType, src, alt)
    document (<u>dID</u>, dName, dType, dDescription, dDate, downloads, wID)
    internal (<u>sourceID, targetID</u>)
    external (<u>wID, sID, followed</u>)
    displays (<u>wID, gID</u>)

22. Which pages contain links to documents named 'emptraining'?
    (wID, wTitle)

23. Which graphics in the database are stored as the type Portable Network Graphics ('png')?
    (gID, gName, alt)

24. Which pages do not contain any links to documents?
    (wID, wTitle)

25. Which pages contain links to external sites?
    (wID, wTitle, sID, sTitle, followed)

26. Which pages display more than one 'gif' graphic?
    (wID, wTitle)

27. Which pages display only one 'jpg' graphic?
    (wID, wTitle)

28. Which document has the fewest downloads?
    (dID, dName, dType, dDescription, downloads)

29. Which pages contain links to all SQL ('sql') documents currently contained in the database?
    (wID, wTitle)

# Answers to Self-Check Questions

1. { E | employee(E) and E.eSalary > 75000 };

2. { C.cTitle | trainingCourse(C) and C.areaID = 'DB' };

3. { C.cID, T.tDate |
       trainingCourse(C) and C.cTitle = 'Big Data' and
       takes(T) and C.cID = T.cID };

4. { T.eID, T.tDate | takes(T) and
       (exists C)
           (trainingCourse(C) and
           C.cTitle = 'Big Data' and
           C.cID = T.cID) };

5. { E.eID | employee(E) and
         not (exists T, C)
              (takes(T) and trainingCourse(C) and
              C.cTitle = 'Big Data' and
              C.cID = T.cID and
              T.eID = E.eID) };

6. { E | employee(E) and
       (exists BD, DS, T1, T2)
            (trainingCourse(BD) and BD.cTitle = 'Big Data' and
            trainingCourse(DS) and DS.cTitle = 'Data Science' and
            takes(T1) and T1.cID = BD.cID and T1.eID = E.eID and
            takes(T2) and T2.cID = DS.cID and T2.eID = E.eID) };

7. { E.eSalary | employee(E) and
         E.eTitle = 'Manager' and
         not (exists M)
              (employee(M) and
              M.eTitle = 'Manager' and
              M.eSalary > E.eSalary) };

8. { E | employee(E) and
       (exists T1, C1, T2, C2)
            (takes(T1) and T1.eID = E.eID and
            trainingCourse(C1) and T1.cID = C1.cID and
            takes(T2) and T2.eID = E.eID and
            trainingCourse(C2) and T2.cID = C2.cID and
            C1.cID <> C2.cID ) };

9. { E | employee(E) and
       (exists T)(takes(T) and T.eID = E.eID and
       not (exists M)
            (trc_moreThanOneTechArea(M) and M.eID = E.eID)) };

10. { EID, ELast, EFirst, ETitle, ESalary |
         employee( EID, ELast, EFirst, ETitle, ESalary) and ESalary > 75000 };

11. { CTitle | trainingCourse(_, CTitle, _, 'DB')  };

12. { CID, TDate | trainingCourse(CID, 'Big Data', _, _) and takes( _, CID, TDate) };

13. { EID, TDate | (exists CID)
         (takes(EID, CID, TDate) and trainingCourse(CID, 'Big Data', _, _)) };

14. { EID | employee(EID, _, _, _, _) and
         not (exists CID)
              (takes(EID, CID, _) and trainingCourse(CID, 'Big Data', _, _)) };

15. { EID, ELast, EFirst, ETitle, ESalary |
         employee(EID, ELast, EFirst, ETitle, ESalary) and (exists BD, DS)
              (trainingCourse(BD, 'Big Data', _, _) and takes(EID, BD, _) and
              trainingCourse(DS, 'Data Science', _, _) and takes(EID, DS, _) ) };

16. { ESalary | employee( _, _, _, 'Manager', ESalary) and not (exists MSalary)
       (employee( _, _, _, 'Manager', MSalary) and MSalary > ESalary) };

17. { EID, ELast, EFirst, ETitle, ESalary |
       employee(EID, ELast, EFirst, ETitle, ESalary) and
       (exists CID1, CID2)
           (takes(EID, CID1, _) and takes(EID, CID2, _) and CID1 <> CID2) };

18. { EID, ELast, EFirst, ETitle, ESalary |
       employee(EID, ELast, EFirst, ETitle, ESalary) and
       takes(EID, _, _) and
       not drc_moreThanOneTechArea(EID, _, _, _, _) };

# Answers to Practice Problems: INVESTMENT PORTFOLIO

TRC:

1. { C.taxPayerID, C.name, S.sTicker, S.sName |
       client(C) and stock(S) and
       (exists P)
           (stockPortfolio(P) and
            S.rating = 'A' and
            S.sTicker = P.sTicker and
            P.taxPayerID = C.taxPayerID) };

2. technologyClients :=
    { P.taxPayerID |
        stockPortfolio(P) and
        (exists S)
            (stock(S) and
             S.prinBus = 'Technology' and
             S.sTicker = P.sTicker) };

   growthClients :=
   { P.taxPayerID |
       mutualFundPortfolio(P) and
       (exists M)
           (mutualFund(M) and
            M.prinObj = 'G' and
            M.mTicker = P.mTicker) };

   { C.taxPayerID, C.name |
       client(C) and
       (exists T,G)
       (technologyClients(T) and T.taxPayerID=C.taxPayerID and
        growthClients(G) and G.taxPayerID=C.taxPayerID) };

3. { C.taxPayerID, C.name |
       client(C) and

```
        not (exists M,P)
            (mutualFund(M) and mutualFundPortfolio(P) and
            M.prinObj='I' and
            M.mTicker=P.mTicker and
            P.taxPayerID=C.taxPayerID) };
```

4. ```
   { C.taxPayerID, C.name |
       client(C) and
       (exists SP)(stockPortfolio(SP) and SP.taxPayerID=C.taxPayerID) and
       not (exists MP)(mutualFundPortfolio(MP) and MP.taxPayerID=
           C.taxPayerID) };
   ```

5. ```
   investNR :=
     { C.taxPayerID, S.sTicker |
         client(C) and stock(S) and S.rating='NR' and
         (exists P)
             (stockPortfolio(P) and
             P.taxPayerID=C.taxPayerID and
             P.sTicker=S.sTicker) };
   ```

   ```
   { C.taxPayerID, C.name |
       client(C) and
       (exists I1, I2)
           (investNR(I1) and I1.taxPayerID=C.taxPayerID and
           investNR(I2) and I2.taxPayerID=C.taxPayerID and
           I1.sTicker <> I2.sTicker) };
   ```

6. ```
   investS(taxPayerID, mTicker) :=
     { P.taxPayerID, P.mTicker |
         mutualFundPortfolio(P) and
         (exists M)
             (mutualFund(M) and
             M.mTicker=P.mTicker and
             M.prinObj='S') };
   ```

   ```
   { C.taxPayerID, C.name |
       client(C) and
       (exists I1)(investS(I1) and I1.taxPayerID=C.taxPayerID and
       not (exists I2)
           (investS(I2) and I2.taxPayerID=C.taxPayerID and
           I1.mTicker<>I2.mTicker)) };
   ```

7. ```
   { M.mTicker, M.mName, M.mCurrent |
       mutualFund(M) and
       not (exists F)(mutualFund(F) and F.mCurrent < M.mCurrent) };
   ```

8. ```
   fictitiousFunds :=
     { M.mTicker | (exists F)
         (mutualFund(M) and fundFamily(F) and
         F.company='Fictitious' and
         F.familyID=M.familyID) };
   ```
   ```

```
{ C.taxPayerID, C.name |
    client(C) and
    not (exists F)
        (fictitiousFunds(F) and
            not (exists P)
                (mutualFundPortfolio(P) and
                    P.taxPayerID=C.taxPayerID and
                    P.mTicker=F.mTicker)) };
```

DRC:

1. { TaxPayerID, Name, STicker, SName |
       client(TaxPayerID, Name, _) and
       stockPortfolio(TaxPayerID, STicker, _) and
       stock(STicker, SName, 'A', _, _, _, _, _, _) };

2. { TaxPayerID, Name | (exists STicker, MTicker)
       (client(TaxPayerID, Name, _) and
       stockPortfolio(TaxPayerID, STicker, _) and
       stock(STicker, _, _, 'Technology', _, _, _, _, _) and
       mutualFundPortfolio(TaxPayerID, MTicker, _) and
       mutualFund(MTicker, _, 'G', _, _, _, _, _)) };

3. { TaxPayerID, Name |
       client(TaxPayerID, Name, _) and
       not (exists MTicker)
           (mutualFundPortfolio(TaxPayerID, MTicker, _) and
               mutualFund(MTicker, _, 'I', _, _, _, _, _)) };

4. { TaxPayerID, Name |
       client(TaxPayerID, Name, _) and
       (exists STicker)
           (stockPortfolio(TaxPayerID, STicker, _) and
               stock(STicker, _, _, _, _, _, _, _, _))
       and not (exists MTicker)
           (mutualFundPortfolio(TaxPayerID, MTicker, _) and
               mutualFund(MTicker, _, _, _, _, _, _)) };

5. investNR :=
   { TaxPayerID, STicker |
       client(TaxPayerID, _, _) and
       stockPortfolio(TaxPayerID, STicker, _) and
       stock(STicker, _, 'NR', _, _, _, _, _, _) };

   { TaxPayerID, Name |
       client(TaxPayerID, Name, _) and
       (exists STicker1, STicker2)
           (investNR(TaxPayerID, STicker1) and
               investNR(TaxPayerID, STicker2) and
               STicker1 <> STicker2) };

6. investS(taxPayerID, mTicker) :=
   { TaxPayerID, MTicker |
       mutualFund(MTicker, _, 'S', _, _, _, _, _) and
       mutualFundPortfolio(TaxPayerID, MTicker, _) };
```
```

```
{ TaxPayerID, Name | (exists MTicker)
    (client(TaxPayerID, Name, _) and
    investS(TaxPayerID, MTicker) and
    not (exists M)
        (investS(TaxPayerID, M) and M<>MTicker)) };
```

7. 
```
{ MTicker, MName, MCurrent |
    mutualFund(MTicker, MName, _, _, _, MCurrent, _, _) and
    not (exists C)
        (mutualFund(_, _, _, _, _, C, _, _)  and C < MCurrent) };
```

8. fictitiousFunds :=
```
{ MTicker | (exists FID)
    (mutualFund(MTicker, _, _, _, _, _, _, FID) and
     fundFamily(FID, 'Fictitious', _))  };
```

```
{ TaxPayerID, Name |
    client(TaxPayerID, Name, _) and
    not (exists MTicker)
        (fictitiousFunds(MTicker) and
         not mutualFundPortfolio(TaxPayerID, MTicker, _)) };
```

# Answers to Practice Problems: New Home

TRC:

1. subdivisionsOfferSingle :=
```
{ O.sName | (exists M)
    (offered(O) and model(M) and
    O.hID=M.hID and O.mID=M.mID and M.story = 1) };
```

subdivisionsOfferOther :=
```
{ O.sName | (exists M)
    (offered(O) and model(M) and
    O.hID=M.hID and O.mID=M.mID and M.story <> 1) };
```

```
{ S | subdivision(S) and
    (exists Single)(subdivisionsOfferSingle(Single) and
        S.sName=Single.sName) and
    not (exists Other)(subdivisionsOfferOther(Other) and
        S.sName=Other.sName) };
```

2. 
```
{ H.hName, H.hPhone | (exists M, O, S)
    (homebuilder(H) and model(M) and offered(O) and subdivision(S) and
    H.hID=M.hID and M.story=1 and M.sqft > 2000 and
    M.hID=O.hID and M.mID=O.mID and
    O.sName=S.sName and S.sCity='Tempe') };
```

3. 
```
{ L.lotNum, L.lStAddr, L.lSize, L.lPremium |
    lot(L) and L.sName='Terraces' and
    not (exists S)(sold(S) and S.sName=L.sName and S.lotNum=L.lotNum) };
```

4. 
```
{ H.hName, M.mName |
    homebuilder(H) and model(M) and H.hID = M.hID and
    not (exists O)(offered(O) and M.hID=O.hID and M.mID=O.mID) };
```

5. { S | subdivision(S) and
    (exists O1, O2)
        (offered(O1) and offered(O2) and
        O1.sName=S.sName and O2.sName=S.sName and O1.hID <> O2.hID) };

6. { H.hName, M.mName | (exists O)
    (homebuilder(H) and
    model(M) and M.hID=H.hID and
    offered(O) and O.hID=M.hID and O.mID=M.mID and
    not (exists F)
        (offered(F) and F.hID=O.hID and F.mID=O.mID and
          F.sName<>O.sName)) };

7. foothillsModels :=
    { M.hID, M.mID, M.sqft |
        model(M) and (exists O)
          (offered(O) and O.sName='Foothills' and O.hID=M.hID and
            O.mID=M.mID) };

    maxSqftFoothillsModels :=
    { F | foothillsModels(F) and
        not (exists M) (foothillsModels(M) and M.sqft > F.sqft) };

    { H.hName, M.mName, S.sqft |
        homebuilder(H) and model(M) and maxSqftFoothillsModels(S) and
        H.hID=S.hID and M.hID=S.hID and M.mID=S.mID };

8. homerModels :=
    { M.hID, M.mID | (exists H)
        (homebuilder(H) and H.hName='Homer' and
        model(M) and M.hID=H.hID) };

    { S | subdivision(S) and
        (exists O,M)
        (offered(O) and homerModels(M) and S.sName=O.sName
          and O.hID=M.hID) and
        not (exists H)
             (homerModels(H) and
              not (exists F)
             (offered(F) and
          F.sName=S.sName and F.hID=H.hID and F.mID=H.mID)) };

DRC:

1. subdivisionsOfferSingle :=
    { SName |(exists HID, MID)
        (offered(SName, HID, MID, _) and
        model(HID, MID, _, _, 1)) };

    subdivisionsOfferOther :=
    { SName |(exists HID, MID, Story)
        (offered(SName, HID, MID, _) and
        model(HID, MID, _, _, Story) and Story<>1) };

```
{ SName, SCity, SZip |
    subdivision(SName, SCity, SZip) and
    subdivisionsOfferSingle(SName) and
    not subdivisionsOfferOther(SName) };
```

2. ```
{ HName, HPhone | (exists HID, MID, SName, Sqft)
    (homebuilder(HID, HName, _, _, _, HPhone) and
    model(HID, MID, _, Sqft, 1) and Sqft > 2000 and
    offered(SName, HID, MID, _) and
    subdivision(SName, 'Tempe', _) ) };
```

3. ```
{ LotNum, LStAddr, LSize, LPremium |
    lot (' Terraces', LotNum, LStAddr, LSize, LPremium) and
    not sold('Terraces', LotNum, _, _, _) };
```

4. ```
{ HName, MName | (exists HID, MID)
    (homebuilder(HID, HName, _, _, _, _) and
    model(HID, MID, MName, _, _) and
    not offered(_, HID, MID, _) ) };
```

5. ```
{ SName, SCity, SZip |
    subdivision(SName, SCity, SZip) and
    (exists HID1, HID2)
        (offered(SName, HID1, _, _) and
        offered(SName, HID2, _, _) and
        HID1 <> HID2 ) };
```

6. ```
{ HName,MName | (exists HID, MID, SName)
    (homebuilder(HID,HName, _, _, _, _) and
    model(HID,MID,MName, _, _) and
    offered(SName,HID,MID, _) and
    not (exists AnotherSName)
        (offered(AnotherSName,HID,MID,_) and SName<>AnotherSName)) };
```

7. foothillsModels :=
   ```
   { HID, MID, Sqft |
       offered('Foothills', HID, MID, _) and
       model(HID, MID, _, Sqft, _) };
   ```

   maxSqftFoothillsModels :=
   ```
   { HID, MID, Sqft |
       foothillsModels(HID, MID, Sqft) and
       not (exists S) (foothillsModels(_, _, S) and S > Sqft) };
   ```

   ```
   { HName, MName, Sqft | (exists HID, MID)
       (maxSqftFoothillsModels(HID, MID, Sqft) and
       homebuilder(HID, HName, _, _, _, _) and
       model(HID, MID, MName, Sqft, _)) };
   ```

8. ```
{ SName,SCity,SZip | (exists HomerHID)
    (subdivision(SName, SCity, SZip) and
    homebuilder(HomerHID, 'Homer', _, _, _, _) and
    offered(SName, HomerHID, _, _) and
    not (exists MID)
        (model(HomerHID, MID, _, _, _) and
        not offered(SName, HomerHID, MID, _))) };
```

# Answers to Practice Problems: WEB PAGE

TRC:

1.  { W.wID, W.wTitle | (exists D)
        (document(D) and D.dType = 'sql' and
        webpage(W) and W.wID = D.wID ) };

2.  { W.wID, W.wTitle | (exists G,D)
        (graphic(G) and G.gName = 'understandingbook' and
        displays(D) and D.gID = G.gID and
        webpage(W) and W.wID = D.wID) };

3.  { W.wID, W.wTitle |
        webpage(W) and
        not (exists D) (displays(D) and D.wID = W.wID) };

4.  jpgPages :=
    { D.wID | displays(D) and (exists G)
                (graphic(G) and G.gType = 'jpg' and G.gID = D.gID) };

    gifPages :=
    { D.wID | displays(D) and (exists G)
                (graphic(G) and G.gType = 'gif' and G.gID = D.gID) };

    { W.wID, W.wTitle |
        webpage(W) and
        (exists J)  (jpgPages(J) and J.wID = W.wID) and
        not (exists G) (gifPages(G) and G.wID = W.wID) };

5.  { W.wID, W.wTitle |
        webpage (W) and
        (exists D1)(document(D1) and D1.wID = W.wID and
        (exists D2)(document(D2) and D2.wID = W.wID and D1.dID <> D2.dID)) };

6.  { W.wID, W.wTitle |
        webpage (W) and
        (exists E1)(external(E1) and E1.wID = W.wID and
        not (exists E2)
            (external(E2) and E2.wID = W.wID and E2.sID <> E1.sID) ) };

7.  { W.wID, W.wTitle, W.hits |
        webpage(W) and
        not (exists P)(webpage(P) and W.hits < P.hits) };

8.  graphicType :=
    { G.gType | graphic(G) };

    displaysGraphicType :=
    { D.wID, G.gType | displays(D) and graphic(G) and D.gID = G.gID };

    { W.wID, W.wTitle |
        webpage(W) and
        not (exists T)(graphicType(T) and
            not (exists G)(displaysGraphicType(G) and G.wID = W.wID and
                G.gType = T.gType)) };

DRC:

1. { WID, WTitle | webpage(WID, WTitle, _, _) and
                document(_, _, 'sql', _, _, _, WID) };

2. { WID, WTitle | (exists GID)
        (graphic(GID, 'understandingbook', _, _, _) and
         displays(WID, GID) and
         webpage(WID, WTitle, _, _) ) };

3. { WID, WTitle | webpage(WID, WTitle, _, _) and
                not displays(WID, _) };

4. jpgPages :=
   { WID | (exists GID) (graphic(GID, _, 'jpg', _, _) and displays(WID, GID) ) };

   gifPages :=
   { WID | (exists GID) (graphic(GID, _, 'gif', _, _) and displays(WID, GID) ) };

   { WID, WTitle | webpage(WID, WTitle, _, _) and
                jpgPages(WID) and not gifPages(WID) };

5. { WID, WTitle | webpage(WID, WTitle, _, _) and
        (exists D1, D2)
        (document(D1, _, _, _, _, _, WID) and
        document(D2, _, _, _, _, _, WID) and
        D1 <> D2) };

6. { WID, WTitle | webpage(WID, WTitle, _, _) and
        (exists SID1)(external (WID, SID1, _) and
        not (exists SID2)(external (WID, SID2, _) and SID1 <> SID2)) };

7. { WID, WTitle, Hits | webpage(WID,WTitle, _, Hits) and
        not (exists BiggerHits)
            (webpage(_, _, _, BiggerHits) and BiggerHits > Hits) };

8. { WID, WTitle | webpage (WID, WTitle, _, _) and
        not (exists GType)(graphic(_, _, GType, _, _) and
            not (exists G)(displays(WID, G) and graphic(G, _, GType, _, _))) };

# Bibliographic Notes

Codd [1972a] defined tuple relational calculus and its equivalence with relational algebra in 1972. Lacroix and Pirotte [1977] described domain relational calculus in 1977. Ullman's texts [1988, 1990] include a formal proof on the equivalence of relational algebra with safe DRC and safe TRC.

The Tuple Relational Calculus language forms the basis of the industry-standard SQL query language, which is explored in the next chapter. The Domain Relational Calculus language is related to the Datalog language of deductive databases, which is a field of study emphasizing the use of a language based on logic to query the database instance stored as logical facts. The Datalog language looked similar to the Prolog (Programming in Logic) language, which was developed in the early 1970s, but the evaluation of the languages was significantly different. While Prolog assumed a particular strategy for the evaluation of the language, the goal of Datalog was to declaratively specify queries in logic and let the database system have the responsibility to determine an efficient evaluation of the declarative query. Ramakrishnan and Ullman [1995] provided a survey of deductive database systems and Ullman's texts [1988, 1990] provide a wealth of knowledge on databases and deductive databases.

## More to Explore

The WinRDBI educational tool (winrdbi.asu.edu) provides an interpreter for relational query languages, including TRC and DRC. This text used WinRDBI's syntax for TRC and DRC so that the example queries can be executed. All of the queries from the chapter, self-check, and practice exercises are available on this book's companion website.

WinRDBI also provides a DRC by name syntax. The by position syntax of theoretical DRC provides a useful language for declaratively specifying the properties of the data to be retrieved by a query. Variables ranging over the domains of attributes provide inherent support for the specification of equality constraints between attributes of different tables by using the same variable name. An equality constraint between an attribute and a domain constant is also inherent by using the domain constant to reference the attribute directly. However, there is a disadvantage to this positional syntax. The query composer must know the position of the attributes within each table in the relational database schema. A by name syntax, such as that offered by relational algebra, does not require the knowledge of the position of the attribute within the table but only the name of the attribute.

Consider the following by name version of a query that finds the training courses offered in the 'Database' technology area:

```
dbCourse(cID:C, cTitle:T, cHours:H) ← (exists A)
    (technologyArea(aTitle:'Database', aID:A) and
    trainingCourse(areaID:A, cID:C, cTitle:T, cHours:H));
```

This by name syntax makes the schema of the resulting table explicit by declaring the attribute names and associating a domain variable with each attribute. The domain variables in the schema result (C, T and H) must appear in a positive atom within the expression to return the query bindings. The pragmatic ← symbol is used instead of the theoretical notation | to separate the free variables from the query expression. The attributes of the technologyArea and trainingCourse tables are referenced by name. The domain constant 'Database' constrains the value of the aTitle attribute of technologyArea. The local domain variable A references both the aID attribute of technologyArea and the areaID attribute of trainingCourse to perform a natural join of the two tables. The result variables are bound by their appearance in the reference to the trainingCourse table.

In fact, WinRDBI is based on deductive database research. The relational database is stored as a collection of Prolog facts. Each of the relational query languages is parsed into Prolog rules, which are then executed. Note that based on Prolog's left-to-right evaluation strategy of goals, the relational calculus languages assume that a variable is bound before checking its value. To explore the deductive database connection, retrieve the EMPLOYEE TRAINING Prolog facts from the companion website and use the Prolog programming language to execute queries.

# SQL: An Introduction to Querying

5

## LEARNING OBJECTIVES

- To understand the mathematical foundations of a declarative SQL query
- To implement fundamental SQL query expressions
- To write SQL statements using nested subqueries and set operators
- To analyze data using SQL's aggregation and grouping capabilities
- To develop SQL query statements to handle null values

This chapter introduces you to SQL – the industry-standard query language for asking questions over data stored in a relational database. SQL is a declarative query language, specifying the tables that contain the information to answer the question along with the conditions that must hold on the data with a list of attributes to display in the answer. In this chapter, you will learn how to write SQL queries to analyze data.

## 5.1 Foundations

Although there are always slight variations of the dialect of SQL provided by a given system, the SQL standard provides a description of the language that allows for the portability of database applications. Typically, identifiers in the SQL standard are limited to a maximum of 128 characters and the first character must be a letter (upper- or lowercase) and the remaining may be any letter, digit or underscore. Usually, identifiers are case insensitive in SQL, meaning that the identifiers tableName and tablename are considered identical. (This is dependent on the installation options of the database product being used.) Thus, the syntax conventions for identifiers used in this book are not inconsistent with the SQL standard. Specifically, the SQL examples continue to use identifiers starting with a lowercase letter to refer to the name of a relation or attribute.

## NOTE 5.1  SQL Syntax

Although SQL is a standard, each database product is an approximation to that standard. This text introduces the SQL standard where queries preceded by a checkmark ($\sqrt{}$) in this chapter have been verified using the MySQL database. See the book's companion website for supporting files. Students are strongly encouraged to run the examples while reading the text and to examine the results of the queries.

> **A basic SQL query consists of select, from, and where clauses, listing the desired attributes from the Cartesian product of the tables where the specified condition holds on the data.**

The basic SQL query expression selects a list of attributes from relations where a condition holds:

```
select   a1, a2, ... , aj
from     r1, r2, ... , rk
where    θ
```

This basic SQL query expression is essentially equivalent to the relational algebra expression:

$$\pi_{a1,\,a2,\,...,\,aj}(\sigma_\theta(r1 \times r2 \times \cdots \times rk))$$

The select clause *projects* the desired attributes from the *Cartesian product* of the tables that satisfy the *selection* condition specified by the where clause. It is interesting to note that the SQL select clause is in fact a relational algebra *projection* and not a *selection*. Another point of interest to note is that the from clause represents a *Cartesian product* of the tables specified. One of the most common mistakes in SQL is the lack of realization that the from clause provides all possible combinations of the tuples from the tables specified in the list. If a relational algebra *join* is desired, then the join condition is specified as part of the where clause, which performs a selection on the result of the Cartesian product.[1]

> **Use * to select all attributes.**

There are slight variations on this SQL syntax. If all attributes are desired in the result, an asterisk (*) provides a convenient shorthand:

```
select   *
from     r1, r2, ... , rk
where    θ
```

> **The where clause is optional.**

If there is no condition for horizontally filtering the result of the from clause, the where clause is optional:

```
select   *
from     r1, r2, ... , rk
```

> **The keyword distinct after select removes duplicates.**

The equivalence of the basic SQL expression to its corresponding relational algebra expression was qualified as *essentially equivalent*. The relational algebra and relational calculus languages assume that relations are *sets* of tuples. A set is a collection of elements without duplicates. Therefore, the formal languages implicitly remove duplicate tuples from the result set. However, SQL assumes that a relation is a *multiset* or *bag* of tuples, which is a collection of elements that may contain duplicates. SQL does not automatically remove duplicate tuples because there is a cost associated with performing duplicate elimination. Use the keyword distinct in the select clause to eliminate duplicate tuples.

```
select   distinct a1, a2, ... , aj
from     r1, r2, ... , rk
where    θ
```

There are also circumstances that require the use of multisets. Consider the situation where the sum of the salaries of employees is needed to determine the salary budget for a company. If the sum is to be performed on a set of employee salaries, rather than a multiset of salaries, then the result of the sum on the set would be incorrect if there were employees earning the same salary.

---

[1] SQL-92 introduced a *join* syntax in the from clause, which will be described later in this chapter.

## SYNTAX 5.2  Basic SQL Query

**Summary:**

| | |
|---|---|
| select | ATTRIBUTE-LIST |
| from | TABLE-LIST |
| where | WHERE-CONDITION |

**Example:** What are the names of employees who are managers?

| | |
|---|---|
| select | eLast, eFirst |
| from | employee |
| where | eTitle = 'Manager' |

This basic SQL query expression is a syntactic variation of the TRC expression:

$$\{ R1, R2, \ldots, RK \mid r1(R1) \text{ and } r2(R2) \text{ and } \ldots \text{ } rk(Rk) \text{ and } \theta \}$$

In the TRC expression, the tuple variables to the left of the vertical bar correspond to the SQL select clause, specifying the schema of the resulting relation. The tables in the SQL from clause correspond to the table references listed to the right of the vertical bar, which specifies that Ri is a tuple variable ranging over the table ri. The condition of the where clause, denoted $\theta$, is part of the condition of the TRC expression.

In this brief comparison of TRC versus SQL, the differences appear minor. The TRC short-cut for including all attributes appearing in the query expression is to list all of the tuple variables, whereas SQL uses an asterisk. When all attributes corresponding to a tuple variable are not desired, dot notation T.a projects the attribute a associated with the tuple variable T. The SQL syntax above shows a list of attribute names. However, since attribute names are only unique within a table, a reference to an attribute name may be ambiguous. SQL also allows the use of dot notation to refer to an attribute and requires dot notation when an attribute reference is ambiguous. For example, if two tables t1 and t2 both contain the attribute a, then the select clause in the following query contains an ambiguous reference to the attribute a.

| | |
|---|---|
| select | a |
| from | t1, t2 |
| where | ... |

However, dot notation t1.a disambiguates the reference by specifying the table of the desired attribute:

| | |
|---|---|
| select | t1.a |
| from | t1, t2 |
| where | ... |

> **Use dot notation to disambiguate an attribute reference.**

SQL allows for the specification of *table aliases* for a table in the from clause. There are several reasons for introducing table aliases. One reason is to provide a short name to reference tables, as in the following example.

| | |
|---|---|
| select | T1.a, T2.b |
| from | longTableName1 T1, longTableName2 T2 |
| where | ... |

> **SQL allows for the specification of *table aliases* for a table in the from clause.**

Another reason is to provide a mechanism by which the same table can be accessed more than once in the same query. These table aliases (sometimes called *range variables*) play a similar role to the tuple variables in TRC. The SQL examples in the remainder of the chapter will follow similar conventions to the TRC examples by using identifiers that begin with an uppercase letter to denote table aliases.

> **Use the as keyword to rename attributes.**

SQL inherently supports the renaming of attributes in the **select** clause using the **as** keyword. The following example renames the attribute a to ta1 and the attribute b to t2b.

```
select   T1.a as t1a, T2.b as t2b
from     longTableName1 as T1, longTableName2 as T2
where    …
```

The **as** keyword can also be used when introducing table aliases. Note that the **as** keyword is required syntax for renaming attributes, whereas it is optional for table aliases. Recall that Chapters 3 and 4 on the formal query languages introduced a different syntax for renaming attributes. When writing SQL queries, use the syntax provided by SQL for renaming.

## Self Check

1.  The relational algebra projection operator corresponds to which clause in SQL?
2.  Which SQL clause corresponds to horizontal filtering or the selection of tuples?
3.  What keyword in the **select** clause removes duplicates?

## 5.2 Fundamental Query Expressions

Learning how to write fundamental **select-from-where** statements in SQL takes practice. In fact, when writing fundamental SQL, the thought process for designing the query is usually from-where-select.

### HOW TO 5.3   Writing a Fundamental Query in SQL

**Step 1:** First determine the tables that have the required data. Which tables have the attributes that need to be returned in the result? How do you relate the tables to answer the question? Only include the tables that are needed; do not include extra tables. Include these tables in the **from** clause.

**Step 2:** Then filter the tuples based on required conditions specified in the **where** clause. These conditions can be filtering based on criteria specified in the question being asked and/or using the primary–foreign key relationships of the relational schema. Note that only constants appearing in the query can be used to filter the results.

**Step 3:** Last, list the desired attributes to answer the question in the **select** clause. Note: If the list of attributes could result in duplicate tuples that the user does not want, then include the keyword **distinct** immediately following the **select** keyword and before the list of attributes.

### 5.2.1 Queries Involving One Table

Let's start by looking at queries that involve only one table to answer the question. This table is listed in the from clause and the filtering conditions involve explicit conditions from the question in the where clause with the select clause listing the desired attributes. Table 5.1 lists various query examples over the EMPLOYEE TRAINING enterprise that involve only one table. The first column gives a label or name to the query along with its English description so that the query can be referenced later. This is similar to the presentation of the formal query languages. Recall that when asking queries, the query design depends on the attributes that are needed in the answer. Therefore, the query specifications list the desired attributes so that there are no ambiguities between the English query description and the expected result.

**Table 5.1   SQL Sample Queries with One Table**

| Query label and description | √ SQL |
|---|---|
| *sql_Managers*:<br>    Which employees are managers,<br>    i.e. have the title 'Manager'?<br>    (eLast, eFirst) | select eLast, eFirst<br>from employee<br>where eTitle = 'Manager' |
| *sql_TitleDB01*:<br>    What is the title of the course with unique id<br>    'DB01'?<br>    (cTitle) | select cTitle<br>from trainingCourse<br>where cID = 'DB01' |
| *sql_TakesDB01*:<br>    Which employees took the course with unique id<br>    'DB01'?<br>    (eID) | select eID<br>from takes<br>where cID = 'DB01' |
| *sql_DatabaseLead*:<br>    What is the employee id of the lead of the<br>    'Database' technology area?<br>    (aLeadID) | select aLeadID<br>from technologyArea<br>where aTitle = 'Database' |

Each of the queries in Table 5.1 horizontally filters the table in the from clause based on the criteria asked in the question in the where clause and then projects the desired attributes in the select clause. In query *sql_DatabaseLead*, the constant 'Database' refers to the title of the technology area, which is used to filter the result. A common mistake in writing SQL queries is using constants that do not appear in the question. For example, the corresponding aID value for the 'Database' technology area is 'DB'. Do not use this 'DB' value for filtering. Some primary–foreign key values are not meant for the end user to see. They are either abbreviations or identifiers generated by the database system. Since a database administrator may have to change these hidden values over time, query solutions should only use the constants given in the question asked. When writing queries, it is also important to think about the number of results the query will return. Note that queries *sql_TitleDB01* and *sql_DatabaseLead* will only yield one result based on the semantics of the enterprise: there is only one title for the course with unique id 'DB01' and there is only one employee who is the lead of a technology area. Queries *sql_Managers* and *sql_TakesDB01* will return multiple tuples: there are many employees who are managers and there are many employees who took the 'DB01' course.

When an SQL query returns multiple tuples, it is returning a set or multiset of tuples based on whether the distinct keyword is used. The term set or multiset implies an *unordered* collection of tuples. However, it is quite useful in practice to display the results of a query in a particular order. SQL provides an order by clause for that purpose. For example, the following *sql_ManagersAlphabetical* query displays the managers ordered by the employee's last name, using the default sort specification, which is ascending.

> **Use an** order by **clause to return results in sorted order.**

*sql_ManagersAlphabetical*:

√        select      eLast, eFirst
         from        employee
         where       eTitle = 'Manager'
         order by    eLast

The order by clause also allows for the ordering of multiple attributes and for the explicit specification of the sort order as ascending or descending. The next query *sql_TitlesAscSalariesDesc* displays the titles of employees in ascending (alphabetical) order and within that displays the salaries of the employees with the same title in descending order. Note that ascending and descending are abbreviated to asc and desc, respectively.

*sql_TitlesAscSalariesDesc:*

√          select     eTitle, eSalary
           from       employee
           order by   eTitle asc, eSalary desc

When your query returns multiple results for a person to examine, you should consider using an order by clause to provide a more meaningful display of the answer.

Ordered results may also be required as part of the answer to a query. For example, the requirements for *sql_ManagersAlphabetical* specifies that the names of managers are returned in alphabetical order. An ordered collection is typically referred to as a *list* in computer science, whereas an unordered collection is either a set or bag depending on whether duplicates are removed or not, respectively. Note that without an order by clause, there is no guaranteed ordering of the results. Just because the query without an order by clause may return the result ordered once, it may not do so on subsequent executions. Therefore, if an ordering of results is required for your query, you must use an order by clause to generate an appropriate list.

When writing queries, it is important to check that the answer is correct. In SQL, instead of just inspecting the data manually, you can write simpler queries to display *sorted* data to facilitate this process. This text calls these queries *reflection queries*, since the query helps to check or reflect on the correctness of the query. Formally, these queries are *verifying* or *validating* that the query results are correct. Table 5.2 shows each query from Table 5.1 along with a *reflection* query. These reflection queries show just enough details to verify the correctness of the original query. These reflection queries return a small list of attributes from the table needed to verify the query without extra filtering and sort the results based on the query specification to support the visual inspection of the query results.

### Table 5.2    **SQL Reflection Queries with One Table**

| Query label and SQL query | √ Reflection SQL query |
| --- | --- |
| *sql_Managers:* | |
|    select eLast, eFirst |    select eTitle, eLast, eFirst |
|    from employee |    from employee |
|    where eTitle = 'Manager' |    order by eTitle, eLast, eFirst |
| *sql_TitleDB01:* | |
|    select cTitle |    select cID, cTitle |
|    from trainingCourse |    from trainingCourse |
|    where cID = 'DB01' |    order by cID |
| *sql_TakesDB01:* | |
|    select eID |    select cID, eID |
|    from takes |    from takes |
|    where cID = 'DB01' |    order by cID, eID |
| *sql_DatabaseLead:* | |
|    select aLeadID |    select aTitle, aLeadID |
|    from technologyArea |    from technologyArea |
|    where aTitle = 'Database' |    order by aTitle |

# Self Check

4. Write a query to find the employees who earn more than $75,000.
   (eID, eLast, eFirst, eTitle, eSalary)

5. What clause would you add to the previous query so that the employee having the highest salary is listed first?

6. Write a simpler reflection query to verify your answer.

## 5.2.2 Queries Involving Multiple Tables

Queries that require more than one table to compute the answer are more complicated and require the consideration of the primary–foreign key relationships between the tables. Recall that the first step in writing an SQL query is to determine the tables that have the data needed to answer the question. Listing these tables in the from clause results in a Cartesian product of the tuples in these tables. A Cartesian product provides all possible combinations of tuples in the list of tables, which is not very useful in general. However, filtering the resulting Cartesian product such that the primary key attributes in one table are equal to the referencing foreign key attributes in another table is useful, and is commonly known as a *join*. Table 5.3 provides sample queries that involve combining two tables from the EMPLOYEE TRAINING enterprise to answer the question asked based on the desired attributes. Note that these sample queries use mnemonic table aliases for all tables although it is not required on some queries. Some prefer to always use table aliases and dot notation as a form of self-documentation.

**Table 5.3  SQL Sample Queries with Two Tables**

| Query label and description | √ SQL |
| --- | --- |
| *sql_NamesTookDB01*: <br> Which employees took the course with unique id 'DB01'? <br> (eLast, eFirst) | select E.eLast, E.eFirst <br> from employee E, takes T <br> where E.eID = T.eID and T.cID = 'DB01' |
| *sql_DatesIntroDB*: <br> Which dates was the course titled 'Introduction to Databases' offered? <br> (tDate) | select distinct T.tDate <br> from takes T, trainingCourse C <br> where T.cID = C.cID and <br>     C.cTitle = 'Introduction to Databases' |
| *sql_DatabaseCourses*: <br> What courses are offered in the 'Database' technology area? <br> (cID, cTitle, cHours) | select C.cID, C.cTitle, C.cHours <br> from trainingCourse C, technologyArea A <br> where C.areaID = A.aID and A.aTitle = 'Database' |
| *sql_NamesAreaLead*: <br> Which employees lead technology areas? <br> (eLast, eFirst) | select E.eLast, E.eFirst <br> from employee E, technologyArea A <br> where E.eID = A.aLeadID |

Table 5.4 provides representative reflection queries for each query in Table 5.3. Again, these queries are simpler, providing a view of the raw data with a smaller list of attributes and ordered

results to aid in checking the answer to the original query. For queries involving multiple tables as shown in Table 5.4, the reflection query joins the tables needed to answer the query but does not include any additional filtering. The ordering of the list of attributes as well as the sorting of results is an important consideration. The goal is to provide a view of the raw data that aids in a visual inspection supporting the verification of the results.

**Table 5.4    SQL Reflection Queries with Two Tables**

| √ Query label and SQL query | √ Reflection SQL Query |
|---|---|
| sql_NamesTookDB01: | |
|    select E.eLast, E.eFirst | select T.cID, E.eLast, E.eFirst |
|    from employee E, takes T | employee E, takes T |
|    where E.eID = T.eID and T.cID = 'DB01' | where E.eID = T.eID |
| | order by T.cID, E.eLast, E.eFirst |
| sql_DatesIntroDB: | |
|    select distinct T.tDate | select C.cTitle, T.tDate |
|    from takes T, trainingCourse C | takes T, trainingCourse C |
|    where T.cID = C.cID and C.cTitle = 'Introduction to Databases' | where T.cID = C.cID |
| | order by C.cTitle, T.tDate |
| sql_DatabaseCourses: | |
|    select C.cID, C.cTitle, C.cHours | select A.aID, C.cID, C.cTitle, C.cHours |
|    from trainingCourse C, technologyArea A | from trainingCourse C, technologyArea A |
|    where C.areaID = A.aID and A.aTitle = 'Database' | where C.areaID = A.aID |
| | order by A.aID, C.cID, C.cTitle |
| sql_NamesAreaLead: | |
|    select E.eLast, E.eFirst | select A.aLeadID, E.eLast, E.eFirst |
|    from employee E, technologyArea A | from employee E, technologyArea A |
|    where E.eID = A.aLeadID | where E.eID = A.aLeadID |
| | order by A.aLeadID |

> **Tables can be joined in the** from **clause using the syntax:** *table1* join *table2* on *condition*.

One of the most common mistakes in forming a query expression in SQL is the omission of the join conditions in the where clause of the query. Consider the *sql_DatabaseCourses* query that is joining the trainingCourse and technologyArea tables on the primary–foreign key relationship between these tables. If the join condition (C.areaID = A.aID) is omitted from the where clause, then the result contains the 'Database' technology area combined in a Cartesian product with all of the rows in the trainingCourse table. The SQL-92 revision of the standard introduced *joined tables* to allow the specification of a join in the from clause of an SQL query. The following query *sql_DatabaseCourses_JoinOn* illustrates the explicit join of the trainingCourse and technologyArea tables in the from clause on their related attributes rather than the implicit join specified in the where clause of query *sql_DatabaseCourses*.

sql_DatabaseCourses_JoinOn:

```
√      select   C.cID, C.cTitle, C.cHours
       from     trainingCourse C join technologyArea A on C.areaID = A.aID
       where    A.aTitle = 'Database'
```

This revision of the standard also allowed for a natural join specification in the from clause. A natural join is a shorthand specification of an equality join, where the attributes having the same name in both tables are joined such that they are equal and only one copy of the attribute is included in the result. Recall the query *sql_NamesTookDB01* that finds the names of employees who took the course with unique id 'DB01'. This query can also be specified using natural joined tables in the from clause, performing a natural join of the employee and takes tables.

> Use a natural join in the from clause to join tables based on equality for common attributes.

*sql_NamesTookDB01_NaturalJoin*

√
```
select   E.eLast, E.eFirst
from     employee E natural join takes T
where    T.cID = 'DB01'
```

All of the sample SQL queries with the join conditions specified in the where clause are still valid SQL queries. The joined tables capability provides an alternative specification of the query, which is usually preferred because the joining of the tables is more obvious. Note that the SQL syntax supported by the database product that you are using may not support the join-on or natural join syntax. Therefore, you may have to specify the join conditions in the where clause.

The samples thus far have shown how to join two tables where the primary keys consist of a single attribute. You can join more than two tables using parenthesized syntax as shown in query *sql_EmpsTookDatabaseCourses* that finds the id of employees who took courses in the 'Database' technology area. Note that this query uses both a join-on and a natural join in the from clause.

*sql_EmpsTookDatabaseCourses*

√
```
select   distinct T.eID
from     (technologyArea A join trainingCourse C on A.aID = C.areaID)
         natural join takes T
where    A.aTitle = 'Database'
order by T.eID
```

## HOW TO 5.4   Writing a Reflection Query

**Step 1:** Similar to writing any query, the first step is to determine the tables that are needed to answer the query without including any unnecessary tables.

**Step 2:** Join these tables using either the appropriate *joined tables* syntax in the from clause or join conditions specified in the where clause. Do not include any additional filtering beyond joining tables.

**Step 3:** List the attributes needed to verify the query in the select clause. Do not include extra attributes. Specify the list in an appropriate order for supporting the validation of the results.

**Step 4:** Use an order by clause to sort the results of the reflection query that supports the visual inspection of the results. The order by clause should include a list of multiple attributes to aid in the verification.

## Self Check

Consider the following query:
> Which employees took the 'Big Data' course and on what date?
> (eID, tDate)

7. Answer the query using a join condition in the where clause.
8. Answer the query using a join in the from clause.
9. Answer the query using a natural join in the from clause.

## 5.3 Nested Queries

> **SQL supports nested queries, which are subqueries appearing within a query.**

The sample SQL queries that you have seen up to this point eagerly find all the answers requested by taking the Cartesian product or join of the tables in the from clause, filtering the results based on the conditions in the where clause, and then projecting the desired attributes in the select clause. SQL also provides support for nested subqueries. If you have looked at the formal declarative query languages, DRC or TRC, nested queries provide support for queries involving existence. In SQL, nested queries also provide support for membership testing and comparisons.

As an example, consider a query that asks for employees who have taken a training course. At this point, you know two solutions to answer this query. One using the where clause to join the employee and takes tables on the primary–foreign key relationship, and another that uses joined tables to accomplish the same task. Both of these solutions require the use of the distinct keyword to remove duplicates, since an employee would be in the result for each training course that they took. These queries are not nested and are shown as queries *sql_empsTookCoursesUnnestedWhere* and *sql_empsTookCoursesUnnestedJoin* in Table 5.5. This table also illustrates two nested solutions to this query. When a nested subquery uses a table from the outer query, it is known as *correlated*; otherwise, it is *uncorrelated*.

> **A *correlated* nested subquery uses a table from the outer query, whereas an *uncorrelated* nested subquery does not.**

The query *sql_empsTookCoursesNestedCorrelated* looks at each employee and checks whether there exists a tuple in the takes table for that employee. The exists evaluates to true if the subquery returns a non-empty result; otherwise, it is false. The query *sql_empsTookCoursesNestedUncorrelated* does not use the employee from the outer query in the nested subquery. The uncorrelated nested query determines the collection of eID values for those employees who have taken a training course. Then the outer query checks whether the employee's eID is in that collection. All of these queries are correct specifications to answer the question.

> **The exists operator supports existential subqueries and the in operator allows for membership testing.**

**Table 5.5    SQL: Which employees have taken a training course?**

| Query label | √ SQL |
| --- | --- |
| *sql_empsTookCoursesUnnestedWhere*: | select distinct E.eID, E.eLast, E.eFirst <br> from employee E, takes T <br> where E.eID = T.eID |
| *sql_empsTookCoursesUnnestedJoin*: | select distinct E.eID, E.eLast, E.eFirst <br> from employee E join takes T on E.eID = T.eID |
| *sql_empsTookCoursesNestedCorrelated*: | select E.eID, E.eLast, E.eFirst <br> from employee E <br> where exists (select * from takes T where T.eID = E.eID) |
| *sql_empsTookCoursesNestedUncorrelated*: | select E.eID, E.eLast, E.eFirst <br> from employee E <br> where E.eID in (select T.eID from takes T) |

Consider a related query that asks for the employees who have *not* taken any training courses. This query involves negation with respect to a relationship and not a specific attribute value. Therefore, the use of the not equal (<>) comparison operator is an incorrect approach as shown in the query *sql_WRONG_empsNoCourses*.

*sql_WRONG_empsNoCourses*:

√      select    distinct E.eID, E.eLast, E.eFirst
           from      employee E join takes T on E.eID <> T.eID

Table 5.6 shows the corresponding nested solutions for this query that use the not keyword to check whether an employee has taken a course. Note that the *difference* set operator introduced in Section 5.4 can also be used to answer queries involving negation.

**Table 5.6**  **SQL: Which employees have not taken a training course?**

| Query label | √ SQL |
| --- | --- |
| *sql_empsNoCoursesNestedCorrelated*: | select E.eID, E.eLast, E.eFirst |
| | from employee E |
| | where not exists (select * from takes T where T.eID = E.eID) |
| *sql_empsNoCoursesNestedUncorrelated*: | select E.eID, E.eLast, E.eFirst |
| | from employee E |
| | where E.eID not in (select T.eID from takes T) |

In addition to existential and membership tests, nested queries are also used in comparisons when a subquery returns a result with exactly one tuple in it and the items being compared are compatible, e.g. comparing primary and foreign key values. Consider a query *sql_dbCoursesEquality* that finds the courses in the 'Database' technology area:

> When a nested subquery returns a result with exactly one tuple in it, the value can be used in a comparison in the outer query.

*sql_dbCoursesEquality*:

√      select    C.cID, C.cTitle, C.cHours
           from      trainingCourse C
           where    C.areaID =
           (select    A.aID
           from        technologyArea A
           where    A.aTitle = 'Database')

The conditional expression in the where clause allows for an equality comparison between the values of the areaID foreign key attribute of the trainingCourse table and the result of a select-from-where expression that returns the primary key attribute value for the 'Database' technology area. The nested subquery of *sql_dbCoursesEquality* is not correlated. The nested subquery is executed once to find the identification number of the technology area with the title 'Database', which is then compared to the areaID attribute of a training course.

Besides comparing a foreign key to the primary key that it references, comparisons are useful in the presence of aggregation, which is introduced in Section 5.5. An example query that will be explored later is finding employee(s) who have the minimum salary.

## SPECIAL TOPIC 5.5   A Glimpse at Query Optimization

In the procedural relational algebra language, the concept of query optimization was introduced to motivate that alternative query specifications may result in varying performance. Heuristics were discussed to perform selections as early as possible and to reorder joins using the theoretical properties of the relational operators to find an alternative specification of the query that was more efficient. Query optimization is also important in declarative languages although the coverage of the declarative query languages (DRC, TRC, SQL) thus far has emphasized the correct specification of a query. After all, the declarative query languages specify what data to retrieve and not how to retrieve the data. However, it is this declarative specification of *what* data to retrieve instead of *how* to retrieve the data that leads to the concept of query optimization for SQL.

There are obviously different ways to specify the characteristics of the data to be retrieved in SQL, and these alternative query specifications may result in query executions having different performance characteristics. Table 5.5 provides various specifications for finding employees who have taken a training course. Which version is more efficient depends on various factors and the database product itself.

Although query optimization is the responsibility of the database system, the performance of the database application is ultimately the responsibility of the database professional. If the performance of certain queries is not acceptable, the database must be tuned based on guidelines for database administration provided for the particular database product employed in the application. There are indexes that can be added on certain attributes or combination of attributes that may improve performance. Essentially, indexing is a mechanism to define a faster way to search the data beyond a simplistic search. Indexes are discussed as a special topic in the next chapter that goes beyond the querying capabilities of SQL. However, revising the specification of a query may also be necessary. Most database products provide the ability to view the plan for evaluating a query, which can be used in conjunction with vendor guidelines to tune the performance of the database application.

## SPECIAL TOPIC 5.6    Views and Inline Views

SQL provides support for views and inline views. A view is a definition of a virtual table, which is a name given to the SQL query to execute to materialize its tuples. Each time that the view name is referenced, its tuples are materialized. The general syntax for defining a view is:

    create view VIEW-NAME as SELECT-FROM-WHERE

The next chapter provides a more detailed exposition of views including their definition and use.

There is also a concept of an inline view, which is a query expression that can be used instead of a table name in the from clause. Queries with inline views are harder to read and will not be used in this introductory coverage of SQL. The *More to Explore* section of the chapter's bibliographic notes provides information for exploring this feature along with other advanced features of SQL.

## Self Check

Consider the same query:
> Which employees took the 'Big Data' course and on what date?
> (eID, tDate)

10. Answer the query using a nested correlated subquery.
11. Answer the query using the in comparison with a nested uncorrelated subquery.
12. Answer the query using the = comparison with a nested uncorrelated subquery.

## 5.4 Set Operators

> **SQL supports the set operators of union, except, and intersect.**

A relationally complete language must provide at least the equivalence of the fundamental relational algebra operators ($\sigma, \pi, \cup, -, \times$). Up to this point, the basic select-from-where SQL expression illustrates the following fundamental operators: $\pi, \times, \sigma$. The fundamental set operators ($\cup, -$) have not yet been explored in the context of SQL. The SQL standard supports the set operators ($\cup, -, \cap$) through the keywords union, except, and intersect, respectively. SQL also provides set semantics for these operators, returning a *set* of tuples by default. To allow duplicates or multisets, the keyword all must be used in combination with the operator. Table 5.7 provides three example queries over the EMPLOYEE TRAINING enterprise to illustrate the use of SQL's set operators.

**Table 5.7  Example SQL Queries for Set Operators**

| Query label | √ SQL |
| --- | --- |
| *sql_ManagersUnionProjectLeads*: | select E.eID from employee E where E.eTitle='Manager'<br>union<br>select E.eID from employee E where E.eTitle='Project Lead' |
| *sql_ManagersExceptCourses*: | select E.eID from employee E where E.eTitle='Manager'<br>except<br>select T.eID from takes T |
| *sql_ManagersIntersectCourses*: | select E.eID from employee E where E.eTitle='Manager'<br>intersect<br>select T.eID from takes T |

Note that although the SQL standard supports these set operators, the particular database product that you are using may not provide all of these operators or use a different keyword for the operator. For example, MySQL does not provide the intersect operator. This does not restrict the expressiveness of MySQL because intersection is not a fundamental operator, and can be defined in terms of difference (see Chapter 3). In addition, all of the above queries in Table 5.7 have alternative solutions in SQL that do not employ the corresponding set operator as shown in Table 5.8.

**Table 5.8  Alternative Example SQL Queries for Set Operators**

| Query label | √ SQL |
| --- | --- |
| *sql_ManagersOrProjectLeads*: | select E.eID<br>from employee E<br>where E.eTitle='Manager' or E.eTitle='Project Lead' |
| *sql_ManagersNoCourses*: | select E.eID<br>from employee E<br>where E.eTitle='Manager' and<br>        E.eID not in (select T.eID from takes T) |
| *sql_ManagersTookCourses*: | select E.eID<br>from employee E<br>where E.eTitle='Manager' and<br>        exists (select * from takes T where E.eID = T.eID) |

## Self Check

Using the set operators, write SQL queries to answer the following questions, simply returning a collection of employee identifiers:

13. Which employees are Database Administrators or took the Data Science course?
14. Which Database Administrators did not take the Data Science course?
15. Which Database Administrators took the Data Science course?

## 5.5 Aggregation and Grouping

> **Aggregate operators** (min, max, avg, sum, count) **provide a single result that** *aggregates* **the detailed data.**

Many important queries over the data in a database involve aggregation of results, such as queries involving minimum, maximum, sum, count, and average. These operators provide a single result that "aggregates" the detailed data. SQL provides inherent support in the language for aggregation constructs. In the previous coverage of the formal query languages of relational algebra and relational calculus, queries involving minimum/maximum and a limited form of counting (more than one/only one) illustrated the use of logic to answer these types of questions. This section explores how to analyze data using SQL's aggregation and grouping capabilities.

Consider the following query that finds the minimum, maximum, and average employee salary as well as the sum of all salaries and a count of the number of employees in the database.

*sql_SalariesAggregationExample*:

```
√       select      min(E.eSalary), max(E.eSalary), avg(E.eSalary),
                    sum(E.eSalary), count(*)
        from        employee E
```

This query returns a single tuple with five attribute values. The min, max, avg and sum aggregate functions return the corresponding value for its argument. The count operator with * as an argument counts the number of tuples in the result. Note that the name of the resulting aggregate attributes is product dependent. Therefore, renaming each attribute with a descriptive name using the **as** keyword is usually recommended, as shown in the following *sql_SalariesAggregationExampleRenaming* query.

*sql_SalariesAggregationExampleRenaming*:

```
√       select      min(E.eSalary) as minsal, max(E.eSalary) as maxsal,
                    avg(E.eSalary) as avgsal,
                    sum(E.eSalary) as totalsal, count(*) as empcount
        from        employee E
```

Aggregation can also be used in nested queries. As mentioned in Section 5.3, consider a query that finds the employees who earn the minimum salary. The query *sql_EmployeesWithMinSalary* illustrates an equality comparison of an employee's salary with the computed minimum salary of all employees.

*sql_EmployeesWithMinSalary*:

```
√       select      *
        from        employee E
        where       E.eSalary =    (select min(M.eSalary) from employee M)
```

The use of comparison operators with nested queries is not limited to equality. Consider the following query *sql_EmployeesLessThanAvgSalary* that finds those employees who earn less than the average employee salary, displaying the result in descending order by salary.

*sql_EmployeesLessThanAvgSalary*:

```
√       select      *
        from        employee E
        where       E.eSalary <    (select avg(M.eSalary) from employee M)
        order by    E.eSalary desc
```

Let's take a closer look at the count aggregate operator. Besides using the * argument to count all tuples, the operator distinct with an attribute name counts the number of unique values of that attribute. Consider the query *sql_CountEmployeesTookCourses* that counts the number of employees who have taken a training course.

*sql_CountEmployeesTookCourses*:

√       select     count(distinct T.eID) as empcount
           from       takes T

Since an employee can take many training courses, the argument to the count aggregate function uses the distinct keyword with the eID attribute to count the number of employees who took a training course, eliminating duplicates.

Consider a variation of the previous query to find the number of managers who have taken a training course.

*sql_CountManagersTookCourses*:

√       select     count(distinct T.eID) as mgrcount
           from       takes T natural join employee E
           where     E.eTitle = 'Manager'

The from - where returns only those managers who have taken a training course and the count(distinct T.eID) counts each manager once. However, what if you wanted to know the count of the employees who took training courses for each title in the database? Characterizing the data based on values to form groups is known as *grouping*.

SQL provides support for *grouping*, applying an aggregate function to groups of tuples that have the same value on a grouping of attributes. The group by clause in SQL specifies the grouping attributes. For example, consider the query *sql_SalaryInfoByTitle* that finds the minimum, maximum, and average salary of employees by title.

> **Use the** group by **clause in SQL to provide an aggregate result for a grouping of attributes.**

*sql_SalaryInfoByTitle*:

√       select     E.eTitle, min(E.eSalary) as mintitle,
                       max(E.eSalary) as maxtitle, avg(E.eSalary) as avgtitle
           from       employee E
           group by  E.eTitle

The database system groups together the tuples that have the same value of eTitle and finds the minimum, maximum, and average salary of the employees in each group. To visualize the execution and to verify the results of the query, consider the following query *sql_SalariesByTitle* that orders the employees by title and then by salary.

*sql_SalariesByTitle*:

√       select     E.eTitle, E.eSalary
           from       employee E
           order by  E.eTitle, E.eSalary

Figure 5.1 shows an abstract representation of the result for the reflection query *sql_SalariesBy Title*. Since the results are ordered first by title, the tuples having the same title represent a group for the original query *sql_SalaryInfoByTitle*. The secondary sort is based on the salary, so the first tuple in the result for that title has the minimum salary, and the last tuple for that title represents the maximum salary. The system computes the average of the salaries in that group of employees having the same title.

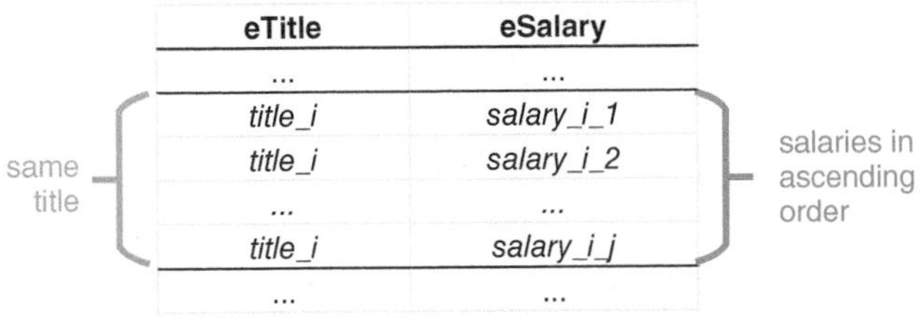

**FIGURE 5.1**
**Abstraction of results for *sql_SalariesByTitle*.**

The following *sql_CountByTitleTookCourses* is the generalized query that finds the number of employees by title who took a training course.

*sql_CountByTitleTookCourses*:

√
```
select    E.eTitle, count(distinct T.eID) as emptookcoursescount
from      takes T natural join employee E
group by  E.eTitle
```

The examples of grouping up to this point have only one attribute. There can be multiple grouping attributes as illustrated by the query *sql_CourseOfferingCount* that computes the count of the number of employees who took a course on a date. The count computes the number of tuples in the grouping that includes both cID and tDate. As a generalization with grouping, the select clause contains the grouping attributes specified in the group by clause and the columns representing the desired aggregation for that group.

*sql_CourseOfferingCount*:

√
```
select    T.cID, T.tDate, count(*) as emptookoffering
from      takes T
group by  T.cID, T.tDate
```

This introductory text follows the semantics for grouping in the SQL standard, requiring that the non-aggregate columns in the select clause must appear in the group by clause as the only grouping attributes. This requirement makes sense because the query is asking for an aggregate result for the same values of those grouping attributes.

SQL also supports the ability to place a selection condition on the results of grouping using the having clause. Essentially a having clause is specifying a filtering, similar to a where clause, for the group. What if you only wanted the titles with the count of the number of employees who took a course such that there are at least four such employees with that title. This query can be answered by appending the following having clause to *sql_CountByTitleTookCourses*:

> A having **clause** **specifies a filtering condition on the result of the grouping.**

```
having    emptookcoursescount >= 4
```

Note that some database products do not recognize the renaming of the attribute within the having clause. In that case, the aggregate operator must be used again:

```
having    count(distinct T.eID) >= 4
```

Note that the having clause is just a shortcut, allowing the use of one query instead of using a second query to filter the result of the grouping. Also, the query can be rewritten with the aggregation query specified as an inline view using a where to filter the result.

## SPECIAL TOPIC 5.7   Arithmetic Expressions

SQL also has the capability of specifying arithmetic expressions in the select clause. Consider a query to find the cost of giving all employees a 2% raise:

You can also use multiple attributes in arithmetic expressions, such as multiplying the item cost by its quantity to find the total cost of the item on an order.

*sql_RaiseSalaries*:

√
```
select    1.02 * sum(E.eSalary) as totalwithraise
from      employee E
```

# Self Check

16. Write a query in SQL to find the average salary of employees who are managers?
    (avgmgrsalary)

17. Write a query in SQL to find the number of employees who took each course that has been offered?
    (cID, emptotal)

18. Write a reflection query for *sql_CourseOfferingCount*. Recall that a reflection query is a simpler query that uses ordering of detailed results that can be used to verify the results of the original query.

## 5.6  Querying with null Values

Up to this point, the assumption has been that the database has values for all of the information stored in each table. In real life, this is not the case. There are times when there is missing data. Relational databases use null to indicate that there is currently no known value. It is important to understand this distinction because null values have an effect on querying.

For the EMPLOYEE TRAINING enterprise, consider a relaxation of the constraint that would allow for a technology area to temporarily not have an employee assigned to lead it. This scenario does not violate the primary–foreign key relationship, which states that if the value of the foreign key is not null, then its value must appear as a primary key in its referenced table. Thus, the value of the aLeadID attribute would be null if there is currently no employee lead. To find the technology areas that do not have leads, the query must use special syntax to test for the presence of null using is.

> **Relational databases use** null **to indicate that an attribute has no known value.**

*sql_AreasWithoutLeads*:

> √        select      aTitle
>          from        technologyArea
>          where       aLeadID is null

> **Use the** is **operator to check whether an attribute value is** null.

Similarly, you could test that an attribute has a non-null value by using is not null.

What if you wanted to count the number of technology areas with leads? Recall that the count aggregate operator has an argument. The argument * results in counting the number of tuples. In the query *sql_CountEmployeesTookCourses*, the syntax distinct T.eID counted the unique number of values of that attribute. In fact, the distinct syntax counts the number of *different* non-null values of the attribute. To count the number of non-null values of an attribute, use that attribute as an argument to count. The query *sql_CountAreasWithLeads* counts the number of aLeadID values in technologyArea that are not null.

> **Use** count(attrname) **to count the number of values for an attribute that are not** null.

*sql_CountAreasWithLeads*:

> √        select      count(aLeadID) as arealeadcount
>          from        technologyArea

Recall the query *sql_NamesAreaLead* that finds the names of employees who lead a technology area. This query is joining on the primary–foreign key relationship between employee and technologyArea. This join requires that the values of the primary and foreign key values are the same and, thus, will only find the employees who are leads of technology areas with non-null values for the aLeadID attribute. In fact, this type of join is also known as an *inner* join. There are also *outer* joins that deal with null values. Consider a variation of *sql_NamesAreaLead*, called *sql_AreaTitlesWithLead*, that displays the area title with the name of the employee who leads that technology area.

*sql_AreaTitlesWithLead*:

√       select     A.aTitle, E.eLast, E.eFirst
              from      technologyArea A left outer join employee E on
                              A.aLeadID = E.eID
              order by  A.aTitle

> **Use an outer join to include** null **values when combining tables in the presence of nulls.**

Rather than using an inner join and only displaying the information for areas having employee leads, the left outer join will include every value in the left table even if there is no matching value in the right table. When there is no match, null values are returned for the attributes in the result from the right table. The query *sql_AreaTitlesWithLead* displays the titles of technology areas in alphabetical order along with the last and first names of the employee lead or null if there currently is no employee assigned to lead that area. Similarly, a right outer join includes every value in the right table with null values for the attributes in the left table when there is no match. A full outer join is essentially a combination of a left and right outer join, returning all rows.

The left outer join operator can also be strategically used to provide counts that include the 0 case. Consider the query *sql_CountEmpCourses* that finds the number of courses taken by each employee.

*sql_CountEmpCourses*:

√       select     T.eID, count(*) as coursecount
              from      takes T
              group by  T.eID

This query computes the count of courses for only those employees who have taken a course. But you would also like to include a count of 0 for those employees who have not taken a course. This can be accomplished by a modification to the query *sql_empsNoCoursesNestedUncorrelated* that returns the numeric literal 0 as the second attribute when the employee satisfies the where filter, as shown in the following query *sql_CountEmpNoCourses*.

*sql_CountEmpNoCourses*:

√       select     E.eID, 0 as coursecount
              from      employee E
              where     E.eID not in (select T.eID from takes T)

These two queries could then be unioned together to answer the question: For each employee in the database, how many courses have they taken? This query can be answered more succinctly using a left outer join in one query.

*sql_CountEmpCoursesLeftOuterJoin*:

√       select     E.eID, count(T.cID) as coursecount
              from      employee E left outer join takes T on E.eID = T.eID
              group by  E.eID

The query *sql_CountEmpCoursesLeftOuterJoin* will only count the non-null values of T.cID, returning 0 for the count when there are only null values for the employees who have not taken any courses. To see how this query works, display the ordered results of the simpler left outer join of the employee and takes tables as shown in the query *sql_EmpLeftOuterJoinTakes*.

*sql_EmpLeftOuterJoinTakes*:

√       select     *
              from      employee E left outer join takes T on E.eID = T.eID
              order by  E.eID

# Self Check

19. What is the operator that is used to test whether a value is equal to null?
20. What does the count(ATTRIBUTE-NAME) in the select clause count?
21. What is the name of the join operator that will include null values for attributes when there is no match on the join?

## 5.7 Relational Completeness

The expressive power of the industry-standard SQL language exceeds that of the fundamental relational algebra operators as shown by its numerous additional features described throughout the chapter. This section illustrates the fundamental and additional relational operators in SQL both at the abstract level as well as by example.

> **SQL is relationally complete, substantially extending its expressive power beyond the capabilities of the formal query languages.**

### 5.7.1 Fundamental Operators

A relationally complete language must provide at least the equivalence of the fundamental relational algebra operators ($\sigma, \pi, \cup, -, \times$). Table 5.9 summarizes the SQL expressions for abstract operations involving the fundamental relational algebra operators.

**Table 5.9   SQL Summary of Fundamental Relational Algebra Operators**

| Algebra | SQL |
|---------|-----|
| $\sigma_\theta(r)$ | select * from r where $\theta$ |
| $\pi_A(r)$ | select distinct A from r |
| $r \cup s$ | select * from r union select * from s |
| $r - s$ | select * from r except select * from s |
| $q \times r$ | select * from q, r |

Table 5.10 provides the SQL queries that correspond to the illustrative examples over the EMPLOYEE TRAINING enterprise using the fundamental operators.

**Table 5.10   SQL Summary of Fundamental EMPLOYEE TRAINING Queries**

| Query | √ SQL |
|-------|-------|
| $Q_\sigma$ | select * from employee E where E.eSalary > 100000 |
| $Q_\pi$ | select distinct E.eLast, E.eFirst, E.eTitle from employee E |
| $Q_\cup$ | select E.eID from employee E where E.eTitle='Manager'<br>union<br>select E.eID from employee E where E.eTitle='Project Lead' |
| $Q_-$ | select E.eID from employee E where E.eTitle='Manager'<br>except<br>select T.eID from takes T |
| $Q_\times$ | select E.eID, C.cID from employee E, trainingCourse C |

Query $Q_\sigma$ is a straightforward selection of an employee having a salary greater than 100,000.

Query $Q_\pi$ projects the desired attributes of the table alias E that ranges over the employee table. Since the key attribute eID of the employee table is not included in the result of the query, duplicates may occur in the result. Therefore, distinct is added to the select clause to return a *set* of tuples to be equivalent to the relational algebra specification.

Query $Q_\cup$ unions together the SQL query expressions that find employees who are managers and employees who are project leads. Note the SQL queries that are operands of the union query are compatible. In general, the union requires that the tables have the same number of attributes, and that the types of the attributes are compatible.

By default, SQL removes duplicate tuples in union queries. To allow duplicates, the option all can be specified after the union. For example,

select * from r union all select * from s

If a tuple $t$ appears $t_r$ times in r and $t_s$ times in s, then $t$ appears $t_r + t_s$ times in the resulting union all. The definition of how an operator deals with duplicates, as just described for the union all, is known as its *duplicate semantics*.

Query $Q_-$ uses the except operator to return the employees who are managers and have not taken a training course. The except operator has similar assumptions to that of the union operator on type compatibility and duplicate removal. The option all is also available on the except operator.

select * from r except all select * from s

The duplicate semantics of the except all for a tuple $t$ appearing $t_r$ times in r and $t_s$ times in s is the maximum of 0 or $t_r - t_s$.

Query $Q_\times$ represents a Cartesian product of the employee and trainingCourse tables. To be consistent with the relational algebra specification for this query, the result of the query includes only the eID and cID attributes of the table aliases E and C, respectively. Recall that the simplifying assumption for the Cartesian product operator in relational algebra requires that the operand relations do not have any attribute names in common so that the result of the Cartesian product does not contain duplicate attribute names.

## 5.7.2  Additional Operators

The additional relational algebra operators $(\cap, \bowtie_\theta, \bowtie, \div)$ provide an abbreviation for frequently used combinations of the fundamental operators. The SQL queries that correspond to the illustrative examples over the EMPLOYEE TRAINING enterprise using these additional operators of relational algebra are summarized in Table 5.11.

**Table 5.11  SQL Summary of Additional EMPLOYEE TRAINING Queries**

| Query | √ SQL |
|---|---|
| $Q_\cap$ | select E.eID from employee E where E.eTitle='Manager'<br>intersect<br>select T.eID from takes T |
| $Q_{\bowtie_\theta}$ | select *<br>from employee E join technologyArea A on E.eID=A.aLeadID |
| $Q_\bowtie$ | select distinct C.cTitle, T.tDate<br>from trainingCourse C natural join takes T |

Query $Q_\cap$ finds the employees who are managers and have taken a training course. The type compatibility and duplicate removal assumptions of the union operator apply to the intersect operator, including the all option.

select * from r intersect all select * from s

If a tuple $t$ appears $t_r$ times in r and $t_s$ times in s, then the duplicate semantics of the intersect all results in the tuple $t$ appearing the minimum of $t_r$ or $t_s$ times.

Query $Q_{\bowtie_\theta}$ illustrates a join of the employee and technologyArea tables such that the employee eID is equal to the aLeadID of the technology area.

Query $Q_\bowtie$ joins the trainingCourse and takes tables on the cID attributes in the where clause. The distinct in the select clause eliminates the many duplicates that otherwise would be included in the result since the multiset version would include a tuple for each employee taking the course on a given date.

In relational algebra, the natural join ($\bowtie$) provides a convenient shorthand for joining two tables such that the value of attributes with the same name in both operand relations are equal. A projection is automatically introduced to include only one copy of the duplicate attributes. DRC provides a shortcut for a natural join by using the same domain variable name in the positions that are to be (natural) joined. TRC does not provide for a natural join shortcut. SQL provided a shortcut when it introduced the natural join syntax in the from clause.

Recall the division example query over the abstract domain, finding the a's from the abTable that are related to *all* of the b's specified in the bTable, where the schema of the tables are abTable(a,b) and bTable(b). There are multiple ways of answering a division-type query using SQL. Since basic SQL is essentially syntactic sugaring of the formal Tuple Relational Calculus language, let's first look at SQL's specification of division using existential quantification.

*sql_divisionExistential*:

```
√    select    distinct T.a
     from      abTable T
     where     not exists
                  (select   *                                    -- β
                   from     bTable B
                   where    not exists
                              (select   *                        -- αβ
                               from     abTable AB
                               where    AB.a=T.a and AB.b=B.b))
```

This division query finds the a's from the abTable such that it is not the case that there exists a b value in the bTable that is *not* related to the a value by the abTable. Recall that the instance of bTable contains the tuples { (b1),(b2) } and the instance of abTable contains the tuples { (a1,b1), (a1,b2), (a2,b2), (a3,b1), (a3,b2), (a3,b3) }. Therefore, the answer to the query is { (a1),(a3) }.

Table 5.12 shows a truth table that corresponds to the specification of division in SQL on the abstract example. There are two nested queries in this example, which are labeled by comments in the SQL specification, which are two dashes followed by a space $--$. The innermost nested query $\alpha\beta$ checks whether the a value from the outermost query (T.a) is related by the abTable to the b value from the inner query (B.b). The nested query $\beta$ checks whether there exists a b value in the bTable that is not related by the abTable to the a value specified in the outermost query (T.a). The truth table indicates that the a1 and a3 values from the abTable are related to *all* of the values in the bTable, i.e. b1 and b2. The value a2 is not included in the result since there exists a b value, specifically b2, that is not related to a2 by the abTable.

Another approach to solving a division-type query is to take advantage of SQL's aggregation capabilities. This solution counts for each a value, the number of b values in the b table to which

**Table 5.12**    **SQL Division Truth Table**

| T.a | B.b | exists $\alpha\beta$ | not exists $\alpha\beta$ | exists $\beta$ | not exists $\beta$ |
|-----|-----|--------------|------------------|----------|----------------|
| a1  | b1  | T | F | F | T |
|     | b2  | T | F |   |   |
| a2  | b1  | T | F | T | F |
|     | b2  | F | T |   |   |
| a3  | b1  | T | F | F | T |
|     | b2  | T | F |   |   |

the a value is related by the abTable. If this count is equal to the number of b values in the b, table, then the a value is related to *all* b values.

*sql_CountAB*:

√    select     AB.a, count(distinct AB.b) as related_bs
       from       abTable AB
       where      AB.b in (select b from bTable)
       group by   AB.a

*sql_divisionCounting*:

√    select     C.a
       from       sql_CountAB C
       where      C.related_bs = (select count(distinct b) as b_Count from bTable)

## Safety

> **The syntax of SQL supports safe query expressions.**

The previous examples have demonstrated the relational completeness of SQL, illustrating how the operators of relational algebra can be expressed in SQL. Recall that a *safe* expression guarantees a finite result, and it is well known that relational algebra and safe TRC (and safe DRC) are equivalent in expressive power. Is SQL safe? Yes. The syntax of SQL guarantees the safety of the SQL language. Since an exists or not exists condition must appear only in a where clause that is associated with a (select and) from clause, a basic SQL query expression limits a table alias to a positive table reference in the from clause.

## Self Check

22. A select clause that lists a subset of the attributes and removes duplicates corresponds to which fundamental relational algebra operator?
23. A from clause that just lists the tables separated by a comma corresponds to the operation of which fundamental relational algebra operator?
24. What keyword is added to a set operator in SQL to return a multiset rather than a set?

## Chapter Notes Summary

### Foundations

- A basic SQL query consists of select, from, and where clauses, listing the desired attributes from the Cartesian product of the tables where the specified condition holds on the data.
- Use * to select all attributes.

- The where clause is optional.
- The keyword distinct after select removes duplicates.
- Use dot notation to disambiguate an attribute reference.
- SQL allows for the specification of *table aliases* for a table in the from clause.
- Use the as keyword to rename attributes.

## Fundamental Query Expressions

- Use an order by clause to return results in sorted order.
- Tables can be joined in the from clause using the syntax: *table1* join *table2* on *condition*.
- Use a natural join in the from clause to join tables based on equality for common attributes.

## Nested Queries

- SQL supports nested queries, which are subqueries appearing within a query.
- The exists operator supports existential subqueries and the in operator allows for membership testing.
- When a nested subquery returns a result with exactly one tuple in it, the value can be used in a comparison in the outer query.

## Set Operators

- SQL supports the set operators of union, except, and intersect.

## Aggregation and Grouping

- Aggregate operators (min, max, avg, sum, count) provide a single result that *aggregates* the detailed data.
- Use the group by clause in SQL to provide an aggregate result for a grouping of attributes.
- A having clause specifies a filtering condition on the result of the grouping.

## Querying with null Values

- Relational databases use null to indicate that an attribute has no known value.
- Use the is operator to check whether an attribute value is null.
- Use count(attrname) to count the number of values for an attribute that are not null.
- Use an outer join to include null values when combining tables in the presence of nulls.

## Relational Completeness

- SQL is relationally complete, substantially extending its expressive power beyond the capabilities of the formal query languages.
- The syntax of SQL supports safe query expressions.

# Chapter Reminders

The industry-standard query language SQL uses a syntactic variation of tuple relational calculus to provide a practical and declarative language to query a relational database. The conventions for the syntax summary use square brackets [...] to denote optional items, | to indicate a choice of one of the items specified, and identifiers in all capital letters to denote items that can be replaced by names or further expanded.

The select statement forms the basis of an SQL query, selecting a list of attributes from a list of tables that optionally satisfy a where condition. The optional keyword distinct returns a set of tuples instead of the default multiset or bag of tuples as the result of the query. The optional group by clause allows for the specification of grouping attributes for the application of aggregate functions (e.g. min, max, avg, sum, count) specified in the select clause. An optional having clause allows for the specification of a condition on the result of the grouping. The result of a query can be optionally ordered using the order by clause, which specifies the columns to be ordered and the sort order (either ascending or descending).

```
select     [distinct] ATTRIBUTE-LIST
from       TABLE-LIST
[where     WHERE-CONDITION]
[group by  GROUPING-ATTRIBUTES
[having    HAVING-CONDITION]]
[order by  COLUMN-NAME [ asc | desc ], ... ]
```

## Practice

There are practice problems for each of the enterprises introduced earlier in the text: INVESTMENT PORTFOLIO, NEW HOME, and WEB PAGE. The answers are provided at the end of the chapter for the WinRDBI educational tool, which has its own syntax for saving intermediate tables. The book's companion website has the scripts to define and populate the enterprises in MySQL. As another learning opportunity, use the WinRDBI answers as a basis for working out the solutions in MySQL.

## Practice Problems: INVESTMENT PORTFOLIO

Answer the following practice problems in SQL over the INVESTMENT PORTFOLIO schema (see Figure 2.18 for the visual relational schema and Figure 2.16 for its conceptual design as an ER diagram):

```
client(taxPayerID, name, address)
stock(sTicker, sName, rating, prinBus, sHigh, sLow, sCurrent, ret1Yr, ret5Yr)
mutualFund(mTicker, mName, prinObj, mHigh, mLow, mCurrent, yield, familyID)
fundFamily(familyID, company, cAddress)
stockPortfolio(taxPayerID, sTicker, sNumShares)
mutualFundPortfolio(taxPayerID, mTicker, mNumShares)
```

1. What clients have invested in which 'A' rated stocks?
   (taxPayerID, name, sTicker, sName)

2. Which clients have invested in both stocks whose principal business is 'Technology' and mutual funds having growth ('G') as a principal objective?
   (taxPayerID, name)

3. What clients have not invested in mutual funds with income ('I') as a principal objective?
   (taxPayerID, name)

4. Which clients have invested in stocks but not in mutual funds?
   (taxPayerID, name)

5. Which clients have more than one no-rating ('NR') stock?
   (taxPayerID, name)

6. Which clients have invested in only one mutual fund with stability ('S') as a principal objective?
   (taxPayerID, name)

7. Which mutual funds have the minimum current rate?
   (mTicker, mName, minCurrent)

8. What clients have invested in all of the mutual funds within the 'Fictitious' fund family?
   (taxPayerID, name)

9. For each client that has invested in stocks, display the average, minimum, and maximum one-year returns on the stocks they own. Display the result such that lowest average of one-year returns is listed first.
   (taxPayerID, name, avgReturn1Yr, minReturn1Yr, maxReturn1Yr)

10. For each client that has invested in mutual funds, display the sum of the number of shares of mutual funds that they own within each principal objective category. Display the result such that the highest total number of shares is listed first.
    (taxPayerID, name, prinObj, numShares)

# Practice Problems: NEW HOME

Answer the following practice problems in SQL over the NEW HOME schema (see Figure 2.21 for the visual relational schema and Figure 2.19 for its conceptual design as an ER diagram):

homebuilder(hID, hName, hStreet, hCity, hZip, hPhone)
model(hID, mID, mName, sqft, story)
subdivision(sName, sCity, sZip)
offered(sName, hID, mID, price)
lot(sName, lotNum, lStAddr, lSize, lPremium)
sold(sName, lotNum, hID, mID, status)

1. Are there subdivisions that only offer single-story homes?
   (sName, sCity, sZip)

2. List all the homebuilders who offer single-story models with at least 2000 square feet in subdivisions located in 'Tempe'.
   (hName, hPhone)

3. Which lots in the 'Terraces' subdivision are available, i.e. not sold?
   (lotNum, lStAddr, lSize, lPremium)

4. Which models are not currently offered in any subdivision?
   (hName, mName)

5. Which subdivisions offer models from more than one homebuilder?
   (sName, sCity, sZip)

6. Which models are offered in only one subdivision?
   (hName, mName)

7. Which models offered in the 'Foothills' subdivision have the maximum square footage?
   (hName, mName, sqft)

8. Which subdivision offers all the models by the homebuilder 'Homer'?
   (sName, sCity, sZip)

9. For each subdivision, find the number of models offered and the average, minimum, and maximum price of the models offered at that subdivision. Display the result such that the subdivision with the highest average price of a home is listed first.
   (sName, sCity, numberOfModels, avgPrice, minPrice, maxPrice)

10. For each subdivision, find the total of lot premiums for lots that are available. Display the result such that the subdivision having the lowest total premiums is listed first.
    (sName, sCity, totalLotPremiums)

# Practice Problems: WEB PAGE

Answer the following practice problems in SQL over the WEB PAGE schema (see Figure 2.24 for the visual relational schema and Figure 2.22 for its conceptual design as an ER diagram):

> webpage (wID, wTitle, wURL, hits)
> site (sID, sTitle, sURL)
> graphic (gID, gName, gType, src, alt)
> document (dID, dName, dType, dDescription, dDate, downloads, wID)
> internal (sourceID, targetID)
> external (wID, sID, followed)
> displays (wID, gID)

1. Which pages contain a link to SQL ('sql') documents?
   (wID, wTitle)

2. Which pages display graphics having the name 'understandingbook'?
   (wID, wTitle)

3. Which pages do not display any graphics?
   (wID, wTitle)

4. Which pages display 'jpg' graphics but not 'gif' graphics?
   (wID, wTitle)

5. Which pages contain more than one document?
   (wID, wTitle)

6. Which pages contain only one link to an external Web page?
   (wID, wTitle)

7. Which pages have the most hits?
   (wID, wTitle, wURL, hits)

8. Which pages display graphics of all graphic types currently stored in the database?
   (wID, wTitle)

9. For each Web page and graphic type, give the number of graphics of that type displayed on that page. Display the results in ascending order on wID, and within that, in ascending order on graphic type.
   (wID, wTitle, gType, cnt)

10. For each type of document in the database, determine the average, minimum, and maximum number of downloads. Display the results such that the document type with the highest average download is first.
    (dType, avgdownloads, mindownloads, maxdownloads)

# End of Chapter Exercises

Answer the following queries in SQL over the EMPLOYEE TRAINING schema:

> employee(eID, eLast, eFirst, eTitle, eSalary)
> technologyArea(aID, aTitle, aURL, aLeadID)
> trainingCourse(cID, cTitle, cHours, areaID)
> takes(eID, cID, tDate)

1. Which employees took the training course with the title 'Introduction to Databases'?
   (eID, eLast, eFirst, eTitle)

2. Which project leads have not taken a training course in the 'Java' technology area?
   (eID, eLast, eFirst)

3. Which employees took *more than one* course in the 'Database' technology area?
   (eID, numberDBcourses)

4. Who is the lowest paid manager?
   (eID, eLast, eFirst, eTitle, eSalary)

5. What are the titles of employees who earn more than the average 'Project Lead' salary?
   (eTitle)

6. What is the schedule of training courses? Display the results in reverse chronological order, i.e. the most recent date is listed first.
   (tDate, aID, aTitle, cID, cTitle)

7. For each technology area that offers a training course, compute the total number of hours of training offered in that technology area. Display the results so that the technology area with the most hours is listed first.
   (aID, aTitle, numberOfHours)

8. Which database administrators have taken *all* of the 'Database' training courses?
   (eID, eLast, eFirst)
   *Hint: Define a view for courses in the Database technology area and use the view to simplify your query.*

9. For each employee that has taken a training course in a technology area, compute the total number of hours taken in that technology area. Display the result so that the employee with the most hours is listed first.
   (eID, eLast, eFirst, aID, aTitle, totalHours)

10. For each training course that has been offered, find the total number of employees who have taken the course. Display the result so that the training course with the fewest employees is listed first.
    (cID, cTitle, totalEmps)

Data validation is an important feature of database systems. For the following constraints over the EMPLOYEE TRAINING schema, write queries in SQL to find violations of the integrity constraint. You may assume that there are no null values in the database instance.

11. Primary Key Constraint
    Choose one of the tables from the EMPLOYEE TRAINING database schema and write a query in SQL to verify the primary key constraint.
    *Hint: Find values of the primary key that appear more than once in the table.*

12. Referential Integrity Constraint
    Choose one of the referential integrity constraints in the EMPLOYEE TRAINING database schema and write a query in SQL to verify the referential integrity constraint.
    *Hint: Find values of the foreign key that do not appear as a value of the primary key to which it is related.*

Answer the following queries in SQL over the INVESTMENT PORTFOLIO schema:

    client(taxPayerID, name, address)
    stock(sTicker, sName, rating, prinBus, sHigh, sLow, sCurrent, ret1Yr, ret5Yr)
    mutualFund(mTicker, mName, prinObj, mHigh, mLow, mCurrent, yield, familyID)
    fundFamily(familyID, company, cAddress)
    stockPortfolio(taxPayerID, sTicker, sNumShares)
    mutualFundPortfolio(taxPayerID, mTicker, mNumShares)

13. What clients own more than 200 shares of which stocks?
    (taxPayerID, name, sTicker, sName, sNumShares)

14. Which stock's one-year return has outperformed its five-year return?
    (sTicker, sName, prinBus, ret1Yr, ret5Yr)

15. What clients have not invested in stocks with 'Technology' as its principal business?
    (taxPayerID, name)

16. Which clients have invested in mutual funds but not in individual stocks?
    (taxPayerID, name)

17. Which clients have invested in more than one mutual fund with growth ('G') as its principal objective?
    (taxPayerID, name)

18. Which fund families have only one mutual fund?
    (familyID, company, cAddress)

19. Which stocks have the maximum one-year return?
    (sTicker, sName, prinBus, ret1Yr)

20. Which clients have invested in *all* stocks having a one-year return greater than its five-year return?
    (taxPayerID, name)

21. For each mutual fund, find the number of clients that have invested in the fund and the total number of shares of the fund invested by all clients. Display the result so that the mutual fund in which most clients invest is listed first.
    (mTicker, mName, numberOfClients, totalShares)

22. For each client that has invested in stocks, find the sum of the number of shares of stock that they own with each stock rating. Display the result alphabetically by client and within client, display the lowest stock rating first.
    (taxPayerID, name, stockRating, numberOfRatingShares)

Answer the following queries in SQL over the NEW HOME schema:

    homebuilder(hID, hName, hStreet, hCity, hZip, hPhone)
    model(hID, mID, mName, sqft, story)
    subdivision(sName, sCity, sZip)
    offered(sName, hID, mID, price)
    lot(sName, lotNum, lStAddr, lSize, lPremium)
    sold(sName, lotNum, hID, mID, status)

23. Which subdivisions offer models with more than 3000 square feet?
    (sName, sCity, sZip)

24. Which lots in the 'Foothills' subdivision are pending ('P')?
    (lotNum, lStAddr, lSize, lPremium)

25. Which subdivisions do not offer any models?
    (sName, sCity, sZip)

26. Which subdivisions do not have any completed ('C') lots?
    (sName, sCity, sZip)

27. Which models are offered in more than one subdivision?
    (hName, mName)

28. Which homebuilders have only one two-story model?
    (hName)

29. Which models in the 'Terraces' subdivision have the lowest price?
    (hName, mName, minPrice)

30. Is there a subdivision that offers at least one model from all the homebuilders in the database?
    (sName, sCity, sZip)

31. For each homebuilder, find the average price of all models offered. Display the result so that the home-builder who has the lowest average price is listed first.
(hName, avgPrice)

32. For each homebuilder, find the number of subdivisions that offer models of that homebuilder. Display the result so that the homebuilder with the most subdivisions is listed first.
(hName, numberOfSubdivisions)

Answer the following queries in SQL over the WEB PAGE schema:

    webpage (wID, wTitle, wURL, hits)
    site (sID, sTitle, sURL)
    graphic (gID, gName, gType, src, alt)
    document (dID, dName, dType, dDescription, dDate, downloads, wID)
    internal (sourceID, targetID)
    external (wID, sID, followed)
    displays (wID, gID)

33. Which pages contain links to documents named 'emptraining'?
(wID, wTitle)

34. Which graphics in the database are stored as the type Portable Network Graphics ('png')?
(gID, gName, alt)

35. Which pages do not contain any links to documents?
(wID, wTitle)

36. Which pages contain links to external sites?
(wID, wTitle, sID, sTitle, followed)

37. Which pages display more than one 'gif' graphic?
(wID, wTitle)

38. Which pages display only one 'jpg' graphic?
(wID, wTitle)

39. Which document has the fewest downloads?
(dID, dName, dType, dDescription, downloads)

40. Which pages contain links to all SQL ('sql') documents currently contained in the database?
(wID, wTitle)

41. For each page that links to a document, determine the number of documents of each type that are available from the page. Display the results in alphabetical order on the title of the page and, within that, display the document type with the highest number first.
(wID, wTitle, dType, numberOfDocumentType)

42. For each page, determine the number of internal sites that link to that page. Display the results so that the Web page with the most hits is listed first.
(wID, wTitle, hits, numberIncomingLinks)

## Answers to Self-Check Questions

1. select

2. where

3. distinct

4. select *
   from employee
   where eSalary > 75000

5. order by eSalary desc

6. select eSalary, eID
   from employee
   order by eSalary, eID

7. select T.eID, T.tDate
   from takes T, trainingCourse C
   where C.cTitle = 'Big Data' and T.cID = C.cID

8. select T.eID, T.tDate
   from takes T join trainingCourse C on T.cID = C.cID
   where C.cTitle = 'Big Data'

9. select T.eID, T.tDate
   from takes T natural join trainingCourse C
   where C.cTitle = 'Big Data'

10. select T.eID, T.tDate
    from takes T
    where exists     (select *
                      from trainingCourse C
                      where C.cTitle = 'Big Data' and T.cID = C.cID)

11. select T.eID, T.tDate
    from takes T
    where T.cID in   (select C.cID
                      from trainingCourse C
                      where C.cTitle = 'Big Data')

12. select T.eID, T.tDate
    from takes T
    where T.cID =    (select C.cID
                      from trainingCourse C
                      where C.cTitle = 'Big Data')

13. (select E.eID
    from employee E
    where E.eTitle = 'Database Administrator')
    union
    (select T.eID
    from takes T natural join trainingCourse C
    where C.cTitle = 'Data Science')

14. (select E.eID
    from employee E
    where E.eTitle = 'Database Administrator')
    except
    (select T.eID
    from takes T natural join trainingCourse C
    where C.cTitle = 'Data Science')

15. (select E.eID
    from employee E
    where E.eTitle = 'Database Administrator')
    intersect
    (select T.eID
    from takes T natural join trainingCourse C
    where C.cTitle = 'Data Science')

16. select avg(eSalary) as avgmgrsalary
    from employee
    where eTitle = 'Manager'

17. select cID, count(*) as emptotal
    from takes
    group by cID

18. select T.cID, T.tDate, T.eID
    from takes T
    order by T.cID, T.tDate

19. is null

20. count(ATTRIBUTE-NAME) counts the number of non-null values for ATTRIBUTE-NAME in the result.

21. outer join

22. $\pi$ (projection)

23. $\times$ (Cartesian product)

24. all

# Answers to Practice Problems: INVESTMENT PORTFOLIO

1. select    C.taxPayerID, C.name, S.sTicker, S.sName
   from      client C, stock S, stockPortfolio P
   where     S.rating = 'A' and
             S.sTicker = P.sTicker and
             P.taxPayerID = C.taxPayerID;

2. technologyClients :=
   select    distinct P.taxPayerID
   from      stock S, stockPortfolio P
   where     S.prinBus = 'Technology' and S.sTicker = P.sTicker;

   growthClients :=
   select    distinct P.taxPayerID
   from      mutualFund M, mutualFundPortfolio P
   where     M.prinObj = 'G' and M.mTicker = P.mTicker;

   technologyGrowthClients :=
   (select *
    from    technologyClients)

```
          intersect
          (select  *
           from    growthClients);

          select    C.taxPayerID, C.name
          from      client C
          where     C.taxPayerID in (select * from technologyGrowthClients);

3.  select    C.taxPayerID, C.name
    from      client C
    where     C.taxPayerID not in
                  (select P.taxPayerID
                   from    mutualFund M, mutualFundPortfolio P
                   where  M.prinObj='I' and M.mTicker=P.mTicker);

4.  select    C.taxPayerID, C.name
    from      client C
    where     C.taxPayerID in
                  (select SP.taxPayerID from stockPortfolio SP) and
              C.taxPayerID not in
                  (select MP.taxPayerID from mutualFundPortfolio MP);

5.  moreThanOneNRstock :=
    select    P.taxPayerID, count(*) as numNRstocks
    from      stock S, stockPortfolio P
    where     S.rating='NR' and P.sTicker=S.sTicker
    group by P.taxPayerID
    having    count(*)>1;

          select    C.taxPayerID, C.name
          from      client C
          where     C.taxPayerID in
                        (select M.taxPayerID
                         from    moreThanOneNRstock M);

6.  countSmutualFunds :=
    select    P.taxPayerID, count(*) as numSmutualFunds
    from      mutualFund M, mutualFundPortfolio P
    where     M.prinObj='S' and P.mTicker=M.mTicker
    group by P.taxPayerID;

          select    C.taxPayerID, C.name
          from      client C, countSmutualFunds S
          where     C.taxPayerID=S.taxPayerID and
                    S.numSmutualFunds=1;

7.  minMFcurrent :=
    select    min(M.mCurrent) as minCurrent
    from      mutualFund M;

          select    M.mTicker, M.mName, M.mCurrent
          from      mutualFund M
          where     M.mCurrent = (select minCurrent from minMFcurrent);
```

8. fictitiousFunds :=
   select    count(*) as numberMutualFunds
   from      mutualFund M natural join fundFamily F
   where     F.company='Fictitious' ;

   clientNumberFictitiousFunds :=
   select    taxPayerID, count(*) as numberMutualFunds
   from      (mutualFundPortfolio natural join mutualFund) natural join
             fundFamily
   where     company='Fictitious'
   group by taxPayerID;

   select    C.taxPayerID, C.name
   from      client C natural join clientNumberFictitiousFunds F
   where     F.numberMutualFunds =
             (select numberMutualFunds from fictitiousFunds);

9. select    C.taxPayerID, C.name, avg(S.ret1Yr) as avgReturn1Yr, min(S.ret1Yr)
             as minReturn1Yr, max(S.ret1Yr) as maxReturn1Yr
   from      client C, stockPortfolio P, stock S
   where     C.taxPayerID=P.taxPayerID and P.sTicker=S.sTicker
   group by C.taxPayerID, C.name
   order by avgReturn1Yr asc;

10. sumSharesByPrincObj :=
    select    P.taxPayerID, M.prinObj, sum(P.mNumShares) as numShares
    from      mutualFundPortfolio P, mutualFund M
    where     P.mTicker=M.mTicker
    group by P.taxPayerID, M.prinObj;

    select    C.taxPayerID, C.name, S.prinObj, S.numShares
    from      sumSharesByPrincObj S, client C
    where     S.taxPayerID=C.taxPayerID
    order by numShares desc;

## Answers to Practice Problems: New Home

1. subdivisionsOfferSingle :=
   select    distinct O.sName
   from      offered O, model M
   where     O.hID=M.hID and O.mID=M.mID and M.story = 1;

   subdivisionsOfferOther :=
   select    distinct O.sName
   from      offered O, model M
   where     O.hID=M.hID and O.mID=M.mID and M.story <> 1;

```
       select  *
       from    subdivision S
       where   exists
                   (select *
                    from    subdivisionsOfferSingle O
                    where   S.sName=O.sName)
               and not exists
                   (select *
                    from    subdivisionsOfferOther D
                    where   S.sName=D.sName);
```

2. 
```
   select  H.hName, H.hPhone
   from    homebuilder H, model M, offered O, subdivision S
   where   H.hID=M.hID and M.story=1 and M.sqft > 2000 and
           M.hID=O.hID and M.mID=O.mID and
           O.sName=S.sName and S.sCity='Tempe';
```

3. 
```
   select  L.lotNum, L.lStAddr, L.lSize, L.lPremium
   from    lot L
   where   L.sName='Terraces' and
           not exists
               (select *
                from    sold S
                where   S.sName=L.sName and S.lotNum=L.lotNum);
```

4. 
```
   select  H.hName, M.mName
   from    homebuilder H, model M
   where   H.hID = M.hID and
           not exists
               (select *
                from    offered O
                where   M.hID=O.hID and M.mID=O.mID);
```

5. 
```
   countBuilders :=
   select  sName, count(distinct hID) as numberBuilders
   from    offered
   group by sName;


   select  *
   from    subdivision S
   where   exists
               (select *
                from    countBuilders C
                where   C.sName= S.sName and C.numberBuilders > 1);
```

6. 
```
   modelsOnlyOneSubdivision :=
   select  hID, mID, count(*) as numberOfSubdivisions
   from    offered O
   group by hID, mID
   having count(*) = 1;


   select  H.hName, M.mName
   from    homebuilder H, model M, modelsOnlyOneSubdivision S
   where   H.hID = M.hID and M.hID=S.hID and M.mID=S.mID;
```

7.  foothillsModels :=
    select   M.hID, M.mID, M.sqft
    from     model M, offered O
    where    M.hID=O.hID and M.mID=O.mID and
                       O.sName = 'Foothills';

    maxSqftFoothills :=
    select   max(sqft) as maxsqft
    from     foothillsModels;

    maxSqftFoothillsModels :=
    select   F.hID, F.mID, F.sqft
    from     foothillsModels F, maxSqftFoothills M
    where    F.sqft=M.maxsqft;

    select   H.hName, M.mName, S.sqft
    from     homebuilder H, model M, maxSqftFoothillsModels S
    where    H.hID=S.hID and M.hID=S.hID and M.mID=S.mID;

8.  homerModels :=
    select   count(distinct M.mID) as numberHomerModels
    from     homebuilder H natural join model M
    where    H.hName='Homer';

    subdivisionsHomerModels :=
    select   O.sName, count(*) as numberHomerModels
    from     offered O natural join model M
    where    M.hID =
             (select H.hID from homebuilder H where H.hName = 'Homer')
    group by O.sName;

    select   S.sName, S.sCity, S.sZip
    from     subdivision S natural join subdivisionsHomerModels H
    where    H.numberHomerModels =
             (select numberHomerModels from homerModels);

9.  select   S.sName, S.sCity, count(*) as numberOfModels, avg(O.price) as
                 avgPrice, min(O.price) as minPrice, max(O.price) as maxPrice
    from     offered O, subdivision S
    where    O.sName=S.sName
    group by S.sName, S.sCity
    order by avgPrice desc;

10. select   S.sName, S.sCity, sum(L.lPremium) as totalLotPremium
    from     subdivision S, lot L
    where    S.sName=L.sName and
             not exists
             (select   *
              from     sold D
              where    D.sName=L.sName and D.lotNum=L.lotNum)
    group by S.sName, S.sCity
    order by totalLotPremium;

# Answers to Practice Problems: WEB PAGE

**1.** select   distinct W.wID, W.wTitle
    from     webpage W natural join document D
    where    D.dType = 'sql';

**2.** select   distinct W.wID, W.wTitle
    from     (graphic G natural join displays D) natural join webpage W
    where    G.gName = 'understandingbook';

**3.** select   W.wID, W.wTitle
    from     webpage W
    where    W.wID not in (select wID from displays);

**4.** jpgGraphics :=
    select   distinct D.wID
    from     displays D
    where    exists
            (select *
             from    graphic G
             where  G.gType = 'jpg' and G.gID = D.gID) ;

    gifGraphics :=
    select   distinct D.wID
    from     displays D
    where    exists
            (select *
             from    graphic G
             where  G.gType = 'gif' and G.gID = D.gID) ;

    select   W.wID, W.wTitle
    from     webpage W
    where    exists (select * from jpgGraphics J where J.wID = W.wID) and
               not exists (select * from gifGraphics G where G.wID = W.wID);

**5.** pagesWithMoreThanOneDoc(wID, cnt) :=
    select   wID, count(*)
    from     document
    group by wID
    having  count(*) > 1;

    select   W.wID, W.wTitle
    from     webpage W natural join pagesWithMoreThanOneDoc P
    order by W.wID asc;

**6.** pagesWithOneLink (wID, cnt) :=
    select   wID, count(*)
    from     external
    group by wID
    having  count(*) = 1;

    select   W.wID, W.wTitle
    from     webpage W natural join pagesWithOneLink P
    order by W.wID asc;

7. mostHits(maxhits) :=
   ```
   select   max(hits)
   from     webpage;

   select   W.wID, W.wTitle, W.wURL, W.hits
   from     webpage W natural join mostHits M
   where    W.hits = M.maxhits;
   ```

8. numberOfGraphicTypes :=
   ```
   select   count(distinct gType) as gTypeCount
   from     graphic;

   numberPageGTypes :=
   select   wID, count(distinct gType) as gTypeCount
   from     displays natural join graphic
   group by wID;

   select   W.wID, W.wTitle
   from     webpage W natural join numberPageGTypes N
   where    N.gTypeCount = (select gTypeCount from numberOfGraphicTypes);
   ```

9. gTypeAndCount (wID, gType, cnt) :=
   ```
   select   D.wID, G.gType, count(*)
   from     displays D natural join graphic G
   group by D.wID, G.gType;

   select   W.wID, W.wTitle, G.gType, G.cnt
   from     webpage W natural join gTypeAndCount G
   order by W.wID, G.gType;
   ```

10. 
    ```
    select   dType, avg(downloads) as avgdownloads,
                 min(downloads) as mindownloads, max(downloads) as
                 maxdownloads
    from     document
    group by dType
    order by avgdownloads desc;
    ```

## Bibliographic Notes

SQL is *the* industry-standard query language. SQL is based on SEQUEL, which was introduced in the mid-1970s as the query language for IBM's System R project (see Chamberlin and Boyce [1974] and Chamberlin et al. [1976]). The original SQL standard was ratified in 1986 by the American National Standards Institute (ANSI) and is informally referred to as SQL-86. The International Standards Organization (ISO) accepted the ANSI standard as an international standard in 1987. This standard was extended to include an integrity enhancement feature in 1989 and is informally referred to as SQL-89. The SQL-92 standard added many features that include explicit support of intersect, except, and join as well as embedded SQL, just to name a few. Additional versions of the standard included support for object-relational databases, XML, and JSON.

Fundamental concepts of querying data are important to understand and extend beyond relational databases. Most big data systems have an SQL-like language available as part of its system architecture. Data scientists who use R, and especially the dplyr package, will see the connection to database querying.

## More to Explore

Practice is essential to understanding the fundamental querying concepts presented in this chapter. SQL is an extensive language with additional features that are outside the scope of this introductory text, such as inline views. To practice fundamental concepts and to explore the additional features of SQL, the author recommends examining the 22 decision support queries of the TPC-H performance benchmark [Council, 2018]. The enterprise is based on customers ordering parts from particular suppliers. The characterization of the 22 queries and a discussion of the use of TPC-H in the database curriculum can be found in Ortiz et al. [2012]. For the more adventurous, there are other languages for querying data besides SQL. For example, the XQuery language is specifically designed to query XML data. LINQ (Language Integrated Query) is a query language that leverages the familiarity with SQL and provides the capability to query collections of tuples, such as in a relational database, a collection of objects, or a collection of XML elements. Dietrich and Chaudhari [2011] illustrate how LINQ can be used in database classes to explore the querying of these various types of collections. Dietrich [2013] overviews the importance of LINQ and why it should be in a computer scientist's toolbox.

# SQL: Beyond the Query Language

**6**

**LEARNING OBJECTIVES**

- To define a relational database schema in SQL satisfying the constraints of the design
- To learn how to manipulate data using insert, update, and delete
- To understand fundamental data security using privileges

Although SQL is short for Structured Query Language, the SQL standard has evolved to include much more than just the query language. There is a data definition language for defining tables and associated constraints on the table and its attributes, including referential integrity. There is also a data manipulation language for inserting, updating, and deleting tuples from tables. In addition, there are language components for defining data access privileges. This chapter highlights these features of a relational database. It is important to note that every database product is an approximation to the SQL standard. When you use a particular database product, it is important to look up the specific syntax it supports.

## 6.1 Data Definition

Chapter 1 introduced the relational data model as a collection of relations. A relation's schema refers to its description, indicating the attributes in the relation. A visual schema of the database includes the tables with their attributes along with yellow gold keys to indicate primary keys and orange keys to denote foreign keys linked to their associated primary keys, illustrating the referential integrity relationship between the tables. Textually, a summary syntax for a relational schema provides the table name with a list of its attributes enclosed in parentheses, underlining the attributes that form the primary key of the table.

The SQL standard provides a sublanguage for defining a database, called a data definition language (DDL). There is a create table statement to define the table attributes with the associated types and constraints, along with any constraints that apply at the table level. Once a table is created, there is support to drop or alter a table's definition. In addition, the DDL supports the ability to define data structures known as indexes to improve the performance of query execution. The create table statement defines tables whose data are stored as facts. There are also virtual tables, called *views*, whose definition is based on a query specification. The view definition is stored as part of the database in a component called a *data dictionary*, which stores the metadata (data about the data) in the database. When the view name is referenced, the query specification is materialized for use in the execution of the referencing query.

> **The SQL DDL specifies the syntax to create, drop, and alter tables.**

> The **create table**
> statement defines
> a table with its
> columns, their
> types, and
> associated
> constraints.
> Composite
> primary or foreign
> key constraints
> must be specified
> as table-level
> constraints.

The **create table** statement defines a table with its attributes, also called columns. Each attribute has a specified type, with the most common types based on character strings and numerics. For example, char(length) denotes a fixed-length character string, whereas varchar(length) means a variable-length character string where length is its maximum size. Examples of numeric types include integer, decimal, float, and numeric. (Check the user manual of the database product for the supported types and descriptions of each type.) Each column has an optional default value specification, which is the word **default** followed by either a literal of the column's type to use as a default value for population or the word null. The optional additional constraints for a column include the constraints mentioned in Chapter 1, which are typically considered part of the relational model, such as the definition of primary keys, referential integrity, unique, not null, and check constraints. Following the list of column definitions is a list of table constraints. If a table has a composite primary or foreign key, these constraints must be defined at the table level since they involve multiple attributes.

## SYNTAX 6.1   Create Table **Statement**

**Summary:**

```
create table TABLE-NAME (
COLUMN-NAME   COLUMN-TYPE
              [DEFAULT-SPEC] [COLUMN-CONSTRAINT],
              ...
[TABLE-CONSTRAINT-LIST] )
```

**Example:**

```
create table employee (
    eID       char(4)       primary key,
    eLast     varchar(25)   not null,
    eFirst    varchar(15)   not null,
    eTitle    varchar(30)   not null,
    eSalary   numeric       not null )
```

> **Part of the**
> **specification of a**
> **referential**
> **integrity**
> **constraint**
> **includes what**
> **action to perform**
> **on a foreign key**
> **when its**
> **referencing**
> **primary key is**
> **updated or**
> **deleted.**

Figure 6.1 shows an abstract specification of column and table-level constraints. Any column or table constraint can be optionally named. The alternatives for column constraints include primary key, not null, unique, check and referential integrity. A check constraint specifies an expression that must evaluate to true for valid data. The specification of a single-attribute foreign key uses the references clause that indicates the referenced table and column name. Recall that referential integrity specifies that if the value of a foreign key attribute is not null, then its value must appear as a primary key value in the referenced table. Therefore, if a foreign key value does not exist as a primary key value, then the database cannot allow the insert or update operation to occur; otherwise, referential integrity would be violated. There are optional clauses when specifying referential integrity that include actions to take when a primary key value is updated or deleted. The decision of what action to take depends on the database application that is being implemented. The no action on an update or delete of a primary key means that if the update/delete would result in a referential integrity violation, then the operation would not be allowed. The cascade option indicates that the update/delete of a referenced primary key would also be applied to the occurrences of the value as a foreign key. (Beware that cascading a delete is a dangerous choice and should only be used when the database application truly warrants this behavior.) The set null action allows the update/delete of the primary key and changes any foreign key references to null, which would not violate referential integrity. Note that this option is only viable if the foreign key attribute is allowed to be null. Another alternative is to

```
COLUMN-CONSTRAINT ::= [constraint CONSTRAINT-NAME]
      primary key | not null | unique | CHECK-CONSTRAINT | COLUMN-REFERENCE
CHECK-CONSTRAINT ::= check (boolean-valued-expression)
COLUMN-REFERENCE ::=
      references REFERENCED-TABLE-NAME [(REFERENCED-COLUMN-NAME)]
      [on update ACTION]
      [on delete ACTION]
ACTION ::= no action | cascade | set null | set default
TABLE-CONSTRAINT-LIST ::= [constraint CONSTRAINT-NAME]
      PRIMARY-KEY-CONSTRAINT | UNIQUE-CONSTRAINT |
      REFERENTIAL-CONSTRAINT | CHECK-CONSTRAINT
PRIMARY-KEY-CONSTRAINT ::=
      primary key (COLUMN-NAME [{,COLUMN-NAME }...])
UNIQUE-CONSTRAINT  ::= unique (COLUMN-NAME [{,COLUMN-NAME}...])
REFERENTIAL-CONSTRAINT ::=
      foreign key (REFERENCING-COLUMN-NAME [{, REFERENCING-COLUMN-NAME }...])
      REFERENCES-SPECIFICATION
REFERENCES-SPECIFICATION ::=
      references REFERENCED-TABLE-NAME
      [(REFERENCED-COLUMN-NAME [{, REFERENCED-COLUMN-NAME }...])]
      [on update ACTION]
      [on delete ACTION]
```

**FIGURE 6.1**  SQL column and table constraints syntax summary.

set the foreign key reference to the column's default value, if specified, which is indicated by the set default option. The table-level constraints are similar to the attribute constraints but involve more than one attribute. Thus, the primary key, unique, and foreign key constraints allow the specification of multiple attributes using a list of attributes separated by commas that are enclosed in parentheses.

A database schema is a collection of relations. Due to referential integrity constraints, the order in which the tables are created is important. For the EMPLOYEE TRAINING enterprise, the employee table should be defined first since it does not have any foreign keys. The technologyArea table includes the foreign key aLeadID that references the eID attribute of an employee. The trainingCourse table references the technology area id so must be defined after technologyArea. The takes table is defined last since it has two foreign keys referencing employee and trainingCourse. Typically, the textual create table commands are created in a text editor and saved in a file with a .sql extension. The file can then be executed as a script to define the database.

> The order of the create table statements is important in the creation of a database due to referential integrity constraints.

Figure 6.2 shows the script for creating the EMPLOYEE TRAINING database. The types used are for the MySQL database product. Note that the script shows a type of char(10) for the tDate attribute of takes, which is an XML-compliant textual representation for dates in the format of yyyy-mm-dd. This format is noted in an SQL comment within the script, which consists of two dashes with no spaces. The example uses the XML-compliant character representation rather than a date type to be consistent with the data in the WinRDBI educational tool. Also, this script shows most constraints except unique and check constraints, which are left for additional learning opportunities.

The debugging of the create table script may require that the created tables are removed from the database, so that they can be recreated. This is called *dropping* a table from the database, using the drop table statement, e.g. drop table takes. The SQL standard supports the

```
create table employee (
      eID        char(3)        primary key,
      eLast      varchar(20)    not null,
      eFirst     varchar(20)    not null,
      eTitle     varchar(30)    not null,
      eSalary    numeric        not null );

create table technologyArea (
      aID        char(2)        primary key,
      aTitle     varchar(20)    not null,
      aURL       varchar(50)    not null,
      aLeadID    char(3),
      foreign key(aLeadID) references employee(eID) );

create table trainingCourse (
      cID        char(4)        primary key,
      cTitle     varchar(30)    not null,
      cHours     integer        not null,
      areaID     char(2)        not null,
      foreign key(areaID) references technologyArea(aID) );

create table takes (
      eID        char(3)        not null,
      cID        char(4)        not null,
      tDate      char(10)       not null, - - yyyy-mm-dd
      primary key(eID,cID),
      foreign key(eID) references employee(eID),
      foreign key(cID) references trainingCourse(cID) );
```

**FIGURE 6.2**
Script for creating the
EMPLOYEE TRAINING
database.

> **The drop table statement removes a table from the database. The order of dropping tables must consider referential integrity.**

specification of an optional restrict or cascade after the table name. The restrict option is the default and is typically not listed, meaning that if the table to be dropped is referenced by an integrity constraint (or view definition), then the drop table command will fail. The cascade option will implicitly drop any referencing integrity constraints (and views) and the implicit drops will also be cascaded, allowing for the success of the specified drop table statement. Again, cascading drops should be used carefully. Typically, drop table statements use the default restrict option and are specified in the reverse order of the create table statements due to referential integrity constraints. For EMPLOYEE TRAINING, the order of the tables to drop is: takes, trainingCourse, technologyArea, employee.

## SYNTAX 6.2   Drop Table Statement

**Summary:**

  drop table TABLE-NAME [restrict | cascade]

**Example:**

  drop table takes

Once tables are created and populated, there may be a need to alter the table's definition, such as adding or dropping a column or a constraint. SQL provides an alter table statement. To add a column to an existing table, the value for the new column must be either null or a specified default value. One can change an existing column by setting or dropping a default value.

An existing column can also be dropped with a restrict or cascade option having similar meaning to these options on a drop table command. Similarly, a table-level constraint can be added or dropped. To drop a table-level constraint, it must be named with the specification of a restrict or cascade option.

## SYNTAX 6.3  Alter Table Statement

**Summary:**

```
alter table TABLE-NAME
    { CHANGE-COLUMN | CHANGE-CONSTRAINT }
CHANGE-COLUMN ::=
    add [column] column-name column-type [DEFAULT-SPEC]
    | alter [column] column-name
    { set DEFAULT-SPEC | drop default }
    | drop [column] column-name { restrict | cascade }
CHANGE-CONSTRAINT ::=
    add TABLE-CONSTRAINT
    | drop constraint CONSTRAINT-NAME { restrict | cascade }
```

**Example:**

```
alter table employee
    add column lastReviewDate char(10)
```

The use of the alter table statement is required when there are referential integrity dependencies that form a cycle. Consider an employee who must work in a department and a department that has a manager who is an employee. There is no way to order the create table statements to satisfy a cyclic dependency. Thus, the referential integrity constraint on the mgrid attribute can be added to the dept table with an alter table statement. The mgrid attribute must be allowed to have a null value so that the database can be populated. The dept table would be populated first, followed by the emp table, and then the value of the mgrid attribute can be assigned a valid employee id value.

> Use alter table statements to add constraints when there are cyclic referential integrity dependencies.

```
create table dept (
    deptid    char(3)        primary key,
    dname     varchar(30)    unique,
    mgrid     char(3)
);
create table emp (
    empid     char(3)        primary key,
    ...,
    deptid    char(3)        references dept(deptid)
);
alter table dept
    add foreign key mgrid references employee(empid);
```

## SPECIAL TOPIC 6.4  Create Index

An index is a data structure that can be created on a column or a combination of columns to improve performance. Instead of searching through all items, the index provides a mechanism to narrow the search. (As an example, the contact list on a cell phone typically provides an index of the letters of the alphabet so that you can jump to that letter to find the contact rather than searching through all contacts.) Note that there is a trade-off in improving querying performance for the cost of maintaining the index during population and updates.

For most database products, the definition of a primary key automatically creates a unique index on the primary key attributes. A unique index means that the data structure is built to take advantage of the fact that primary key values are unique. Indexes may be useful to other attributes besides the primary key. For example, defining an index on a foreign key can improve the efficiency of joining tables on the primary–foreign key relationship. In this case, the index is not unique since a foreign key value may appear multiple times in the table.

The capabilities of each database product for the definition of indexes vary, as well as the specifics of the syntax. Consult the manual for the database product to determine the details for creating an appropriate index.

---

> **The create view statement defines a name given to an SQL query that is executed to compute its tuples on each reference to the virtual table.**

A view is a definition of a virtual table, which is a name given to the SQL query to execute to compute its tuples. Each time the view name is referenced, the view's defining expression from the data dictionary is executed. The general syntax for defining a view is

create view VIEW-NAME [(COLUMN-LIST)] as VIEW-EXPRESSION

The COLUMN-LIST is optional. If not specified, the database system infers the names of the attributes from the list of attributes in the select clause. However, any columns that have an implementation-dependent name, such as the result of aggregation, should be renamed.

### SYNTAX 6.5    Create View Statement

Summary:

create view VIEW-NAME [(COLUMN-LIST)] as
    VIEW-EXPRESSION

Example:

create view dbas as
    select *
    from employee
    where eTitle = 'Database Administrator'

---

Similarly, a view can be dropped from the data dictionary using the following syntax:

drop view VIEW-NAME { restrict | cascade }

The restrict option will not remove the view if it is referenced by another view (or integrity constraint), whereas cascade will drop any referencing components as well so that the drop will always succeed.

## Self Check

1. Assuming that the EMPLOYEE TRAINING database has been defined using the script shown in Figure 6.2, write a statement that will succeed in removing the employee table.

2. Assuming that the dept table has been created as shown earlier in this section, write an alter table statement to enforce a constraint that a manager can manage at most one department.

3. Write a view definition that finds the number of employees who took each course in the database, having schema cID and empTotal, where empTotal is the name of the resulting column for the aggregation.

> **The SQL DML specifies the syntax for insert, update, and delete of table data.**

## 6.2  Data Manipulation

The SQL standard also provides a sublanguage for insert, update, and delete, called the data manipulation language (DML). (Technically, the select statement of the query language is part of the DML but Chapter 5 covered the querying aspect.) The insert statement adds new rows to a table, either with explicit values or the result of a query expression. The update statement modifies rows in a table, with a single update statement potentially revising multiple rows. Similarly, delete removes potentially many rows from a table.

# Insert

The insert into statement provides a mechanism to insert tuples into the named table according to an optional ATTRIBUTE-LIST using the specified SOURCE.

> insert into TABLE-NAME [(ATTRIBUTE-LIST)]
> SOURCE

> **The** insert into **statement inserts tuples into the named table, using either a list of explicit values or a query expression.**

The SOURCE of the insert into statement is either a list of explicit values or a select expression. In either case, if a column of TABLE-NAME is not included in the ATTRIBUTE-LIST, then a default value is assigned for that column. Note that if an omitted column does not have a default value specified in the DDL for TABLE-NAME, then the insert results in an error. If ATTRIBUTE-LIST is not specified, then a left-to-right ordering of the attributes within that table is assumed.

## SYNTAX 6.6    Insert into **Statement**

Summary:

    insert into TABLE-NAME [(ATTRIBUTE-LIST)]
    values (EXPLICIT-VALUES)

or

    insert into TABLE-NAME [(ATTRIBUTE-LIST)]
    SELECT-STATEMENT

Examples:

    insert into employee(eID, eLast, eFirst, eTitle, eSalary)
    values ('222', 'Last222', 'First222',
            'Software Engineer', 51722)

or

    insert into managers
    select eID
    from employee
    where eTitle = 'Manager'

Recall that the order of the create table statements is an important consideration when creating the database schema due to referential integrity constraints. Similarly, referential integrity constraints impact the order in which the tables are populated. For an insert to succeed, any of its non-null foreign key values must appear as a value in its referenced primary key. In the EMPLOYEE TRAINING database, employee must be populated before technologyArea, which must be populated before trainingCourse. The table takes is populated last because it needs its foreign key values for eID and cID to be in the employee and trainingCourse tables, respectively.

> **Referential integrity constraints also impact the order of data population.**

The insert into values syntax inserts a single row in the table. To insert multiple rows at the same time, most database products support listing multiple tuples separated by a comma. As an example, consider the following multi-row insert in MySQL for the rows shown in Figure 1.7 of the employee table:

    insert into employee(eID, eLast, eFirst, eTitle, eSalary)
    values    ('222', 'Last222', 'First222', 'Software Engineer', 51722),
              ('321', 'Last321', 'First321', 'Database Administrator', 68321),
              ('666', 'Last666', 'First666', 'Project Lead', 66666),
              ('999', 'Last999', 'First999', 'Manager', 100999)

The insert into select syntax is inserting multiple rows that are the result of a query expression. The table into which the rows are inserted must be already defined by a create table statement. A simple scenario is to use the statement to copy one table to another or to save a copy of some of the rows of another table. The column names of the resulting select query should match the table. If the scenario is to use the select attributes to populate only some of the attributes in the table, then the column list must be specified with the remaining columns being populated through a default or null value.

Another scenario for insert into select is to maintain a snapshot or materialized view. Recall that a view represents a derived query expression. This query can be quite complex and, based on the size of the database, can be costly to recompute on each reference. Based on the database application requirements, it may be more efficient to store the result of the derived query expression in a table and just use the table. However, note that if the data in the tables referenced by the select changes, then the snapshot is out-of-date. This snapshot approach may be chosen if the underlying data does not change dynamically but at fixed points in time, at which point, the rederivation of the materialized view can be recomputed. An example of this may be a scientific database that is populated with curated models on a recurring basis, perhaps weekly. But in the interim, there are numerous Web searches over this database that need the derived query expression to return a result in a reasonable amount of time.

## SPECIAL TOPIC 6.7   Database Population

Besides the insert into statement in SQL, most database products support the import of data from a csv file, for example. The table has to be created in the database and the columns in the spreadsheet need to match the order of the attributes in the table. Although this sounds straightforward, there are many practical concerns, such as the type of quote used to represent strings and date-time formats. For example, some databases use a single quote for strings, another uses double quotes, and yet another uses either single or double quotes. With respect to representing date-time, it is highly recommended to refer to the manual for the specific format of the database that you are using as well as to determine what the default format setting is for the date-time.

## Update

| |
|---|
| The update statement modifies a table using a set clause for assignment statements with an optional where clause. |

An update statement specifies the table to update. The set clause consists of a list of assignment statements separated by commas that assigns the value specified to the named column of the table. The value is a literal or expression that has a single value or one of the keywords: default or null. There is an optional where clause that restricts the rows of the table to be updated. If the where clause is not present, then all rows of the table are updated.

## SYNTAX 6.8   Update Statement

**Summary:**

```
update    TABLE-NAME
set       COLUMN-NAME = VALUE-EXPRESSION, ...
[where    UPDATE-CONDITION]
```

**Example:**

```
update technologyArea
set aLeadID = '888'
where aTitle = 'Database'
```

Multiple columns can be modified with one update statement. Consider the promotion of an employee that requires both a change in title and salary:

```
update employee
set eTitle = 'Sr Software Engineer', eSalary = eSalary * 1.10
where eID = '222'
```

The sample update promotes employee with id '222' to a 'Sr Software Engineer' with a 10% raise. This example illustrates that the VALUE-EXPRESSION can be a string literal value or a mathematical expression.

The VALUE-EXPRESSION of an update can also be an SQL query that returns a single row having a single column. Consider a university example, where a student's major is stored in the database as a specific code. Assume there is a majormap table that contains the mapping of the majortitle to majorcode, where majorcode is the primary key and majortitle has a unique constraint because there cannot exist two different major codes for the same major title. The following example updates a student's major to the result of looking up the major code for 'Interdisciplinary Studies':

```
update student
set majorcode =      (select majorcode
                     from majormap
                     where majortitle = 'Interdisciplinary Studies')
where sID = '234'
```

If the query does not return a single value for a single row, then a run-time exception will occur and the update statement will fail.

The update example of a student's major illustrated the use of a lookup of a primary key value to assign to a foreign key. If an update statement is assigning a foreign key based on a literal value that does not appear as a referenced primary key value, then referential integrity would be violated. Thus, such an update would not be allowed.

> **Updating the value of a foreign key must satisfy referential integrity.**

Besides the update statement, an update can also occur if the on update clause of the referential integrity constraint specified an action other than no action. For a cascade specification, when a primary key value is updated, then all of its occurrences as a foreign key value would be automatically updated. For the set null or set default actions, an update to a primary key results in setting its corresponding foreign keys to either null or its default value, respectively.

## Delete

The delete statement removes tuples from the table specified. The optional where clause restricts the delete operation to the rows that satisfy the DELETE-CONDITION. If the where clause is not specified, then all rows of the table are deleted.

> **The delete statement removes tuples from a table with an optional where clause.**

**SYNTAX 6.9   Delete Statement**

| Summary: | Example: |
|---|---|
| delete   from TABLE-NAME<br>[where   DELETE-CONDITION] | delete   from takes<br>where   eID = '123' |

| A delete of a primary key value uses the referential integrity specification to determine the action to take. |
| :--- |

Recall that there is an on delete clause specification when declaring a referential integrity constraint. The no action option means that a delete statement will fail if the delete removed the value of a primary key referenced by a foreign key. For the options set null or set default, the referencing foreign key value would automatically be set to null or the attribute's default value, respectively. The cascade option cascades the delete by removing all rows having a foreign key referencing the deleted primary key. This is a dangerous option to use and should only be used when warranted by the application.

## Self Check

4. For the Employee Training database, insert a new employee with attribute values of your choice.

5. Assuming the dept table defined earlier with schema dept(deptid, dname, mgrid), update the manager of the 'Research' department to the employee with id '123'.

6. For the Employee Training database, write a statement to remove all rows in the takes table.

## 6.3 Database User Privileges

| Use grant and revoke statements to manage privileges on a database table. |
| :--- |

The security component of a database system is responsible for enforcing the access rules based on the discretionary privileges on a database object. There are account-level privileges for creating, dropping, or altering database components, such as tables and views. These would be typically granted by a database administrator. This discussion covers the table privileges that are granted to or revoked from an authorized database user on a table. In this exposition, the table refers to either a stored table or a virtual table. The owner of the database table is the authorized database user who created the table. The table owner is automatically granted all table privileges on the created table. The owner of the table may then use the grant and revoke statements to manage the privileges on the database table.

The table privileges include select, insert, update, delete and references. An authorized database user must have the select table privilege to access any column of a table. To insert data into a table requires the insert table privilege, which can be restricted to specify a list of named columns. Similarly, the update privilege allows a user to update data in a table, and this privilege can be restricted to specify the columns of the table that the authorized user is allowed to update. An authorized database user must have the delete table privilege to delete any tuples from a table. The references table privilege, which may be restricted to columns of a table, allows the referencing of the table columns in the specification of an integrity constraint. There is also an all privileges option, i.e. all of the privileges that the authorized database user has on the table, which is not all possible privileges for the table unless they are the owner of the table. Table 6.1 provides a list of table privileges, indicating whether that privilege can be restricted to some of the columns in the table.

The grant statement adds the list of privileges on the given tables, with optional column restrictions, to the list of users specified. Note that the keyword public refers to all authorized database users but providing privileges to public is not common. Assume that there is a training group that is responsible for the technical training courses and enrollment for those courses within the company, and that the training database user is the owner of the takes, trainingCourse, and technologyArea tables. The example in Syntax 6.10 for the grant statement shows the granting of the select privilege on the these tables to humanResources so that they can determine the skill set of an employee.

Table 6.1 **Table Privileges**

| Privilege | Restrict to a list of columns |
|---|---|
| select | |
| insert | √ |
| update | √ |
| delete | |
| references | √ |
| all privileges | |

## SYNTAX 6.10 Grant Statement

**Summary:**

| grant | PRIVILEGE-LIST |
|---|---|
| on | TABLE-COLUMN-LIST |
| to | USER-LIST |
| [with grant option] | |

**Example:**

| grant | select |
|---|---|
| on | takes, trainingCourse, technologyArea |
| to | humanResources |

When granting privileges, the user granting the privileges may optionally specify the with grant option, which allows the user to grant these privileges (or a subset thereof) to other authorized database users. Assume that humanResources is the owner of the employee table. In order for the training group to be able to populate the takes table, the humanResources user must have granted the references privilege on the eID attribute of the employee table to the training user so that the employee identification number entered in the takes table can be verified for referential integrity. The with grant option allows the training user to grant this references privilege on eID to another authorized database user.

> **The** with grant option **allows users to grant their privileges to other users.**

| grant | reference(eID) |
|---|---|
| on | employee |
| to | trainingCoordinator |
| with grant option | |

The revoke statement removes the list of privileges on the given tables from the list of users specified. There is an optional grant option for clause that just removes the user's ability to grant that privilege, essentially dropping the initial with grant option. The SQL standard specifies a restrict or cascade option on the revoke that is related to privileges granted by an authorized database user who is not the owner. If a user was granted a privilege with grant option and granted that privilege to another user, then the transitive grant of the privilege is known as a *dependent* privilege. The restrict specification on a revoke will fail if there are dependent privileges. A revoke with a cascade specification will succeed if there are any dependent privileges by cascading the revocation by dropping the dependent privileges.

## SYNTAX 6.11 Revoke Statement

**Summary:**

| revoke | [grant option for] PRIVILEGE-LIST |
|---|---|
| on | TABLE-COLUMN-LIST |
| from | USER-LIST { cascade | restrict } |

**Example:**

| revoke | select |
|---|---|
| on | takes |
| from | humanResources |

> **Use views in conjunction with privileges for data security to restrict select access to columns of a table.**

Views also provide a mechanism that works in conjunction with privileges for data security. The insert, update, and reference table privileges can be restricted to specify a list of named columns. However, the select table privilege gives the user access to any column of a table. To restrict a user's access to only some of the columns of a table, a view can be defined on that table to project the desired attributes. A grant statement of the select table privilege on the view allows select access to only those columns provided in the view.

The training department would like the ability to print out a roster of the employees taking a training course on a particular date, which includes the employee names. To allow this capability, humanResources creates an employeenames view with the eID, eLast, and eFirst attributes and grants the select access privilege on the view. The training department can then join takes with employeenames to produce a roster.

```
create    view employeenames as
select    eID, eLast, eFirst
from      employee;

grant     select
on        employeenames
to        training;
```

## Self Check

7.  What privileges would an authorized database user need in order to execute the update statement that promotes employee with id '222' to a 'Sr Software Engineer' with a 10% raise?

8.  Assume that the training department created a view named roster that has just the employee names for a particular course. Write a statement that allows the user instructor to access the roster.

9.  Write a statement that removes the instructor's access to the roster by the training department after the course is taught.

## Chapter Notes Summary

### Data Definition

*   The SQL DDL specifies the syntax to create, drop, and alter tables.
*   The create table statement defines a table with its columns, their types, and associated constraints. Composite primary or foreign key constraints must be specified as table-level constraints.
*   Part of the specification of a referential integrity constraint includes what action to perform on a foreign key when its referencing primary key is updated or deleted.
*   The order of the create table statements is important in the creation of a database due to referential integrity constraints.
*   The drop table statement removes a table from the database. The order of dropping tables must consider referential integrity.
*   Use alter table statements to add constraints when there are cyclic referential integrity dependencies.
*   The create view statement defines a name given to an SQL query that is executed to compute its tuples on each reference to the virtual table.

## Data Manipulation

- The SQL data manipulation language specifies the syntax for insert, update, and delete of table data.
- The insert into statement inserts tuples into the named table, using either a list of explicit values or a query expression.
- Referential integrity constraints also impact the order of data population.
- The update statement modifies a table using a set clause for assignment statements with an optional where clause.
- Updating the value of a foreign key must satisfy referential integrity.
- The delete statement removes tuples from a table with an optional where clause.
- A delete of a primary key value uses the referential integrity specification to determine the action to take.

## Database User Privileges

- Use grant and revoke statements to manage privileges on a database table.
- The with grant option allows users to grant their privileges to other users.
- Use views in conjunction with privileges for data security to restrict select access to columns of a table.

# Chapter Reminders

Figure 6.3 provides a syntax summary of the SQL statements that comprise the heart of its DDL (create, drop, alter), its data manipulation language (insert, update, delete), and data security with respect to access privileges (grant, revoke).

# Practice

There are practice questions related to each of the enterprises introduced earlier in the text: INVESTMENT PORTFOLIO, NEW HOME, and WEB PAGE. The book's companion website has the scripts to define and populate the enterprises in MySQL. There are sample answers provided at the end of the chapter after the solutions to the self-check questions.

# Practice Problems: INVESTMENT PORTFOLIO

Answer the following practice problems over the INVESTMENT PORTFOLIO schema (see Figure 2.18 for the visual relational schema and Figure 2.16 for its conceptual design as an ER diagram):

```
client(taxPayerID, name, address)
stock(sTicker, sName, rating, prinBus, sHigh, sLow, sCurrent, ret1Yr, ret5Yr)
mutualFund(mTicker, mName, prinObj, mHigh, mLow, mCurrent, yield, familyID)
fundFamily(familyID, company, cAddress)
stockPortfolio(taxPayerID, sTicker, sNumShares)
mutualFundPortfolio(taxPayerID, mTicker, mNumShares)
```

1. Provide the order in which the create table statements should be executed, taking into consideration the primary–foreign key dependencies.

2. Write the definition of the primary key for stockPortfolio as a table-level constraint.

3. Write the definition of all foreign key constraints for stockPortfolio as table-level constraints.

```
create table TABLE-NAME (
COLUMN-NAME   COLUMN-TYPE
                   [DEFAULT-SPEC] [COLUMN-CONSTRAINT],
                   …
[TABLE-CONSTRAINT-LIST] )
```

```
drop table TABLE-NAME [restrict | cascade]
```

```
alter table TABLE-NAME { CHANGE-COLUMN | CHANGE-CONSTRAINT }
CHANGE-COLUMN ::=
                   add [column] column-name column-type [DEFAULT-SPEC]
                   | alter [column] column-name { set DEFAULT-SPEC | drop default }
                   | drop [column] column-name { restrict | cascade }
CHANGE-CONSTRAINT ::=
                   add TABLE-CONSTRAINT
                   | drop constraint CONSTRAINT-NAME { restrict | cascade }
```

```
create view VIEW-NAME [(COLUMN-LIST)] as VIEW-EXPRESSION
```

```
insert into TABLE-NAME [(ATTRIBUTE-LIST)]
values (EXPLICIT-VALUES)
```

```
update          TABLE-NAME
set             COLUMN-NAME = VALUE-EXPRESSION, …
[where          UPDATE-CONDITION]
```

```
delete          from TABLE-NAME
[where          DELETE-CONDITION]
```

```
grant              PRIVILEGE-LIST
on                 TABLE-COLUMN-LIST
to                 USER-LIST
[with grant option]
```

```
revoke             [grant option for] PRIVILEGE-LIST
on                 TABLE-COLUMN-LIST
from               USER-LIST { cascade | restrict }
```

**FIGURE 6.3**   Syntax summary: DDL, DML, and user access privileges.

4. Provide the order in which the drop table statements should be executed, taking into consideration the primary–foreign key dependencies.

5. Write an alter table statement to add a check constraint validating the rating of a stock.

6. Write an insert statement to insert a new stock with attribute values of your choice.

7. Write an update statement to change the rating of a stock in the database.

8. Write a delete statement to remove the stock that you just inserted since it will not be involved in relationship instances.

9. Write a grant statement to provide the select privilege and the ability to change the client's address to adminassistant for the client table.

10. Write a revoke statement to remove the update privileges that were granted in the previous question.

# Practice Problems: New Home

Answer the following practice problems over the New Home schema (see Figure 2.21 for the visual relational schema and Figure 2.19 for its conceptual design as an ER diagram):

> homebuilder(<u>hID</u>, hName, hStreet, hCity, hZip, hPhone)
> model(<u>hID, mID</u>, mName, sqft, story)
> subdivision(<u>sName</u>, sCity, sZip)
> offered(<u>sName, hID, mID</u>, price)
> lot(<u>sName, lotNum</u>, lStAddr, lSize, lPremium)
> sold(<u>sName, lotNum</u>, hID, mID, status)

1. Provide the order in which the create table statements should be executed, taking into consideration the primary–foreign key dependencies.

2. Write the definition of the primary key for offered as a table-level constraint.

3. Write the definition of all foreign key constraints for offered as table-level constraints.

4. Provide the order in which the drop table statements should be executed, taking into consideration the primary–foreign key dependencies.

5. Write an alter table statement to add a check constraint validating the status of a sold lot.

6. Write an insert statement to insert a new subdivision with attribute values of your choice.

7. Write an update statement to change the status of a sold lot from pending to complete.

8. Write a delete statement to remove the subdivision that you just inserted since it will not be involved in relationship instances.

9. Write a grant statement to provide the select privilege and the ability to change the status of a sold lot to salesassociate for the sold table.

10. Write a revoke statement to remove the update privileges that were granted in the previous question.

# Practice Problems: Web Page

Answer the following practice problems over the Web Page schema (see Figure 2.24 for the visual relational schema and Figure 2.22 for its conceptual design as an ER diagram):

> webpage (<u>wID</u>, wTitle, wURL, hits)
> site (<u>sID</u>, sTitle, sURL)
> graphic (<u>gID</u>, gName, gType, src, alt)
> document (<u>dID</u>, dName, dType, dDescription, dDate, downloads, wID)
> internal (<u>sourceID, targetID</u>)
> external (<u>wID, sID</u>, followed)
> displays (<u>wID, gID</u>)

1. Provide the order in which the create table statements should be executed, taking into consideration the primary–foreign key dependencies.

2. Write the definition of the primary key for internal as a table-level constraint.

3. Write the definition of all foreign key constraints for internal as table-level constraints.

4. Provide the order in which the drop table statements should be executed, taking into consideration the primary–foreign key dependencies.

5. Write an alter table statement to add a check constraint validating the gType of graphic.

6. Write an insert statement to insert a new graphic with attribute values of your choice.

7. Write an update statement to change the title of a Web page in the database.

8. Write a delete statement to remove the graphic that you just inserted since it will not be involved in relationship instances.

9. Write a grant statement to provide the select privilege and the ability to change the title of a Web page to webassistant for the webpage table.

10. Write a revoke statement to remove the update privileges that were granted in the previous question.

# End of Chapter Exercises

Recall the MLS Practice Scenario from Chapter 1 about selling houses. There is a multiple listing service (MLS) that provides information about homes for sale. A unique MLS number is assigned to the listing, along with the date and price of the listing. Other required properties to post the listing include the address (street, city, state, zip) and the listing agent with realty. The MLS must also maintain a history of price changes, which is displayed on the Web page with the date and price on that date. Look at the practice answers for a reminder of the suggested tables and constraints on the tables.

1. Write a ddl script to define the tables, including all constraints: primary key, foreign key, not null, and check.

2. Write an insert script to populate the tables with sample data, exercising the constraints defined on the tables.

3. Write a drop script to remove all tables.

4. Write an insert statement to illustrate a price change on an mls listing in your database instance.

5. Write an update statement to illustrate a change in listing agent from the same realty company.

6. Write a delete statement to remove the price change just added. (Note that in reality, the mls service probably does not allow information to be deleted, just changed.)

7. Write a grant statement to the realty's office manager providing the capability to process a price change.

8. Write a revoke statement to remove the privilege just granted.

Recall the COURSE SCHEDULE Practice Scenario from Chapter 1 about university courses that are described in a course catalog with a unique course id, a title, a catalog description, and the number of credits. The schedule for course registration provides a unique line number for a course offering, the course id for the course, the date and time that the course is offered, along with the classroom and the instructor of record. Look at the practice answers for a reminder of the suggested tables and constraints on the tables.

9. Write a ddl script to define the tables, including all constraints: primary key, foreign key, not null, and check.

10. Write an insert script to populate the tables with sample data, exercising the constraints defined on the tables.

11. Write a drop script to remove all tables.

12. Write an insert statement to add another offering of a course in your database instance.

13. Write an update statement to revise the classroom and instructor for the course offering just added.

14. Write a delete statement to remove the course offering that you just added.

15. Write a grant statement to the department's office manager providing the capability to revise the instructor for a course offering.

16. Write a revoke statement to remove the privilege just granted.

Recall the WAREHOUSE Scenario from Chapter 1 described by an ER diagram at the end of chapter exercises that you mapped to a collection of tables represented by the textual summary syntax.

17. Write a ddl script to define the tables, including all constraints: primary key, foreign key, not null, and check.

18. Write an insert script to populate the tables with sample data, exercising the constraints defined on the tables.

19. Write a drop script to remove all tables.

20. Write an insert statement to add another order of a customer for an item, both of which are in your current database instance.

21. Write an update statement to revise the quantity in stock of the item just ordered from one of the warehouses that has enough quantity to fulfill the order.

22. Write a delete statement to remove the order that you just added.

23. Write a grant statement to the warehouse manager providing the capability to revise the quantity in stock of an item in the warehouse.

24. Write a revoke statement to remove the privilege just granted.

# Answers to Self-Check Questions

1. `drop table employee cascade;`

2. `alter table dept`
   `add managesone unique(mgrid);`

3. `create view coursescnt as`
   `select cID, count(*) as empTotal from takes;`

4. `insert into employee`
   `values ('864', 'Last864', 'First864', 'Database Administrator', 86400);`

5. `update dept`
   `set mgrid = '123'`
   `where dname = 'Research';`

6. `delete from takes;`

7. update (at least on the eTitle and eSalary attributes) and select since the salary is referenced on the right-hand side of the expression to compute the raise.

8. `grant select on roster to instructor;`

9. `revoke select on roster from instructor;`

## Answers to Practice Problems: INVESTMENT PORTFOLIO

1. Note that multiple orderings exist. One possible ordering is: client, stock, fundFamily, mutualFund, mutualFundPortfolio, stockPortfolio

2. primary key (taxPayerID, sTicker)

3. foreign key (taxPayerID) references myclient(taxPayerID),
   foreign key (sTicker) references stock(sTicker)

4. Note that multiple orderings exist. One possible ordering is: stockPortfolio, mutualFund Portfolio, mutualFund, fundFamily, stock, client

5. alter table stock add constraint stockrating check (rating in ('NR', 'C', 'A'));

6. insert into stock values ('YZA', 'Stock YZA', 'C', 'Consumer', 2, 12, 20, 8, 2);

7. update stock set rating = 'A' where sTicker='YZA';

8. delete from stock where sTicker='YZA';

9. grant select, update(name, address) on client to adminassistant;

10. revoke update on client from adminassistant;

## Answers to Practice Problems: NEW HOME

1. Note that multiple orderings exist. One possible ordering is: homebuilder, subdivision, lot, model, offered, sold

2. primary key (sName, hID, mID)

3. foreign key (sName) references subdivision(sName),
   foreign key (hID, mID) references model(hID, mID)

4. Note that multiple orderings exist. One possible ordering is: sold, offered, model, lot, subdivision, homebuilder

5. alter table sold add constraint soldstatus check (status in ('P', 'C'));

6. insert into subdivision values ('New Subdivision', 'Phoenix', 85858);

7. update sold set status = 'C' where sName='Terraces' and lotNum=1 and hID='H01' and mID='01';

8. delete from subdivision where sName='New Subdivision';

9. grant select, update(status) on sold to salesassociate;

10. revoke update on sold from salesassociate;

## Answers to Practice Problems: WEB PAGE

1. Note that multiple orderings exist. One possible ordering is: webpage, site, graphic, document, internal, external, displays

2. primary key (sourceID, targetID)

3. foreign key (sourceID) references webpage(wID),
   foreign key (targetID) references webpage(wID)

4. Note that multiple orderings exist. One possible ordering is: displays, external, internal, document, graphic, site, webpage

5. alter table graphic add constraint graphicTypeCheck check (gType in ('jpg', 'png', 'gif'));

6. insert into graphic values ('G20', 'asulogo', 'jpg', 'images', 'ASU logo');

7. update webpage set wTitle = 'WinRDBI Frequently Asked Questions' where wTitle= 'WinRDBI FAQs';

8. delete from graphic where gID='G20';

9. grant select, update(wTitle) on webpage to webassistant;

10. revoke update on webpage from webassistant;

## Bibliographic Notes

The bibliographic notes for Chapter 5 provided several references to foundational articles on SQL. Note that each database product is an approximation to the SQL standard so it is important to reference the User Manual for the particular database product and version that you are using for its syntax and supported features.

## More to Explore

There are several features of SQL that were not covered as part of the chapter. The SQL standard specifies a general create assertion statement, which is essentially specifying an *assertion* that must hold true on the database. The constraints that you learned in the chapter covering primary keys, referential integrity, unique, not null, and check constraints are common constraints that the database system can verify efficiently. A general assertion may be quite complex and would be expensive to validate effectively. Most database systems do not support general assertions. However, there are features, called *triggers*, that can be employed by database professionals to assist in maintaining the integrity of the data by defining actions to perform on specific insert, update, or delete operations to the database. The actions are typically specified by calling stored procedures defined using the programming language for the database product. There is also a field of database research known as *active* databases, which specify event–condition–action rules that when an *event* occurs, if a *condition* holds, then perform the specified *action*.

# 7

# Database Programming

**LEARNING OBJECTIVES**

- To understand how procedural language extensions provide support for stored procedures

- To explain the architecture, security, and resources associated with a call-level interface to databases

- To utilize a call-level interface from a programming language

Up to this point in the text, interactions with the database have been in an ad hoc manner, using client software to issue SQL statements and receiving the results. However, building a database application requires the expressiveness of a general-purpose programming language with additional capabilities, e.g. named blocks, decisions, and iteration. Therefore, every database product has its associated programming language that is tightly coupled with the database system. The SQL standard refers to this capability as *persistent stored modules*. The named block of statements are called *stored procedures*, which provide the ability to encapsulate business logic for maintainability and increased security as well as improved performance.

Besides building a database application, there are many applications written in various programming languages that utilize databases because the amount of data to process will not fit in main memory. Access to the database is through a *call-level interface* in which the program establishes a connection to the database and with that connection, the program can issue statements and call stored procedures based on the program's access privileges. The collection of answers from the database are returned to the programming language, which uses the call-level interface routines to process the answers one tuple at a time. This disparity between database set processing and programming languages is called an *impedance mismatch*.

The goal of this chapter is to provide an overview of stored procedures, call-level interfaces, and, specifically, example call-level interfaces for the Java and Python programming languages. Note that there are also frameworks for call-level interfaces that provide an abstraction layer over these routines to assist in the handling of resources. It is assumed that the reader has some familiarity with programming and, in particular, either Java or Python. Note that the examples provided in this chapter use syntax for the MySQL database. As always, check the user guide for the database product and version that you are using.

## 7.1 Persistent Stored Modules

The term *persistent stored modules* essentially refers to the general-purpose programming language that is closely coupled with the database. One of the most used features is the definition of named blocks of code, generally called *stored procedures*. Just like the use of methods, functions, or procedures in any programming language, one can define a block of code with a name that can take parameters and be called to accomplish a specific task. The stored procedure is compiled and saved as part of the database in the data dictionary. There are multiple advantages to using a stored procedure in addition to encapsulation and maintainability. The stored procedure is now a component of the database to which access privileges are granted for data security. Also, calling a stored procedure residing on the server from a client sending parameters reduces the amount of network traffic compared to sending the entire query each time.

**Persistent stored modules refer to the general-purpose programming language that is tightly coupled with the database product.**

Let's first look at a simple stored procedure to get the names of the employees who lead technology areas. This procedure does not use parameters since it retrieves all employee leads.

```
create procedure get_employee_leads()
    begin
        select eLast, eFirst
        from employee
        where eID in (select aLeadID from technologyArea);
    end
```

Once created, use client software to call the stored procedure: call get_employee_leads().

Now consider generalizing this to a procedure named get_employee_lead that takes a technology area title as a parameter and returns the name of the employee who leads that area. Recall that the title of a technology area is unique. The example component of Syntax 7.1 illustrates the creation of the get_employee_lead procedure. Parameter passing modes in MySQL are in, out, or inout. An in mode means that the procedure must be called with a value for the input parameter, and any changes to the parameter in the procedure will not be returned. An out parameter does not have an initial value that is accessible to the procedure and its assignment in the procedure is returned. An inout parameter may have an initial value and its assignments in the procedure are returned. The type of the parameter should be appropriately defined. In this example, the type of the parameter areaTitle is the same as the type of the aTitle attribute of technologyArea. Use the call statement to call the procedure with the technology area title as a parameter, e.g. call get_employee_lead('Database').

**Stored procedures are named blocks of code with in, out, and inout modes of passing parameters.**

## SYNTAX 7.1  Create Procedure Statement

**Summary:**

```
create procedure PROC-NAME(PARAMETER-LIST)
    begin
        statements;
    end
```

**Example:**

```
create procedure get_employee_lead(in areaTitle varchar(20))
    begin
        select eLast, eFirst
        from employee
        where eID =    (select aLeadID
                        from technologyArea
                        where aTitle= areaTitle);
    end
```

Consider another example stored procedure to illustrate an out parameter, get_course_count, that finds the number of courses available in a technology area given its title. The out parameter is bound to the count. This example also illustrates another version of the select statement, select into, which stores the value in a variable. Note that due to the select into statement, this procedure does not return a result set.

```
create procedure get_course_count(in areaTitle varchar(20), out areaCount int)
    begin
        select count(*) into areaCount
        from trainingCourse
        where areaID = (select aID from technologyArea where aTitle = areaTitle);
    end
```

To call a stored procedure with out parameters in the client, introduce a session variable, which uses the @ symbol before an identifier to denote a variable. The following lines issued in the MySQL client first call the stored procedure and then retrieve the value of the session variable:

```
call get_course_count('Database', @dbcoursecnt);
select @dbcoursecnt;
```

> **Stored functions are named blocks of code that return a value. All parameters to a stored function are input parameters.**

Some databases also allow for stored functions, which is a named block that takes input parameters and returns a value. As illustrated in the last stored procedure, get_course_count, it is common to write a subquery to find the primary key associated with a more readable unique value from the query. Consider writing a stored function to provide a lookup function for this purpose. Note that any parameter to a function must be an in parameter, so there are no mode specifications for a function's parameters. In addition to the main characteristics of declaring a procedure, the function must declare a type to return and return a value at the end of the function. In addition, there is a declaration of whether the function is deterministic, which means given the same input will the function always return the same value. The get_aID function shown in the example of Syntax 7.2 that finds the unique aID based on the unique aTitle is a deterministic function. Using the get_aID function, the last line of the get_course_count stored procedure can be rewritten as where areaID = get_aID(areaTitle).

## SYNTAX 7.2    Create Function Statement

**Summary:**

```
create function FUNC-NAME(PARAMETER-LIST)
returns type
[not] deterministic
    begin
        statements;
        return(value);
    end
```

**Example:**

```
create function get_aID(areaTitle varchar(20))
returns varchar(2)
deterministic
    begin
        declare areaID varchar(2);

        select aID into areaID
        from technologyArea
        where aTitle = areaTitle;
        return(areaID);
    end
```

To call a stored function in the MySQL client, use a set command to assign the value of the stored function to the session variable followed by a select of the session variable to display its value:

```
set @db_aID = get_aID('Database');
select @db_aID;
```

As illustrated in the get_aID function, stored procedures and functions can define variables. In fact, the programming language that is tightly coupled with the database can have compound statements with decisions and iteration. If the procedure has to process a result set from a query inside its body, the language has the concept of a cursor to iterate over the result set. A MySQL cursor points to the actual data in read-only mode and can only process the results from beginning to end. A cursor is first declared for a select statement, followed by handler code for when there is no more data to be retrieved in the result set. An open statement initializes the result set by executing the select statement. A fetch statement retrieves the next row in the result set. Once the entire result set has been processed in its entirety, a close statement closes the cursor and releases it resources, such as memory. The example code shows a procedure that, given a title, returns an email list of all employees with that title as the value of an out variable.

> A cursor provides the ability to iterate over the result set of a query inside the body of a stored procedure or function.

```
create procedure title_email_list(in title varchar(30), out email_list varchar(1000))
begin
      declare done boolean default 0;
      declare email varchar(75) default "";
      declare fname, lname varchar(20);
      declare emp_cursor cursor for
            select eFirst, eLast from employee where eTitle = title order by eLast desc;
      declare continue handler for sqlstate '02000' set done = −1;
      open emp_cursor;
      set email_list = "";
      repeat
          fetch emp_cursor into fname, lname;
          if not done then
                set email = concat(fname,".",lname,"@company.com");
                set email_list = concat(email, ";", email_list);
          end if;
      until done end repeat;
      close emp_cursor;
end
```

This section highlighted the programming language that is tightly coupled with the MySQL database for creating stored procedures and functions that encapsulate business logic and commonly used queries, increasing maintainability and security. The rest of the chapter illustrates how to connect to a database from within a general-purpose programing language using a call-level interface with examples for Java and Python.

## Self Check

1. What is the database terminology for a named block of code in the programming language that is tightly coupled with the database?
2. What are the possible parameter passing modes for stored procedures in MySQL?
3. What is the name of the concept that allows a routine to iterate over a result set from a query inside its body?

## 7.2 Call-Level Interface

> A CLI is a library of routines that the application program calls to interact with the database.

Databases are used by many applications, including Web-based applications, written in a variety of programming languages. A call-level interface (CLI) is a library of routines that the application program calls to interact with the database. This is typical in a client/server environment where the application program running on one machine (the client) calls the routines in the library to interact with the database, residing on a different machine (the server) across a network. Each CLI is programming-language specific although the functionality is similar. There is an additional translation layer between the CLI API and the database that provides DBMS-specific functionality. This component is usually called a driver although adapter and connector are also terms that are used to describe this feature. Figure 7.1 provides an abstraction of the architecture. Specific examples of the use of the Java and Python programming languages to access a database appear later in the chapter.

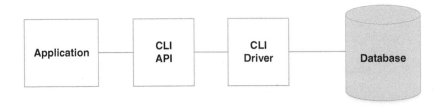

**FIGURE 7.1**
Abstraction of architecture for database application programming.

The application uses the CLI routines to first establish a connection with the database by providing appropriate credentials. Then, using that connection, the application sends SQL requests to the database and processes the results. It is important to note that the application program needs to close the connection to the database before it exits. There are only a certain number of connections allowed to the database, and establishing a connection with the database takes time and resources. In practice, there are libraries that programmers can use to implement *connection pools*, which means that a connection object is placed into a collection and can be reused by the application rather than creating a new one. Also, when dealing with any resources, including database connections, it is best practice to implement exception handling where the handler releases any verified, open resources.

Besides the access privileges already discussed in Chapter 6, there are many concerns regarding database security that must be addressed, especially when the database is connected to a Web application. A significant security vulnerability that must be considered when sending requests from an application to a database is known as *SQL injection*, sometimes abbreviated to SQLi. When user data obtained from the client is sent as part of an SQL request to the database, a malicious user could *inject* code in their input to change the SQL statement being sent from the Web application to the database. The results could compromise the database and even the operating system. SQL injection can be prevented by a database programmer who is knowledgeable about the threat and uses best practices, especially parameterized queries. The specific examples later in the chapter in Java and Python will use parameterized queries for user input.

> SQL injection is a significant security vulnerability for a database Web application that can be mitigated by using best practices.

## Self Check

4.  What is the term used to describe the component that is a translation layer between the API of the CLI and the specific database management system?
5.  What is the name of the security vulnerability in which SQL requests can be modified by malicious user's input?
6.  What is the term used to refer to a collection of resources that are maintained for reuse, such as in database connections?

## 7.3 Java and JDBC

JDBC is a CLI for Java that provides the routines for a Java program to interact with a database. A Java program imports the java.sql package to access these routines. In addition, the system running the Java program must have a driver for the CLI that is specific to the database product being accessed. This should be available from the database product's website for a specific version of the database. Establishing a connection with the database typically requires a url specification and a database username and password. For example,

Connection dbConnection = DriverManager.getConnection(url, username, password);

The url is a string that represents a combination of the driver, the database server, and the port on which to communicate with the database. All interactions with the database should be enclosed within exception handling code to deal with possible exceptions returned from the database.

After establishing a connection to the database, use the Connection object to create an SQL statement to send to the database for execution. There are three types of statement objects for querying the database: Statement, PreparedStatement, and CallableStatement.

> **JDBC is a CLI for Java that provides the routines for a Java program to interact with a database.**

- Statement createStatement()
  A Statement object allows for the execution of SQL statements without any parameters.

- PreparedStatement prepareStatement(String sql)
  A PreparedStatement precompiles the SQL query with input parameters. The value of the input parameters are set using methods of the PreparedStatement interface.

- CallableStatement prepareCall(String sql)
  A CallableStatement allows for SQL queries using stored procedures with input and output parameters. In addition to setting the value of the input parameters, the type of the output parameters must be registered.

A Statement allows the execution of SQL statements without any parameters. The createStatement method on the established database connection instance creates a Statement object. The executeQuery method on the Statement object takes a parameter string, which is the SQL query that is sent to the database. The results are returned in a ResultSet. Remember that a query returns a collection of tuples that represents all answers to the query asked. The programming language must then iterate over each tuple and get the attribute values from the tuple. A ResultSet has a next method that is an iterator over the results. To get the value of an attribute in the current tuple, use the appropriate getTTTT method, e.g. getString, getInt, getLong, for the type of the attribute with the name of the attribute as a parameter. When done processing the ResultSet, it is important to close it to release its resources.

> **A Statement allows the execution of SQL statements without any parameters.**

An example of a simple query using a Statement is shown that simply iterates over the results, calling a method to display the values in a readable format. Note that the code snippet would be enclosed in exception handling code.

```
String query = "select * from employee order by eSalary desc";
Statement stmt = dbConnection.createStatement();
ResultSet rs = stmt.executeQuery(query);
while (rs.next())
{
    String eID = rs.getString("eID");
    String eLast = rs.getString("eLast");
    String eFirst = rs.getString("eFirst");
    String eTitle = rs.getString("eTitle");
    long eSalary = rs.getLong("eSalary");
    // process tuple ...
}
rs.close();
```

Use a
PreparedStatement
to execute SQL
with input
parameters.

A PreparedStatement allows the execution of SQL with input parameters. If the program needs to call the same query multiple times with different parameter values, then it is more efficient to use this construct. The prepareStatement method on the database connection creates an instance of a PreparedStatement with the input SQL query that has the parameter values indicated by a ? in the specification. For example, the following query finds the name of the employee who is the lead for a given technology area where the title of the technology area is a parameter: select eLast, eFirst from employee where eID = (select aLeadID from technology Area where aTitle= ?. The prepareStatement method sends this query to the server, which is then compiled and cached for reuse. Before calling the executeQuery method on the prepared statement, the input parameter values must be initialized. These values are established using setTTTT methods of the appropriate type based on the parameter with the first argument being the indexed position of the ? to which the value is being provided and the second argument being the actual value. The example code below assigns the value of the areaTitle variable to the parameter of the prepared statement and then executes the query. Similarly to a statement, the result set is processed and closed when finished. Again, this code must be enclosed within an exception handling block.

```java
String query = "select eLast, eFirst from employee where eID =" +
    "(select aLeadID from technologyArea where aTitle= ?)";
PreparedStatement pstmt = dbConnection.prepareStatement(query);
pstmt.setString(1, areaTitle);
ResultSet rs = pstmt.executeQuery();
while (rs.next())
{
    String eLast = rs.getString("eLast");
    String eFirst = rs.getString("eFirst");
    // process tuple ...
}
rs.close();
```

Recall that SQL injection is a significant security vulnerability in which user input may inject malicious code changing the SQL query. This could happen when using a Statement object in which the programmer concatenates the user input to the SQL query being sent to the server. *NEVER* concatenate user input to create a query. One of the best practices for dealing with user input is to use parameterized queries in the CLI. For Java, this means using a PreparedStatement. The compilation of the SQL on the prepareStatement call means that the values supplied to the executeQuery method call are treated as parameters and not part of the SQL code. Another approach to parameterized queries for avoiding SQL injection is to call a stored procedure that uses a parameterized query.

Call a stored
procedure using a
CallableStatement.

A CallableStatement allows for calling a stored procedure with input or output parameters. The prepareCall method on the connection instance sends the procedure call with the stored procedure name and a ? for each parameter. In addition to setting the values of input parameters, the types of the output parameters must be *registered*. The registerOutParameter method takes the position of the parameter in the query string as its first argument and the type of the parameter as its second argument. The execute command executes the call of the stored procedure. The getTTTT() method retrieves the value of the output parameter. Consider as an example, the following code snippet to call the get_course_count stored procedure defined earlier in the chapter that finds the count of the number of training courses available in a technology area. The first parameter is the title of the technology area and the second parameter is the output count. Remember that this code snippet would be enclosed in an exception handling block since it interacts with the database.

```
String query = "Call get_course_count(?, ?)";
CallableStatement cstmt = dbConnection.prepareCall(query);
cstmt.setString(1, areaTitle);
cstmt.registerOutParameter(2, Types.INTEGER) ;
cstmt.execute();
int courseCount = cstmt.getInt(2);
```

Chapter 6 covered the data definition and data manipulation components of the SQL language. These DDL and DML commands are handled in JDBC using an executeUpdate method, which returns the number of rows affected. Consider a snippet of code that illustrates the execution of an update statement from Chapter 6, changing the area lead of the 'Database' technology area to a different employee.

```
String query = "update technologyArea set aLeadID='888' where aTitle='Database'";
Statement stmt = dbConnection.createStatement();
int updateCount = stmt.executeUpdate(query);
```

Table 7.1 provides an abbreviated summary of the JDBC API. Note that executeUpdate appears in the Statement interface and it is also available for both a PreparedStatement and a CallableStatement based on inheritance. The JDBC API includes many more features that are beyond the coverage of an introductory text. For example, there are interfaces for determining information about tables, attributes, and result sets. Metadata is a term that means data about data. There are interfaces called DatabaseMetaData and ResultSetMetaData for determining this information dynamically through JDBC.

**Table 7.1  Abbreviated JDBC API**

| Interface *Connection* | |
|---|---|
| Statement | createStatement() |
| PreparedStatement | prepareStatement(String sql) |
| CallableStatement | prepareCall(String sql) |
| **Interface *Statement*** | |
| ResultSet | executeQuery(String sql) |
| int | executeUpdate(String sql) |
| void | close() |
| **Interface *ResultSet*** | |
| *TTTT* | get*TTTT*(String columnName) |
| *TTTT* | get*TTTT*(int columnIndex) |
| void | close() |
| **Interface *PreparedStatement* extends *Statement*** | |
| void | set*TTTT*(int parameter, *TTTT* x) |
| boolean | execute(String sql) |
| **Interface *CallableStatement* extends *PreparedStatement*** | |
| *TTTT* | get*TTTT*(int i) |
| *TTTT* | get*TTTT*(String parameterName) |
| void | registerOutParameter(int parameter, int sqlType) |

## Self Check

7.  What are the components of the url for establishing a connection to a database using JDBC?
8.  When sending queries to the database that incorporate user input in JDBC, should a Statement or PreparedStatement be used? Explain.
9.  What JDBC class should be used to execute a stored procedure?

## 7.4 Python and DB-API

> The DB-API defines a specification for implementations of connectors for accessing databases from Python.

Python has a specification that defines an implementation of database connectivity to increase consistency and portability of Python database applications. This Python Database API (DB-API) defines a specification for implementations of drivers/adapters/connectors accessing databases from Python. There are many choices of modules for interfacing Python with databases. Since MySQL is the database product used for examples in this text, this section uses the MySQLdb module, which is the MySQL implementation of the Python DB-API, to illustrate connectivity to a MySQL database from Python. All operations to the database must be enclosed in exception handling code. Note that the exception handling code has been omitted from the code snippets presented in this section to increase readability.

The first step in accessing a database is to establish a connection. The connect method has named parameters for user, passwd, host, db, and port. For example,

MySQLdb.connect(user=username, passwd=password, host=DBSERVER, db=DATABASE)

creates a connection to the DBSERVER for the user specified. This call assumes the default port for a MySQL database. In MySQL, you can define tables in the context of a named database. Thus, the db parameter specifies the database to which the user wants to connect, which for this example is the employee_training database.

> A cursor object uses the established connection to issue operations to the database.

Using the returned connection object, a cursor method creates a cursor for issuing operations to the database. There are essentially two methods for sending a database command: execute and callproc. The first executes SQL statements and the latter calls a stored procedure. The first argument of the execute method is a string representation of the SQL statement to execute, and the optional second argument is a Python sequence providing parameters, usually represented as a tuple. Similarly, for callproc, its first argument is the name of the stored procedure to call with its second argument providing any optional parameters. There are fetch methods for processing the result set returned by either method. The fetchone method returns the next row in the query result as a sequence or None when the result set is exhausted. There is also a fetchall method that returns the result set (from its current position) as a list of tuples. Once finished processing the result set, close the cursor.

> Use the execute method on a cursor object to execute a query.

Let's first explore a sample query to the database that does not require any parameters. In the code snippet below, the variable dbconnection represents the established connection object to the MySQL database. In this example, the fetchall method called on the cursor object returns a list of tuples, which the code iterates over to access the attributes of each tuple.

```
query = "select * from employee order by eSalary desc";
cursor = dbconnection.cursor()
cursor.execute(query)
results = cursor.fetchall()
for row in results:
    eID, eLast, eFirst, eTitle, eSalary = row[0], row[1], row[2], row[3], row[4]
    # process tuple ...
cursor.close()
```

Parameterized queries also use the execute method of the cursor object with parameter values sent as a sequence in the optional second argument. The specification of the parameter format for the SQL query string is database-specific. MySQL uses the format paramstyle, which means that the percent sign followed by a character designating its type indicates a parameter in the query string. The example parameterized query finds the name of the employee who is the area lead for a technology area given the title of the technology area. This query example illustrates the use of the fetchone method because there is only one lead for a technology area.

```
query = """select eLast, eFirst from employee
     where eID = (select aLeadID from technologyArea where aTitle= %s)""";
cursor = dbconnection.cursor()
cursor.execute(query, (areaTitle,))
result = cursor.fetchone()
# process tuple ...
cursor.close()
```

Recall that parameterized queries are essential for avoiding the SQL injection security vulnerability. In the above example, the parameters are sent to the execute function as its second argument and are, therefore, treated as parameters by the database and must match the specified type. It is important to note here that concatenation as well as string interpolation should *not* be used in Python to create a query specification with user input. The % operator denotes string interpolation, which just concatenates the parameters in the position specified, converting any values into strings. Calling a stored procedure that is parameterized is also another method of avoiding SQL injection.

The callproc method provides the ability to call a stored procedure by name, with the parameters specified as a tuple in the second argument. Input variables just need to have a value before the call. Accessing an output variable requires an additional query to the server. The callproc may return a result set that requires processing in addition to retrieving the values of the output variables. The variables associated with the callproc are stored as server variables that can be queried once the result set has been processed. The server name variables are in the following format: @_procname_#, where procname is the name of the stored procedure and # represents the position of the variable to be accessed relative to 0. In the example stored procedure get_course_count, the first parameter is the input variable and the second parameter is the answer count. Thus, the line cursor.execute('select @_get_course_count_1') queries the database for the server variable in the second position to retrieve the number of courses in that technology area.

> **Call a stored procedure using the callproc method on a cursor object.**

```
cursor = dbconnection.cursor()
cursor.callproc("get_course_count", (areaTitle, areaCount))
# NOTE: No result set for this stored procedure; need to get output variable value
cursor.execute('select @_get_course_count_1')
result = cursor.fetchone()
# process value
cursor.close()
```

The DDL and DML SQL statements are also submitted using the execute method on the cursor. To retrieve the number of rows affected by the statement, there is an affected_rows method on the database connection object. The following code snippet performs the sample update operation from Chapter 6 to update the employee lead for the 'Database' technology area.

```
update = "update technologyArea set aLeadID='888' where aTitle='Database'"
cursor = dbconnection.cursor()
cursor.execute(update)
```

```
update_count = dbconnection.affected_rows()
print("Updated count: " + str(update_count))
cursor.close()
```

This section provided an overview of connecting to databases in Python, using the MySQLdb module that is an implementation of the Python Database API specification. There are additional capabilities that the reader is encouraged to explore.

## Self Check

10. In MySQLdb, what is the name of the method on a connection instance that creates an object for query execution?

11. How is a parameterized query called in MySQLdb?

12. Which MySQLdb method should be used to execute a stored procedure?

## Chapter Notes Summary

### Persistent Stored Modules

- Persistent stored modules refer to the general-purpose programming language that is tightly coupled with the database product.
- Stored procedures are named blocks of code with in, out, and inout modes of passing parameters.
- Stored functions are named blocks of code that return a value. All parameters to a stored function are input parameters.
- A cursor provides the ability to iterate over the result set of a query inside the body of a stored procedure or function.

### Call-Level Interface

- A CLI is a library of routines that the application program calls to interact with the database.
- SQL injection is a significant security vulnerability for a database Web application that can be mitigated by using best practices.

### Java and JDBC

- JDBC is a CLI for Java that provides the routines for a Java program to interact with a database.
- A Statement allows the execution of SQL statements without any parameters.
- Use a PreparedStatement to execute SQL with input parameters.
- Call a stored procedure using a CallableStatement.

### Python and DB-API

- The DB-API defines a specification for implementations of connectors for accessing databases from Python.
- A cursor object uses the established connection to issue operations to the database.
- Use the execute method on a cursor object to execute a query.
- Call a stored procedure using the callproc method on a cursor object.

# Chapter Reminders

Tables 7.2 and 7.3 provide an abstraction of the chapter examples illustrating JDBC and the MySQLdb implementation of the Python DB-API.

**Table 7.2  JDBC Abstraction**

| | |
|---|---|
| Establishing connection | Connection dbconn = DriverManager.getConnection(*url, user, pass*) |
| Executing queries without parameters | Statement stmt = dbconn.createStatement();<br>ResultSet rs = stmt.executeQuery(*query*);<br>while (rs.next())<br>    process result set ...<br>      use get*TTTT*(*attrname*) to retrieve value<br>rs.close() |
| Executing queries with parameters | PrepareStatement pstmt = dbconn.prepareStatement(*query*);<br>use setTTTT(position, value) for input parameter values<br>ResultSet rs = pstmt.executeQuery();<br>process result set as shown for Statement |
| Calling stored procedures | CallableStatement cstmt = dbconn.prepareCall(*query*);<br>use setTTTT(position, value) for input parameter values<br>use registerOutParameter(position, type) for output parameters<br>cstmt.execute()<br>retrieve output parameter values using getTTTT |
| Executing update | int updateCount = stmt.executeUpdate(*query*); |

**Table 7.3  MySQLdb Abstraction**

| | |
|---|---|
| Establishing connection | dbconn = MySQLdb.connect (*user, pass, host, db, port*) |
| Executing queries without parameters | mycursor = dbconn.cursor();<br>mycursor.execute(*query*);<br>results = cursor.fetchall()<br>*process result set ...*<br>mycursor.close() |
| Executing queries with parameters | Similar except parameter values sent as tuple in 2nd argument<br>mycursor.execute(*query, parameters*); |
| Calling stored procedures | mycursor.callproc(*procname, parameters*)<br>retrieve output parameter values using a subsequent select<br>mycursor.execute('*select @_procname_#*') |
| Executing update | mycursor.execute(*update*);<br>updateCount = dbconn.affected_rows() |

# Practice

There are practice problems related to each of the enterprises introduced earlier in the text: INVESTMENT PORTFOLIO, NEW HOME, and WEB PAGE. The book's companion website has the scripts and code to support the sample answers provided at the end of the chapter for these practice problems.

# Practice Problems: INVESTMENT PORTFOLIO

Answer the following practice problems over the INVESTMENT PORTFOLIO schema (see Figure 2.18 for the visual relational schema and Figure 2.16 for its conceptual design as an ER diagram):

```
client(taxPayerID, name, address)
stock(sTicker, sName, rating, prinBus, sHigh, sLow, sCurrent, ret1Yr, ret5Yr)
mutualFund(mTicker, mName, prinObj, mHigh, mLow, mCurrent, yield, familyID)
fundFamily(familyID, company, cAddress)
stockPortfolio(taxPayerID, sTicker, sNumShares)
mutualFundPortfolio(taxPayerID, mTicker, mNumShares)
```

1. Write a stored procedure client_amount_prinObj that finds the clients who have invested more than the input amount in mutual funds having the input prinObj. Return a result set with the client tax-PayerID, name, and total amount invested, illustrating a sample call of the stored procedure from a MySQL client.

2. Write a stored procedure client_stock that, given a stock's name as input, returns the total number of clients that have invested in that stock as an output parameter. Illustrate a sample call of the stored procedure from a MySQL client.

3. Write a function mutual_fund_ticker to find the ticker associated with a mutual fund given its name, illustrating a sample call of the function from a MySQL client.

4. Using JDBC, answer the following query: Which clients have invested in which 'A' rated stocks?

5. Using JDBC, answer the following parameterized query: Given a principal objective as input, which clients have invested in mutual funds with that principal objective?

6. Using JDBC, illustrate a call to the client_stock stored procedure using in and out parameters.

7. Using JDBC, illustrate an update statement to modify the current rate of return for the 'Blue Chip' mutual fund that uses the mutual_fund_ticker function defined earlier.

8. Using MySQLdb, answer the following query: Which clients have invested in which 'A' rated stocks?

9. Using MySQLdb, answer the following parameterized query: Given a principal objective as input, which clients have invested in mutual funds with that principal objective?

10. Using MySQLdb, illustrate a call to the client_stock stored procedure using in and out parameters.

11. Using MySQLdb, illustrate an update statement to modify the current rate of return for the 'Blue Chip' mutual fund that uses the mutual_fund_ticker function defined earlier.

# Practice Problems: NEW HOME

Answer the following practice problems over the NEW HOME schema (see Figure 2.21 for the visual relational schema and Figure 2.19 for its conceptual design as an ER diagram):

```
homebuilder(hID, hName, hStreet, hCity, hZip, hPhone)
model(hID, mID, mName, sqft, story)
subdivision(sName, sCity, sZip)
offered(sName, hID, mID, price)
lot(sName, lotNum, lStAddr, lSize, lPremium)
sold(sName, lotNum, hID, mID, status)
```

1. Write a stored procedure subdivisions_city_sqft that, given a city and a square footage, returns a result set of subdivisions with their zip codes that offer models having at least the input square footage specified and are located in the input city. Illustrate a sample call of the stored procedure from a MySQL client.

2. Write a stored procedure available_lots that, given a subdivision name as input, returns the total number of lots still available for sale. Illustrate a sample call of the stored procedure from a MySQL client.

3. Write a function homebuilder_id to find the unique id associated with a homebuilder given its name, illustrating a sample call of the function from a MySQL client.

4. Using JDBC, answer the following query: Which subdivisions offer lot sizes greater than 20,000 square feet?

5. Using JDBC, answer the following parameterized query: Which subdivisions offer homes by a given homebuilder specified by name? Use the homebuilder_id function defined earlier.

6. Using JDBC, illustrate a call to the available_lots stored procedure using in and out parameters.

7. Using JDBC, illustrate an update statement to modify the lot premiums of unsold lots in the 'Terraces' subdivision by 10%.

8. Using MySQLdb, answer the following query: Which subdivisions offer lot sizes greater than 20,000 square feet?

9. Using MySQLdb, answer the following parameterized query: Which subdivisions offer homes by a given homebuilder specified by name? Use the homebuilder_id function defined earlier.

10. Using MySQLdb, illustrate a call to the available_lots stored procedure using in and out parameters.

11. Using MySQLdb, illustrate an update statement to modify the lot premiums of unsold lots in the 'Terraces' subdivision by 10%.

# Practice Problems: Web Page

Answer the following practice problems over the Web Page schema (see Figure 2.24 for the visual relational schema and Figure 2.22 for its conceptual design as an ER diagram):

```
webpage (wID, wTitle, wURL, hits)
site (sID, sTitle, sURL)
graphic (gID, gName, gType, src, alt)
document (dID, dName, dType, dDescription, dDate, downloads, wID)
internal (sourceID, targetID)
external (wID, sID, followed)
displays (wID, gID)
```

1. Write a stored procedure graphics_on_page that, given a name, returns a result set of Web pages that display that image. Illustrate a sample call of the stored procedure from a MySQL client.

2. Write a stored procedure document_type that, given a type of document, returns the total number of documents of that type. Illustrate a sample call of the stored procedure from a MySQL client.

3. Write a function graphic_id to find the unique id associated with an image given its name, illustrating a sample call of the function from a MySQL client.

4. Using JDBC, answer the following query: Which pages display 'gif' graphics?

5. Using JDBC, answer the following parameterized query: Which pages do not display a graphic specified by name? Use the graphic_id function defined earlier.

6. Using JDBC, illustrate a call to the document_type stored procedure using in and out parameters.

7. Using JDBC, illustrate an update statement to increment by 1 the number of hits for the Web page with id 'W06'.

8. Using MySQLdb, answer the following query: Which pages display 'gif' graphics?

9. Using MySQLdb, answer the following parameterized query: Which pages do not display a graphic specified by name? Use the graphic_id function defined earlier.

10. Using MySQLdb, illustrate a call to the document_type stored procedure using in and out parameters.

11. Using MySQLdb, illustrate an update statement to increment by 1 the number of hits for the Web page with id 'W06'.

# End of Chapter Exercises

Answer the following exercises over the EMPLOYEE TRAINING schema:

    employee(eID, eLast, eFirst, eTitle, eSalary)
    technologyArea(aID, aTitle, aURL, aLeadID)
    trainingCourse(cID, cTitle, cHours, areaID)
    takes(eID, cID, tDate)

1. Write a stored procedure titled_employees that finds the employees who have the given title. Return a result set of employees, illustrating a sample call of the stored procedure from a MySQL client.

2. Write a function course_id to find the course id associated with a training course given its title, illustrating a sample call of the function from a MySQL client.

3. Write a stored procedure emp_course_count that, given a training course title as input, returns the total number of employees who took that course as an output parameter. Use the course_id function in the stored procedure. Illustrate a sample call of the stored procedure from a MySQL client.

4. Using JDBC, answer the following query: For each employee title in the database, find the number of employees having that title.

5. Using JDBC, answer the following parameterized query: Given a course title, find the number of times that the course has been offered.

6. Using JDBC, illustrate a call to the emp_course_count stored procedure using in and out parameters.

7. Using JDBC, illustrate an update statement to modify the number of hours for the 'JDBC' course to 16 hours that uses the course_id function defined earlier.

8. Using MySQLdb, answer the following query: For each employee title in the database, find the number of employees having that title.

9. Using MySQLdb, answer the following parameterized query: Given a course title, find the number of times that the course has been offered.

10. Using MySQLdb, illustrate a call to the emp_course_count stored procedure using in and out parameters.

11. Using MySQLdb, illustrate an update statement to modify the number of hours for the 'JDBC' course to 16 hours that uses the course_id function defined earlier.

Answer the following exercises over the INVESTMENT PORTFOLIO schema:

    client(taxPayerID, name, address)
    stock(sTicker, sName, rating, prinBus, sHigh, sLow, sCurrent, ret1Yr, ret5Yr)
    mutualFund(mTicker, mName, prinObj, mHigh, mLow, mCurrent, yield, familyID)
    fundFamily(familyID, company, cAddress)
    stockPortfolio(taxPayerID, sTicker, sNumShares)
    mutualFundPortfolio(taxPayerID, mTicker, mNumShares)

12. Write a stored procedure clients_stock_invest that finds the clients who have invested in the stock, given the stock's name. Return a result set with the client taxPayerID, name, and number of shares, illustrating a sample call of the stored procedure from a MySQL client.

13. Write a stored procedure fund_family_count that given a fund family name as input, returns the total number of funds in that fund family as an output parameter. Illustrate a sample call of the stored procedure from a MySQL client.

14. Write a function stock_ticker to find the ticker associated with a stock given its name, illustrating a sample call of the function from a MySQL client.

15. Using JDBC, answer the following query: Which mutual funds are in the 'Fictitious' fund family?

16. Using JDBC, answer the following parameterized query: Given a principal business as input, which clients have invested in stock with that principal business?

17. Using JDBC, illustrate a call to the fund_family_count stored procedure using in and out parameters.

18. Using JDBC, illustrate an update statement to modify the current rate of return for the 'Stock ABC' stock that uses the stock_ticker function defined earlier.

19. Using MySQLdb, answer the following query: Which mutual funds are in the 'Fictitious' fund family?

20. Using MySQLdb, answer the following parameterized query: Given a principal business as input, which clients have invested in stock with that principal business?

21. Using MySQLdb, illustrate a call to the fund_family_count stored procedure using in and out parameters.

22. Using MySQLdb, illustrate an update statement to modify the current rate of return for the 'Stock ABC' stock that uses the stock_ticker function defined earlier.

Answer the following exercises over the NEW HOME schema:

    homebuilder(hID, hName, hStreet, hCity, hZip, hPhone)
    model(hID, mID, mName, sqft, story)
    subdivision(sName, sCity, sZip)
    offered(sName, hID, mID, price)
    lot(sName, lotNum, lStAddr, lSize, lPremium)
    sold(sName, lotNum, hID, mID, status)

23. Write a stored procedure models_gtsqft that finds the models by a homebuilder specified by name that are greater than the input square footage. Return a result set with the model name, square footage, and number of stories. Illustrate a sample call of the stored procedure from a MySQL client.

24. Write a stored procedure pending_count that given a subdivision name as input, returns the total number of lots having a pending status as an output parameter. Recall that a pending status means that the lot has been sold and the house has not completed the construction process. Illustrate a sample call of the stored procedure from a MySQL client.

25. Write a function model_id to find the unique model id given its name and the name of the homebuilding. Illustrate a sample call of the function from a MySQL client.

26. Using JDBC, answer the following query: Which subdivisions offer homes under $300,000?

27. Using JDBC, answer the following parameterized query: Which homebuilders build models greater than a specified square footage?

28. Using JDBC, illustrate a call to the pending_count stored procedure using in and out parameters.

29. Using JDBC, illustrate an update statement to modify the status of a pending lot to completed.

30. Using MySQLdb, answer the following query: Which subdivisions offer homes under $300,000?

31. Using MySQLdb, answer the following parameterized query: Which homebuilders build models greater than a specified square footage?

32. Using MySQLdb, illustrate a call to the pending_count stored procedure using in and out parameters.

33. Using MySQLdb, illustrate an update statement to modify the status of a pending lot to completed.

Answer the following exercises over the Web Page schema:

```
webpage (wID, wTitle, wURL, hits)
site (sID, sTitle, sURL)
graphic (gID, gName, gType, src, alt)
document (dID, dName, dType, dDescription, dDate, downloads, wID)
internal (sourceID, targetID)
external (wID, sID, followed)
displays (wID, gID)
```

34. Write a stored procedure graphics_type that finds the graphics that are of the input type. Return a result set with the graphic id, name, src, and alt. Illustrate a sample call of the stored procedure from a MySQL client.

35. Write a stored procedure webgraphics_count that given a webpage id, returns the total number of distinct graphics displayed on that page as an output parameter. Illustrate a sample call of the stored procedure from a MySQL client.

36. Write a function document_id that given a unique document description returns its unique document id. Illustrate a sample call of the function from a MySQL client.

37. Using JDBC, answer the following query: Which pages contain links to documents?

38. Using JDBC, answer the following parameterized query: Which pages display graphics of the input type?

39. Using JDBC, illustrate a call to the webgraphics_count stored procedure using in and out parameters.

40. Using JDBC, illustrate an update statement to update the date of a document in the database.

41. Using MySQLdb, answer the following query: Which pages contain links to documents?

42. Using MySQLdb, answer the following parameterized query: Which pages display graphics of the input type?

43. Using MySQLdb, illustrate a call to the webgraphics_count stored procedure using in and out parameters.

44. Using MySQLdb, illustrate an update statement to update the date of a document in the database.

## Answers to Self-Check Questions

1. stored procedure

2. in, out, inout

3. cursor

4. drive, adapter, or connector

5. SQL injection

6. pool

7. driver, database host server, and port

8. A PreparedStatement must be used to send values to a parameterized query to avoid SQL injection.

9. CallableStatement

10. cursor()

11. After establishing a parameterized query string using the required format, call the execute method, sending the values of the parameters in a tuple as the second argument of the method.

12. callproc

# Answers to Practice Problems: INVESTMENT PORTFOLIO

(See book's companion website for complete code with exception handling.)

1. 
```
create procedure client_amount_prinObj(in amount int, in prinObj char(1))
    begin
        select c.taxPayerID, c.name, sum(mf.mCurrent * mfp.mNumShares) as
            client_total
        from (mutualFund mf natural join mutualFundPortfolio mfp) natural join
            myclient
        where mf.prinObj = prinObj
        group by c.taxPayerID
        having client_total > amount;
        end
```
Call in MySQL Workbench:
```
    call client_amount_prinObj(500, 'G');
```

2. 
```
create procedure client_stock(in stock varchar(20), out client_count int)
    begin
        select count(*) into client_count
        from stock natural join stockportfolio
        where sName = stock;
    end
```
Call in MySQL Workbench:
```
    call client_stock('Stock STU', @number_of_clients);
    select @number_of_clients;
```

3. 
```
create function mutual_fund_ticker(mfname varchar(25))
    returns varchar(5)
    deterministic
    begin
        declare mfticker varchar(5);
        select mTicker into mfticker
        from mutualFund
        where mName = mfname;
        return(mfTicker);
    end
```

4.
```
String query = "select c.taxPayerID, c.name, s.sTicker, s.sName"
    + "from (myclient c natural join stockPortfolio sp) natural join stock s"
    + "where s.rating = 'A' ";
Statement stmt = dbConnection.createStatement();
ResultSet rs = stmt.executeQuery(query);
while (rs.next())
{
    String cTaxPayerID = rs.getString("taxPayerID");
    String cName = rs.getString("name");
    String sTicker = rs.getString("sTicker");
    String sName = rs.getString("sName");
    // process tuple ...
}
rs.close();
```

5.
```
String query = "select distinct taxPayerID " +
    "from mutualFund natural join mutualFundPortfolio " +
    "where prinObj= ?";
String principalObjective = "G";
PreparedStatement pstmt = dbConnection.prepareStatement(query);
pstmt.setString(1, principalObjective);
ResultSet rs = pstmt.executeQuery();
while (rs.next())
{
    String cTaxPayerID = rs.getString("taxPayerID");
    // process tuple ...
}
rs.close();
```

6.
```
String query = "call client_stock(?, ?)";
String stockName = "Stock STU";
CallableStatement cstmt = dbConnection.prepareCall(query);
cstmt.setString(1, stockName);
cstmt.registerOutParameter(2, Types.INTEGER);
cstmt.execute();
int clientCount = cstmt.getInt(2);
System.out.println("ClientCount: " + stockName + " – " + clientCount);
```

7.
```
String query = "update mutualFund" +
    "set mCurrent = 7 "+"where mTicker = mutual_fund_ticker('Blue Chip')";
Statement stmt = dbConnection.createStatement();
int updateCount = stmt.executeUpdate(query);
System.out.println("Update Count: " + updateCount);
```

8.
```
query = """select c.taxPayerID, c.name, s.sTicker, s.sName
    from (myclient c natural join stockPortfolio sp) natural join stock s
    where s.rating = 'A' """
cursor = self.dbconnection.cursor()
cursor.execute(query)
```

```
        results = cursor.fetchall()
        for row in results:
            taxPayerID, name, sTicker, sName = row[0], row[1], row[2], row[3]
            # process tuple ...
        cursor.close()
```

9.
```
        query = """select distinct taxPayerID
            from mutualFund natural join mutualFundPortfolio
            where prinObj=%s"""
        principal_objective = 'G'
        cursor = self.dbconnection.cursor()
        cursor.execute(query, (principal_objective,))
        results = cursor.fetchall()
        for row in results:
            taxPayerID = row[0]
            # process tuple ...
        cursor.close()
```

10.
```
        stockName = 'Stock STU'
        clientCount = 0
        cursor = self.dbconnection.cursor()
        cursor.callproc("client_stock", (stockName, clientCount))
        # NOTE: No result set for this stored procedure; get output variable value
        cursor.execute('select @_client_stock_1')
        result = cursor.fetchone()
        if result is not None:
            clientCount = result[0]
            # process value
        cursor.close()
```

11.
```
        update = """update mutualFund set mCurrent = 8
                    where mTicker = mutual_fund_ticker('Blue Chip')"""
        cursor = self.dbconnection.cursor()
        cursor.execute(update)
        update_count = self.dbconnection.affected_rows()
        print("Updated count: " + str(update_count))
        cursor.close()
```

## Answers to Practice Problems: NEW HOME

(See book's companion website for complete code with exception handling.)

1.
```
create procedure subdivisions_city_sqft(in icity varchar(10), in isqft decimal(10))
    begin
        select sName, sZip
        from subdivision s
        where sCity=icity and
            exists (select *
            from offered o natural join model m
            where o.sName = s.sName and m.sqft>isqft);
    end
call subdivisions_city_sqft('Tempe', 3000);
```

2. create procedure available_lots(in sub varchar(15), out available int)
```
        begin
            select count(*) into available
            from lot l
            where l.sName = sub and
                not exists ( select *
                from sold d
                where d.sName = l.sName and d.lotNum = l.lotNum);
        end call available_lots('Terraces', @number_of_lots);
    select @number_of_lots;
```

3. create function homebuilder_id(hbname varchar(10))
```
        returns char(3)
        deterministic
        begin
            declare hbid char(3);
            select hid into hbid
            from homebuilder
            where hName = hbname;
            return(hbid);
        end
    set @hbid = homebuilder_id('Homer');
    select @hbid;
```

4.
```
    String query = "select * from subdivision s"
            + "where exists (select * from lot l"
            + "where l.sName = s.sName and l.lSize>20000)";
    Statement stmt = dbConnection.createStatement();
    ResultSet rs = stmt.executeQuery(query);
    while (rs.next())
    {
        String sName = rs.getString("sName");
        String sCity = rs.getString("sCity");
        String sZip = rs.getString("sZip");
        // process tuple ...
    }
    rs.close();
```

5.
```
    String query = "select * from subdivision s" +
            "where exists (select * from offered o" +
            "where s.sName = o.sName and o.hID = homebuilder_id(?))";
    String hbName = "Homer";
    PreparedStatement pstmt = dbConnection.prepareStatement(query);
    pstmt.setString(1, hbName);
    ResultSet rs = pstmt.executeQuery();
    while (rs.next())
    {
        String sName = rs.getString("sName");
        String sCity = rs.getString("sCity");
```

```
                String sZip = rs.getString("sZip");
                // process tuple ...
        }
        rs.close();

6.      String query = "call available_lots(?, ?)";
        String subdivisionName = "Terraces";
        CallableStatement cstmt = dbConnection.prepareCall(query);
        cstmt.setString(1, subdivisionName);
        cstmt.registerOutParameter(2, Types.INTEGER);
        cstmt.execute();
        int availableCount = cstmt.getInt(2);
        System.out.println("Available Lots: " + subdivisionName + " - " + availableCount);

7.      String query = "update lot set lPremium = 1.1 * lPremium" +
                "where sName = 'Terraces' and not exists (select * from sold d" +
                "where d.sName = lot.sName and d.lotNum = lot.lotNum)";
        Statement stmt = dbConnection.createStatement();
        int updateCount = stmt.executeUpdate(query);
        System.out.println("Update Count: " + updateCount);

8.      query = """select *
                from subdivision s
                where exists (select *
                        from lot l
                        where l.sName = s.sName and l.lSize>20000)"""
        cursor = self.dbconnection.cursor()
        cursor.execute(query)
        results = cursor.fetchall()
        for row in results:
                sName, sCity, sZip = row[0], row[1], row[2]
                # process tuple ...
        cursor.close()

9.      query = """select *
                from subdivision s
                where exists (select *
                        from offered o
                        where s.sName = o.sName and o.hID = homebuilder_id(%s))"""
        hbname = 'Homer'
        cursor = self.dbconnection.cursor()
        cursor.execute(query, (hbname,))
        results = cursor.fetchall()
        for row in results:
                sName, sCity, sZip = row[0], row[1], row[2]
                # process tuple ...
        cursor.close()

10.     subdivisionName = 'Terraces'
        availableCount = 0
        cursor = self.dbconnection.cursor()
```

```
cursor.callproc("available_lots", (subdivisionName, availableCount))
# NOTE: No result set for this stored procedure; get output variable value
cursor.execute('select @_available_lots_1')
result = cursor.fetchone()
if result is not None:
availableCount = result[0]
print("Available Lots Count for" + subdivisionName + ": " + str(availableCount))
cursor.close()
```

11.
```
update = """update lot
    set lPremium = 1.1 * lPremium
    where sName = 'Terraces' and
    not exists (select *
        from sold d
        where d.sName = lot.sName and d.lotNum = lot.lotNum)"""
cursor = self.dbconnection.cursor()
cursor.execute(update)
update_count = self.dbconnection.affected_rows()
print("Updated count: " + str(update_count))
cursor.close()
```

## Answers to Practice Problems: WEB PAGE

(See book's companion website for complete code with exception handling.)

1. 
```
create procedure graphics_on_pages(in name varchar(15))
    begin
        select w.*
        from (webpage w natural join displays d) natural join graphic g
        where g.gName = name;
    end
```

2. 
```
create procedure document_type(in itype char(1), out dcount int)
    begin
        select count(*) into dcount
        from document d
        where d.dType = itype;
    end
```

3. 
```
create function graphic_id(iname varchar(15))
    returns varchar(5)
    deterministic
    begin
        declare id char(3);
        select gId into id
        from graphic
        where gName = iname;
        return(id);
    end
```

4.
```
String query = "select w.* " +
        "from (webpage w natural join displays d) natural join graphic g" +
        "where g.gType = 'gif'" ;
Statement stmt = dbConnection.createStatement();
ResultSet rs = stmt.executeQuery(query);
while (rs.next())
{
    String wID = rs.getString("wID");
    String wTitle = rs.getString("wTitle");
    String url = rs.getString("wURL");
    int hits = rs.getInt("hits");
    // process tuple ...
}
rs.close();
```

5.
```
String query = "select w.* from webpage w" +
        "where not exists (select * from graphic g natural join displays d" +
        "where w.wID = d.wID and d.gID = graphic_id(?))";
System.out.println("Web Page Prepared Statement: " + query);
String grName = "asulogo";
PreparedStatement pstmt = dbConnection.prepareStatement(query);
pstmt.setString(1, grName);
ResultSet rs = pstmt.executeQuery();
while (rs.next())
{
    String wID = rs.getString("wID");
    String wTitle = rs.getString("wTitle");
    String url = rs.getString("wURL");
    int hits = rs.getInt("hits");
    // process tuple ...
}
rs.close();
```

6.
```
String query = "call document_type(?, ?)";
System.out.println("Callable Statement: " + query);
String dtype = "gif";
CallableStatement cstmt = dbConnection.prepareCall(query);
cstmt.setString(1, dtype);
cstmt.registerOutParameter(2, Types.INTEGER);
cstmt.execute();
int typeCount = cstmt.getInt(2);
System.out.println("Document type: " + dtype + " - " + typeCount);
```

7.
```
String query = "update webpage set hits = hits + 1 where wID = 'W06'";
System.out.println("Update Statement: " + query);
Statement stmt = dbConnection.createStatement();
int updateCount = stmt.executeUpdate(query);
System.out.println("Update Count: " + updateCount);
```

8.
```
query = """select w.*
        from (webpage w natural join displays d) natural join graphic g
        where g.gType = 'gif'""";
```

```
        cursor = self.dbconnection.cursor()
        cursor.execute(query)
        results = cursor.fetchall()
        for row in results:
            wID, wTitle, url, hits = row[0], row[1], row[2], row[3]
            # process tuple ...
        cursor.close()
```

9.
```
        query = """select w.*
            from webpage w
            where not exists (select *
            from graphic g natural join displays d
            where w.wID = d.wID and d.gID = graphic_id(%s))"""
        grname = 'asulogo'
        cursor = self.dbconnection.cursor()
        cursor.execute(query, (grname,))
        results = cursor.fetchall()
        for row in results:
            wID, wTitle, url, hits = row[0], row[1], row[2], row[3]
            # process tuple ...
        cursor.close()
```

10.
```
        dtype = 'gif'
        typeCount = 0
        cursor = self.dbconnection.cursor()
        cursor.callproc("document_type", (dtype, typeCount))
        # NOTE: No result set for this stored procedure; get output variable value
        cursor.execute('select @_document_type_1')
        result = cursor.fetchone()
        if result is not None:
            typeCount = result[0]
            print("Document Count for " + dtype + ": " + str(typeCount))
        cursor.close()
```

11.
```
        update = """update webpage set hits = hits + 1 where wID = 'W06'"""
        cursor = self.dbconnection.cursor()
        cursor.execute(update)
        update_count = self.dbconnection.affected_rows()
        print("Updated count: " + str(update_count))
        cursor.close()
```

## Bibliographic Notes

Database programming relies heavily on the current capabilities of the programming language and database product, as well as on available implementations of drivers that act as bridges between the programming language and the specific database system. Therefore, the system documentation available online for these technologies must be consulted when building the application. Also, the current best practices for avoiding SQL injection from reputable sites on the Web must be researched. OWASP – Open Web Application Security Project at owasp.org provides a wealth of information on the topic. For a readable overview of database security including SQL injection, see Murray [2010].

# More to Explore

There are many avenues to explore based on the database programming introduction in this chapter, including the following:

- The specification of triggers in the programming language tightly coupled with the database to encapsulate reactions to changes in the database

- The capabilities of call-level interfaces for retrieving metadata about the database and the result sets

- Best practices for avoiding SQL injection in database applications in various languages and frameworks, including the Web

- Object-relational wrappers that automatically generate classes wrapping the access of a relational database for a programming language (e.g. Hibernate for Java, LINQ to SQL for C#) or Web application (e.g. Ruby on Rails)

# XML and Databases

- To describe and recognize well-formed XML
- To read and write DTD and XSD specifications for the validation of well-formed XML documents
- To explain how the structure of XML facilitates data exchange

HyperText Markup Language (HTML) is the primary language for writing Web pages. HTML contains opening and closing tags that the Web browser interprets for directions on how to display the text within the tags. HTML has a fixed collection of tags to use. The Extensible Markup Language (XML) is a markup language that is flexible since it allows user-defined tags. XML was originally developed for the presentation of documents. Due to its simplicity and ease of use, XML is a universal language for representing data and the semantics of the data.

XML is also widely used in configuration files for software. Rather than specifying information to programs on the command line or using standard input, XML provides a self-documenting mechanism for specifying parameters and other information required by programs.

Most relational database products are now *XML-enabled*. XML-enabled databases provide the capability to transfer data between XML documents and the data structures of the database itself. This transfer capability typically relies on the specification of the structure of the XML document. Initially, the Document Type Definition (DTD) language was introduced to describe the structure of an XML document. DTDs are a succinct representation but lack the granularity of types that are typically available in the specification of a database schema. Therefore, the XML Schema language, which is also known as the XML Schema Definition (XSD) language, was developed to provide more detailed requirements. An XSD looks like XML and has specific tags for defining the structure of the XML document. XML Schema is quite diverse and has myriad features, so a thorough exposition is beyond the scope of this book. However, XML Schema is covered in enough detail to illustrate the similar features for describing documents that are provided by DTDs and how XSDs extend that specification to include user-defined types. The chapter concludes with a motivating example that illustrates the use of XML for exchanging data.

## 8.1 Overview of XML

**A *tag* is a label enclosed in angle brackets (< and >).**

Figure 8.1 provides a simple, motivational example of an XML document containing information about employees. A tag is a label enclosed in angle brackets (< and >). The first tag has the label employees, indicating the intended semantics that the content will contain information about multiple employees. The tag <employees> is called an opening tag. Its corresponding closing tag is </employees>, formed by preceding the label with a slash character (/). The next opening tag is employee. The tags empid, lastname, firstname, title, and salary document the information that is represented for each employee. Opening tags may include attributes to provide additional information. For example, the opening tag for employee has an attribute active, describing the status of the employee. There are only two employee instances shown in the figure for an introduction with additional instances omitted for brevity of presentation. This is also documented in the XML code using a comment, which starts with <! - - and concludes with - ->.

```
<employees>
      <employee active="true">
            <empid>123456789</empid>
            <lastname>Smith</lastname>
            <firstname>John</firstname>
            <title>Software Engineer</title>
            <salary effective="2019-02-14" moneyFormat="dollars">50000</salary>
      </employee>
      <employee active="false">
            <empid>987654321</empid>
            <lastname>Doe</lastname>
            <firstname>Jane</firstname>
            <title>Manager</title>
            <salary effective="2021-01-04" moneyFormat="dollars">98765</salary>
      </employee>
      <! - -Additional employees not shown for brevity - ->
      ...
</employees>
```

**FIGURE 8.1**
XML employees sample.

XML requires that every opening tag has an associated closing tag. The tags in XML are case sensitive and may *not* contain white space. Tags must start with a letter or underscore (_) and may contain letters, digits, or the following characters: period (.), underscore (_), or hyphen (-). Since XML is a semantic markup language, it is strongly suggested that tag names are descriptive.

The term *element* refers to an opening tag, its enclosed information, and its corresponding closing tag. For example,

<lastname>Smith</lastname>

represents an element in the example shown in Figure 8.1. The data appearing between the opening and closing tags of an element is called the *content* of an element.

Opening tags in an element may contain *attributes*. An attribute has a name and a value, which is enclosed in quotes:

<label attributeName="attributeValue">enclosed text</label>

For example, an employee's salary can be annotated with an attribute named effective, which indicates the effective date of the salary specified:

<salary effective="2019-02-14">50000</salary>

Recall that all XML elements must have a closing tag. If an element is empty, then XML allows an abbreviated closing tag:

<emptyElement attributeName="attributeValue" />

> An *element* consists of an opening tag, its content, and a corresponding closing tag.

> An *attribute* appears only in an opening tag of an element and its value must be enclosed in quotes.

instead of:

<emptyElement attributeName="attributeValue"></emptyElement>

When an element is empty, there is typically an attribute that is providing information about the element.

In addition to the syntax rules already specified for the definition of elements and attributes, a *well-formed* XML document must also contain a distinguished root element that contains the entire document, and all elements within the document must be properly nested. The distinguished root element has a unique opening and closing tag having the whole document as its enclosed text. In the example shown in Figure 8.1, **employees** represents the distinguished root element. All elements within a well-formed XML document must be properly nested. This nesting structure for XML documents is hierarchical in nature. Typically, the outer element is called a *parent* and an element nested within it is called a *child* element.

> A ***well-formed*** **XML document adheres to the specified syntax rules, contains a distinguished root element, and is properly nested.**

The requirements of a distinguished root element and proper nesting enforce a hierarchical computer science tree structure for the XML document, which is why the distinguished element that is enclosing the entire document is called a *root* element. The proper nesting of elements ensures a subtree structuring of the document. Figure 8.2 illustrates a pictorial tree representation of the elements of the motivational XML employees sample shown in Figure 8.1, with only the first employee element being expanded in the tree. There is an important observation regarding this structure for XML. XML is inherently ordered, which is different from the unordered set of tuples in a relational table. There is a suite of XML technology that supports searching and querying XML data that traverse this ordered tree structure although the details of this technology are beyond the scope of this introductory text.

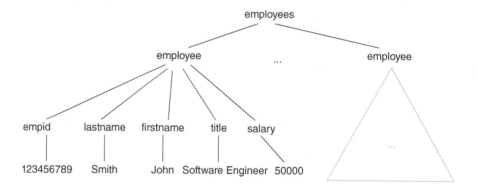

**FIGURE 8.2**
Tree structure of XML.

> A ***valid*** **XML document is a well-formed XML document that also follows a set of rules given by its corresponding DTD or XSD.**

Just having a well-formed XML document with an instance of data having self-describing tags is not enough to facilitate data sharing. The structure of the XML to be shared must be specified so that the data conforms to the specification for data exchange. A DTD or XSD specification defines the structure of an XML document. A *valid* XML document is a well-formed XML document that also follows a set of rules given by its corresponding DTD or XSD, which are defined in the following sections.

## Self Check

1. What is the term used to refer to a name enclosed in < and > brackets?
2. What is an element?
3. What is well-formed XML?

# 8.2 DTD

A DTD gives metadata information about the data contained in an XML document. A DTD is an initial approach for representing the structure of an XML document, defining the name of the distinguished root element as well as the structure and associated content of each element. XML Schema, which is presented in the next section, was developed after DTDs to provide a richer description of the schema of an XML document. XML Schema is written in XML, whereas DTD has its own structure.

> **A DTD is an initial approach for representing the structure of an XML document.**

The DTD may appear in the XML document itself before the opening root tag or in a separate file, which is referenced in the XML document. The former is known as an internal declaration:

<!DOCTYPE rootElement [elementDeclarations]>

where rootElement is the name of the distinguished root element of the XML document and elementDeclarations represents the DTD for declaring the elements. The latter is called an external declaration:

> **DOCTYPE specifies the name of the distinguished root element.**

<!DOCTYPE rootElement SYSTEM "filename.dtd">

where rootElement is the name of the distinguished root element of the XML document and filename.dtd represents the name of the filename that defines the DTD for the XML document. All elements and attributes are declared within the DTD.

## SYNTAX 8.1  DTD Overview

Distinguished Root Element:
    <!DOCTYPE rootElement [elementDeclarations]>

Element Declarations:
    <!ELEMENT elementName contentSpecification>

Attribute Declarations:
    <!ATTLIST elementName attributeName attributeType defaultValue>

Each element declaration consists of an element name and its content:

<!ELEMENT elementName contentSpecification>

> **ELEMENT declares the element name and its content.**

The contentSpecification is either character data or the specification of nested elements. The content specification for character data is PCDATA. PCDATA represents parsed character strings, i.e. the character strings will be parsed as XML. If the content of an element includes symbols used by XML, such as <, >, ", ', and &, these symbols must be represented using the following strings, which are prefixed by an ampersand (&) and suffixed by a semicolon: &lt;, &gt;, &quot;, &apos;, and &amp;. The parsing of the XML data changes these strings into the associated symbol.

Nested elements represent more complex types of information. A sequence of elements, similar to a tuple in a table, is represented in a DTD using a comma-separated list enclosed in parentheses:

<!ELEMENT sequencedElements (element1, element2, element3)>

Each nested element (element1, element2, and element3) must appear exactly once in the order specified. However, a DTD also allows for the specification of the number of occurrences of nested elements using the suffixes +, * and ?. A + suffix indicates that the element occurs one or more times. A * suffix indicates that the element occurs zero or more times. A ? suffix indicates that the element may appear at most once, which essentially means that the element is optional.

Consider the DTD specification of occurrenceConstraintsExSeq:

```
<!ELEMENT occurrenceConstraintsExSeq (element1+, element2*, element3?)>
```

The nested elements still must appear in order. However, element1 must appear at least once but may appear any number of times. The element element2 may not appear or may appear any number of times, whereas element3 is optional but if included, it occurs once.

DTDs also provide for the specification of a choice of elements:

```
<!ELEMENT choiceOfElements (elementA | elementB | elementC)>
```

The element declaration for choiceOfElements denotes that only one of the nested elements (elementA, elementB, or elementC) can appear in a valid XML document.

Figure 8.3 gives the DTD for the XML document shown in Figure 8.1. The XML document must contain at least one occurrence of employee. Each employee element consists of the sequence of elements: empid, lastname, firstname, title, and salary. The DTD also defines the attributes associated with the elements employee and salary.

```
<!DOCTYPE employees [
    <!ELEMENT employees (employee)+>
    <!ELEMENT employee (empid, lastname, firstname, title, salary)>
    <!ATTLIST employee active (true | false) #REQUIRED>
    <!ELEMENT empid (#PCDATA)>
    <!ELEMENT lastname (#PCDATA)>
    <!ELEMENT firstname (#PCDATA)>
    <!ELEMENT title (#PCDATA)>
    <!ELEMENT salary (#PCDATA)>
    <!ATTLIST salary effective CDATA #IMPLIED
                     moneyFormat CDATA #FIXED "dollars">
]>
```

**FIGURE 8.3**
DTD for employees
XML document.

> **Use ATTLIST to declare an attribute for an element, including its type and default value or requirements for its value (#REQUIRED, #IMPLIED, #FIXED).**

The attribute for an element has a type and a default value.

```
<!ATTLIST elementName attributeName attributeType defaultValue>
```

The type of an attribute can be character data (CDATA), an enumerated value, or one of the following: ID, IDREF, or IDREFS. The defaultValue is either a default value for the attribute enclosed in quotes, or a specification for the requirements of the attribute value: #REQUIRED, #IMPLIED, or #FIXED. A value of a #REQUIRED attribute must be specified. If the attribute is #IMPLIED, then the attribute is optional. A #FIXED attribute means that the value of the attribute must be the value given in quotes following #FIXED.

The DTD of Figure 8.3 shows a required (#REQUIRED) attribute named active for an employee element and two attributes for the salary element. As shown, multiple attributes for an element can be defined in one ATTLIST. The effective date is optional (#IMPLIED) and the moneyFormat has a fixed (#FIXED) value of dollars for this fictitious company. If an optional attribute can have a default value, then the default value itself follows the attributeType. Consider as an example using a rate attribute for salary that specifies whether the salary value is a yearly or hourly rate. By default, it is assumed that the rate is a yearly specification.

```
<!ATTLIST salary rate (yearly | hourly) "yearly">
```

The type of an attribute that is a simple character string is CDATA. There is a distinction between the CDATA and PCDATA types. The character data represented by CDATA are not parsed. The textual data is treated "as is". Therefore, the special characters such as &, <, >, ", and ' can appear in a CDATA value.

Recall that elements defined as PCDATA represent parsed character strings and cannot include the XML characters: &, <, >, ", and '. However, these characters could appear in attribute values within a database. For example, there are many names that include a ' or titles that use an ampersand to represent the word and. Thus, to represent data values that are not to be parsed, data can be enclosed in a CDATA section as follows:

<![CDATA [this text won't be parsed]]>

The syntax appears somewhat awkward, but it allows for data to be represented *as is* for an element whose content is PCDATA.

> **Enclose the text of an element in a CDATA section to represent data that may contain characters that are parsed by XML, e.g. <, >, ", ', and &.**

Another attributeType specification is ID. The value of an attribute of type ID must be unique for the declared element in the XML document. For example, each employee can include an eID attribute of type ID.

<employee eID="e01"> ... </employee>

> **ID is a special attribute type indicating that the value must be unique for the declared element in the XML document.**

These attribute values can later be used to refer to the XML elements of interest. Consider extending the employee example to include departments. A department element can include nested elements called manager and hasEmployees. The manager element has an mgrid attribute of type IDREF, referencing the ID value of the employee who is the manager. The hasEmployees element has an attribute emps of type IDREFS, specifying a list of employee references who work in the department.

```
<department>
    ...
    <manager mgrid="e06" />
    <hasEmployees emps="e01 e02 e06" />
</department>
```

> **IDREF and IDREFS are special attribute types that reference ID values. For IDREFS, the ID values are separated by white space.**

The attribute value of an IDREF is an ID value and IDREFS is given by ID values separated by white space enclosed in quotes. This use of references within the XML document also provides examples of the use of empty elements, e.g. manager and hasEmployees in this example. The following snippet of DTD illustrates the structure of the above XML having an eID attribute for employee and empty manager and hasEmployees elements that include mgrid and emps attributes, respectively, referencing the employees.

```
...
<!ATTLIST employee eid ID #REQUIRED>
...
<!ELEMENT department (..., manager, hasEmployees)>
<!ELEMENT manager EMPTY>
<!ATTLIST manager mgrid IDREF #REQUIRED>
<!ELEMENT hasEmployees EMPTY>
<!ATTLIST hasEmployees emps IDREFS #REQUIRED>
```

After seeing the specifications of an element and attribute definition, it is worth mentioning when an element is used versus an attribute. An element is typically a nested or structured specification of data, which can have multiple occurrences. An attribute has a single value that is simple, since its value is given in quotes. As seen in the effective date of the salary of an employee, an attribute value tends to be metadata about the value of the element.

## DTDs and Relational Databases

There is a canonical table-based mapping approach for representing a relational database instance in XML. Figure 8.4 gives a snippet of a DTD for this table-based mapping approach. The element database forms the distinguished root element of the XML document. The database shown in Figure 8.4 contains two tables: table1 and table2. The element table1 contains any number of tuples for table1, which is given by the table1Tuple element. The table table1 has three attributes: t1Attr1, t1Attr2, and t1Attr3. Therefore, each element representing a tuple or row of table1 contains three elements, named t1Attr1, t1Attr2, and t1Attr3.

**FIGURE 8.4**
DTD for a table-based mapping to an XML document.

```
<!ELEMENT database (table1 , table2)>
<!ELEMENT table1 (table1Tuple)*>
<!ELEMENT table1Tuple (t1Attr1, t1Attr2, t1Attr3)>
<!ELEMENT t1Attr1 (#PCDATA)>
<!ELEMENT t1Attr2 (#PCDATA)>
<!ELEMENT t1Attr3 (#PCDATA)>
...    <! - -table2 not shown for brevity - ->
```

Figure 8.5 gives a sample XML instance for the DTD given in Figure 8.4. The data instance only shows one tuple of table1: (attr1Value, attr2Value, attr3Value). The rest of the instance is omitted for brevity of presentation. Note that the value of an attribute in the table is shown within a CDATA section.

**FIGURE 8.5**
Sample data for a table-based mapping to XML.

```
<database>
    <table1>
        <table1Tuple>
            <t1Attr1><![CDATA[attr1Value]]></t1Attr1>
            <t1Attr2><![CDATA[attr2Value]]></t1Attr2>
            <t1Attr3><![CDATA[attr3Value]]></t1Attr3>
            ...
        </table1Tuple>
        ...
        <! - - The rest of the tuples for table1 omitted.  - ->
    </table1>
    ...
    <! - - The data for table2 omitted for brevity.  - ->
</database>
```

## Self Check

4.  In a DTD, what term indicates that the value of an attribute is optional?

5.  What is the name of the section in which characters will not be parsed?

6.  What is the name of the special attribute that denotes *references* to unique identifiers?

# 8.3 XML Schema

Although DTDs provide some information about the structure of an XML document, the W3C organization introduced XML Schema as a language specifically designed for defining schemas of XML documents. XSDs have several advantages over DTDs, while building on some of its strengths. XML Schema is written using XML syntax and has the capability to define simple and complex data types. Simple types contain only text, whereas complex types contain other elements or attributes. Elements can have simple or complex types, but attributes are always of a simple type since they are textual.

Another advantage of XSDs over DTDs is the ability of XML Schema to have both global and local declarations. In DTDs, all declarations are global. For databases, this global declaration restriction for DTDs may cause an issue. In a database schema, attribute names are unique within the scope of the table in which it is defined. Therefore, multiple tables can have an attribute with the same name. This scenario can be validated using XSDs but not with DTDs since DTD declarations are global and will not allow for more than one element of the same name.

XML Schema also uses namespaces to provide a collection of related element names. The name of a namespace must be unique. The design of a namespace name follows the format of a URL. For example, the namespace denoting the XML Schema standard is

http://www.w3.org/2001/XMLSchema

> **XSD has several advantages over DTDs for representing the structure of an XML document, including user-defined types, global and local declarations, namespace support, and XML syntax.**

The URL is not meant to be dereferencable but to be a unique name that does not change. The elements globally declared in a namespace are uniquely identifiable by a combination of the namespace and the element name. The use of namespaces allows for multiple XML documents to be used in one document without having to worry about name clashes.

Figure 8.6 shows the outline of an XML Schema specification. An optional XML version declaration can appear before the beginning of the schema declaration. The schema is enclosed in the distinguished root element named xsd:schema. The xsd:schema element has an attribute to define the XML namespace or namespaces referenced in the schema, which in this example is the default namespace given by W3C. The xmlns:xsd attribute defines xsd: as the prefix for any element or type that refers to this namespace. An xsd:annotation element allows for the inclusion of additional descriptions of schema components. The nested xsd:documentation element provides the text of a comment that is meant to be read by a person. There is also a nested element xsd:appinfo to allow the inclusion of application-specific information that is meant to be recognized by an application. The rules for the schema being defined will appear within the scope of the xsd:schema element.

```
<? xml version="1.0" ?>
<xsd:schema xmlns:xsd="http://www.w3.org/2001/XMLSchema">
<xsd:annotation>
    <xsd:documentation>
    The rules for validation will appear within the xsd:schema element.
    </xsd:documentation>
</xsd:annotation>
...
</xsd:schema>
```

**FIGURE 8.6**
XML schema outline.

XML Schema allows for the declaration of elements and attributes to be of a specified data type to allow for the validation of the element content and attribute values. Data types can be simple or complex. A simple type is a type that contains only text. A complex type may contain child elements or attributes. The specification of a data type is referred to as a definition.

> **Element and attribute definitions specify a name and a data type.**

## SYNTAX 8.2   XSD Overview of Element and Attribute Declarations

This overview shows the structure of the declaration of elements and attributes using named and anonymous types. There are additional attributes on element and attribute declarations not shown here, which will be described by examples in the text.

*Using named types*:

Element Declarations:

```
<xsd:element name="elementName" type="typeName" />
```

Attribute Declarations:

```
<xsd:attribute name="elementName" type="typeName" />
```

*Using anonymous types*:

Element Declarations:

```
<xsd:element name="elementName">
local type definition
</xsd:element>
```

Attribute Declarations:

```
<xsd:attribute name="elementName">
local type definition
</xsd:attribute>
```

The declaration of elements and attributes and the definition of data types may be global or local. Global declarations or definitions must appear at the top level of the document as a child of the xsd:schema element. Global components must have unique names in the schema within the type of that component. For example, a schema *may not* contain two global elements of the same name, but a schema *may* contain a global element declaration and a global complex type definition that have the same name. Local declarations or definitions appear within the scope of the complex type in which they are being declared. Data type definitions that are locally defined cannot be used outside of the scope of the declaration in which they are defined. Local data type definitions need not be named. Unnamed data type definitions are referred to as *anonymous*. Examples will appear throughout the chapter.

## Simple Types

> **A simple type is a type that contains only text.**

XML Schema provides built-in simple types and allows for the user to define custom simple types. A simple type is a type that contains only text. Some examples of built-in simple types are string, integer, decimal, float, boolean, date, and time. For example, consider the declaration of an element named dateOfBirth of type date:

```
<xsd:element name="dateOfBirth" type="xsd:date" />
```

Note that an XML-compliant date is a 10-character string in the format: yyyy-mm-dd.

Custom simple types can define restrictions on a simple type and are defined using the simpleType element. Figure 8.7 shows an example of the definition of the salaryRange simple type. The restriction element indicates the base type on which the simple type is being built. The elements minInclusive and maxInclusive provide the value of the minimum and maximum salary allowable. Note that inclusive means that the values specified are allowed. So minInclusive means greater than or equal to the value given. XSDs also allow for the elements minExclusive and

**FIGURE 8.7**
XSD example of a custom simple type.

```
<xsd:simpleType name="salaryRange">
    <xsd:restriction base="xsd:integer">
        <xsd:minInclusive value="25000" />
        <xsd:maxInclusive value="100000" />
    </xsd:restriction>
</xsd:simpleType>
```

maxExclusive to specify a greater than or less than relationship, respectively. It is not necessary to specify both a minimum and a maximum unless that is required by the semantics of the data.

The restriction element allows for the specification of various types of restrictions, which are also called *facets* in the literature. Figure 8.8 illustrates some of the additional types of restrictions. The enumeration element restricts the value of the type to be one of the enumerated values. Figure 8.8 provides an example of the enumeration of undergraduate student classifications, from Freshman indicating a first year student to Senior indicating a fourth year student. The length, minLength, and maxLength elements restrict the length of the type. The abbreviation for a department code is restricted to be a string of length 3 in Figure 8.8. Alternatively, the minLength and maxLength elements can be used to restrict the value to a required minimum length or maximum length, or both. The totalDigits and fractionDigits elements specify the total number of digits and the number of digits appearing to the right of the decimal point, respectively. Figure 8.8 illustrates a gpaType, which restricts a decimal to have a total of three digits with two digits to the right of the decimal point. The value of the pattern element provides a regular expression to specify the restriction on a value of the type. Regular expressions are a pattern matching technology frequently used throughout computer science. The most commonly used specifications are \d for digit, \w for a word character (letter, digit, underscore), or \s for white space (e.g. space, tab). Note that the symbols described for occurrence constraints in a DTD (+ for one or more, * for zero or more, and ? for once or none) are also used in regular expressions. When the number of occurrences is known, the number can be used in the regular expression. For example, the usaTelephoneNumberType in Figure 8.8 is restricted to be a string value consisting of 10 digits.

```
<xsd:simpleType name="studentClassification">
    <xsd:restriction base="xsd:string">
        <xsd:enumeration value="Freshman" />
        <xsd:enumeration value="Sophomore" />
        <xsd:enumeration value="Junior" />
        <xsd:enumeration value="Senior" />
    </xsd:restriction>
</xsd:simpleType>

<xsd:simpleType name="deptType">
    <xsd:restriction base="xsd:string">
        <xsd:length value="3" />
    </xsd:restriction>
</xsd:simpleType>

<xsd:simpleType name="gpaType">
    <xsd:restriction base="xsd:decimal">
        <xsd:totalDigits value="3" />
        <xsd:fractionDigits value="2" />
    </xsd:restriction>
</xsd:simpleType>

<xsd:simpleType name="usaTelephoneNumberType">
    <xsd:restriction base="xsd:string">
        <xsd:pattern value="\d{10}" />
    </xsd:restriction>
</xsd:simpleType>
```

**FIGURE 8.8**
Additional examples of restrictions in XSD.

## Complex Types

A complex type may contain child elements or attributes.

An element that has attributes or that can contain other elements has a *complex type*. A complex type definition is enclosed within the content of the complexType element.

```
<xsd:complexType name="complexTypeName">
...
</xsd:complexType>
```

XML Schema allows for defining a complex type with nested elements using the elements sequence and choice. A sequence is similar to the comma (,) specification in DTDs, defining a sequence of elements in the given order.

```
<!ELEMENT sequencedElements (element1, element2, element3)>
```

A choice corresponds to the usage of the vertical bar (|) in DTDs, providing a choice of one of the elements.

```
<!ELEMENT choiceOfElements (elementA | elementB | elementC)>
```

Use sequence to define a group of elements in the specified order.

Figure 8.9 provides examples of defining complex types based on a sequence or choice of nested elements. The example definition of the sequencedElementsType shows three nested elements (element1, element2, and element3) each of type string defined within the sequence. The group of elements declared within the sequence is called a sequence group. The elements in a sequence must appear in the specified order. The element sequencedElements is then defined to be of type sequencedElementsType.

```
<xsd:element name="sequencedElements" type="sequencedElementsType" />
```

Use choice to define a group of elements providing a choice of one of the elements.

The example definition of the choiceOfElementsType shows a choice of three elements (elementA, elementB, and elementC) each of type string defined within the choice group. Only one of these elements can appear. The declaration of the element choiceOfElements is of type choiceOfElementsType.

```
<xsd:element name="choiceOfElements" type="choiceOfElementsType" />
```

```
<xsd:complexType name="sequencedElementsType">
    <xsd:sequence>
        <xsd:element name="element1" type="xsd:string" />
        <xsd:element name="element2" type="xsd:string" />
        <xsd:element name="element3" type="xsd:string" />
    </xsd:sequence>
</xsd:complexType>
<xsd:complexType name="choiceOfElementsType">
    <xsd:choice>
        <xsd:element name="elementA" type="xsd:string" />
        <xsd:element name="elementB" type="xsd:string" />
        <xsd:element name="elementC" type="xsd:string" />
    </xsd:choice>
</xsd:complexType>
```

**FIGURE 8.9** Examples of complex types based on sequence and choice.

In the examples presented so far, elements must appear once. In XSDs, occurrence constraints are specified using built-in attributes named minOccurs and maxOccurs having default values of 1. The attribute minOccurs has the built-in type nonnegativeInteger. The maxOccurs attribute value is either a nonnegativeInteger or unbounded. Figure 8.10 illustrates the use of occurrence constraints in the definition of occurrenceConstraintsExSeq, having occurrence constraints based on the earlier DTD given:

```
<!ELEMENT occurrenceConstraintsExSeq (element1+, element2*, element3?)>
```

```
<xsd:complexType name="occurrenceConstraintsExSeqType">
    <xsd:sequence>
        <xsd:element name="element1" type="xsd:string"
            minOccurs="1" maxOccurs="unbounded" />
        <xsd:element name="element2" type="xsd:string"
            minOccurs="0" maxOccurs="unbounded" />
        <xsd:element name="element3" type="xsd:string"
            minOccurs="0" maxOccurs="1" />
    </xsd:sequence>
</xsd:complexType>
```

**FIGURE 8.10**
XSD example of sequence complex type with occurrence constraints.

The occurrence constraints on element declarations may be included on locally declared elements within complex type definitions, as shown in the illustrative example of Figure 8.10. Occurrence constraints are not allowed on the declaration of global elements, which appear at the top level of the schema. Elements declared globally are going to be referenced within an XML document. The references to the global elements may then specify occurrence constraints. Figure 8.11 shows a definition of a complex type similar to that shown in Figure 8.10. However, Figure 8.11 references the three globally declared elements: element1, element2, and element3. Instead of specifying a name and type attribute for the element declaration, the value of the ref attribute specifies the name of the referenced global element.

```
<xsd:element name="element1" type="xsd:string">
<xsd:element name="element2" type="xsd:string">
<xsd:element name="element3" type="xsd:string">
<xsd:complexType name="occurrenceConstraintsExSeqType">
    <xsd:sequence>
        <xsd:element ref="element1" minOccurs="1" maxOccurs="unbounded" />
        <xsd:element ref="element2" minOccurs="0" maxOccurs="unbounded" />
        <xsd:element ref="element3" minOccurs="0" maxOccurs="1" />
    </xsd:sequence>
</xsd:complexType>
```

**FIGURE 8.11**
XSD example of sequence complex type with element references.

The complex types illustrated thus far are structured using sequence and choice groups having nested elements. XSDs also support deriving a complex type from an existing type using the complexType element. If the complex type is derived from a simple type, then the complex type has simple content. A complex type derived from another complex type has complex content.

Figure 8.12 provides examples of defining complex types. The type salaryRangeAndDate extends the simple salaryRange type to include the effective attribute to record the associated date. The simpleContent element indicates that the content model for the complex type contains only textual data and no elements. The type salaryRangeDateFormat extends the complex type

```
<xsd:complexType name="salaryRangeAndDate">
    <xsd:simpleContent>
        <xsd:extension base="salaryRange">
            <xsd:attribute name="effective" type="xsd:date" />
        </xsd:extension>
    </xsd:simpleContent>
</xsd:complexType>
<xsd:complexType name="salaryRangeDateFormat">
    <xsd:complexContent>
        <xsd:extension base="salaryRangeAndDate">
            <xsd:attribute name="moneyFormat" type="moneyFormatType" />
        </xsd:extension>
    </xsd:complexContent>
</xsd:complexType>
```

**FIGURE 8.12**
XSD examples of complex types with simple and complex content.

> **Attribute declarations can also include attributes specifying** use **participation constraints and** default **or** fixed **values.**

salaryRangeAndDate to include the attribute moneyFormat and is, therefore, defined using the complexContent element. Both declarations use the extension element with the attribute base to indicate the base type that is being extended into the declared complex type. The moneyFormat attribute is of type moneyFormatType, which is assumed to be an enumeration of different monetary formats, such as dollars or euros.

The examples in Figure 8.12 are adding attribute declarations. There are additional attributes that can be specified on an attribute declaration, which include use, default, fixed. The use attribute defines a participation constraint on the attribute, which is either required or optional. Both attributes defined in Figure 8.12, effective and moneyFormat are optional, based on the default value of the use attribute when not specified. The default attribute specifies a default value and the fixed attribute specifies the value used as either a default or required value.

## SYNTAX 8.3   XSD Attribute Declarations: use, default, fixed

XSD attribute declarations can specify additional attributes: use, default, fixed. Every attribute declaration can specify a use attribute. However, an attribute declaration can specify a default or fixed attribute but not both.

use:
The use attribute value is either required or optional, with optional being its default value.

```
<xsd:attribute name="active" type="xsd:boolean"
    use="required" />
<xsd:attribute name="effective" type="xsd:date" use="optional" />
```

default:
A default value provides a value for an attribute if the attribute is absent. Therefore, an attribute declaration that has a default value cannot be required.

```
<xsd:attribute name="rate" type="salaryRateType"
    default="yearly" />
```

fixed:
A fixed value indicates that the attribute must have the value specified. If the attribute is absent, then the fixed value is used, as in a default value. However, if the attribute is present, it must be the same as the fixed value, otherwise, the instance is invalid.

```
<xsd:attribute name="moneyFormat" type="xsd:string"
    fixed="dollars" />
```

Empty elements are elements that do not contain elements nor text and possibly contain attributes. There are several ways to define a type for an empty element that only contains an attribute in XSDs. Figure 8.13 shows two methods. The first definition is the long version, which extends the built-in wild card type, called anyType, with the attribute declaration.

```
<xsd:complexType name="emptyElementTypeLongVersion">
    <xsd:complexContent>
        <xsd:extension base="xsd:anyType">
            <xsd:attribute name="attrName" type="xsd:string" />
        </xsd:extension>
    </xsd:complexContent>
</xsd:complexType>

<xsd:complexType name="emptyElementTypeAbbreviated">
    <xsd:attribute name="attrName" type="xsd:string" />
</xsd:complexType>
```

**FIGURE 8.13**
XSD examples of empty
element type
definitions.

The second definition is the abbreviated version, which indicates that the complex type only contains an attribute.

Note that XSDs also support the ID and IDREF types. Figure 8.14 shows a snippet of the declarations for an employee element having an attribute eid of type ID and a department element with nested manager and hasEmployees empty elements. The manager element has an mgrid attribute of type IDREF to reference the employee who is the manager of the department. The hasEmployees element has an attribute emps of type IDREFS to reference the employees working in that department. XSDs also have a more generalized key specification, but it uses an XPath expression, which is beyond the scope of this text.

```
        ...
        <xsd:element name="employee">
            <xsd:complexType>
                <xsd:sequence>
                    ...
                </xsd:sequence>
                <xsd:attribute name="eid" type="xsd:ID" use="required" />
            </xsd:complexType>
        </xsd:element>
        ...
        <xsd:element name="department">
            <xsd:complexType>
                <xsd:sequence>
                    ...
                    <xsd:element name="manager">
                        <xsd:complexType>
                            <xsd:attribute name="mgrid" type="xsd:IDREF" use="required" />
                        </xsd:complexType>
                    </xsd:element>
                    <xsd:element name="hasEmployees">
                        <xsd:complexType>
                            <xsd:attribute name="emps" type="xsd:IDREFS" use="required" />
                        </xsd:complexType>
                    </xsd:element>
                    ...
                </xsd:sequence>
            </xsd:complexType>
        </xsd:element>
```

**FIGURE 8.14**   XSD examples of definitions using ID, IDREF, and IDREFS.

Figure 8.15 shows the missing pieces of the XSD for the employee XML given in Figure 8.1 that is consistent with the DTD provided in Figure 8.3. The ellipsis is omitting the sample type declarations for salaryRange in Figure 8.7 as well as salaryRangeDate and salaryRangeDateFormat in Figure 8.12. Putting these pieces together is left as an end of chapter exercise.

```xml
<xsd:schema xmlns:xsd="http://www.w3.org/2001/XMLSchema">
    <xsd:element name="employees">
        <xsd:complexType>
            <xsd:sequence>
                <xsd:element ref="employee" minOccurs="1" maxOccurs="unbounded" />
            </xsd:sequence>
        </xsd:complexType>
    </xsd:element>

    <xsd:element name="employee">
        <xsd:complexType>
            <xsd:sequence>
                <xsd:element name="empid" type="xsd:string" />
                <xsd:element name="lastname" type="xsd:string" />
                <xsd:element name="firstname" type="xsd:string" />
                <xsd:element name="title" type="xsd:string" />
                <xsd:element name="salary" type="salaryRangeDateFormat" />
            </xsd:sequence>
            <xsd:attribute name="active" type="xsd:boolean" use="required" />
        </xsd:complexType>
    </xsd:element>
    ...
</xsd:schema>
```

**FIGURE 8.15**   XSD for employee XML document.

## XSDs and Relational Databases

Figure 8.16 gives an XSD for the table-based mapping of relational tables to XML data. The global database element has a local type given by the complexType element within its content. The type of the database element is a sequence of references to the tables in the database. The reference to element table1 is a reference to the global element declaration for table1, which appears later in the XML document. The declaration for table2 is not shown for brevity of presentation. The table1 element has a local complex type consisting of a sequence of only one element, which is a reference to the table1Tuple element. The occurrence constraints indicate that there can be an unbounded number of occurrences of table1Tuple. Each table1Tuple element consists of a sequence of references to the attributes appearing in table1 (t1Attr1, t1Attr2, t1Attr3). Note that in this example approach all elements that correspond to the table names, the attribute names, and the tuples of the tables are declared globally and referenced with appropriate occurrence constraints within the complex type definitions.

XML Schema is a powerful language for expressing the schema of XML documents. A discussion of the entire XML Schema specification is quite intricate and beyond the scope of this book. This section provided an overview of XSDs for representing structured database content.

```
<xsd:schema xmlns:xsd="http://www.w3.org/2001/XMLSchema">
<xsd:element name="database">
    <xsd:complexType>
        <xsd:sequence>
            <xsd:element ref="table1" />
            <xsd:element ref="table2" />
        </xsd:sequence>
    </xsd:complexType>
</xsd:element>
<xsd:element name="t1Attr1" type="xsd:string" />
<xsd:element name="t1Attr2" type="xsd:string" />
<xsd:element name="t1Attr3" type="xsd:string" />
<xsd:element name="table1">
    <xsd:complexType>
        <xsd:sequence>
            <xsd:element ref="table1Tuple" minOccurs="0" maxOccurs="unbounded" />
        </xsd:sequence>
    </xsd:complexType>
</xsd:element>
<xsd:element name="table1Tuple">
    <xsd:complexType>
        <xsd:sequence>
            <xsd:element ref="t1Attr1" />
            <xsd:element ref="t1Attr2" />
            <xsd:element ref="t1Attr3" />
        </xsd:sequence>
    </xsd:complexType>
</xsd:element>
...
</xsd:schema>
```

**FIGURE 8.16**  XSD for table-based mapping.

## Self Check

7.  How is the distinguished root element identified in an XSD?
8.  If an element has a built-in simple type and an attribute, is the element considered to be a simple type or a complex type?
9.  What are the default values of the minOccurs and maxOccurs attributes?

## 8.4  Structuring XML for Data Exchange

XML has become a de facto industry standard for data exchange. Up to this point, the chapter has looked at the details of how to write a well-formed XML document based on its syntax rules and the specification of a valid XML document using DTDs and XSDs. The perspective presented how to represent relational databases in XML. However, relational databases and XML are very different. The features of XML support a richer representation that include nested and repeated elements. These capabilities along with XML being textual and self-documenting support an effective technology for data exchange.

> XML's self-documenting textual format facilitates data exchange with an inherently ordered structure that supports nested and repeated elements.

To motivate the differences between relational and XML structuring, consider the ONLINE RETAILER visual schema of Figure 1.11 discussed in Chapter 1 to provide a more complex example of primary and foreign keys. The visual schema shows six tables that are linked by referential integrity: customer, item, supplier, item_supplier, orders, and lineitem. The customer, item, and supplier tables represent the corresponding concepts. The item_supplier table provides the information regarding an item, its supplier, the quantity available, and the price that the supplier supplies the item. An order consists of the items on the order, which is represented by a lineitem, giving the quantity purchased of the item supplied by the indicated supplier.

The structure of the data representing this enterprise can be quite different in XML. Recall that XSDs support ID and IDREF attributes. Assume that each order, customer, item, and supplier has an associated ID value. Figure 8.17 shows a possible structuring of XML data with these assumptions, where oid, cid, iid, and sid represent the ID attribute for order, customer, item, and supplier, respectively.

```xml
<order oid="o123" cust_id="c111">
    <order_date>2020-08-20</order_date>
    <order_total>123.45</order_total>
    <order_info>represents misc info indicated by ellipsis in figure</order_info>
    <lineitems>
        <lineitem item_id="i111" supp_id="s111">2</lineitem>
    </lineitems>
</order>
<customer cid="c111">
    <cust_name>Customer 111</cust_name>
    <cust_info>represents misc info indicated by ellipsis in figure</cust_info>
    <cust_orders>
        <cust_order order_id="o123" odate="2020-08-20" ototal="123.45" />
        <!- - ... - ->
    </cust_orders>
</customer>
<item iid="i111">
    <item_name>Item 111</item_name>
    <item_info>represents misc info indicated by ellipsis in figure</item_info>
    <item_suppliers>
        <item_supplier supp_id="s111">
            <qty_available>100</qty_available>
            <supp_price>9.87</supp_price>
        </item_supplier>
        <!- - ... - ->
    </item_suppliers>
</item>
<supplier sid="s111" supplies_items="i111">
    <supp_name>Supplier 111</supp_name>
    <supp_info>represents misc info indicated by ellipsis in figure</supp_info>
</supplier>
```

**FIGURE 8.17**
ONLINE RETAILER XML structure.

An order element represents most relational attributes in the order table as a nested element. The referential integrity to its associated customer is represented as an attribute cust_id in the order opening element. The concept of a lineitem can be integrated into an order by nesting.

A lineitem element has attributes, item_id and supp_id, referencing the associated item and supplier of the item purchased, with the content of the element being the quantity purchased.

The representation of a customer can also nest order summary information for that customer. Each cust_order for a customer is represented by an empty element nested within cust_orders that uses attributes to provide the order reference, its date, and total. The reference to the unique ID of the order, given by the attribute order_id, can be used by the application, if additional details about the order are needed.

When structuring the item element, it may be reasonable to nest the information about the suppliers of that item. Since a purchase is item-centric, it may be useful to know the available quantity of that item by each supplier. Thus, the information given by the item_supplier table in the relational database can be represented within the item element itself as a nested item_suppliers element. Each item_supplier is represented by referencing the unique id of the supplier as an attribute supp_id. Nested elements qty_available and supp_price correspond to the available quantity of the item by that supplier and the price of the item by that supplier, respectively.

The supplier element is the simplest in this proposed design. Since the details of the items supplied are stored within the items, there is no need to repeat the details within the supplier. The items that the supplier supplies could be represented as an attribute supplies_items that has the references to the items supplied by that supplier.

Most relational database products are now XML-enabled, providing various capabilities: importing and exporting of XML; supporting XML as a data type in the database with searching functions using XML technology; extending SQL to return query results in XML; and including XML features in the programming language that is tightly coupled with the database. Each product has different capabilities with varying syntax. Thus, the details are beyond the scope of this introductory text.

## Self Check

10. Briefly describe two fundamental differences between relational and XML data structuring.
11. How can referential integrity be represented within XML?
12. The relational schema for the ONLINE RETAILER has six tables (customer, item, supplier, item_supplier, orders, lineitem), but the XML design only has four high-level elements (order, customer, item, supplier). How does the XML design presented represent the lineitem and item_supplier data?

## Chapter Notes Summary

### Overview of XML

- A *tag* is a label enclosed in angle brackets (< and >).
- An *element* consists of an opening tag, its content, and a corresponding closing tag.
- An *attribute* appears only in an opening tag of an element and its value must be enclosed in quotes.
- A *well-formed* XML document adheres to the specified syntax rules, contains a distinguished root element, and is properly nested.
- A *valid* XML document is a well-formed XML document that also follows a set of rules given by its corresponding DTD or XSD.

### DTD

- A DTD is an initial approach for representing the structure of an XML document.
- DOCTYPE specifies the name of the distinguished root element.

- ELEMENT declares the element name and its content.
- Use ATTLIST to declare an attribute for an element, including its type and default value or requirements for its value (#REQUIRED, #IMPLIED, #FIXED).
- Enclose the text of an element in a CDATA section to represent data that may contain characters that are parsed by XML, e.g. <, >, ", ', and &.
- ID is a special attribute type indicating that the value must be unique for the declared element in the XML document.
- IDREF and IDREFS are special attribute types that reference ID values. For IDREFS, the ID values are separated by white space.

### XSD

- XSD has several advantages over DTDs for representing the structure of an XML document, including user-defined types, global and local declarations, namespace support, and XML syntax.
- Element and attribute definitions specify a data type.
- A simple type is a type that contains only text.
- A complex type may contain child elements or attributes.
- Use sequence to define a group of elements in the specified order.
- Use choice to define a group of elements providing a choice of one of the elements.
- Use the minOccurs and maxOccurs attributes to define occurrence constraints.
- Complex types can be derived from an existing type, having either simple or complex content.
- Attribute declarations can also include attributes specifying use participation constraints and default or fixed values.

### Structuring XML for Data Exchange

- XML's self-documenting textual format facilitates data exchange with an inherently ordered structure that supports nested and repeated elements.

## Chapter Reminders

Table 8.1 summarizes the correspondence between the DTD suffix and the values of the minOccurs and maxOccurs attributes in XSDs.

**Table 8.1    Occurrence Constraints in DTDs versus XSDs**

| DTD suffix | minOccurs value | maxOccurs value |
|---|---|---|
| + | 1 | unbounded |
| * | 0 | unbounded |
| ? | 0 | 1 |
| no suffix | 1 | 1 |

Table 8.2 summarizes the example attribute declarations in both DTDs and XSDs, including optional and required examples as well as default and fixed values.

XSDs build on the strengths of DTDs by declaring elements and attributes to be of specific data types. XSDs support the definition and use of both simple and complex types. Table 8.3 summarizes some of the restrictions available for the definition of custom simple types in XSDs. A summary of the definition of complex types is given in Table 8.4.

**Table 8.2  DTD and XSD Example Attribute Declaration Constraints**

| | |
|---|---|
| DTD: | `<!ATTLIST salary effective CDATA #IMPLIED>` |
| XSD: | `<xsd:attribute name="effective" type="xsd:date" use="optional" />` |
| DTD: | `<!ATTLIST salary rate (yearly | hourly) "yearly">` |
| XSD: | `<xsd:attribute name="rate" type="salaryRateType" default="yearly" />` |
| DTD: | `<!ATTLIST employee active (true | false) #REQUIRED>` |
| XSD: | `<xsd:attribute name="active" type="xsd:boolean" use="required" />` |
| DTD: | `<!ATTLIST salary moneyFormat #FIXED "dollars">` |
| XSD: | `<xsd:attribute name="moneyFormat" type="xsd:string" fixed="dollars" />` |

**Table 8.3  Summary of XSD Simple Type Restrictions**

| | |
|---|---|
| `<xsd:simpleType>` | Custom simple type definition |
| `<xsd:restriction base="`*baseType*`">` | Restriction of a simple base type |
| `<xsd:minInclusive value="`*minValue*`" />` | numeric base type greater than or equal to *minValue* |
| `<xsd:maxInclusive value="`*maxValue*`" />` | numeric base type less than or equal to *maxValue* |
| `<xsd:minExclusive value="`*minValue*`" />` | numeric base type greater than *minValue* |
| `<xsd:maxExclusive value="`*maxValue*`" />` | numeric base type less than *maxValue* |
| `<xsd:enumeration value="`*enumValue*`" />` | *enumValue* is one of the enumerated values given |
| `<xsd:length value="`*lenValue*`" />` | string of at most *lenValue* in length |
| `<xsd:minLength value="`*minValue*`" />` | string of at least *minValue* in length |
| `<xsd:maxLength value="`*maxValue*`" />` | string of at least *maxValue* in length |
| `<xsd:totalDigits value="`*tdValue*`" />` | *tdValue* is the number of digits in a decimal |
| `<xsd:fractionDigits value="`*fdValue*`" />` | *fdValue* is the number of digits to the right of the decimal point |
| `<xsd:pattern value="`*patternValue*`" />` | value follows the specified regular expression *patternValue* |

**Table 8.4  Summary of XSD Complex Type Definitions**

| | |
|---|---|
| `<xsd:complexType>` | Custom complex type definition |
| `<xssd:sequence>` | A sequence of elements in the given order |
| `<xsd:choice>` | A choice of one of the elements |
| `<xsd:simpleContent>` | A complex type derived from a simple type, such as extending a simple type to include an attribute |
| `<xsd:complexContent>` | A complex type derived from a complex type, such as extending a complex type to include another attribute or element |

# Practice

Use the ONLINE RETAILER enterprise to practice your understanding of XML, DTDs, and XSDs.

## Practice Problems

Extend the sample XML data given in Section 8.4 for the ONLINE RETAILER enterprise to create a complete XML document, adding instances of the elements that satisfy the following constraints.

1. customer: 0 orders, one order, two orders

2. item: 0 suppliers, one supplier, two suppliers

3. supplier: 0 items, one item, two items

4. order: one lineitem, two lineitems, three lineitems

Define the DTD for the various components of the XML document

5. the overall structure

6. the order element

7. the customer element

8. the item element

9. the supplier element

Validate the XML document with respect to the defined DTD

10. After refining the DTD structure specifications to represent the valid XML document, create various versions of the XML data that violate the constraints to verify the completeness of the DTD specification.

Define the XSD for the various components of the XML document

11. the overall structure

12. the order element

13. the customer element

14. the item element

15. the supplier element

Validate the XML document with respect to the defined XSD

16. After refining the XSD structure specifications to represent the valid XML document, create various versions of the XML data that violate the constraints to verify the completeness of the XSD specification.

## End of Chapter Exercises

Give a brief justification for why the following snippets of XML are not well-formed.

1. <employee> emp1 </Employee>

2. <last name> emp1 </last name>

3. <employee> emp1 </employee> <employee> emp2 </employee>

4. <salary effective=2017-02-20> emp1 </salary>

5. <name>
   <lastname>
   Smith
   <firstname>
   John
   </lastname>
   </firstname>
   </name>

For each of the following, determine whether the XML snippet is valid with respect to the DTD shown. If not valid, provide a brief justification.

6. <!DOCTYPE skills [
   <!ELEMENT skills (skill)*>
   <!ELEMENT skill (#PCDATA)>
   ]>

7. <!ELEMENT salary (#PCDATA)>
   <!ATTLIST salary effective CDATA #IMPLIED>

   ...
   <salary>
   50000
   </salary>

8. <!ELEMENT salary (#PCDATA)>
   <!ATTLIST salary moneyFormat CDATA #FIXED "dollars">

   ...
   <salary moneyformat="dollars">
   50000
   </salary>

9. ...
   <!ELEMENT name (lastname, firstname)>
   <!ELEMENT lastname (#PCDATA)>
   <!ELEMENT firstname (#PCDATA)>

   ...
   <name>
   <firstname>John</firstname>
   <lastname>Smith</lastname>
   </name>

10. <!ELEMENT employee (name)>
    <!ATTLIST employee active (true | false) #REQUIRED>
    <!ELEMENT name (#PCDATA)>

    ...
    <employee active=true>
    <name>John Smith</name>
    </employee>

Consider the DTD specification for employees given in Figure 8.3:

11. Create a well-formed and valid XML document of the data shown in Table 8.5 for the given DTD.

Table 8.5 **Data for XML Document**

| Empid | Active | Last | First | Title | Salary | Effective |
|-------|--------|------|-------|-------|--------|-----------|
| 123 | Yes | Smith | John | Engineer | $50,000 | 2017-09-07 |
| 987 | Yes | Doe | Jane | Manager | $75,000 | 2019-07-09 |
| 111 | No | Redbeard | Gene | Assistant | $30,000 | 2018-05-15 |

12. Write an XSD that corresponds to the given DTD for employees, including the additional constraints on the data as shown in the chapter. Validate the XML for the previous question against the XSD. Since the XSD is more restrictive, identify additional employee XML data that is valid with respect to the DTD but not the more descriptive XSD.

Consider the following DTD for online banking:

```
<!DOCTYPE onlinebanking [
<!ELEMENT onlinebanking (item)*>
<!ATTLIST onlinebanking balance CDATA #REQUIRED>
<!ELEMENT item (checknum?, date, description, amount)>
<!ELEMENT checknum (#PCDATA)>
<!ELEMENT date (#PCDATA)>
<!ELEMENT description (#PCDATA)>
<!ELEMENT amount (#PCDATA)>
<!ATTLIST amount type (credit | debit) #REQUIRED>
]>
```

13. Is the following XML snippet well-formed? Is it valid with respect to the DTD? Provide a brief justification.
```
<item>
<date>2019-12-01</date>
<description>Deposit</description>
<amount type="credit">100.00</amount>
</item>
<item>
<checknum>229</checknum>
<amount type="debit">156.28</amount>
<date>2019-12-05</date>
<description>Electricity</description>
</item>
```

14. Is the following XML snippet well-formed? Is it valid with respect to the DTD? Provide a brief justification.
```
<item>
<date>2019-12-01</date>
<description>Deposit</description>
<amount type="credit">100.00</amount>
</item>
<item>
<checknum>228</checknum>
<date>2019-11-30</date>
<description>Water</description>
<amount type="debit">56.28</amount>
</item>
```

15. Is the following XML snippet well-formed? Is it valid with respect to the DTD? Provide a brief justification.

```
<item>
<date>2019-12-01</date>
<description>Deposit</description>
<amount type="credit">100.00</amount>
</item>
<item>
<checknum>227</checknum>
<date>2019-12-05</date>
<description>ISP</description>
<amount type=debit>59.65</amount>
</item>
```

16. Is the following XML snippet well-formed? Is it valid with respect to the DTD? Provide a brief justification.

```
<item>
<checknum>230</checknum>
<date>2019-12-30</date>
<description>Phone</description>
<amount type="debit">56.28</amount>
</item>
<item>
<description>Deposit</description>
<amount type="credit">150.00</amount>
</item>
```

17. Write an XSD that corresponds to the given DTD for online banking that captures more constraints by specifying types for the textual data.

Consider the representation of your favorite sports Web page statistics for a given year. For this question, find the statistics on the Web for the most recent standings for Major League Baseball, which consists of the American and National leagues and within each league the East, Central, and West divisions. For each team, make sure that you include at least the following information: location, name, wins, losses, percentage, and the win and loss records for both home and away.

18. Create an XML document that reflects the standings. Do not use a flat relational structure. Attempt to represent the information in the hierarchical and nested manner as presented on the Web page.

19. Create a DTD to validate the XML document of the MLB standings.

20. Create an XSD to validate the XML document of the MLB standings that captures additional constraints by specifying types for the textual data.

Using a database product, explore its XML capabilities.

21. Export a table into XML format and examine the resulting XML.

22. Create a small XML document that you can import into a relational table.

## Answers to Self-Check Questions

1. tag

2. An element consists of its opening tag, its content, and its closing tag.

3. Well-formed XML is an XML document that adheres to XML syntax rules, contains a distinguished root element, and is properly nested.

4. IMPLIED

5. CDATA

6. IDREF denotes a single reference, whereas IDREFS denotes a space-separated string containing multiple references.

7. The first global element defined within the xsd:schema element is the distinguished root element.

8. An element with an attribute or nested elements is considered to have a complex type.

9. The default values for minOccurs and maxOccurs is 1, similar to the occurrence constraints in a DTD.

10. Relational tables are sets of tuples and therefore unordered, whereas XML data is inherently ordered. The data values in relational tables must be simple values, whereas XML elements can have nested elements with repetition.

11. Referential integrity can be represented in XML by assigning an ID value to each element and referencing that value through IDREF and IDREFS.

12. The lineitem of an order is nested within the order element itself. Similarly, the item_supplier data is nested within the item element and the items supplied by a supplier are also incorporated as an attribute supplies_items of type IDREFS to more easily find the items from the supplier element.

## Answers to Practice Problems:

1. customer: see companion website for XML document

2. item: see companion website for XML document

3. supplier: see companion website for XML document

4. order: see companion website for XML document

5. `<!ELEMENT online_retailer (orders, customers, items, suppliers)>`

6. 
```
<!ELEMENT orders (order)*>
<!ELEMENT order (order_date, order_total, order_info, lineitems)>
<!ATTLIST order oid ID #REQUIRED
                cust_id IDREF #REQUIRED>
<!ELEMENT order_date #PCDATA>
<!ELEMENT order_total #PCDATA>
<!ELEMENT order_info #PCDATA>
<!ELEMENT lineitems (lineitem)+>
<!ELEMENT lineitem #PCDATA>
<!ATTLIST lineitem item_id ID #REQUIRED supp_id IDREF #REQUIRED>
```

7. 
```
<!ELEMENT customers (customer)*>
<!ELEMENT customer (cust_name, cust_info, cust_orders)>
<!ATTLIST customer cid ID #REQUIRED>
<!ELEMENT cust_name #PCDATA>
<!ELEMENT cust_info #PCDATA>
<!ELEMENT cust_orders (cust_order)+>
<!ELEMENT cust_order EMPTY>
```

8. 
```
<!ELEMENT items (item)*>
<!ELEMENT item (item_name, item_info, item_suppliers)>
<!ATTLIST item iid ID #REQUIRED>
<!ELEMENT item_name #PCDATA>
<!ELEMENT item_info #PCDATA>
<!ELEMENT item_suppliers (item_supplier)+>
<!ELEMENT item_supplier (qty_available, supp_price)>
<!ELEMENT qty_available #PCDATA>
<!ELEMENT supp_price #PCDATA>
```

9. 
```
<!ELEMENT suppliers (supplier)*>
<!ELEMENT supplier (supp_name, supp_info)>
<!ATTLIST supplier sid ID #REQUIRED>
<!ELEMENT supp_name #PCDATA>
<!ELEMENT supp_info #PCDATA>
```

10. See companion website.

11. 
```
<xsd:element name="online_retailer">
  <xsd:complexType>
    <xsd:sequence>
      <xsd:element name="orders">
        <xsd:complexType>
          <xsd:sequence>
            <xsd:element ref="order" minOccurs="0"
              maxOccurs="unbounded" />
          </xsd:sequence>
        </xsd:complexType>
      </xsd:element>
      <xsd:element name="customers">
        <xsd:complexType>
          <xsd:sequence>
            <xsd:element ref="customer" minOccurs="0"
              maxOccurs="unbounded" />
          </xsd:sequence>
        </xsd:complexType>
      </xsd:element>
      <xsd:element name="items">
        <xsd:complexType>
          <xsd:sequence>
            <xsd:element ref="item" minOccurs="0"
              maxOccurs="unbounded" />
          </xsd:sequence>
        </xsd:complexType>
      </xsd:element>
      <xsd:element name="suppliers">
        <xsd:complexType>
          <xsd:sequence>
            <xsd:element ref="supplier" minOccurs="0"
              maxOccurs="unbounded" />
          </xsd:sequence>
        </xsd:complexType>
```

```
                </xsd:element>
            </xsd:sequence>
        </xsd:complexType>
    </xsd:element>

12.     <xsd:element name="order">
            <xsd:complexType>
                <xsd:sequence>
                    <xsd:element name="order_date" type="xsd:string" />
                    <xsd:element name="order_total" type="xsd:float" />
                    <xsd:element name="order_info" type="xsd:string" />
                    <xsd:element name="lineitems">
                        <xsd:complexType>
                            <xsd:sequence>
                                <xsd:element name="lineitem">
                                    <xsd:complexType>
                                        <xsd:simpleContent>
                                            <xsd:extension base="xsd:int">
                                                <xsd:attribute name="item_id" type="xsd:IDREF"
                                                    use="required" />
                                                <xsd:attribute name="supp_id" type="xsd:IDREF"
                                                    use="required" />
                                            </xsd:extension>
                                        </xsd:simpleContent>
                                    </xsd:complexType>
                                </xsd:element>
                            </xsd:sequence>
                        </xsd:complexType>
                    </xsd:element>
                </xsd:sequence>
                <xsd:attribute name="oid" type="xsd:ID" use="required" />
                <xsd:attribute name="cust_id" type="xsd:IDREF" use="required" />
            </xsd:complexType>
        </xsd:element>

13.     <xsd:element name="customer">
            <xsd:complexType>
                <xsd:sequence>
                    <xsd:element name="cust_name" type="xsd:string" />
                    <xsd:element name="cust_info" type="xsd:string" />
                    <xsd:element name="cust_orders">
                        <xsd:complexType>
                            <xsd:sequence>
                                <xsd:element name="cust_order" maxOccurs="unbounded">
                                    <xsd:complexType>
                                        <xsd:attribute name="order_id" type="xsd:IDREF"
                                            use="required" />
                                        <xsd:attribute name="odate" type="xsd:date"
                                            use="required" />
                                        <xsd:attribute name="ototal" type="xsd:float"
                                            use="required" />
```

```
                      </xsd:complexType>
                  </xsd:element>
                </xsd:sequence>
              </xsd:complexType>
          </xsd:element>
        </xsd:sequence>
        <xsd:attribute name="cid" type="xsd:ID" use="required" />
      </xsd:complexType>
  </xsd:element>
```

14.
```
    <xsd:element name="item">
      <xsd:complexType>
        <xsd:sequence>
          <xsd:element name="item_name" type="xsd:string" />
          <xsd:element name="item_info" type="xsd:string" />
          <xsd:element name="item_suppliers">
            <xsd:complexType>
              <xsd:sequence>
                <xsd:element name="item_supplier" maxOccurs="unbounded">
                  <xsd:complexType>
                    <xsd:sequence>
                      <xsd:element name="qty_available" type="xsd:int" />
                      <xsd:element name="supp_price" type="xsd:float" />
                    </xsd:sequence>
                    <xsd:attribute name="supp_id" type="xsd:IDREF"
                        use="required" />
                  </xsd:complexType>
                </xsd:element>
              </xsd:sequence>
            </xsd:complexType>
          </xsd:element>
        </xsd:sequence>
        <xsd:attribute name="iid" type="xsd:ID" use="required" />
      </xsd:complexType>
    </xsd:element>
```

15.
```
    <xsd:element name="supplier">
      <xsd:complexType>
        <xsd:sequence>
          <xsd:element name="supp_name" type="xsd:string" />
          <xsd:element name="supp_info" type="xsd:string" />
        </xsd:sequence>
        <xsd:attribute name="sid" type="xsd:ID" use="required" />
        <xsd:attribute name="supplies_items" type="xsd:IDREFS"
            use="required" />
      </xsd:complexType>
    </xsd:element>
```

16. See companion website.

## Bibliographic Notes

There are numerous resources on XML. The World Wide Web Consortium (W3C)'s website provides a wealth of information and links related to XML. Although HTML was used as a motivation for XML, XML is derived from the Standard Generalized Markup Language (SGML). There are numerous books available on XML-related information including definitive reference books on XML Schema (e.g. Walmsley [2013]). The SQL:2003 standard added the SQL/XML specification (Eisenberg and Melton [2004]), which includes the import and storage of XML data in a relational database, the manipulation of XML within the database, and the export of XML.

## More to Explore

There are many avenues to explore within the suite of XML technologies. With respect to databases, XQuery is the query language for XML, which also utilizes the XPath language. The Extensible Stylesheet Language Transformation (XSLT) navigates XML and supports the transformation to other forms, such as HTML for presentation in a Web browser or an XML format that can be imported into a database product. In addition, most database products are XML-enabled so that you can explore the various XML capabilities supported by the database product that you are using.

# Transaction Management

**9**

**LEARNING OBJECTIVES**

- To describe the ACID properties of a transaction
- To understand how databases recover from failures
- To express how databases provide support for concurrent access
- To explain how database recovery and concurrency control support the ACID properties of a transaction

One of the fundamental features of a database system is the inherent support for the properties of a transaction in the presence of concurrent execution and system failures. A transaction is a unit of code that takes the database state from one consistent state to another. However, during the execution of the transaction, the database may be in a temporarily inconsistent state. What if there is a system failure at that point in time when the database is inconsistent? How does the concurrent execution of transactions by the operating system of the computer affect the outcome of the transactions? This chapter describes how the recovery and concurrency control mechanisms of a relational database support transactions in the presence of system failures and concurrent execution so that the database remains in a consistent state.

## 9.1 ACID Properties of a Transaction

The properties of a transaction that guarantee the correctness of the database for concurrent execution and system failures are known as its ACID properties: Atomicity, Consistency, Isolation, Durability.

- **Atomicity:** The individual operations of a transaction must be performed in their entirety or not at all.
- **Consistency:** The concurrent execution of transactions maintains the correctness of the database.
- **Isolation:** The transaction should not reveal its uncommitted results to other transactions.
- **Durability:** The effects of a committed transaction must be preserved.

Table 9.1 shows the pseudocode for sample transactions over an online banking scenario, including TransferFunds, ATMWithdrawal, Dashboard, GetBalance, DepositFunds. The rightmost column of the table provides an abstraction of the read and write operations for each transaction. The ACID properties of a database rely on the read and write operations of the database being defined within the scope of transactions, so that a system log records the read and write

**Table 9.1    Pseudocode for Example Banking Transactions**

| Transaction pseudocode | Read–write **abstraction** |
|---|---|
| TransferFunds(amount, from, to) | |
|     begin transaction | |
|         if fromBalance >= amount | Read(fromBalance) |
|             fromBalance ← fromBalance − amount | Write(fromBalance) |
|             toBalance ← toBalance + amount | Read(toBalance) |
| | Write(toBalance) |
|         else | |
|             Insufficient Funds | |
|     end transaction | |
| | |
| ATMWithdrawal(amount, account) | |
|     begin transaction | |
|         if accountBalance >= amount | Read(accountBalance) |
|             accountBalance ← accountBalance − amount | Write(accountBalance) |
|         dispense money | |
|         else | |
|             Insufficient Funds | |
|     end transaction | |
| | |
| Dashboard(account1, account2) | |
|     begin transaction | |
|         display account1 | Read(account1) |
|         display account2 | Read(account2) |
|     end transaction | |
| | |
| GetBalance(account) | |
|     begin transaction | |
|         display accountBalance | Read(accountBalance) |
|     end transaction | |
| | |
| DepositFunds(amount, account) | |
|     begin transaction | |
|         accountBalance ← accountBalance + amount | Read(accountBalance) |
| | Write(accountBalance) |
|     end transaction | |

operations on the data to ensure that the recovery and concurrency control mechanisms can guarantee these properties.

> **Atomicity guarantees that all of the operations for a transaction are executed or none of them are executed.**

The atomicity property must guarantee that all of the operations for a transaction are executed or none of them are executed. Recall that a database transaction is a unit of code that takes the database state from one consistent state to another, but within the lines of code for that transaction, the database may temporarily be in an inconsistent state. For example, in the TransferFunds transaction, the database is in an inconsistent state between the statements that deduct the amount from one account and add the amount to the other account. If there was an error that caused the database system to fail at that point, then the database would be inconsistent. As another example, consider an ATMWithdrawal transaction that includes a physical operation to dispense the money to the customer. What if there was a hardware error that failed to disburse the money or that the ATM had run out of physical bills? The system must guarantee that there are no operations affecting the data if the transaction does not complete successfully.

The consistency property refers to maintaining the correctness of the database in the presence of concurrent transactions. Table 9.2 illustrates a side-by-side representation of concurrent transactions, showing a possible interleaving of the individual operations of the transactions by the operating systems scheduler. Transaction 1 is transferring funds between the savings and checking account, and Transaction 2 is an ATM withdrawal from savings. The interleaving of operations shows that T1 reads the savings balance, then T2 reads the savings balance. T1 and T2 have both read the same balance. T1 then updates the savings balance by the transfer amount and reads the checking balance. T2 then updates the savings balance by the withdrawal amount. Ending with T1 updating the checking balance to reflect the transferred funds. Due to the interleaving, the database is inconsistent. The last write of the savings balance was by ATMWithdrawal, which was the starting balance minus the amount withdrawn. However, the TransferFunds transaction withdrew the transfer amount from the savings account, which is not reflected in the final savings account balance.

> **Consistency** guarantees the correctness of the database in the presence of concurrent transactions.

**Table 9.2   Concurrent Transactions Illustrating Consistency Violation**

| T1: TransferFunds(1000, Savings, Checking) | T2: ATMWithdrawal(200, Savings) |
| --- | --- |
| Read(SavingsBalance) | |
| | Read(SavingsBalance) |
| Write(SavingsBalance) | |
| Read(CheckingBalance) | |
| | Write(SavingsBalance) |
| Write(CheckingBalance) | |

The isolation property guarantees that the results of uncommitted transactions should not be seen by other transactions. Consider the same two TransferFunds and ATMWithdrawal transactions but with a different interleaving of operations as shown in Table 9.3. In this scenario, T2 reads the savings account balance updated by T1 and completes the withdrawal process. However, in the scenario shown, T1 does not complete due to a system error, such as a power failure, and T1 does not complete. The atomicity property would guarantee that none of T1's partial operations would leave any effects on the data. But T2 has read the uncommitted results of T1, resulting in the deduction of both the transfer and withdrawal amounts from the savings account balance when the transfer was not successful.

> **Isolation** guarantees that the results of uncommitted transactions should not be seen by other transactions.

**Table 9.3   Concurrent Transactions Illustrating Isolation Violation**

| T1: TransferFunds(1000, Savings, Checking) | T2: ATMWithdrawal(200, Savings) |
| --- | --- |
| Read(SavingsBalance) | |
| Write(SavingsBalance) | |
| | Read(SavingsBalance) |
| | Write(SavingsBalance) |
| Read(CheckingBalance) | |
| System goes down! | |

Durability ensures that the effects of committed transactions are preserved. In the example shown in Table 9.4, the system goes down *after* T1 has completed. Therefore, the effects of the deposit transaction should not be lost by the system when a failure occurs. Thus, the system must be able to recover from failures and guarantee that committed transactions are persistent. Some examples of possible system failures besides power include the failure of memory or persistent storage, such as a hard drive.

**Table 9.4    Concurrent Transactions for Durability Discussion**

| T1: DepositFunds(500, Checking) | T2: ATMWithdrawal(200, Savings) |
| --- | --- |
| Read(CheckingBalance) | |
| Write(CheckingBalance) | |
| | Read(SavingsBalance) |
| | System goes down! |

These ACID properties of transactions are guaranteed by the recovery and concurrency control mechanisms of the database system. The remainder of the chapter describes these mechanisms in more detail, illustrating how the ACID properties are maintained.

## Self Check

1. Name the ACID properties of a transaction.
2. Define the ACID properties of a transaction without using the name of the property in its definition.
3. Which mechanism (recovery control or concurrency control) is responsible for guaranteeing each property?

## 9.2 Recovery Control

The recovery control mechanism is an integral component of a database system and is responsible for the detection of failures and the restoration of the database to a consistent state prior to failure. Thus, recovery control guarantees the atomicity and durability properties of a transaction. The system log is an essential part of the system, which records all transaction operations that affect the value of any database item. The log is kept on persistent storage and backed up to another storage device because a database system must be resilient from single failures. If the system log was only written on one hard drive, for example, the database would not be able to recover from the failure of that one drive. Therefore, the term *stable storage* refers to having the system log stored in multiple places so that the database can recover.

The system log records when a transaction begins and ends as well as the reading and writing of data items by the transaction. The corresponding log entries of the transaction are written out to stable storage before the read or write operations on the database take place. Table 9.5 illustrates the format of the corresponding system log entries. Note that this exposition assumes

**Table 9.5    Format of System Log Entries**

| Description | Format |
| --- | --- |
| begin transaction | [start, T] |
| read(item) | [read, T, item] |
| write(item) | [write, T, itemold, itemnew] |
| end transaction | [commit, T] |

both an *immediate update* of the database during the transaction execution and the *constrained write assumption*, which means that any transaction that will be writing a data item will first be reading its value. The recovery control mechanism needs to know the previous value of the data item if a failure occurs. With respect to updating the database, there are some systems that use a *deferred update* approach, deferring the commands until the commit point of the transaction. Rather than look at all alternatives, the coverage of recovery control will focus on understanding the essential aspects of the process.

When a failure occurs, the recovery control process uses the system log to determine the state of transactions as either *active* or *committed*. An active transaction started but does not have a corresponding commit log entry. Therefore, the atomicity property of a transaction must guarantee that none of the partially executed operations leave any effects on the data. Assume the existence of an UNDO(T) operation that uses the system log in a *backward* manner to undo the partial operations of an active transaction T. Since the log maintains both the old and new values on a write, the undo process assigns the old value to the data item.

> UNDO an *active* transaction that has not committed to guarantee atomicity.

For a *committed* transaction, assume there is a REDO(T) operation that enforces the durability property of a committed transaction T. The redo uses the system log in a *forward* direction to process the updates of the transaction. The redo process assigns the new value in the write log entry to the data item. It may seem counterintuitive that a committed transaction must be redone. However, a database system sends a write request for the immediate update of the database to the operating system of the computer, which schedules the write in an output buffer. The database system does not know whether the write request was completed before the failure, so it must redo all of the transaction's operations.

> REDO a *committed* transaction to guarantee durability.

## HOW TO 9.1  **Recovery Control:** UNDO **and** REDO

Given a system log, when recovering from failure, identify uncommitted transactions that have started ([start, Ti]) that do not have a matching commit entry in the log and committed transactions that have a start ([start, Tj]) with a matching commit ([commit, Tj]) entry in the system log. UNDO uncommitted transactions using the log backwards. REDO committed transactions using the log forwards.

**UNDO(Ti):** Uncommitted transaction Ti
  Iterate through the log backwards and for each [write, Ti, dataitem_old, dataitem_new] entry, assign data item its old value: dataitem ← dataitem_old

**REDO(Tj):** Committed transaction Tj
  Iterate through the log forwards and for each [write, Ti, dataitem_old, dataitem_new] entry, assign data item its new value: dataitem ← dataitem_new

For practical reasons, a system log cannot have all of the transactions ever in the history of the database system. Checkpoint log entries are introduced to improve the performance of recovery control. Before a [checkpoint] entry is written out to the system log, the database system requests that the operating system *flush* its output buffers and waits for a response before requesting the write of the checkpoint. Upon recovery from a failure, the database system uses the system log to determine the transactions that committed before or after the checkpoint. If a transaction committed before the checkpoint, then the recovery control system does not need to redo the transaction because its updates were guaranteed to be written to the database. However, it still needs to redo any transaction that committed after the checkpoint to maintain the durability property. As part of the checkpoint log entry, the database system can include information to improve the search in the system log by including a list of active transactions since the last checkpoint along with the earliest entry in the system log that the recovery control needs to access.

> Checkpoint entries are added to the system log to improve performance so that there is no need to REDO a transaction that committed before the checkpoint.

## Self Check

Consider the abstraction of a system log below:

[start, T1]

...

[commit, T1]

[start, T2]

A: ...

[checkpoint]

B: ...

[commit, T2]

C: ...

4. For each transaction, indicate the recovery control process (**UNDO/REDO**) if the system fails at point A.

5. For each transaction, indicate the recovery control process (**UNDO/REDO**) if the system fails at point B.

6. For each transaction, indicate the recovery control process (**UNDO/REDO**) if the system fails at point C.

## 9.3 Concurrency Control

**Concurrency control is responsible for the consistency and isolation properties of transactions.**

Concurrency control is responsible for the consistency and isolation properties of transactions. The consistency property of a transaction maintains the correctness of the database in the presence of concurrent transactions. The isolation property does not reveal the results of uncommitted transactions.

Section 9.1 introduced example concurrent executions of transactions to describe the consistency and isolation properties. In Table 9.2, a concurrent execution of two transactions illustrates a violation of the consistency property. An important component of looking at the concurrent execution of transactions is realizing that the operations within a given transaction cannot be changed. Table 9.1 provides a collection of transaction pseudocode with its corresponding read–write abstractions. Table 9.6 shows a summary of these read–write abstractions in a left-to-right manner. The left-to-right order of these operations is given for a transaction because it is showing the sequence of program statements needed to execute the transaction. For example, TransferFunds reads and writes the balance of the from account before it reads and writes the balance of the to account. However, a concurrent execution of the operations of multiple transactions can be interleaved by the scheduler of the operating system while preserving the order in which the instructions appear in each individual transaction. A sequence of such operations is called a *schedule*.

**A *schedule* is a sequence of operations that preserve the order in which instructions appear in each individual transaction.**

**Table 9.6    Abstraction of Example Banking Transactions**

| Transaction header | Read–write abstraction |
| --- | --- |
| TransferFunds(amount, from, to) | R(from) W(from) R(to) W(to) |
| ATMWithdrawal(amount, account) | R(account) Write(account) |
| Dashboard(account1, account2) | R(account1) Read(account2) |
| GetBalance(account) | R(account) |
| DepositFunds(amount, account) | R(account) Write(account) |

Note that a schedule of interleaving operations of transactions, described as a *concurrent schedule*, can be written in a left-to-right manner, too. For example, the interleaving operations of T1: TransferFunds(1000, Savings, Checking) and T2: ATMWithdrawal(200, Savings) shown in Table 9.2 can be abstracted more succinctly as shown inline below where R indicates a read operation, W indicates a write operation, the numbered suffix to the operation indicates the transaction associated with the read/write operation, and the identifier in parentheses represents the data item with S being a mnemonic for the Savings account and C for Checking:

Schedule A: R1(S) R2(S) W1(S) R1(C) W2(S) W1(C)

In the above schedule labeled Schedule A, the operations of the individual transactions are preserved. For T1: TransferFunds, the operations are R1(S) W1(S) R1(C) W1(C) and for T2: ATMWithdrawal, its operations are R2(S) W2(S). When all of the operations of one transaction occur before the operations of another transaction, the schedule is called a *serial* schedule. For the T1 and T2 transactions, there are two possible equivalent serial schedules, labeled Schedules B and C below:

> **A *serial* schedule has all of the operations of one transaction occurring before the operations of another transaction.**

Schedule B: R1(S) W1(S) R1(C) W1(C) R2(S) W2(S)
Schedule C: R2(S) W2(S) R1(S) W1(S) R1(C) W1(C)

Schedule B represents an execution sequence where T1 occurs before T2, and, similarly, Schedule C is an execution sequence where T2 occurs before T1. Thus, both are serial schedules. Since transactions by definition take the database state from a consistent state to another consistent state, Schedules B and C are consistent schedules. However, the concurrent Schedule A, which interleaves the operations in a particular manner, is not a serial schedule. In fact, Table 9.2 illustrates that Schedule A leaves the database in an inconsistent state. How does a database system take advantage of the performance gain from concurrent execution yet guarantee the consistency property of a transaction?

## 9.3.1 Serializability

Theoretically, if the system could determine that the concurrent schedule is equivalent to a serial schedule, then the concurrent execution of the transactions is consistent. Thus, *serializability* refers to the determination of a concurrent execution being computationally equivalent to running the same set of transactions in a serial execution. At a high level, two schedules S1 and S2 can be considered computationally equivalent if the following holds:

1. The set of transactions participating in S1 and S2 are the same.

2. The read–write dependencies of the same data items holds in S1 and S2.

3. The last transaction writing the same data item holds in S1 and S2.

A *serializable* schedule is computationally equivalent to a serial schedule.

To better visualize the read–write dependencies of the concurrent transactions, a *precedence graph* is introduced where an edge from transaction Ti to Tj implies that in any serial schedule that is equivalent to the concurrent schedule, Ti must appear before Tj. For the following definition of the precedence graph, it is important to note that the exposition still assumes the *constrained write assumption*, where a data item must be read by a transaction before it is written. Again, this allows understanding fundamental concepts without overcomplication and simplifies the construction of the precedence graph to looking for read–write and write–read conflicts.

> **A *serializable* schedule is computationally equivalent to a serial schedule.**

> **A precedence graph visualizes the read–write dependencies of a concurrent schedule, which is serializable if the graph does not contain a cycle.**

A precedence graph is a directed graph having nodes that correspond to each transaction participating in the schedule and directed edges from Ti to Tj for which one of the following holds:

1.  Ti executes a write(D) before Tj executes read(D), only when Tj reads the value written by Ti.

2.  Ti executes a read(D) before Tj executes write(D).

The schedule corresponding to the precedence graph is *serializable* if the precedence graph does not contain a cycle.

## HOW TO 9.2    Create a Precedence Graph

Given a concurrent schedule S of transaction operations, create a precedence graph to determine whether it is serializable. For each transaction appearing in the schedule, add a node to the precedence graph. For each operation appearing in the schedule S from left to right, perform the described action based on the type of the operation:

**Ri(D):** Transaction i is reading data item D.
Starting at the next operation, scan the operations from left to right to look for the first read–write conflict. Look for a *write* operation by a *different* transaction for the *same* data item, e.g. Wj(D). If a conflict is found and there is no existing directed edge from Ti to Tj, add a directed edge to the precedence graph from Ti to Tj.

**Wi(D):** Transaction i is writing data item D.
Starting at the next operation, scan the operations from left to right to look for the first write–read conflict. Look for a *read* operation by a *different* transaction for the *same* data item, e.g. Rj(D). If a conflict is found and there is no existing directed edge from Ti to Tj, add a directed edge to the precedence graph from Ti to Tj.

As an example, let's build the precedence graph for the concurrent Schedule A having transactions T1 and T2 from Table 9.2.

Schedule A: R1(S) R2(S) W1(S) R1(C) W2(S) W1(C)

Looking at the first operation R1(S), there is a read–write conflict with the fifth operation W2(S), adding an edge in the precedence graph from T1 to T2. The second operation R2(S) has a read–write conflict with the third operation W1(S), adding an edge in the precedence graph from T2 to T1. The remainder of the operations in the concurrent schedule do not have any conflicts. Figure 9.1 shows the resulting precedence graph for Schedule A, along with the schedule itself, showing the read–write conflicts in the schedule with different colors to indicate which conflict contributed to which edge in the precedence graph. Since there exists a cycle in the precedence graph, Schedule A is not serializable. This cycle indicates that T1 has to occur before T2 and T2 has to occur before T1, representing a contradiction. Thus, Schedule A is not equivalent to a serial schedule.

Schedule A: R1(S) R2(S) W1(S) R1(C) W2(S) W1(C)

T1             T2

**FIGURE 9.1**    Precedence graph for Schedule A.

Let's introduce a new concurrent Schedule D for the same set of transactions and build its precedence graph.

Schedule D: R1(S) W1(S) R2(S) R1(C) W1(C) W2(S)

The first operation R1(S) has a read–write conflict with the last operation W2(S), adding a directed edge from T1 to T2 in the precedence graph. The second operation W1(S) has a write–read conflict with the third operation R2(S). This conflict does not add an edge to the precedence graph since there already exists an edge from T1 to T2. None of the remaining operations have conflicts, so the precedence graph is complete as shown in Figure 9.2. There is no cycle in the precedence graph. Therefore, Schedule D is serializable. It is equivalent to the serial schedule in which T1 occurs before T2, which is shown by the directed edges in the precedence graph. Thus, Schedule D is equivalent to the serial Schedule B shown earlier in which all T1 operations occur before T2. To describe the order of the transactions in the equivalent serial schedule, indicate a serializability order of transactions using the < symbol. For example, the serializability order for Schedule D is T1 < T2.

Schedule D: R1(S) W1(S) R2(S) R1(C) W1(C) W2(S)

T1          T2

**FIGURE 9.2**  Precedence graph for Schedule D.

The theoretical definition of serializability illustrates the fundamental concept that concurrent schedules must be serializable in order to be consistent. However, drawing precedence graphs for each operation as it occurs is not practical for the database system. Therefore, databases use protocols that are an approximation to serializability. These protocols are implemented algorithms such that if the protocol allows the execution of the concurrent schedule, then the concurrent schedule is serializable. However, the protocol may not allow all possible serializable schedules. Two of the most common protocols for concurrency control are locking and timestamps.

> **Locking and timestamps are two common protocols that only allow serializable schedules, but not *all* serializable schedules.**

## Self Check

7. The consistency property of a transaction is specifically referring to the correctness in the presence of concurrent transactions. Which term presented in this chapter describes a consistent concurrent schedule?

8. Explain the process of creating a precedence graph for the execution of concurrent transactions with the constrained write assumption.

9. Given a precedence graph for a concurrent execution of transactions, explain how to determine whether the concurrent schedule is serializable.

## 9.3.2 Locking

Locking is the most common concurrency control protocol. If a transaction is going to access a data item, it must request a lock on the data item and wait for the lock to proceed. There are two types of locks: shared and exclusive. A shared lock is essentially a lock to read the data item. Since there can be multiple readers of a data item at the same time, the read lock is called a shared lock.

An exclusive lock is required to write a data item as only one transaction can write a data item at a time. The lock request by a transaction is sent to a software component known as a *lock manager*. If a data item is locked by a shared lock, then the lock manager can authorize a shared lock but not an exclusive lock. A transaction requesting an exclusive lock request must wait until all locks are released. Any request for a lock of a data item on which there is an exclusive lock must wait until the write lock is released.

## Well-Formed

> **Locking assumes that transactions are well-formed, requesting a shared lock for reading and an exclusive lock for writing.**

The underlying assumption of locking is that transactions are well-formed, requesting the appropriate type of lock for a data item before it accesses that data item. A simplifying assumption for introducing this concept is that a transaction asks for only one type of lock based on how it will be using the data item. A transaction requests a shared lock only if it is going to be reading the data item. If the transaction will be reading and writing the data item, the transaction requests an exclusive lock.

Consider the concurrent Schedule E of transactions T1:TransferFunds(1000, Savings, Checking) and T3: Dashboard(Savings, Checking). Recall that Dashboard reads the savings and checking account balances to display the information on the customer dashboard.

Schedule E: R3(S) R1(S) W1(S) R1(C) W1(C) R3(C)

Is this concurrent schedule allowable by the locking protocol assuming that transactions are well-formed? To represent the locking and unlocking of data items by transactions, additional operations are introduced:

- SLi(D) denotes that transaction i requests a shared or read lock on data item D.

- XLi(D) denotes an exclusive or write lock request on data item D by transaction i.

- ULi(D) unlocks or releases the lock held on data item D by transaction i.

Table 9.7 illustrates a possible concurrent execution with lock and unlock operations added. The header of the table has the interleaving operations in the concurrent schedule. Each row represents the shown transaction with lock and unlock operations added for its read or write operation. For example, the first operation R3(S) represents a read operation by transaction T3 for the savings account balance. Since the Dashboard transaction only reads the account balances, it gets a shared lock for the savings account balance. After it reads the balance, T3 then unlocks the savings account because it no longer needs access to that data item. Therefore, the cell in the table for the operation R3(S) for T3 shows the sequence of operations: SL3(S) R3(S) UL3(S). Similarly, the second operation R1(S) indicates the exclusive lock request by T1 for the savings account balance

**Table 9.7    Well-formed Transactions Releasing Locks When Done with Data Item**

| | 1 | 2 | 3 | 4 | 5 | 6 |
|---|---|---|---|---|---|---|
| Schedule E | R3(S) | R1(S) | W1(S) | R1(C) | W1(C) | R3(C) |
| T1: TransferFunds | | XL1(S) | | XL1(C) | | |
| | | R1(S) | W1(S) | R1(C) | W1(C) | |
| | | | UL1(S) | | UL1(C) | |
| T3: Dashboard | SL3(S) | | | | | SL3(C) |
| | R3(S) | | | | | R3(C) |
| | UL3(S) | | | | | UL3(C) |

before its first access: XL1(S). After writing the savings balance as part of the third operation, T1 releases its lock: UL1(S). The remaining operations illustrate the lock and unlock requests associated with the read and write operations that allow this concurrent schedule.

Although Schedule E is allowed by well-formed transactions, it is not serializable. T3 reads the savings account before T1 writes it, and T1 writes the checking account balance before T3 reads it. Thus, well-formed transactions that release the locks immediately after their last access of the data item do not ensure serializability.

## Two-Phase Locking (2PL)

To guarantee serializability, a lock cannot be requested by a transaction after it has released another lock. This is called *two-phase locking* (2PL) in which a transaction has a growing phase of obtaining locks following by a shrinking phase of releasing locks. If all transactions in a concurrent schedule are two-phase locked, then the concurrent schedule is two-phase locked. If the 2PL protocol allows a concurrent schedule, then the schedule is serializable, which ensures the consistency property of a transaction.

Consider the concurrent Schedule F of the same transactions, T1: TransferFunds(1000, Savings, Checking) and T3: Dashboard(Savings, Checking), but with a different interleaving of operations:

> Schedule F: R1(S) W1(S) R3(S) R1(C) W1(C) R3(C)

Table 9.8 shows the concurrent execution of Schedule F with locking. In order for the transactions to be both well-formed and two-phase locked, T1 must obtain its exclusive lock on the checking account *before* it releases its exclusive lock on the savings account as shown under the second operation. Similarly, T3 must hold onto its shared lock on the savings account until after it has obtained its shared lock on the checking account as shown in the last operation. Schedule F is serializable with serializability order of T1 < T3. Although two-phase locked transactions ensure the consistency of the concurrent execution of transactions, the isolation property is not guaranteed. For example, in the third operation of Schedule F, T3 reads the uncommitted results of T1 from the second operation.

> A transaction is *two-phase locked* if it has a growing phase of obtaining locks and a shrinking phase of releasing locks. If the 2PL protocol allows a concurrent schedule, then the schedule is serializable, which ensures the consistency property of a transaction.

### Table 9.8 **Two-Phase Locked Transactions**

|  | 1 | 2 | 3 | 4 | 5 | 6 |
|---|---|---|---|---|---|---|
| Schedule F | R1(S) | W1(S) | R3(S) | R1(C) | W1(C) | R3(C) |
| T1: TransferFunds | XL1(S) | | | | | |
| | R1(S) | W1(S) | | R1(C) | W1(C) | |
| | | XL1(C) | | | UL1(C) | |
| | | UL1(S) | | | | |
| T3: Dashboard | | | SL3(S) | | | SL3(C) |
| | | | R3(S) | | | R3(C) |
| | | | | | | UL3(S) |
| | | | | | | UL3(C) |

## Isolation

To guarantee the isolation property, two-phase locked transactions must hold their locks until the commit point of the transaction. The transaction releases its acquired locks only after it has completed all of its read and write operations. Visually, check that all of the unlock operations appear at the end of each transaction to verify the isolation property of the schedule.

> To guarantee the isolation property, two-phase locked transactions must hold their locks until the commit point of the transaction.

Consider the concurrent Schedule G that includes T1 and T3 but adds another transaction T4: GetBalance(Savings):

Schedule G: R3(S) R4(S) R3(C) R1(S) W1(S) R1(C) W1(C)

Table 9.9 shows a concurrent execution of Schedule G with locking. The transactions T3 and T4 can both have a shared lock on the savings account. Since T4 only gets the savings account balance, it can release its lock after it is done reading. However, T3 must hold the shared lock on the savings account balance until it has completed, which is shown as part of the third operation of the concurrent schedule. T3 must release the lock before T1 can acquire the lock in the fourth operation of Schedule G. T1 holds the exclusive locks on the savings and checking accounts until the transaction has completed, releasing the locks in the last column of Schedule G. Since each of the three transactions is two-phase locked and isolated, the concurrent Schedule G satisfies the consistency and isolation properties.

**Table 9.9    Two-Phase Locked with Isolation**

|  | 1 | 2 | 3 | 4 | 5 | 6 | 7 |
|---|---|---|---|---|---|---|---|
| Schedule G | R3(S) | R4(S) | R3(C) | R1(S) | W1(S) | R1(C) | W1(C) |
| T1: TransferFunds |  |  |  | XL1(S) |  | XL1(C) |  |
|  |  |  |  | R1(S) | W1(S) | R1(C) | W1(C) |
|  |  |  |  |  |  |  | UL1(C) |
|  |  |  |  |  |  |  | UL1(S) |
| T3: Dashboard | SL3(S) |  | SL3(C) |  |  |  |  |
|  | R3(S) |  | R3(C) |  |  |  |  |
|  |  |  | UL3(C) |  |  |  |  |
|  |  |  | UL3(S) |  |  |  |  |
| T4: GetBalance |  | SL4(S) |  |  |  |  |  |
|  |  | R4(S) |  |  |  |  |  |
|  |  | UL4(S) |  |  |  |  |  |

Figure 9.3 shows the precedence graph for Schedule G. Note that there is no cycle, confirming the serializability of the schedule. There is a read–write conflict between T3 and T1, and another read–write conflict between T4 and T1. There is no conflict between T3 and T4, which are only reading account balances. Thus, there are two serializability orders: T3 < T4 < T1 and T4 < T3 < T1. Schedule G is computationally equivalent to the serial schedules in which T3 and T4 occur before T1.

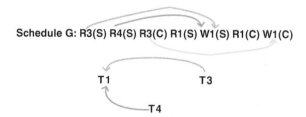

**FIGURE 9.3**   Precedence graph for Schedule G.

## Deadlock and Livelock

There are important considerations to be aware of when using a locking approach. Specifically, using 2PL and holding the locks until the commit point of the transaction may result in a *deadlock*. Consider a concurrent Schedule H of the transactions T1: TransferFunds(1000, Savings, Checking) and T3: Dashboard(Checking, Savings). Note that this call to T3 accesses the checking account first before the savings account.

Schedule H: R3(C) R1(S) W1(S) R1(C) W1(C) R3(S)

Table 9.10 shows an attempt at adding lock and unlock instructions following the 2PL protocol with isolation. For the first operation, T3 obtains a shared lock on the checking account balance to read it, holding on to the lock until the transaction completes. In the second operation, T1 acquires an exclusive lock on the savings account balance because it is going to update the balance with the transfer amount. T1 also needs to hold on to its exclusive lock until the commit point of the transaction. In the fourth operation, T1 requests an exclusive lock on the checking account, which it cannot get because T3 is holding on to a shared lock on C. At this point, the concurrent schedule cannot proceed as given. Similarly, when T3 requests a shared lock on the savings account, it must wait because T1 holds an exclusive lock on S. This is a deadlock situation in which there is a circular wait of exclusive resources held until completion.

> The term *deadlock* refers to a situation in which there is a circular wait of exclusive resources held until completion.

Table 9.10    **Deadlock Illustration**

|  | 1 | 2 | 3 | 4 | 5 | 6 |
|---|---|---|---|---|---|---|
| Schedule H | R3(C) | R1(S) | W1(S) | R1(C) | W1(C) | R3(S) |
| T1: TransferFunds |  | XL1(S) |  | XL1(C) |  |  |
|  |  | R1(S) | W1(S) |  |  |  |
| T3: Dashboard | SL3(C) |  |  |  |  | SL3(S) |
|  | R3(C) |  |  |  |  |  |

There are two main approaches to dealing with deadlock. One approach is to use a timeout interval, setting a predetermined amount of time that transactions wait for a lock. If the wait time is exceeded, then the transaction must be aborted, which means that the partial transaction must be undone and its locks released. There are issues with this approach since a transaction may be aborted if it is not in a deadlock situation due to system overload. The abort of the transaction introduces additional work on the database system that may be already overloaded, creating a cascading effect of more transactions being aborted. Another approach is to have the lock manager be responsible for detecting when the system is in a deadlock situation. The lock manager chooses one of the transactions to be aborted, releasing its locks and allowing the other transactions to complete. Theoretically, there is a possibility of a *livelock* situation as well, where livelock means that a transaction never gets a chance to complete. What if the aborted transaction that is restarted is again unlucky and is chosen by the lock manager as the victim to be aborted? Thus, the lock manager software component must be written so that it is *fair*, providing priorities to previously aborted transactions so that they can eventually complete.

> The term *livelock* refers to a situation in which a transaction never gets a chance to complete due to a cyclic restart.

Deadlock occurs in 2PL with isolation because the transactions are holding on to resources as they wait for additional ones. Another concurrency control approach, known as *timestamps*, avoids deadlock by preventing it in the first place. Similar to locking, the timestamp protocol is an approximation to serializability, in which it allows only serializable schedules but does not allow all possible serializable schedules.

# Self Check

10. Draw the precedence graph for Schedule E and comment on the properties of the schedule.

11. Draw the precedence graph for Schedule F and comment on the properties of the schedule.

12. Consider the following concurrent execution of the transactions

> T0: DepositFunds(500,Checking) and T1: TransferFunds(1000, Savings, Checking):
>     Schedule SC: R0(C) R1(S) W1(S) W0(C) R1(C) W1(C)

> Attempt to add lock and unlock instructions that will allow this concurrent schedule to occur. Is it allowed under 2PL? It is allowed under 2PL with isolation?

> | A timestamp is a unique identifier assigned by the database system to a transaction when it starts. |

## 9.3.3 Timestamps

> | The basic timestamp protocol determines whether a read or write execution should be allowed based on the timestamp of the transaction requesting the operation compared to the maximum timestamp recorded by the system for a conflicting operation. |

A timestamp is a unique identifier assigned by the database system to a transaction when it starts. The database system must guarantee that for two transactions Ti and Tj, if Tj started after Ti, then the timestamp of Ti is less than the timestamp of Tj. The basic timestamp approach to concurrency control uses timestamps to guarantee serializability. A transaction is aborted and restarted with a new timestamp if the execution of its next operation would potentially violate the serializability order. Thus, concurrency control based on timestamps does not suffer from deadlock. However, a livelock situation can occur if a transaction is continually aborted and restarted and is never allowed to complete.

The basic timestamp protocol essentially looks for read–write or write–read conflicts based on timestamps. Therefore, for each data item, the protocol must know the maximum value of a timestamp that has read or written a data item. Let's use the notation MRT(D) to denote the maximum read timestamp for the data item D, and MWT(D) for the maximum write timestamp for the data item D. Again, the exposition continues to assume the constrained write assumption in order to focus on essential concepts. For each operation, the basic timestamp protocol checks whether the timestamp of the transaction requesting the operation is less than the maximum timestamp recorded for the conflicting operation. If so, then there is a potential that a transaction would read/write a data item that was read/written by a transaction that started after it. Thus, the protocol aborts the transaction requesting the operation, undoing its partially completed operations, and restarts the transaction assigning it a new timestamp.

## ALGORITHM 9.3   Basic Timestamp Protocol

```
Read(D, TS):                              Write(D, TS):
    if TS < MWT(D)                            if TS < MRT(D)
        reject operation, abort transaction and       reject operation, abort transaction and
        restart with new timestamp                    restart with new timestamp
    else                                      else
        execute read                              execute write
        MRT(D) = max(MRT(D), TS)                  MWT(D) = max(MWT(D), TS)
```

Let's examine some of the concurrent schedules covered in the locking discussion. Recall that Schedules A, E, and H were not serializable and, hence, cannot be recognized by locking nor timestamps. Table 9.11 illustrates a trace of the basic timestamp protocol for Schedule D. For simplicity, assume that the timestamp assigned to Ti is its index i. For the concurrent schedule given, assume that the first operation in the schedule for a data item initializes its MRT and MWT

Table 9.11   **Trace of Basic Timestamp Protocol on** Schedule D

|  | 1 | 2 | 3 | 4 | 5 | 6 |
|---|---|---|---|---|---|---|
| Schedule D | R1(S) | W1(S) | R2(S) | R1(C) | W1(C) | W2(S) |
| MRT(S) | 1 |  | 2 |  |  |  |
| MWT(S) |  | 1 |  |  |  | 2 |
| MRT(C) |  |  |  | 1 |  |  |
| MWT(C) |  |  |  |  | 1 |  |

values. For each operation in the schedule, Table 9.11 shows the updated value of the MRT/MWT for the S and C data items, representing the savings and checking account balances. Since all operations successfully complete, Schedule D is also allowed under the basic timestamp protocol.

As a counterexample, Table 9.12 shows a trace of the basic timestamp protocol on Schedule E, which is known to be not serializable. The first read operation by T3 initializes MRT(S) to the value 3. The subsequent read by T1 is successful but it does not update the MRT because its timestamp is less than the current value of MRT(S). When T1 attempts to write the savings account balance, the timestamp protocol rejects the operation because T1 that started before T3 is attempting to write a data item already read by T3, which started after T1.

Table 9.12   **Trace of Basic Timestamp Protocol on** Schedule E

|  | 1 | 2 | 3 | 4 | 5 | 6 |
|---|---|---|---|---|---|---|
| Schedule E | R3(S) | R1(S) | W1(S) | R1(C) | W1(C) | R3(C) |
| MRT(S) | 3 |  |  |  |  |  |
| MWT(S) |  |  | REJECT! |  |  |  |
| MRT(C) |  |  |  |  |  |  |
| MWT(C) |  |  |  |  |  |  |

If the basic timestamp protocol allows a concurrent schedule, then it is serializable and guarantees the consistency property of transactions, which means that the database is correct in the presence of concurrent execution. However, the basic timestamp protocol does not guarantee the isolation property because the partial results of uncommitted transactions are revealed to other transactions. The implementation of the isolation property when using timestamps requires a more complicated approach that includes the system log and the recovery control mechanism. Technically, if a transaction read the uncommitted results of another transaction, it cannot commit until the transaction on which it depends commits. Thus, the database system must record these dependencies in order to guarantee the ACID properties of its transactions.

Both timestamps and 2PL are approximations to the theoretical concept of serializability. If the protocol allows a concurrent schedule, then the schedule is serializable. However, the protocols do not allow *all* serializable schedules. Consider the example Schedule I that illustrates a concurrent schedule of three transactions: T0: TransferFunds(1500, Savings, Checking), T1: TransferFunds(1000, Savings, Checking), and T2: ATMWithdrawal(500, Savings).

> Schedule I: R0(S) W0(S) R1(S) W1(S) R2(S) W2(S) R0(C) W0(C) R1(C) W1(C)

Table 9.13 shows the trace of the basic timestamp protocol for Schedule I, which allows the schedule shown. However, Table 9.14 illustrates that in the locking protocol, T1 must unlock the savings

> The basic timestamp protocol reveals the partial results of uncommitted transactions, requiring the database system to ensure that a transaction reading the results of an uncommitted transaction cannot commit until the transaction on which it depends commits.

Table 9.13    **Trace of Basic Timestamp Protocol on** Schedule I

|            | 1     | 2     | 3     | 4     | 5     | 6     | 7     | 8     | 9     | 10    |
|------------|-------|-------|-------|-------|-------|-------|-------|-------|-------|-------|
| Schedule I | R0(S) | W0(S) | R1(S) | W1(S) | R2(S) | W2(S) | R0(C) | W0(C) | R1(C) | W1(C) |
| MRT(S)     | 0     |       | 1     |       | 2     |       |       |       |       |       |
| MWT(S)     |       | 0     |       | 1     |       | 2     |       |       |       |       |
| MRT(C)     |       |       |       |       |       |       | 0     |       | 1     |       |
| MWT(C)     |       |       |       |       |       |       |       | 0     |       | 1     |

Table 9.14    **Two-Phase Locking Protocol on** Schedule I

|            | 1      | 2      | 3      | 4      | 5      | 6      | 7      | 8      | 9      | 10     |
|------------|--------|--------|--------|--------|--------|--------|--------|--------|--------|--------|
| Schedule I | R0(S)  | W0(S)  | R1(S)  | W1(S)  | R2(S)  | W2(S)  | R0(C)  | W0(C)  | R1(C)  | W1(C)  |
| T0         | XL0(S) | XL0(C) |        |        |        |        |        |        |        |        |
|            | R0(S)  | W0(S)  |        |        |        |        | R0(C)  | W0(C)  |        |        |
|            |        | UL0(S) |        |        |        |        |        | UL0(C) |        |        |
| T1         |        |        | XL1(S) |        |        |        |        |        | XL1(C) |        |
|            |        |        | R1(S)  | W1(S)  |        |        |        |        | R1(C)  | W1(C)  |
|            |        |        |        | UL1(S) |        |        |        |        |        | UL1(C) |
| T2         |        |        |        |        | XL2(S) |        |        |        |        |        |
|            |        |        |        |        | R2(S)  | W2(S)  |        |        |        |        |
|            |        |        |        |        |        | UL2(S) |        |        |        |        |

account balance in the fourth operation so that T2 can acquire its lock in the following step. Since T1 has to request a lock in the ninth operation, T1 violates the 2PL protocol. Therefore, although Schedule I is serializable, it is not allowed under 2PL.

There are also schedules allowed under 2PL but not timestamps. Consider as an example a simpler Schedule J of the transactions T0: Dashboard(Savings, Checking) and T2: ATMWithdrawal(200, Checking).

Schedule J: R0(S) R2(C) W2(C) R0(C)

Table 9.15 shows the lock and unlock instructions that allow this concurrent execution, whereas Table 9.16 traces the basic timestamp protocol, which does not allow this schedule.

Table 9.15    **Two-Phase Locking Protocol on** Schedule J

|                    | 1      | 2      | 3      | 4      |
|--------------------|--------|--------|--------|--------|
| Schedule J         | R0(S)  | R2(C)  | W2(C)  | R0(C)  |
| T0: Dashboard      | SL0(S) |        |        | SL0(C) |
|                    | R0(S)  |        |        | R0(C)  |
|                    |        |        |        | UL0(C) |
|                    |        |        |        | UL0(S) |
| T2: ATMWithdrawal  |        | XL2(C) |        |        |
|                    |        | R2(C)  | W2(C)  |        |
|                    |        |        | UL2(C) |        |

**Table 9.16   Trace of Basic Timestamp Protocol on** Schedule J

|            | 1      | 2      | 3      | 4       |
| ---------- | ------ | ------ | ------ | ------- |
| Schedule J | R0(S)  | R2(C)  | W2(C)  | R0(C)   |
| MRT(S)     | 0      |        |        |         |
| MWT(S)     |        |        |        |         |
| MRT(C)     |        | 2      |        | REJECT! |
| MWT(C)     |        |        | 2      |         |

## Self Check

13. Trace the basic timestamp protocol for Schedule A.
14. Consider the following concurrent execution of the transactions
    T0: DepositFunds(500, Checking) and T1: TransferFunds(1000, Savings, Checking):

    Schedule SC: R0(C) R1(S) W1(S) W0(C) R1(C) W1(C)

    Trace the basic timestamp protocol for this schedule. Is it allowed under timestamps?
15. Assume that $MRT(D) = 5$ and $MWT(D) = 3$. For each of the following operation requests using these initial values in each case, indicate the result of the basic timestamp protocol.
    a. Read(D, 4)
    b. Write(D, 4)
    c. Write(D, 5)
    d. Read(D, 2)
    e. Read(D, 6)

## Chapter Notes Summary

### ACID Properties of a Transaction

- *Atomicity* guarantees that all of the operations for a transaction are executed or none of them are executed.
- *Consistency* guarantees the correctness of the database in the presence of concurrent transactions.
- *Isolation* guarantees that the results of uncommitted transactions should not be seen by other transactions.
- *Durability* guarantees that the effects of committed transactions are preserved.

### Recovery Control

- Recovery control detects failures and restores the consistency of the database, supporting the atomicity and durability properties of transactions.
- Recovery control uses a system log of the execution of transactions that is written to stable storage.
- UNDO an *active* transaction that has not committed to guarantee atomicity.
- REDO a *committed* transaction to guarantee durability.
- Checkpoint entries are added to the system log to improve performance so that there is no need to REDO a transaction that committed before the checkpoint.

### Concurrency Control

- Concurrency control is responsible for the consistency and isolation properties of transactions.
- A *schedule* is a sequence of operations that preserve the order in which instructions appear in each individual transaction.

- A *serial* schedule has all of the operations of one transaction occurring before the operations of another transaction.
- A *serializable* schedule is computationally equivalent to a serial schedule.
- A precedence graph visualizes the read–write dependencies of a concurrent schedule, which is serializable if the graph does not contain a cycle.
- Locking and timestamps are two common protocols that only allow serializable schedules, but not *all* serializable schedules.
- Locking assumes that transactions are well-formed, requesting a shared lock for reading and an exclusive lock for writing.
- A transaction is *two-phase locked* if it has a growing phase of obtaining locks and a shrinking phase of releasing locks. If the 2PL protocol allows a concurrent schedule, then the schedule is serializable, which ensures the consistency property of a transaction.
- To guarantee the isolation property, two-phase locked transactions must hold their locks until the commit point of the transaction.
- The term *deadlock* refers to a situation in which there is a circular wait of exclusive resources held until completion.
- The term *livelock* refers to a situation in which a transaction never gets a chance to complete due to a cyclic restart.
- A timestamp is a unique identifier assigned by the database system to a transaction when it starts.
- The basic timestamp protocol determines whether a read or write execution should be allowed based on the timestamp of the transaction requesting the operation compared to the maximum timestamp recorded by the system for a conflicting operation.
- The basic timestamp protocol reveals the partial results of uncommitted transactions, requiring the database system to ensure that a transaction reading the results of an uncommitted transaction cannot commit until the transaction on which it depends commits.

## Chapter Reminders

Locking and timestamps are two common concurrency protocols that approximate serializability. Table 9.17 summarizes the lock operations on a data item, and Table 9.18 summarizes the bookkeeping required for the basic timestamp protocol for a data item D.

**Table 9.17   Locking Operations on a Data Item D**

| Operation | Description |
| --- | --- |
| SLi(D) | Shared lock request by transaction i to read data item D |
| XLi(D) | Exclusive lock request by transaction i to write data item D |
| ULi(D) | Unlock request by transaction i to release its lock on data item D |

**Table 9.18   Bookkeeping for Timestamps on a Data Item D**

| Information | Description |
| --- | --- |
| MRT(D) | Maximum read timestamp of a transaction that read data item D |
| MWT(D) | Maximum write timestamp of a transaction that wrote data item D |

# Practice

Use the problems below to practice your understanding of the recovery and concurrency control mechanisms of a relational database.

## Practice Problems

Consider the system log entries shown in Figure 9.4, with three different points in time shown as A, B, and C.

```
[start, T1]
[read, T1, Savings1]
[start, T2]
[write, T1, Savings1_old, Savings1_new]
[commit, T1]
[read, T2, Checking2]
[write, T2, Checking2_old, Checking2_new]
A: ---------------------------------------------------
[read, T2, Savings2]
[write, T2, Savings2_old, Savings2_new]
[checkpoint]
B: ---------------------------------------------------
[commit, T2]
C: ---------------------------------------------------
```

**FIGURE 9.4**
**System log for Practice Problems.**

1. At point A, for each transaction, indicate the high-level recovery control process for the transaction and the detailed operations to undo/redo the transaction.

2. At point B, for each transaction, indicate the high-level recovery control process for the transaction and the detailed operations to undo/redo the transaction.

3. At point C, for each transaction, indicate the high-level recovery control process for the transaction and the detailed operations to undo/redo the transaction.

Consider the following Schedule P: R1(S) W1(S) R1(C) R2(S) W1(C) R3(C) R2(C) W3(C), which is a concurrent execution of the following transactions: T1: TransferFunds(500, Savings, Checking), T2: Dashboard(Savings, Checking), T3: DepositFunds(250, Checking).

4. Draw the precedence graph for Schedule P. Is it serializable? If so, what is the serializability order?

5. Attempt to add well-formed lock and unlock instructions to the concurrent Schedule P. Is Schedule P allowed under 2PL with isolation? If not, is the schedule allowed under 2PL? If not, is it at least well-formed?

6. Trace the basic timestamp protocol for Schedule P. Is the schedule allowed under the basic timestamp protocol?

# End of Chapter Exercises

Consider the system log entries shown in Figure 9.5, with three different points in time shown as A, B, and C.

1. At point A, for each transaction, indicate the high-level recovery control process for the transaction and the detailed operations to undo/redo the transaction.

```
[start, T3]
[read, T3, Savings3]
[start, T4]
[write, T3, Savings3_old, Savings3_new]
[read, T4, Savings4]
[commit, T3]
A: ---------------------------------------------------
[read, T4, Checking4
[write, T4, Checking4_old, Checking4_new]
[checkpoint]
B: ---------------------------------------------------
[commit, T4]
C: ---------------------------------------------------
```

**FIGURE 9.5**
System log for End of
Chapter Exercises.

2. At point B, for each transaction, indicate the high-level recovery control process for the transaction and the detailed operations to undo/redo the transaction.

3. At point C, for each transaction, indicate the high-level recovery control process for the transaction and the detailed operations to undo/redo the transaction.

For each of the following interleaving of operations for the banking transactions T2: DepositFunds(500, Checking) and T3: Dashboard(Checking, Savings), indicate whether the interleaving is a concurrent schedule of those transactions, respecting the order of operations within each transaction.

4. R2(C) R3(S) R3(C) W2(C)

5. R2(C) R3(C) W2(C) R3(S)

6. R3(C) R2(S) W2(S) R3(C)

Consider the Schedule EX2: R2(C) W2(C) R1(S) W1(S) R2(S) W2(S), representing a concurrent schedule of the following two transactions:

T1: DepositFunds(250, Savings) and T2: TransferFunds(350, Checking, Savings).

7. Draw the precedence graph for Schedule EX2. Is it serializable? If so, what is the serializability order?

8. Attempt to add well-formed lock and unlock instructions to the concurrent Schedule EX2. Is Schedule EX2 allowed under 2PL with isolation? If not, is the schedule allowed under 2PL? If not, is it at least well-formed?

9. Trace the basic timestamp protocol for Schedule EX2. Is the schedule allowed under the basic timestamp protocol?

Consider the Schedule EX3: R2(S) R3(S) R1(S) W1(S) R2(C) R1(C) W1(C) representing a concurrent schedule of the following three transactions:

T1: TransferFunds(400, Savings, Checking, T2: Dashboard(Savings, Checking), and
T3: GetBalance(Savings).

10. Draw the precedence graph for Schedule EX3. Is it serializable? If so, what is the serializability order?

11. Attempt to add well-formed lock and unlock instructions to the concurrent Schedule EX3. Is Schedule EX3 allowed under 2PL with isolation? If not, is the schedule allowed under 2PL? If not, is it at least well-formed?

12. Trace the basic timestamp protocol for Schedule EX3. Is the schedule allowed under the basic timestamp protocol?

Assuming initial MRT and MWT values for a data item D with MRT(D) = 7 and MWT(D) = 5, indicate the result of the basic timestamp protocol for each of the following operation requests using these initial values in each case.

13. Write(D, 6)

14. Read(D, 4)

15. Read(D, 6)

16. Write(D, 7)

17. Read(D, 8)

# Answers to Self-Check Questions

1. ACID: Atomicity, Consistency, Isolation, Durability

2. Definition of ACID properties without using the name of the property in its definition:
   **Atomicity:** The individual operations of a transaction must be performed in their entirety or not at all.
   **Consistency:** The concurrent execution of transactions maintains the correctness of the database.
   **Isolation:** The transaction should not reveal its uncommitted results to other transactions.
   **Durability:** The effects of a committed transaction must be preserved.

3. Atomicity and durability are typically handled by the recovery control mechanism and the concurrency control is responsible for consistency and isolation.

4. A: REDO(T1); UNDO(T2)

5. B: UNDO(T2)

6. C: REDO(T2)

7. serializability

8. Create a graph with transactions as nodes and directed edges between nodes showing the read–write/write–read dependencies within the concurrent execution of transactions.

9. If the directed edges of the precedence graph do not form a cycle, then the concurrent schedule is serializable.

10. The precedence graph for Schedule E is shown in Figure 9.6. The cycle in the precedence graph means that Schedule E is not serializable.

Schedule E: R3(S) R1(S) W1(S) R1(C) W1(C) R3(C)

T1    T3

**FIGURE 9.6** Precedence graph for Schedule E.

11. The precedence graph for Schedule F is shown in Figure 9.7. There is no cycle in the precedence graph. Therefore, Schedule F is equivalent to a serial schedule where T1 < T3.

Schedule F: R1(S) W1(S) R3(S) R1(C) W1(C) R3(C)

**FIGURE 9.7** Precedence graph for
Schedule F.           T1         T3

12. Schedule SC is allowed under 2PL with isolation as shown in Table 9.19 in which all transactions hold their locks until the commit point of the transaction.

Table 9.19    **Two-Phase Locking** Schedule SC

|  | 1 | 2 | 3 | 4 | 5 | 6 |
|---|---|---|---|---|---|---|
| Schedule SC | R0(C) | R1(S) | W1(S) | W0(C) | R1(C) | W1(C) |
| T0: DepositFunds | XL0(C) |  |  |  |  |  |
|  | R0(C) |  |  | W0(C) |  |  |
|  |  |  |  | UL0(C) |  |  |
| T1: TransferFunds |  | XL1(S) |  |  | XL1(C) |  |
|  |  | R1(S) | W1(S) |  | R1(C) | W1(C) |
|  |  |  |  |  |  | UL1(C) |
|  |  |  |  |  |  | UL1(S) |

13. The concurrent Schedule A is not serializable and cannot be recognized by the timestamp protocol. Table 9.20 illustrates the point at which the timestamp protocol rejects the write operation, disallowing the concurrent schedule.

Table 9.20    **Trace of Basic Timestamp Protocol for** Schedule A

|  | 1 | 2 | 3 | 4 | 5 | 6 |
|---|---|---|---|---|---|---|
| Schedule SC | R1(S) | R2(S) | W1(S) | R1(C) | W2(S) | W1(C) |
| MRT(S) | 1 | 2 |  |  |  |  |
| MWT(S) |  |  | REJECT! |  |  |  |
| MRT(C) |  |  |  |  |  |  |
| MWT(C) |  |  |  |  |  |  |

14. Schedule SC is also allowed under the basic timestamp protocol as shown by the trace in Table 9.21.

**Table 9.21** **Trace of Basic Timestamp Protocol for** Schedule SC

| | 1 | 2 | 3 | 4 | 5 | 6 |
|---|---|---|---|---|---|---|
| Schedule SC | R0(C) | R1(S) | W1(S) | W0(C) | R1(C) | W1(C) |
| MRT(S) | | 1 | | | | |
| MWT(S) | | | 1 | | | |
| MRT(C) | 0 | | | | 1 | |
| MWT(C) | | | | 0 | | 1 |

15. Assuming that MRT(D) = 5 and MWT(D) = 3 for each operation below:

   a. Read(D, 4): Read executes with NO changes to MRT

   b. Write(D, 4): Write rejected since 4 < MRT(D)

   c. Write(D, 5): Write executes and updates MWT(D) to 5

   d. Read(D, 2): Read rejected since 2 < MWT(D)

   e. Read(D, 6): Read executes and updates MRT(D) to 6

# Answers to Practice Problems:

1. When the system goes down at point A:

   REDO(T1): Savings1 ← Savings1_new
   UNDO(T2): Checking2 ← Checking2_old

2. When the system goes down at point B:

   UNDO(T2): Savings1 ← Savings1_old
   Checking2 ← Checking2_old

3. When the system goes down at point C:

   REDO(T2): Checking2 ← Checking2_new
   Savings1 ← Savings1_new

4. The precedence graph for Schedule P is shown in Figure 9.8. There is no cycle in the precedence graph. Therefore, Schedule P is equivalent to a serial schedule where T1 < T2 < T3.

Schedule P: R1(S) W1(S) R1(C) R2(S) W1(C) R3(C) R2(C) W3(C)

**FIGURE 9.8** Precedence graph for Schedule P.

5. Schedule P is not allowed under 2PL as shown in Table 9.22. T3 requires an exclusive lock on C in step 6, which it must hold on to for the write operation in step 8. Thus, the shared

**Table 9.22** **Two-Phase Locking Protocol on** Schedule P

|  | 1 | 2 | 3 | 4 | 5 | 6 | 7 | 8 |
|---|---|---|---|---|---|---|---|---|
| Schedule P | R1(S) | W1(S) | R1(C) | R2(S) | W1(C) | R3(C) | R2(C) | W3(C) |
| T1 | XL1(S) | XL1(C) | | | | | | |
|  | R1(S) | W1(S) | R1(C) | | W1(C) | | | |
|  | | | UL1(S) | | UL1(C) | | | |
| T2 | | | | SL2(S) | | | SL2(C) | |
|  | | | | R2(S) | | | | |
| T3 | | | | | | XL3(C) | | |
|  | | | | | | R3(C) | | |

lock request in step 7 by T2 is not granted and the concurrent execution stops at this point. Thus, the concurrent schedule is not even possible for well-formed transactions.

6. Schedule P is allowed under the basic timestamp protocol as shown by the trace in Table 9.23.

**Table 9.23** **Trace of Basic Timestamp Protocol for** Schedule P

|  | 1 | 2 | 3 | 4 | 5 | 6 | 7 | 8 |
|---|---|---|---|---|---|---|---|---|
| Schedule P | R1(S) | W1(S) | R1(C) | R2(S) | W1(C) | R3(C) | R2(C) | W3(C) |
| MRT(S) | 1 | | | 2 | | | | |
| MWT(S) | | 1 | | | | | | |
| MRT(C) | | | 1 | | | 3 | 3 | |
| MWT(C) | | | | | 1 | | | 3 |

# Bibliographic Notes

The landmark papers in the area of transactions, recovery, and concurrency control are from the mid-1970s to 1980s. Serializability and 2PL can be found in Gray et al. [1975] and Eswaran et al. [1976]. Reed [1983] presents the basic timestamp protocol. The transaction concept is described in Gray [1981], and the ACID properties are discussed further in Haerder and Reuter [1983]. Lewis et al. [2002] is a comprehensive textbook on databases and transaction processing, providing a wealth of details available regarding this important topic in database systems.

# More to Explore

This chapter provided only a brief overview of some of the fundamental concepts and approaches in this overall topic: flat transaction model using an incremental log with immediate updates for recovery control and pessimistic concurrency control, such as 2PL and the basic timestamp protocol. There are other transaction models, recovery control approaches, and optimistic concurrency control mechanisms to explore.

# More on Database Design

10

**LEARNING OBJECTIVES**

- To explain the goals of a database design
- To describe the database requirements using functional dependency notation
- To determine whether a relational database schema is dependency preserving
- To verify that a relational database schema has the lossless-join property
- To analyze the relational schema to determine its normal form

Chapter 2 covered the conceptual design of a database using ER diagrams to pictorially represent the concepts in the database and their associations. Chapter 2 also presented an approach to map ER diagrams to a collection of relations for storing the data. The database design resulting from the correct application of this approach provides a schema that represents a *good* design. Each table represents a specific concept or relationship without unnecessarily repeated data and captures the constraints associated with the data in the table. The tables can also be joined together on primary–foreign key relationships to answer a query requiring the combined view of the data. However, there are numerous existing databases that need to be modified in response to changes to user requirements or evolution of business needs. This chapter introduces techniques for examining the properties of an existing database design.

## 10.1 Database Design Goals

Let's assume that the EMPLOYEE TRAINING enterprise has not been defined yet and that the company is just using a spreadsheet to represent this information. For brevity of presentation, consider a part of this enterprise that represents employees and the training courses that they have taken with the date that they took the course. The company also requires that there are no empty cells, as shown by the fragment of data in Table 10.1.

There are several observations to note about the organization of the data. An employee's information is repeated for each training course that they have taken. The information for a training course is repeated for each employee taking the course. This repeated information may cause anomalous situations to occur when data are updated, deleted, or inserted. Consider a scenario in which an employee's title changes. In Table 10.1, the employee with id 369 who took two courses receives a promotion from Software Engineer to Sr Software Engineer. Due to the employee's information being repeated for each training course that they have taken, every row associated with the employee must update the employee's title. This is called an update anomaly.

> **An update anomaly occurs when there are multiple copies of the same data that must be changed.**

**Table 10.1**    **Sample Spreadsheet Data**

| eID | eLast | eFirst | eTitle | eSalary | cID | cTitle | cHours | tDate |
|-----|-------|--------|--------|---------|-----|--------|--------|-------|
| 777 | Last777 | First777 | Database Administrator | 77777 | DB04 | Big Data | 8 | 2019-08-01 |
| 369 | Last369 | First369 | Software Engineer | 36369 | DB04 | Big Data | 8 | 2019-08-01 |
| 369 | Last369 | First369 | Software Engineer | 36369 | JA04 | JDBC | 8 | 2018-03-09 |
| 654 | Last654 | First654 | Project Lead | 60654 | WW03 | XSLT | 24 | 2020-09-14 |
| ... | | | | | | | | |

> **A delete anomaly results in a loss of information.**

Consider another scenario in the data where only one employee is enrolled in a training course. In Table 10.1, the employee with id 654 is the only one registered to take the WW03 course. If the employee drops the course, then the information about the training course is lost. This is called a delete anomaly.

What if the company wants to add a new training course, e.g. on the LINQ query language? Based on the requirements that a row cannot have any empty cells, a training course cannot be represented. This is called an insert anomaly.

> **An insert anomaly occurs when certain information cannot be added to the database.**

One goal of a database design is to avoid unnecessarily repeated data so that anomalous situations do not occur when data are updated, deleted, or inserted. The characterization of the amount of repeated data is represented by *normal forms*, which are discussed in Section 10.4. Databases remove redundancy by breaking down a larger table into smaller tables, introducing primary and foreign keys. These referential integrity associations provide a method to join the smaller tables together when needed to answer a query. The *lossless-join* property describes a collection of smaller relations that when joined together result in a correct view of the data. Lossless join is described in Section 10.3. How does one know how to correctly break down a larger table into smaller ones that capture the constraints on the data correctly and efficiently? Functional dependencies are introduced in the next section to describe data constraints, which are used throughout the rest of the chapter. Functional dependencies assist in the determination of whether a database schema has the lossless-join property as well as its normal form. In addition, the efficient verification of the data constraints as functional dependencies is another desired property of a database design, and is called *dependency preservation*, which is discussed in Section 10.3. Therefore, a database schema should be dependency preserving, have the lossless-join property, and limit the amount of redundant information.

> **The goals of a database design include the correct representation of the data (*lossless-join*) with its constraints (*functional dependencies*), limiting redundancy (characterized by *normal forms*), and checking constraints efficiently (*dependency preserving*).**

## Self Check

1. Which term describes a situation where one change results in having to modify multiple copies of the data?
2. Which term describes the property of a database schema where joining the smaller tables together results in a correct view of the combined data?
3. Which term describes the property of a database schema referring to the efficient verification of the data constraints?

## 10.2 Functional Dependencies

> **Functional dependencies represent constraints on the data.**

Functional dependencies are a formal way to specify certain constraints on the data. In fact, a functional dependency can represent a superkey. Recall that a superkey is a set of attributes such that no two tuples have the same values for the superkey attributes: A *superkey* for a relation having schema $r(a_1, a_2, ..., a_n)$ is defined to be any set of attributes $\{a_i, ..., a_j\}$ satisfying $\{a_i, ..., a_j\} \subseteq R$ such that for any two distinct tuples $t_1$ and $t_2$, $t_1.(a_i, ..., a_j) \neq t_2.(a_i, ..., a_j)$. The superkey represents a uniqueness constraint on the relation.

Recall that the dot notation t1.a references the value of the attribute a of the tuple t1, and the dot notation on a tuple of attributes t1.(ai, ..., aj) refers to a tuple of values (t.ai, ..., t.aj). A tuple has an implicit list of attributes. Consider extending the dot notation to work on a set of attributes S without an explicit listing of the attributes using the syntax t.(S). Then, the definition of a superkey can be restated as for S ⊆ R and any two distinct tuples t1 and t2, t1.(S) ≠ t2.(S).

A functional dependency is defined over sets of attributes. The notation A → B denotes that the value of the set of attributes A *functionally determines* the value of the set of attributes B. More formally, a functional dependency A → B, where A ⊆ R and B ⊆ R, holds on R, if for any legal relation r(R) for all pairs of tuples t1 and t2 in r such that t1.(A) = t2.(A), it is also the case that t1.(B) = t2.(B). Therefore, if S is a superkey holding on R, then S → R because the value of the superkey attributes uniquely determines a tuple in the relation. Note that if K ⊆ L, then the functional dependency L → K is trivial.

Functional dependencies give us a way to represent some constraints on the data. For example, the data shown in the spreadsheet of Table 10.1 has the following nontrivial functional dependencies:

$f_1$: eID → eLast eFirst eTitle eSalary
Those tuples with the same eID values must agree on the values of the employee's other properties, such as name, title, and salary.

$f_2$: cID → cTitle cHours
Similarly, those tuples representing the same cID must have the same values for the title and hours of that course.

$f_3$: eID cID → tDate
The semantics of the enterprise dictates that an employee can take a particular training course at most once.

Given these functional dependencies, is there a way to determine a candidate key for the data represented by the spreadsheet? Yes, using the properties of functional dependencies, there are inference rules to reason about functional dependencies derived from the given functional dependencies.

Table 10.2 summarizes some of the inference rules for functional dependencies. Reflexivity derives functional dependencies based on the definition of a trivial functional dependency, where the attributes forming the right-hand side of a functional dependency is a subset of the attributes forming the left-hand side. For example, if B ⊆ A then A → B. Augmentation derives a functional dependency by adding the same set of attributes to both sides of a given functional dependency; if A → B then AC → BC. Transitivity indicates that *functionally determines* is a transitive

**Table 10.2  Functional Dependency Inference Rules**

| Name | Rule | Description |
| --- | --- | --- |
| Reflexivity | if B ⊆ A then A → B | Trivial functional dependency |
| Augmentation | if A → B then AC → BC | The same attributes can be added to both sides of the functional dependency |
| Transitivity | if A → B and B → C then A → C | Functional dependencies are transitive |
| Union | if A → B and if A → C then A → BC | Functional dependencies with the same left-hand side can be combined together into one |
| Decomposition | if A → BC then A → B and A → C | If there are multiple attributes on the right-hand side of the functional dependency, then the functional dependency can be broken down into two functional dependencies |

relationship; if A → B and B → C then the functional dependency A → C holds. The reflexivity, augmentation, and transitivity rules are called Armstrong's axioms. These are a complete set of inference rules needed to derive functional dependencies. However, there are two additional inference rules, union and decomposition, that are useful, although they can be proven in terms of Armstrong's axioms. Union derives a functional dependency by combining two functional dependencies that have the same attributes in the left-hand side into one; if A → B and if A → C then A → BC. Decomposition derives multiple functional dependencies by breaking down a functional dependency with multiple attributes on the right-hand side into multiple functional dependencies that have the same left-hand side. For example, if A → BC then A → B and A → C.

> **Inference rules can be applied to functional dependencies F to derive the closure of that set, denoted F⁺.**

Given a set of functional dependencies F, these inference rules can be applied to generate the *closure* of F, which is denoted $F^+$, which are all the functional dependencies derivable from F. These inference rules can also be applied to a given set of attributes A to determine the closure of A, denoted $A^+$, in the context of the given set of functional dependencies F. Determining the closure of a set of attributes A would be useful for determining a superkey of a table r. If $A^+ = R$, then A is a superkey of R.

> **Attribute closure, denoted A⁺, determines the set of attributes functionally determined by the given set of attributes A with respect to a set of functional dependencies.**

The *Attribute Closure Algorithm* determines the closure of a set of attributes with respect to a given set of functional dependencies F. The algorithm initializes the attribute closure to the set of attributes A given as input, using the reflexivity inference rule. Each iteration of the algorithm examines each functional dependency in the given set of functional dependencies F. If the attributes in the left-hand side of the functional dependency are in the current attribute closure, then the attributes on the right-hand side of the functional dependency are added via a union to the attribute closure computed thus far. Note that the algorithm uses the notation of two functions, LHS and RHS. Each function takes a functional dependency as input and returns the set of attributes on the side of the functional dependency denoted by the function name. The algorithm terminates when there is an iteration in which no changes are made to the attribute closure.

## ALGORITHM 10.1    Attribute Closure

Given a set of attributes A and a set of functional dependencies F, find the closure of A, denoted $A^+$.

```
attribute_closure = A
changes = true
while changes
    changes = false
    for each functional dependency fᵢ in F
        if LHS(fᵢ) ⊆ attribute_closure
            if there exists an attribute in RHS(fᵢ) that is not in attribute_closure
                attribute_closure = attribute_closure ∪ RHS(fᵢ)
                changes = true
return attribute_closure
```

Table 10.3 traces the execution of the attribute closure algorithm for the set of attributes { eID, cID } for the spreadsheet example of Table 10.1 using the functional dependencies { $f_1, f_2, f_3$ }. Iteration 0 indicates the initialization of the attribute_closure to the given attributes. Iteration 1 examines each functional dependency, adding the attributes shown via a union to the attribute_closure. Iteration 2 does not add any attributes so the algorithm terminates. Since { eID, cID }⁺ includes all attributes of the spreadsheet table, it is a superkey. Since no subset of { eID, cID } is a superkey, then { eID, cID } is a candidate key for the spreadsheet table.

**Table 10.3  Trace of Attribute Closure Algorithm**

| Iteration | Functional dependency | attribute_closure |
|-----------|-----------------------|-------------------|
| 0 | | eID, cID |
| 1 | $f_1$ | eLast, eFirst, eTitle, eSalary |
| | $f_2$ | cTitle, cHours |
| | $f_3$ | tDate |
| 2 | $f_1$ | |
| | $f_2$ | |
| | $f_3$ | |

Determining the candidate key of a table is an important component of relational database design theory. There is a heuristic approach that can help determine a candidate key using the functional dependencies that apply on a table. The quality of the functional dependencies is an important consideration in this approach. For example, does the set of functional dependencies have extraneous or redundant information? Special Topic 10.2 discusses extraneous attributes and redundant functional dependencies.

> Determining the candidate key of a table is an important component of relational database design theory.

## SPECIAL TOPIC 10.2   Minimal Set of Functional Dependencies

Recall that the functional dependency inference rules can derive many functional dependencies from the given set. Theoretically, a minimal set of functional dependencies can be obtained by first using the decomposition inference rule so that each functional dependency has a single attribute on the right-hand side; then removing any extraneous attributes from the left-hand side; and finally, removing any redundant functional dependencies. An extraneous attribute on the left-hand side of a functional dependency is one whose removal does not affect the closure of the functional dependencies. For example, if there was a functional dependency $f_4$: eID cID cTitle → tDate, the attribute cTitle is extraneous in $f_4$ due to $f_3$, which is eID cID → tDate. Similarly, a redundant functional dependency is one that can be removed without affecting the closure of the functional dependencies. Removing the extraneous cTitle attribute from $f_4$ yields a redundant functional dependency that is the same as $f_3$, and thus, should be removed.

## HOW TO 10.3   Heuristic Determination of a Candidate Key

Given a set of functional dependencies that apply to the table:

**Step 1:** Union together the attributes appearing on the left-hand side of all functional dependencies that apply to the table.

**Step 2:** If there are any attributes in the table that do not appear in a functional dependency (either LHS or RHS), add the attributes to the set. This set of attributes is a superkey.

**Step 3:** Remove all extraneous attributes from the set to determine the candidate key, where an attribute is extraneous on the left-hand side of a functional dependency if its removal does not affect the closure of the functional dependencies. *(Hint: If an attribute appears on the right-hand side of a nontrivial functional dependency, it is potentially extraneous.)*

Note that this approach finds one candidate key. There may be multiple candidate keys for a relation. This typically happens in the presence of unique constraints on attributes in a table, such as when an employee can be uniquely identified by both the employee id number and the assigned phone number at the company. For example, eID → ePhone and ePhone → eID. The candidate key found first depends on the order in which the functional dependencies are examined in the process above.

Figures 10.1 and 10.2 provide examples of determining a candidate key. The supplier table in Figure 10.1 has two functional dependencies: the name of the supplier determines the supplier's address; and the supplier name and item determine the price of the item for that supplier. The determination of the candidate key starts with the union of the left-hand side of the functional dependencies: { sName, item }, which is a superkey. Since no subset is a superkey, then { sName, item } is the candidate key. Figure 10.2 shows the empdept table having three functional dependencies: the employee's id determines the name of the employee and the number of the department in which the employee works; the unique department number determines the name of the department; since department names are also unique for this company, the name of the department determines the department number. The determination of the candidate key starts with the set of attributes { eID, dNum, dName }, which is the union of the left-hand sides of the functional dependencies. The set of attributes is confirmed as a superkey. The determination in Figure 10.2 shows the attribute closure for subsets of length 2 and then subsets of length 1. The candidate key for this empdept table is the eID attribute. Note that the hint in How To 10.3 suggests that dNum and dName may be extraneous since these attributes appeared on the right-hand side of a functional dependency. However, let's consider yet another example. Figure 10.3 shows the department having its own table with just the dNum and dName attributes

Table: supplier(sName, sAddr, item, price)

FDs: { sName → sAddr, sName item → price }

Candidate key: { sName, item }

| Candidate key | Attributes | Attribute closure |
|---|---|---|
| √ | { sName, item } | sName, item, sAddr, price |
| X | { sName } | sName, sAddr |
| X | { item } | item |

**FIGURE 10.1**
supplier **candidate key determination example.**

Table: empdept(eID, eName, dNum, dName)

FDs: { eID → eName dNum, dNum → dName, dName → dNum }

Candidate key: { eID }

| Candidate key | Attributes | Attribute closure |
|---|---|---|
| Superkey | { eID, dNum, dName } | eID, eName, dNum, dName |
| Superkey | { eID, dNum } | eID, eName, dNum, dName |
| Superkey | { eID, dName } | eID, dName, eName, dNum |
| X | { dNum, dName } | dNum, dName |
| √ | { eID } | eID, eName, dNum, dName |
| X | { dNum } | dName, dNum |
| X | { dName } | dName, dNum |

**FIGURE 10.2**
empdept **candidate key determination example.**

Table: department(dNum, dName)

FDs: { dNum → dName, dNum → dName }

Candidate keys: { dNum }, { dName }

| Candidate key | Attributes | Attribute closure |
|---|---|---|
| Superkey | { dNum, dName } | dNum, dName |
| √ | { dNum } | dNum, dName |
| √ | { dName } | dName, dNum |

**FIGURE 10.3**
department **candidate key determination example.**

with two functional dependencies: { dNum → dName, dNum → dName }. In this scenario, the department table has two candidate keys: dNum and dName.

Most of the table examples of this section (spreadsheet table, supplier, empdept) have issues with their design. Intuitively, the unnecessary repetition of information in these tables should have hinted at that. Using functional dependencies, the rest of the chapter examines the properties of a relational database schema: lossless join, dependency preservation, and normal forms.

## Self Check

4. What term describes a functional dependency A → B where B ⊆ A?

5. What is the name of the inference rule that breaks down eID → eName dNum into two functional dependencies: eID → eName and eID → dNum?

6. What does attribute closure mean?

## 10.3 Decomposition

Database design strategies break down tables with unnecessarily repeated data into smaller tables to avoid anomalies, associating the resulting tables using referential integrity. When the combined view of the data is needed to answer a query, the required smaller tables are joined together. This section covers the formal definition of a decomposition of a table and the dependency preservation and lossless-join properties of a decomposition.

Recall that the set of attributes for a relation r is denoted by R. A collection of relation schemes { $R_1$, ..., $R_n$ } is a *decomposition* of a relation r if the union of all of the $R_i$ = R.

> A collection of relation schemes { $R_1$, ..., $R_n$ } is a *decomposition* of a relation r if the union of all of the $R_i$ = R.

$$R = \bigcup_{i=1}^{n} R_i$$

This is a formal way of indicating that all of the attributes in r must appear at least once in the breakdown of r into a collection of smaller tables for it to be considered a decomposition of r.

Given a set of functional dependencies F on the relation r, these functional dependencies must also be broken down to apply to the appropriate tables in the decomposition. If all of the attributes in a functional dependency, including both the left-hand side and right-hand side attributes, appear in a table, then the functional dependency is associated with that table.

# HOW TO 10.4    Determine Breakdown of F for a Decomposition

Given a decomposition $\{ R_1, ..., R_n \}$ of r and the set of functional dependencies F that apply to r, determine the breakdown of F.

**Step 1:** Use the decomposition inference rule to modify the given set F to $F^d$ such that each functional dependency has only one attribute on the right-hand side.

**Step 2:** For each $R_i$ in the decomposition, define $F_i$ as the set of functional dependencies that apply to $R_i$.

$$F_i = \{ f \mid f \in F^d \text{ and } LHS(f) \cup RHS(f) \subseteq R_i \}$$

**Step 3:** Define $F^\cup$ as the union of all of the $F_i$.

$$F^\cup = \bigcup_{i=1}^{n} F_i$$

---

> $F_i$ **is the set of functional dependencies in F that apply to a relation** $R_i$ **in the decomposition, and** $F^\cup$ **is the union of all of the** $F_i$.

There are several observations to make regarding $F^\cup$. These are the functional dependencies that can be checked efficiently using the tables in the decomposition without having to perform joins. A decomposition is *dependency preserving* if $(F^\cup)^+ = F^+$. If $F^\cup = F$, then no functional dependencies were lost and the decomposition is trivially dependency preserving. What if $F^\cup$ is not equivalent to F? Computing and comparing the closures of $F^\cup$ and F using Armstrong's axioms is a lot of work. The simpler approach is to examine each functional dependency in $F - F^\cup$ to determine whether the functional dependency is already in the closure with respect to $F^\cup$ and is, therefore, a redundant functional dependency.

> **A decomposition is** *dependency preserving* **if** $(F^\cup)^+ = F^+$.

Figures 10.4 and 10.5 provide two examples of decompositions using the earlier supplier and empdept examples illustrating functional dependencies and the determination of candidate keys. In Figure 10.4, the supplier table is broken down into two tables: one with the supplier name and address; the second having the supplier name, item, and price. As shown, $F^\cup = F$ and, therefore,

Table: supplier(sName, sAddr, item, price)

F: { sName → sAddr, sName item → price }

| Decomposition | Attributes | Functional dependencies |
|---|---|---|
| $R_1$ | { sName, sAddr } | $F_1$ = sName → sAddr |
| $R_2$ | { sName, item, price } | $F_2$ = sName item → price |

Determination of dependency preservation:
$F^\cup = F$
Dependency preserving $\sqrt{}$

**FIGURE 10.4**
supplier **dependency preserving** decomposition example.

Table: empdept(eID, eName, dNum, dName)

F: { eID → eName dNum dName, dNum → dName, dName → dNum }

| Decomposition | Attributes | Functional dependencies |
|---|---|---|
| $R_1$ | { eID, eName, dNum } | $F_1$ = eID → eName |
| | | eID → dNum |
| $R_2$ | { dNum, dName } | $F_2$ = dNum → dName |
| | | dName → dNum |

Determination of dependency preservation:
$F - F^\cup$ = eID → dName
$(eID)^+$ with respect to $F^\cup$ = eID, eName, dNum, dName
Dependency preserving $\sqrt{}$

**FIGURE 10.5**
empdept **dependency preserving** decomposition example.

is trivially dependency preserving since no functional dependencies were lost. Figure 10.5 breaks down empdept into two tables: one with the employee id, name, and department number in which the employee works; the other contains the department number and name. The original functional dependency eID → eName dNum dName is broken down into three: eID → eName, eID → dNum, and eID → dName. Note that eID → dName does not apply to R$_1$ because dName does not appear in the table, and thus, represents a lost functional dependency. However, since the attribute closure of eID with respect to the remaining functional dependencies contains dName, this is a redundant functional dependency that is logically determined by F$^\cup$. Therefore, the decomposition is dependency preserving.

Another property to examine for a decomposition is whether it has the lossless-join property, which essentially means that joining together the smaller tables in the decomposition of a larger table will result in that original table. A decomposition { R$_1$, ..., R$_n$ } of a relation r is a *lossless-join decomposition* if for all legal relations r(R) the following holds:

$$r = \bowtie_{i=1}^{n} \pi_{R_i}(r)$$

> **Intuitively, a lossless-join decomposition means that the result of joining the smaller tables in the decomposition results in the original table.**

How do you correctly breakdown a table to remove unnecessary repetition of data? Consider a table representing the addresses of employees in the United States, which has a postal code, known as a zipcode, that is associated with exactly one city and state. Since this employer is located in only one state and employees must live in this state, the table consists of the following fields: the employee id, name, street address, city, and zip code. The company notices that the city is repeated for every employee living in that zip code. Therefore, the company wants to break down this table into two tables: one with city and zipcode; the other with the employee's id, name, street address, and city. There are issues with this breakdown when the two tables are joined together on their common attribute, which is city. Although a zipcode is associated with only one city, a city has many zip codes. Thus, a join of the broken down tables results in a table with more tuples than the original one. This decomposition is *lossy* because information was lost.

> **The pairwise decomposition of R into R$_1$ and R$_2$ is lossless if R$_1$ ∩ R$_2$ → R$_1$ or R$_1$ ∩ R$_2$ → R$_2$.**

There is a straightforward test to check whether the breakdown of one table into two smaller ones is lossless or not. Breaking down one table into two is called a *pairwise decomposition*. If the attributes in common between the two smaller tables form a candidate key of one of the tables, then the pairwise decomposition is lossless.

## HOW TO 10.5    Determine Lossless Pairwise Decomposition

Given a decomposition { R$_1$, R$_2$ } of r and the set of functional dependencies F that apply to r, determine whether the pairwise decomposition has the lossless-join property.

**Step 1:** Using the functional dependencies F$_i$ that apply to each table in the decomposition, determine the candidate key(s) for R$_i$.

**Step 2:** The pairwise decomposition is lossless if R$_1$ ∩ R$_2$ is a candidate key for either R$_1$ or R$_2$.

$$R_1 \cap R_2 \to R_1 \text{ or } R_1 \cap R_2 \to R_2$$

Figures 10.6 and 10.7 illustrate that the supplier and empdept dependency-preserving decompositions also have the lossless-join property. Figure 10.8 shows that the proposed decomposition of empaddr into { eID eName street city, city zip } is *not* lossless because the city attribute is not a candidate key of one of the tables. A lossless-join decomposition for empaddr would be { eID eName street zip, city zip } because the zip common attribute is a candidate key for the { city zip } table.

What if you have an existing database design and want to confirm that the tables can be joined correctly to answer the processing needs of the application? The algorithm essentially applies the functional dependencies to the schema to determine whether the database has the lossless-join property.

> **To determine the lossless-join property for a database schema, apply the functional dependencies at the schema level.**

Table: supplier(sName, sAddr, item, price)

F: { sName → sAddr, sName item → price }

| Decomposition | Attributes | Functional dependencies | Candidate key(s) |
|---|---|---|---|
| $R_1$ | { sName, sAddr } | $F_1$ = sName → sAddr | { sName } |
| $R_2$ | { sName, item, price } | $F_2$ = sName item → price | { sName, item } |

Determination of lossless join:
$R_1 \cap R_2$ = sName
sName → $R_1$
Lossless join √

**FIGURE 10.6**    supplier **lossless-join pairwise decomposition example.**

Table: empdept(eID, eName, dNum, dName)

F: { eID → eName dNum dName, dNum → dName, dName → dNum }

| Decomposition | Attributes | Functional dependencies | Candidate key(s) |
|---|---|---|---|
| $R_1$ | { eID, eName, dNum } | $F_1$ = eID → eName<br>eID → dNum | { eID } |
| $R_2$ | { dNum, dName } | $F_2$ = dNum → dName<br>dName → dNum | { dNum }, { dName } |

Determination of lossless join:
$R_1 \cap R_2$ = dNum
dNum → $R_2$
Lossless join √

**FIGURE 10.7**    empdept **lossless-join pairwise decomposition example.**

Table: empaddr(eID, eName, street, city, zip)

F: { eID → eName street city zip, zip → city }

| Decomposition | Attributes | Functional dependencies | Candidate key(s) |
|---|---|---|---|
| $R_1$ | { eID, eName, street, city } | $F_1$ = eID → eName<br>eID → street<br>eID → city | { eID } |
| $R_2$ | { city, zip } | $F_2$ = zip → city | { zip } |

Determination of lossless join:
$R_1 \cap R_2$ = city
$city^+$ → city
Lossless join X

**FIGURE 10.8**    empaddr **lossless-join pairwise decomposition counterexample.**

# ALGORITHM 10.6  Lossless-Join Property for Database Schema

Given a relational database schema { $R_1$, ..., $R_m$ } and the set of functional dependencies F, determine whether the database schema has the lossless-join property.

```
n = | R₁ ∪ ... ∪ Rₘ |
matrix = m rows by n columns
for i = 1 to m
    for j = 1 to n
        if jᵗʰ attribute ∈ Rᵢ
            matrix[i, j] = aⱼ
        else
            matrix[i, j] = bᵢⱼ
changes = true
while changes
    changes = false
    for each functional dependency f in F
        for all rows that agree on the symbols of LHS(f)
            equate the symbols on the RHS(f),
            choosing a symbols over b symbols
            if updates, changes = true
lossless_join = exists a row in the matrix with all a values
return lossless_join
```

Figures 10.9 and 10.10 illustrate the trace of Algorithm 10.6 on the supplier and empdept examples, respectively, confirming the lossless-join property. The initial matrix is shown as Iteration 0 in the figures. Iteration 1 shows the first application of the functional dependencies to the database schema. When a symbol changes in the table, it is noted by a prefix indicating the functional dependency that was applied. Iteration 2 in both figures does not result in any change, and, thus, the algorithm terminates. The trace of the counterexample of empaddr is shown in Figure 10.11. There is no change to the initial matrix when applying the functional dependencies, and there does not exist a row in the table with all $a$ symbols. Thus, it does not have the lossless-join property. This illustrates that there is a problem in the decomposition of the original

$R_1 = \{$ sName, sAddr $\}$

$R_2 = \{$ sName, item, price $\}$

F: $\{ f_1:$ sName $\rightarrow$ sAddr, $f_2:$ sName item $\rightarrow$ price $\}$

| Iteration | Table | 1: sName | 2: sAddr | 3: item | 4: price |
|-----------|-------|----------|----------|---------|----------|
| 0 | $R_1$ | $a_1$ | $a_2$ | $b_{13}$ | $b_{14}$ |
|   | $R_2$ | $a_1$ | $b_{22}$ | $a_3$ | $a_4$ |
| 1 | $R_1$ | $a_1$ | $a_2$ | $b_{13}$ | $b_{14}$ |
|   | $R_2$ | $a_1$ | $f_1: a_2$ | $a_3$ | $a_4$ |
| 2 | $R_1$ | $a_1$ | $a_2$ | $b_{13}$ | $b_{14}$ |
|   | $R_2$ | $a_1$ | $a_2$ | $a_3$ | $a_4$ √ |

**FIGURE 10.9**
supplier lossless-join decomposition algorithm trace.

$R_1 = \{$ eID, eName, dNum $\}$

$R_2 = \{$ dNum, dName $\}$

F: $\{ f_1$: eID $\rightarrow$ eName dNum dName, $f_2$: dNum $\rightarrow$ dName, $f_3$: dName $\rightarrow$ dNum $\}$

| Iteration | Table | 1: eID | 2: eName | 3: dNum | 4: dName |
|-----------|-------|--------|----------|---------|----------|
| 0 | $R_1$ | $a_1$ | $a_2$ | $a_3$ | $b_{14}$ |
|   | $R_2$ | $b_{21}$ | $b_{22}$ | $a_3$ | $a_4$ |
| 1 | $R_1$ | $a_1$ | $a_2$ | $a_3$ | $f_2$: $a_4$ |
|   | $R_2$ | $b_{21}$ | $b_{22}$ | $a_3$ | $a_4$ |
| 2 | $R_1$ | $a_1$ | $a_2$ | $a_3$ | $a_4$ $\checkmark$ |
|   | $R_2$ | $b_{21}$ | $b_{22}$ | $a_3$ | $a_4$ |

**FIGURE 10.10**
empdept **lossless-join** decomposition algorithm trace.

$R_1 = \{$ eID, eName, street, city $\}$

$R_2 = \{$ city, zip $\}$

F: $\{ f_1$: eID $\rightarrow$ eName street city zip, $f_2$: zip $\rightarrow$ city $\}$

| Iteration | Table | 1: eID | 2: eName | 3: street | 4: city | 5: zip |
|-----------|-------|--------|----------|-----------|---------|--------|
| 0 | $R_1$ | $a_1$ | $a_2$ | $a_3$ | $a_4$ | $b_{15}$ |
|   | $R_2$ | $b_{21}$ | $b_{22}$ | $b_{23}$ | $a_4$ | $a_5$ |
| 1 | $R_1$ | $a_1$ | $a_2$ | $a_3$ | $a_4$ | $b_{15}$ |
|   | $R_2$ | $b_{21}$ | $b_{22}$ | $b_{23}$ | $a_4$ | $a_5$ |

**FIGURE 10.11**
empaddr **lossless-join** decomposition algorithm trace.

empaddr table into smaller tables. The next section provides an approach to guide the decomposition of a table into smaller ones such that the decomposition will be lossless.

There is an intuitive approach that confirms the results of the lossless-join decomposition algorithm, which is looking at all of the attributes in the decomposition for the set of relation schemes given. This collection of attributes has been called the *universal* relation. The algorithm applies the functional dependencies at the schema level to this universal relation. The insight is that if one of the relations in the decomposition contains a candidate key of the universal relation, then the decomposition will be lossless. Use the determination of a candidate key from How To 10.3 with the universal relation and its functional dependencies to determine its candidate key.

As another counterexample for lossless join, extend the empdept decomposition shown in Figures 10.7 and 10.10 to include another table that represents the many locations of a department. Specifically, add the table deptlocations(dNum, dLocation) with the functional dependency dNum dLocation $\rightarrow$ dNum dLocation that indicates a department has many locations. This extension adds another column for dLocation and another row for deptlocations. The lossless-join decomposition algorithm will not yield a row of all $a$ symbols because there is no way to determine the dLocation. This is confirmed by determining the candidate key of the extended example, which is the combination of eID and dLocation. This candidate key is not contained in one of the tables. Semantically, the issue in this design is that the location of the department in which an employee works is not represented. Thus, if this information is needed, then the relational schema for the employee must be updated to include both the department number and location in which the employee works.

A database schema may or may not have the lossless-join property across the entire database. This may be due to the database storing a wide range of related data, such as employee personal information, project and work hours, dependents, and benefits. There is no need in the application to combine all of this information to answer a single query. However, for the information that must be joined together for the processing needs of the application, the set of relation schemes must be lossless, which can be determined by running the lossless-join decomposition algorithm on a subset of relation schemes from the database scheme.

## Self Check

7. Explain how to determine if a given breakdown of a relation is a decomposition.
8. What is the method used to determine whether a decomposition is dependency preserving?
9. What is the shortcut to check whether a pairwise decomposition of R into R1 and R2 is lossless?

## 10.4 Normal Forms

One of the goals of database design is to limit the amount of unnecessarily repeated data. As motivated earlier in Section 10.1, redundant data may result in anomalous situations when data are modified. Formally, how can unnecessarily repeated data be identified in a table, and, once identified, how should the table be broken down to eliminate the redundant data? The data constraints represented by functional dependencies introduced in Section 10.2 help in this determination. Using functional dependencies that apply on a table, the amount of redundancy in the table is characterized using the definition of *normal forms* on the data. By definition of the relational data model previously discussed in Section 1.3, each attribute of a relation must have an associated domain of basic or simple values. This underlying assumption is called *first normal form*, which is abbreviated as 1NF.

> 1NF is the underlying assumption of the relational data model that each attribute of a relation must have a simple value.

In Section 10.2, the supplier(sName, sAddr, item, price) table was introduced to represent a supplier's name and address along with the items that they supply and the price of the items that they supply. The data constraints are given by the set of functional dependencies F = { sName → sAddr, sName item → price }. Based on these constraints, the address of the supplier is repeated for every item supplied by the supplier. Formally, Figure 10.1 illustrates that the candidate key for the supplier table is a composite key consisting of the attributes sName and item. Since the sAddr attribute is functionally determined by part of the candidate key, only sName, the sAddr is repeated. A relation is in *second normal formal (2NF)* if every attribute in the relation either appears in a candidate key or is fully functionally determined by every candidate key, i.e. no partial dependency exists. The attributes sName and item appear in a candidate key. The attribute price is functionally determined by the entire candidate key. However, sAddr is functionally determined by only *part* of the candidate key, sName. Therefore, the table does not satisfy the definition of 2NF, but is in 1NF based on the definition of the relational data model.

> Informally, 2NF does not allow a partial dependency.

Consider a table workson(eID, pID, plocation) with the functional dependencies F = { eID → pID, pID → plocation }. The data constraints indicate that an employee can only work on one project and a project has only one location. Based on these constraints, the project's location is repeated for each employee working on the project. The candidate key for workson is the attribute eID. Note that plocation is transitively dependent on eID. The workson table is in 2NF since there are no partial dependencies. A relation is in *third normal formal (3NF)* if for each functional dependency f in $F^d$ one of the following holds: f is trivial, the left-hand side is a superkey

> Informally, a relation is in 3NF if it satisfies 2NF and there is no transitive dependency.

or the right-hand side is contained in a candidate key. Recall that $F^d$ just applies the decomposition inference rule to the functional dependencies in F so that there is only one attribute on the right-hand side. The use of $F^d$ instead of F facilitates the check that the right-hand side of the functional dependency is contained in a candidate key. The functional dependency pID → plocation violates 3NF since pID is not a superkey and plocation is not contained in a candidate key.

Consider a modified version of a table recording the number of hours that an employee works on a project: hoursworked(eID, pID, hours, email) with F = { eID pID → hours, eID → email, email → eID }. The functional dependencies for this scenario indicate that an employee can work on many projects because it is the combination of the employee id and project id that determine the number of hours that an employee worked on that project. The last two functional dependencies identify that an employee has a unique email and the email uniquely identifies the employee. The hoursworked table has unnecessarily repeated data. The email of an employee is repeated for each project on which an employee works. Note that there are two candidate keys for the hoursworked table: { eID, pID } and { email, pID }. The hoursworked table is in 3NF since the functional dependencies satisfy the definition of 3NF: the left-hand side is a superkey or the right-hand side is contained in a candidate key. A relation is in *Boyce–Codd normal form (BCNF)* if for each functional dependency $f$ that applies on the table, either $f$ is a trivial functional dependency or the left-hand side of $f$ is a superkey. Since both functional dependencies eID → email and email → eID violate this rule, hoursworked is not in BCNF.

> A relation is in BCNF if for each nontrivial functional dependency $f$ that applies on the table, the left-hand side of $f$ is a superkey.

Each normal form introduced removes additional potential redundancy. Based on the given definitions of the normal forms, a relation in BCNF is also in 3NF, and a 3NF relation is also in 2NF. Thus, the normal form of a relation is the highest normal form condition that the relation and its functional dependencies meet.

## HOW TO 10.7    Determine the Normal Form of a Relation

Given a relation schema and the set of functional dependencies that apply to the table:

**Step 1:** Determine the candidate key(s) for the table.

**Step 2:** Determine the highest normal form by applying the conditions for the normal form definitions in the following order: BCNF, 3NF, 2NF.

**Step 3:** If none of the conditions are met, then the table is in 1NF, which is the underlying assumption of the relational data model since attributes must have simple atomic values.

> *Normalization* is the process of breaking down a table into smaller ones to remove redundancy.

The process of breaking down a table into smaller ones to remove redundancy is called *normalization*. The goal of the normalization process is for each relational schema in a database to satisfy BCNF, or at least 3NF, which will be discussed later. The BCNF decomposition algorithm uses the functional dependencies that violate BCNF to direct the normalization process. The intuition is that a functional dependency violating BCNF guides the replacement of the original table with two tables: one that has all of the attributes of the functional dependency and another that removes the attributes on the right-hand side of the functional dependency from the original table. The first table in the pairwise decomposition is in BCNF since it was formed using the functional dependency so its left-hand side is a superkey. The determination of the normal form of the second table in the pairwise decomposition is based on the applicable functional dependencies and its candidate key(s). If this table is not in BCNF, then the algorithm breaks down this table as well. The algorithm terminates when there no longer exists a table in the decomposition that is not in BCNF.

# ALGORITHM 10.8  BCNF Decomposition Algorithm

Given a relational schema R and a set of functional dependencies F, determine a BCNF decomposition of R.

decomposition = R
done = false
while not done
    if there exists an $R_i$ in decomposition that is not in BCNF
        let $f$ = a nontrivial functional dependency
            such that LHS($f$) is not a superkey of $R_i$
        $R_{i1}$ = LHS($f$) $\cup$ RHS($f$)
        $R_{i2}$ = $R_i$ − RHS($f$)
        decomposition = decomposition − { $R_i$ } $\cup$ { $R_{i1}$, $R_{i2}$ }
    else
        done = true
return decomposition

The BCNF decomposition algorithm guarantees the lossless-join property since it is performing a pairwise decomposition at each step such that the intersection of attributes in the decomposition forms a key of one of tables, i.e. the table created using the violating functional dependency. Note that there can be multiple functional dependencies for the schema R such that the left-hand side is not a superkey. Since the algorithm removes the attributes from the original table that appear on the right-hand side of the functional dependency, there can be multiple BCNF decompositions of a relational schema based on the order in which the violating functional dependencies are chosen. Typically, a more intuitive decomposition results when the violating functional dependency chosen does not have any attributes on its right-hand side that appear on the left-hand side of another functional dependency. This will be the approach illustrated in the application of the BCNF decomposition algorithm to the various examples.

Recall the supplier(sName, sAddr, item, price) table having the functional dependencies: { sName → sAddr, sName item → price }. Figure 10.1 determines that the candidate key for the table is the combination of sName and item. This table is not even in 2NF because of the partial dependency. The attribute sAddr depends only on part of the candidate key, namely, sName. The functional dependency that violates BCNF is sName → sAddr because sName is not a superkey. Thus, the application of the BCNF decomposition algorithm results in two relations: one with schema { sName, sAddr } and the other with schema { sName, item, price }. In fact, it is this decomposition that was shown to have the dependency preservation property in Figure 10.4 and the lossless-join property in Figures 10.6 and 10.9. Each relational schema in the decomposition is in BCNF since the left-hand sides of the functional dependencies that apply to each table are a superkey of the table. Therefore, the database schema given by the decomposition is in BCNF.

The earlier workson(eID, pID, plocation) table with the functional dependencies F = { eID → pID, pID → plocation } is in 2NF but not in 3NF and, therefore, not BCNF. The functional dependency that violates BCNF is pID → plocation because pID is not a superkey of the table. Figure 10.12 summarizes the resulting decomposition using the BCNF decomposition algorithm and also verifies the dependency preservation and lossless-join properties. The resulting decomposition is BCNF, dependency preserving, and lossless.

Similarly, the hoursworked(eID, pID, hours, email) table with F = { eID pID → hours, eID → email, email → eID } is in 3NF but not in BCNF. Recall that there are two candidate keys: { eID, pID } and { email, pID } because both eID and email uniquely identify an employee.

Table: workson(eID, pID, plocation)

F: { eID → pID, pID → plocation }

Candidate key: { eID }

Violating functional dependency: pID → plocation

| Decomposition | Attributes | Functional dependencies |
| :---: | :---: | :--- |
| $R_1$ | { pID, plocation } | $F_1 = pID \rightarrow plocation$ |
| $R_2$ | { eID, pID } | $F_2 = eID \rightarrow pID$ |

**FIGURE 10.12**
workson **BCNF**
decomposition example.

Dependency preservation: $F^\cup = F$ √
Lossless join: $R_1 \cap R_2 = pID$ and $pID \rightarrow R_1$ √

Table: hoursworked(eID, pID, hours, email)

F: { eID pID → hours, eID → email, email → eID }

Candidate keys: { eID, pID }, { email, pID }

Violating functional dependency: eID → email

| Decomposition | Attributes | Functional dependencies |
| :---: | :---: | :--- |
| $R_1$ | { eID, email } | $F_1 = eID \rightarrow email, email \rightarrow eID$ |
| $R_2$ | { eID, pID, hours } | $F_2 = eID \ pID \rightarrow hours$ |

**FIGURE 10.13**
hoursworked **BCNF**
decomposition example.

Dependency preservation: $F^\cup = F$ √
Lossless join: $R_1 \cap R_2 = eID$ and $eID \rightarrow R_1$ √

Figure 10.13 illustrates the resulting BCNF decomposition using the violating functional dependency eID → email. The decomposition shown is in BCNF and also has the dependency preservation and lossless-join properties.

The goal of the normalization process is to remove redundancy to avoid anomalies. However, the impact of normalization on the performance of database applications must also be considered. For example, the normalization of an employee's address into two tables requires a join of these tables for every retrieval of an address. Storing the city in the same table as the rest of the address is trading off limited redundancy for improved performance. The process of introducing limited redundancy in the tuning of database applications is called *denormalization*.

> **The process of introducing limited redundancy in the tuning of database applications is called *denormalization*.**

Theoretically, it is possible to determine a database schema that is lossless, dependency preserving, and 3NF. However, this is not the case for BCNF. As a possible example, consider a scenario with faculty who may have a joint appointment in multiple departments. For each department in which they work, faculty are assigned a mentor. A faculty mentor is associated with one department. The table facultydeptmentors(faculty, dept, mentor) has the following functional dependencies: faculty dept → mentor, mentor → dept. The candidate key for facultydeptmentors is composite, consisting of faculty and dept. This table is in 3NF since faculty dept is a superkey for the table and dept is contained in a candidate key. However, using the violating functional dependency mentor → dept to decompose facultydeptmentors via the BCNF decomposition algorithm results in the tables: mentordept(mentor, dept) and facultydept(faculty, dept). Each table in the decomposition is in BCNF, but the functional dependency faculty dept → mentor is lost. If a database administrator had to choose between a 3NF, lossless, and dependency-preserving decomposition versus a BCNF and lossless decomposition that did not preserve dependencies, which design should be chosen? Essentially, it is a choice between limited redundancy versus a high-performance penalty for data integrity. Thus, the limited redundancy in the 3NF design is a reasonable trade-off for the high-performance penalty of the BCNF design that is not dependency preserving.

## Self Check

10. What is the term used to describe the process of breaking down tables into smaller ones to remove potential redundancy?
11. Summarize the process of determining the normal form of a relation.
12. Does the BCNF decomposition algorithm guarantee the lossless-join property? Explain your answer.

## Reflections: Employee Training

Let's examine how the tools presented in this chapter provide an opportunity to reflect on the design of the Employee Training schema. Figure 10.14 shows the summary of the schema with the functional dependencies that apply on each table with its candidate keys underlined. Recall that the ER diagram in Figure 2.4 shows that an employee can be the area lead of at most one technology area. Therefore, aLeadID is also a candidate key for technologyArea.

| Table | Functional dependencies |
|---|---|
| employee(eID, eLast, eFirst, eTitle, eSalary) | $f_1$: eID → eLast eFirst eTitle eSalary |
| technologyArea(aID, aTitle, aURL, aLeadID) | $f_2$: aID → aTitle aURL aLeadID |
| | $f_3$: aLeadID → aID |
| trainingCourse(cID, cTitle, cHours, areaID) | $f_4$: cID → cTitle cHours areaID |
| takes(eID, cID, tDate) | $f_5$: eID cID → tDate |

**FIGURE 10.14**
Employee Training database schema with functional dependencies.

The Employee Training schema is dependency preserving. All of the functional dependencies can be verified on the relations in the database schema without requiring a join of the tables. Each table in the database schema is in BCNF since the left-hand side of each functional dependency that applies on a table is a candidate key. The database schema has the lossless-join property, as shown in Figure 10.15, and supported by the candidate key of the universal database relation { eID, cID } being in the takes table.

| | Table | 1: eID/aLeadID | 2: eLast | 3: eFirst | 4: eTitle | 5: eSalary | 6: aID/areaID | 7: aTitle | 8: aURL | 9: cID | 10: cTitle | 11: cHours | 12: inst | 13: length | 14: tDate |
|---|---|---|---|---|---|---|---|---|---|---|---|---|---|---|---|
| INITIAL | 1: employee | $a_1$ | $a_2$ | $a_3$ | $a_4$ | $a_5$ | $b_{1,6}$ | $b_{1,7}$ | $b_{1,8}$ | $b_{1,9}$ | $b_{1,10}$ | $b_{1,11}$ | $b_{1,12}$ | $b_{1,13}$ | $b_{1,14}$ |
| | 2: technologyArea | $a_1$ | $b_{2,2}$ | $b_{2,3}$ | $b_{2,4}$ | $b_{2,5}$ | $a_6$ | $a_7$ | $a_8$ | $b_{2,9}$ | $b_{2,10}$ | $b_{2,11}$ | $b_{2,12}$ | $b_{2,13}$ | $b_{2,14}$ |
| | 3: trainingCourse | $b_{3,1}$ | $b_{3,2}$ | $b_{3,3}$ | $b_{3,4}$ | $b_{3,5}$ | $b_{3,6}$ | $b_{3,7}$ | $b_{3,8}$ | $a_9$ | $a_{10}$ | $a_{11}$ | $a_{12}$ | $a_{13}$ | $b_{3,14}$ |
| | 4: takes | $a_1$ | $b_{4,2}$ | $b_{4,3}$ | $b_{4,4}$ | $b_{4,5}$ | $b_{4,6}$ | $b_{4,7}$ | $b_{4,8}$ | $a_9$ | $b_{4,10}$ | $b_{4,11}$ | $b_{4,12}$ | $b_{4,13}$ | $a_{14}$ |
| | | | | | | | | | | | | | | | |
| FINAL | 1: employee | $a_1$ | $a_2$ | $a_3$ | $a_4$ | $a_5$ | f3: $a_6$ | f2: $a_7$ | f2: $a_8$ | $b_{1,9}$ | $b_{1,10}$ | $b_{1,11}$ | $b_{1,12}$ | $b_{1,13}$ | $b_{1,14}$ |
| | 2: technologyArea | $a_1$ | f1: $a_2$ | f1: $a_3$ | f1: $a_4$ | f1: $a_5$ | $a_6$ | $a_7$ | $a_8$ | $b_{2,9}$ | $b_{2,10}$ | $b_{2,11}$ | $b_{2,12}$ | $b_{2,13}$ | $b_{2,14}$ |
| | 3: trainingCourse | $b_{3,1}$ | $b_{3,2}$ | $b_{3,3}$ | $b_{3,4}$ | $b_{3,5}$ | $b_{3,6}$ | $b_{3,7}$ | $b_{3,8}$ | $a_9$ | $a_{10}$ | $a_{11}$ | $a_{12}$ | $a_{13}$ | $b_{3,14}$ |
| | 4: takes | $a_1$ | f1: $a_2$ | f1: $a_3$ | f1: $a_4$ | f1: $a_5$ | f3: $a_6$ | f2: $a_7$ | f2: $a_8$ | $a_9$ | f4: $a_{10}$ | f4: $a_{11}$ | f4: $a_{12}$ | f4: $a_{13}$ | $a_{14}$ |

**FIGURE 10.15** Employee Training lossless-join determination.

# Chapter Notes Summary

### Database Design Goals

- An update anomaly occurs when there are multiple copies of the same data that must be changed.
- A delete anomaly results in a loss of information.
- An insert anomaly occurs when certain information cannot be added to the database.
- The goals of a database design include the correct representation of the data (*lossless join*) with its constraints (*functional dependencies*), limiting redundancy (characterized by *normal forms*), and checking constraints efficiently (*dependency preserving*).

### Functional Dependencies

- Functional dependencies represent constraints on the data.
- Inference rules can be applied to functional dependencies F to derive the closure of that set, denoted $F^+$.
- Attribute closure, denoted $A^+$, determines the set of attributes functionally determined by the given set of attributes A with respect to a set of functional dependencies.
- Determining the candidate key of a table is an important component of relational database design theory.

### Decomposition

- A collection of relation schemes { $R_1$, ..., $R_n$ } is a *decomposition* of a relation r if the union of all of the $R_i$ = R.
- $F_i$ is the set of functional dependencies in F that apply to a relation $R_i$ in the decomposition, and $F^{\cup}$ is the union of all of the $F_i$.
- A decomposition is *dependency preserving* if $(F^{\cup})^+ = F^+$.
- Intuitively, a *lossless-join decomposition* means that the result of joining the smaller tables in the decomposition results in the original table.
- The pairwise decomposition of R into $R_1$ and $R_2$ is lossless if $R_1 \cap R_2 \rightarrow R_1$ *or* $R_1 \cap R_2 \rightarrow R_2$.
- To determine the lossless-join property for a database schema, apply the functional dependencies at the schema level.

### Normal Forms

- 1NF is the underlying assumption of the relational data model that each attribute of a relation must have a simple value.
- Informally, 2NF does not allow a partial dependency.
- Informally, a relation is in 3NF if it satisfies 2NF and there is no transitive dependency.
- A relation is in BCNF if for each nontrivial functional dependency *f* that applies on the table, the left-hand side of *f* is a superkey.
- *Normalization* is the process of breaking down a table into smaller ones to remove redundancy.
- The process of introducing limited redundancy in the tuning of database applications is called *denormalization*.

# Chapter Reminders

Table 10.4 summarizes the determination of the three main database design goals of dependency preservation, lossless join, and normal forms.

**Table 10.4    Summary: Determination of Database Design Goals**

**Dependency preserving**

| | |
|---|---|
| $F_i$ | The set of functional dependencies in F that apply to a relation $R_i$ in the decomposition |
| $F^U$ | The union of all of the $F_i$ |
| $F - F^U$ | Potential lost dependencies; dependency preserving if $F = F^U$ or each fd in $F - F^U$ is logically implied by $F^U$ |

**Lossless join**

| | |
|---|---|
| Pairwise | The pairwise decomposition of R into $R_1$ and $R_2$ is lossless if $R_1 \cap R_2 \rightarrow R_1$ or $R_1 \cap R_2 \rightarrow R_2$ |
| Schema | Apply functional dependencies at the schema level with matrix consisting of a row for each relation in the decomposition and a column for each attribute in the database schema |

**Normal forms** Apply definitions in order: BCNF, 3NF, 2NF, 1NF

| | |
|---|---|
| BCNF | If for each nontrivial functional dependency $f$ that applies on the table, the left-hand side of $f$ is a superkey |
| 3NF | If for each functional dependency $f$ in $F^d$ one of the following holds: $f$ is trivial, the left-hand side is a superkey or the right-hand side is contained in a candidate key |
| 2NF | If every attribute in the relation either appears in a candidate key or is fully functionally determined by every candidate key, i.e. no partial dependency exists |
| 1NF | The underlying assumption of the relational data model that each attribute of a relation must have a simple value |

# Practice

This section reflects on the database designs for the three practice enterprises in the book: Investment Portfolio, New Home, and Web Page.

## Practice Problems: Investment Portfolio

Determine and justify the answer to the following problems over the Investment Portfolio enterprise (see Figure 2.18 for the visual relational schema and Figure 2.16 for its conceptual design as an ER diagram):

1. What are the functional dependencies that apply to each table?

2. What are the candidate keys for each table?

3. What is the normal form of each table?

4. Is the database schema dependency preserving?

5. Does the database schema have the lossless-join property? Justify the answer using the lossless-join matrix algorithm.

## Practice Problems: New Home

Determine and justify the answer to the following problems over the New Home enterprise (see Figure 2.21 for the visual relational schema and Figure 2.19 for its conceptual design as an ER diagram):

1. What are the functional dependencies that apply to each table?

2. What are the candidate keys for each table?

3. What is the normal form of each table?

4. Is the database schema dependency preserving?

5. Does the database schema have the lossless-join property? Justify the answer using the lossless-join matrix algorithm.

## Practice Problems: Web Page

Determine and justify the answer to the following problems over the Web Page enterprise (see Figure 2.24 for the visual relational schema and Figure 2.22 for its conceptual design as an ER diagram):

1. What are the functional dependencies that apply to each table?

2. What are the candidate keys for each table?

3. What is the normal form of each table?

4. Is the database schema dependency preserving?

5. Does the database schema have the lossless-join property? Justify the answer using the lossless-join matrix algorithm.

## End of Chapter Exercises

Recall the MLS Practice Scenario from Chapter 1 about selling houses. There is a multiple listing service (MLS) that provides information about homes for sale. A unique MLS number is assigned to the listing, along with the date and price of the listing. Other required properties to post the listing include the address (street, city, state, zip) and the listing agent with realty. The MLS must also maintain a history of price changes, which is displayed on the Web page with the date and price on that date.

Determine and justify the answer to the following exercises, given the database schema:

> mls(mlsnum, listprice, listdate, street, city, state, zip, listagent, listrealty)
>
> pricehistory(mlsnum, pricedate, amount)

1. What are the functional dependencies that apply to each table?

2. What are the candidate keys for each table?

3. What is the normal form of each table?

4. Is the database schema dependency preserving?

5. Does the database schema have the lossless-join property? Justify the answer using the lossless-join matrix algorithm.

Recall the Course Schedule Practice Scenario from Chapter 1 about university courses that are described in a course catalog with a unique course id, a title, a catalog description, and the number of credits. The schedule for course registration provides a unique line number for a course offering, the course id for the course, the date and time that the course is offered, along with the classroom and the instructor of record.

Determine and justify the answer to the following exercises, given the database schema:

> catalog(courseid, title, description, credits)
>
> schedule(linenumber, courseid, classdatetime, classroom, instructor)

6. What are the functional dependencies that apply to each table?

7. What are the candidate keys for each table?

8. What is the normal form of each table?

9. Is the database schema dependency preserving?

10. Does the database schema have the lossless-join property? Justify the answer using the lossless-join matrix algorithm.

In the United States, there is an election every four years to elect a president. Each presidential candidate has a designated vice presidential candidate and is affiliated with exactly one political party. A political party has exactly one presidential candidate on the ballot. Each state in the country has a name, a two-character abbreviation, and a designated number of electoral votes. The candidate that receives the most popular votes of the citizens in the state secures the state's electoral votes. The candidate with a majority of the electoral votes becomes the next president of the United States.

Determine and justify the answer to the following exercises, given the database schema:

> candidate(president, vp, party)
>
> state(name, st, electoral)
>
> votes(president, st, popular)

11. What are the functional dependencies that apply to each table?

12. What are the candidate keys for each table?

13. What is the normal form of each table?

14. Is the database schema dependency preserving?

15. Does the database schema have the lossless-join property? Justify the answer using the lossless-join matrix algorithm.

# Answers to Self-Check Questions:

1. update anomaly

2. lossless join

3. dependency preserving

4. trivial

5. decomposition

6. To determine the set of attributes that are functionally determined by the given set of attributes using the given functional dependencies.

7. A given breakdown of a table into multiple tables is a decomposition if none of the attributes are lost.

8. A decomposition is dependency preserving if the only functional dependencies that are lost are logically implied by the remaining functional dependencies.

9. A pairwise decomposition of a table r into r1 and r2 is lossless if the intersection of the attributes in $R_1$ and $R_2$ is a candidate key of one of the tables.

10. normalization

11. After determining the candidate key(s) for the table, find its highest normal form starting with BCNF, then 3NF, then 2NF. All relations are at least in 1NF.

12. The BCNF decomposition algorithm guarantees the lossless-join property because it uses all of the attributes in the violating functional dependency to form one of the tables. Thus, the intersection of the resulting pairwise decomposition is the left-hand side of the violating functional dependency, which is a candidate key of the table.

# Answers to Practice Problems: INVESTMENT PORTFOLIO

1. Functional dependencies: see Figure 10.16.

2. Candidate keys: see Figure 10.16.

3. Normal forms: BCNF since the left-hand side of every functional dependency is a superkey.

4. Dependency preserving: The database schema is dependency preserving.

5. Lossless join: Using the intuition of the universal candidate key { taxPayerID, sTicker, mTicker }, the database schema is not lossless because there does not exist a table containing that key. Figure 10.17 shows the justification using the lossless-join algorithm.

---

## Table and functional dependencies

client(<u>taxPayerID</u>, name, address)
  $f_1$: taxPayerID → name address

stock(<u>sTicker</u>, sName, rating, prinBus, sHigh, sLow, sCurrent, ret1Yr, ret5Yr)
  $f_2$: sTicker → sName rating prinBus sHigh sLow sCurrent ret1Yr ret5Yr

mutualFund(<u>mTicker</u>, mName, prinObj, mHigh, mLow, mCurrent, yield, familyID)
  $f_3$: mTicker → mName prinObj mHigh mLow mCurrent yield familyID

fundFamily(<u>familyID</u>, company, cAddress)
  $f_4$: familyID → company cAddress

stockPortfolio(<u>taxPayerID, sTicker</u>, sNumShares)
  $f_5$: taxPayerID sTicker → sNumShares

mutualFundPortfolio(<u>taxPayerID, mTicker</u>, mNumShares)
  $f_6$: taxPayerID mTicker → mNumShares

**FIGURE 10.16** INVESTMENT PORTFOLIO database schema with functional dependencies.

---

| | Table | 1: taxPayerID | 2–3: name, address | 4: sTicker | 5–12: sTicker, sName, rating, prinBus, sHigh, sLow, sCurrent, ret1Yr, ret5Yr | 13: mTicker | 14–19: mName, prinObj, mHigh, mLow, mCurrent | 20: familyID | 21–22: company, cAddress | 23: sNumShares | 24: mNumShares |
|---|---|---|---|---|---|---|---|---|---|---|---|
| INITIAL | 1: client | $a_1$ | $a_{2-3}$ | $b_{1,4}$ | $b_{1,5-12}$ | $b_{1,13}$ | $b_{1,14-19}$ | $b_{1,20}$ | $b_{1,21-22}$ | $b_{1,23}$ | $b_{1,24}$ |
| | 2: stock | $b_{2,1}$ | $b_{2,2-3}$ | $a_4$ | $a_{5-12}$ | $b_{2,13}$ | $b_{2,14-19}$ | $b_{2,20}$ | $b_{2,21-22}$ | $b_{2,23}$ | $b_{2,24}$ |
| | 3: mutualFund | $b_{3,1}$ | $b_{3,2-3}$ | $b_{3,4}$ | $b_{3,5-12}$ | $a_{13}$ | $a_{14-19}$ | $a_{20}$ | $b_{3,21-22}$ | $b_{3,23}$ | $b_{3,24}$ |
| | 4: fundFamily | $b_{4,1}$ | $b_{4,2-3}$ | $b_{4,4}$ | $b_{4,5-12}$ | $b_{4,13}$ | $b_{4,14-19}$ | $a_{20}$ | $a_{21-22}$ | $b_{4,23}$ | $b_{4,24}$ |
| | 5: stockPortfolio | $a_1$ | $b_{5,2-3}$ | $a_4$ | $b_{5,5-12}$ | $b_{5,13}$ | $b_{5,14-19}$ | $b_{5,20}$ | $b_{5,21-22}$ | $a_{23}$ | $b_{5,24}$ |
| | 6: mutualFundPortfolio | $a_1$ | $b_{6,2-3}$ | $b_{6,4}$ | $b_{6,5-12}$ | $a_{13}$ | $b_{6,14-19}$ | $b_{6,20}$ | $b_{6,21-22}$ | $b_{6,23}$ | $a_{24}$ |
| | | | | | | | | | | | |
| FINAL | 1: client | $a_1$ | $a_{2-3}$ | $b_{1,4}$ | $b_{1,5-12}$ | $b_{1,13}$ | $b_{1,14-19}$ | $b_{1,20}$ | $b_{1,21-22}$ | $b_{1,23}$ | $b_{1,24}$ |
| | 2: stock | $b_{2,1}$ | $b_{2,2-3}$ | $a_4$ | $a_{5-12}$ | $b_{2,13}$ | $b_{2,14-19}$ | $b_{2,20}$ | f4: $a_{21-22}$ | $b_{2,23}$ | $b_{2,24}$ |
| | 3: mutualFund | $b_{3,1}$ | $b_{3,2-3}$ | $b_{3,4}$ | $b_{3,5-12}$ | $a_{13}$ | $a_{14-19}$ | $a_{20}$ | $b_{3,21-22}$ | $b_{3,23}$ | $b_{3,24}$ |
| | 4: fundFamily | $b_{4,1}$ | $b_{4,2-3}$ | $b_{4,4}$ | $b_{4,5-12}$ | $b_{4,13}$ | $b_{4,14-19}$ | $a_{20}$ | $a_{21-22}$ | $b_{4,23}$ | $b_{4,24}$ |
| | 5: stockPortfolio | $a_1$ | f1: $a_{2-3}$ | $a_4$ | f2: $a_{5-12}$ | $b_{5,13}$ | $b_{5,14-19}$ | $b_{5,20}$ | $b_{5,21-22}$ | $a_{23}$ | $b_{5,24}$ |
| | 6: mutualFundPortfolio | $a_1$ | f1: $a_{2-3}$ | $b_{6,4}$ | $b_{6,5-12}$ | $a_{13}$ | f3: $a_{14-19}$ | f3: $a_{20}$ | $b_{6,21-22}$ | $b_{6,23}$ | $a_{24}$ |

**FIGURE 10.17** INVESTMENT PORTFOLIO lossless-join determination.

# Answers to Practice Problems: New Home

1. Functional dependencies: see Figure 10.18.

2. Candidate keys: see Figure 10.18.

3. Normal forms: BCNF since the left-hand side of every functional dependency is a superkey.

4. Dependency preserving: The database schema is dependency preserving.

5. Lossless join: Figure 10.19 shows the justification using the lossless-join algorithm that the schema has the lossless-join property since row 6 representing the sold table has all a sym- bols. The intuition of the universal candidate key of { sName, lotNum } supports the trace.

## Table and functional dependencies

homebuilder(<u>hID</u>, hName, hStreet, hCity, hZip, <u>hPhone</u>)

$f_1$: hID → hName hStreet hCity hZip hPhone

$f_2$: hPhone → hID

model(<u>hID, mID</u>, mName, sqft, story)

$f_3$: hID mID → mName sqft story

subdivision(<u>sName</u>, sCity, sZip)

$f_4$: sName → sCity sZip

offered(<u>sName, hID, mID</u>, price)

$f_5$: sName, hID, mID → price

lot(<u>sName, lotNum</u>, lStAddr, lSize, lPremium)

$f_6$: sName, lotNum → lStAddr, lSize, lPremium

sold(<u>sName, lotNum</u>, hID, mID, status)

$f_7$: sName, lotNum → hID, mID, status

**FIGURE 10.18**
New Home database schema with functional dependencies.

| | Table | 1: hID | 2–5: hName, hStreet, hCity, hZip | 6: hPhone | 7: mID | 8–10: mName, sqft, story | 11: sName | 12–13: sCity, sZip | 15: price | 16: lotNum | 17–19: lStAddr, lSize, lPremium | 20: status |
|---|---|---|---|---|---|---|---|---|---|---|---|---|
| **INITIAL** | 1: homebuilder | $a_1$ | $a_{2-5}$ | $a_6$ | $b_{1,7}$ | $b_{1,8-10}$ | $b_{1,11}$ | $b_{1,12-13}$ | $b_{1,15}$ | $b_{1,16}$ | $b_{1,17-19}$ | $b_{1,20}$ |
| | 2: model | $a_1$ | $b_{2,2-5}$ | $b_{2,6}$ | $a_7$ | $a_{8-10}$ | $b_{2,11}$ | $b_{2,12-13}$ | $b_{2,15}$ | $b_{2,16}$ | $b_{2,17-19}$ | $b_{2,20}$ |
| | 3: subdivision | $b_{3,1}$ | $b_{3,2-5}$ | $b_{3,6}$ | $b_{3,7}$ | $b_{3,8-10}$ | $a_{11}$ | $a_{12-13}$ | $b_{3,15}$ | $b_{3,16}$ | $b_{3,17-19}$ | $b_{3,20}$ |
| | 4: offered | $a_1$ | $b_{4,2-5}$ | $b_{4,6}$ | $a_7$ | $b_{4,8-10}$ | $a_{11}$ | $b_{4,12-13}$ | $a_{15}$ | $b_{4,16}$ | $b_{4,17-19}$ | $b_{4,20}$ |
| | 5: lot | $b_{5,1}$ | $b_{5,2-5}$ | $b_{5,6}$ | $b_{5,7}$ | $b_{5,8-10}$ | $a_{11}$ | $b_{5,12-13}$ | $b_{5,15}$ | $a_{16}$ | $a_{17-19}$ | $b_{5,20}$ |
| | 6: sold | $a_1$ | $b_{6,2-5}$ | $b_{6,6}$ | $a_7$ | $b_{6,8-10}$ | $a_{11}$ | $b_{6,12-13}$ | $b_{6,15}$ | $a_{16}$ | $b_{6,17-19}$ | $a_{20}$ |
| **FINAL** | 1: homebuilder | $a_1$ | $a_{2-5}$ | $a_6$ | $b_{1,7}$ | $b_{1,8-10}$ | $b_{1,11}$ | $b_{1,12-13}$ | $b_{1,15}$ | $b_{1,16}$ | $b_{1,17-19}$ | $b_{1,20}$ |
| | 2: model | $a_1$ | f1: $a_{2-5}$ | f1: $a_6$ | $a_7$ | $a_{8-10}$ | $b_{2,11}$ | $b_{2,12-13}$ | $b_{2,15}$ | $b_{2,16}$ | $b_{2,17-19}$ | $b_{2,20}$ |
| | 3: subdivision | $b_{3,1}$ | $b_{3,2-5}$ | $b_{3,6}$ | $b_{3,7}$ | $b_{3,8-10}$ | $a_{11}$ | $a_{12-13}$ | $b_{3,15}$ | $b_{3,16}$ | $b_{3,17-19}$ | $b_{3,20}$ |
| | 4: offered | $a_1$ | f1: $a_{2-5}$ | f1: $a_6$ | $a_7$ | f3: $a_{8-10}$ | $a_{11}$ | f4: $a_{12-13}$ | $a_{15}$ | $b_{4,16}$ | $b_{4,17-19}$ | $b_{4,20}$ |
| | 5: lot | $b_{5,1}$ | $b_{5,2-5}$ | $b_{5,6}$ | $b_{5,7}$ | $b_{5,8-10}$ | $a_{11}$ | f4: $a_{12-13}$ | $b_{5,15}$ | $a_{16}$ | $a_{17-19}$ | f7: $a_{20}$ |
| | 6: sold | $a_1$ | f1: $a_{2-5}$ | f1: $a_6$ | $a_7$ | f3: $a_{8-10}$ | $a_{11}$ | f4: $a_{12-13}$ | f5: $a_{15}$ | $a_{16}$ | f6: $a_{17-19}$ | $a_{20}$ |

**FIGURE 10.19** New Home lossless-join determination.

# Answers to Practice Problems: WEB PAGE

1. Functional dependencies: see Figure 10.20.

2. Candidate keys: see Figure 10.20.

---

## Table and functional dependencies

webpage (<u>wID</u>, wTitle, <u>wURL</u>, hits)
$f_1$: wID → wTitle wURL hits
$f_2$: wURL → wID

site (<u>sID</u>, sTitle, <u>sURL</u>)
$f_3$: sID → sTitle sURL
$f_4$: sURL → sID

graphic (<u>gID</u>, gName, gType, src, alt)
$f_5$: gID → gName gType src alt

document (<u>dID</u>, dName, dType, dDescription, dDate, downloads, wID)
$f_6$: dID → dName dType dDescription dDate downloads wID

internal (<u>sourceID</u>, <u>targetID</u>)
$f_7$: sourceID targetID → sourceID targetID

external (<u>wID</u>, <u>sID</u>, followed)
$f_8$: wID sID → followed

displays (<u>wID</u>, <u>gID</u>)
$f_9$: wID gID → wID gID

**FIGURE 10.20**
WEB PAGE database schema with functional dependencies.

| | Table | 1: wID/sourceID/ targetID | 2–3: wTitle, hits | 4: wURL | 5: sID | 6: sTitle | 7: sURL | 8: gID | 9–12: gName, gType, src, alt | 13: dID | 14–18: dName, dType, dDescription, dDate, downloads | 19: followed |
|---|---|---|---|---|---|---|---|---|---|---|---|---|
| **INITIAL** | 1: webpage | $a_1$ | $a_{2-3}$ | $a_4$ | $b_{1,5}$ | $b_{1,6}$ | $b_{1,7}$ | $b_{1,8}$ | $b_{1,9-12}$ | $b_{1,13}$ | $b_{1,14-18}$ | $b_{1,19}$ |
| | 2: site | $b_{2,1}$ | $b_{2,2-3}$ | $b_{2,4}$ | $a_5$ | $a_6$ | $a_7$ | $b_{2,8}$ | $b_{2,9-12}$ | $b_{2,13}$ | $b_{2,14-18}$ | $b_{2,19}$ |
| | 3: graphic | $b_{3,1}$ | $b_{3,2-3}$ | $b_{3,4}$ | $b_{3,5}$ | $b_{3,6}$ | $b_{3,7}$ | $a_8$ | $a_{9-12}$ | $b_{3,13}$ | $b_{3,14-18}$ | $b_{3,19}$ |
| | 4: document | $a_1$ | $b_{4,2-3}$ | $b_{4,4}$ | $b_{4,5}$ | $b_{4,6}$ | $b_{4,7}$ | $b_{4,8}$ | $b_{4,9-12}$ | $a_{13}$ | $a_{14-18}$ | $b_{4,19}$ |
| | 5: internal | $a_1$ | $b_{5,2-3}$ | $b_{5,4}$ | $b_{5,5}$ | $b_{5,6}$ | $b_{5,7}$ | $b_{5,8}$ | $b_{5,9-12}$ | $b_{5,13}$ | $b_{5,14-18}$ | $b_{5,19}$ |
| | 6: external | $a_1$ | $b_{6,2-3}$ | $b_{6,4}$ | $a_5$ | $b_{6,6}$ | $b_{6,7}$ | $b_{6,8}$ | $b_{6,9-12}$ | $b_{6,13}$ | $b_{6,14-18}$ | $a_{19}$ |
| | 7: displays | $a_1$ | $b_{7,2-3}$ | $b_{7,4}$ | $b_{7,5}$ | $b_{7,6}$ | $b_{7,7}$ | $a_8$ | $b_{7,9-12}$ | $b_{7,13}$ | $b_{7,14-18}$ | $b_{7,19}$ |
| | | | | | | | | | | | | |
| **FINAL** | 1: webpage | $a_1$ | $a_{2-3}$ | $a_4$ | $b_{1,5}$ | $b_{1,6}$ | $b_{1,7}$ | $b_{1,8}$ | $b_{1,9-12}$ | $b_{1,13}$ | $b_{1,14-18}$ | $b_{1,19}$ |
| | 2: site | $b_{2,1}$ | $b_{2,2-3}$ | $b_{2,4}$ | $a_5$ | $a_6$ | $a_7$ | $b_{2,8}$ | $b_{2,9-12}$ | $b_{2,13}$ | $b_{2,14-18}$ | $b_{2,19}$ |
| | 3: graphic | $b_{3,1}$ | $b_{3,2-3}$ | $b_{3,4}$ | $b_{3,5}$ | $b_{3,6}$ | $b_{3,7}$ | $a_8$ | $a_{9-12}$ | $b_{3,13}$ | $b_{3,14-18}$ | $b_{3,19}$ |
| | 4: document | $a_1$ | f1: $a_{2-3}$ | f1: $a_4$ | $b_{4,5}$ | $b_{4,6}$ | $b_{4,7}$ | $b_{4,8}$ | $b_{4,9-12}$ | $a_{13}$ | $a_{14-18}$ | $b_{4,19}$ |
| | 5: internal | $a_1$ | f1: $a_{2-3}$ | f1: $a_4$ | $b_{5,5}$ | $b_{5,6}$ | $b_{5,7}$ | $b_{5,8}$ | $b_{5,9-12}$ | $b_{5,13}$ | $b_{5,14-18}$ | $b_{5,19}$ |
| | 6: external | $a_1$ | f1: $a_{2-3}$ | f1: $a_4$ | $a_5$ | f3: $a_6$ | $b_{6,7}$ | $b_{6,8}$ | $b_{6,9-12}$ | $b_{6,13}$ | $b_{6,14-18}$ | $a_{19}$ |
| | 7: displays | $a_1$ | f1: $a_{2-3}$ | f1: $a_4$ | $b_{7,5}$ | $b_{7,6}$ | $b_{7,7}$ | $a_8$ | f5: $a_{9-12}$ | $b_{7,13}$ | $b_{7,14-18}$ | $b_{7,19}$ |

**FIGURE 10.21** WEB PAGE lossless-join determination.

3. Normal forms: BCNF since the left-hand side of every functional dependency is a superkey.

4. Dependency preserving: The database schema is dependency preserving.

5. Lossless join: Using the intuition of the universal candidate key { sID, gID, dID }, the database schema is not lossless because there does not exist a table containing that key. Figure 10.21 shows the justification using the lossless-join algorithm.

## Bibliographic Notes

Codd's original relational database paper included functional dependencies [Codd, 1970]. Additional papers by Codd introduced normal forms [Codd, 1972b, 1974]. The lossless-join algorithm is from Aho et al. [1979]. Maier [1983] is an excellent reference on the theory of relational databases.

## More to Explore

There are additional normal forms beyond BCNF for a relational schema that are based on multivalued dependencies and join dependencies.

# WinRDBI

## A.1 Overview

Relational databases are the focus of most introductory courses on database management systems. An important part of the curriculum in such a course is the coverage of formal query languages for the retrieval of information from a database. Understanding the formal relational query languages (relational algebra, domain relational calculus, and tuple relational calculus) is essential to comprehending the industry-standard relational query language SQL. As a student, it is difficult to know whether your queries expressed on paper in the formal languages are correct. As an instructor, it is often difficult to grade creative queries, especially those that have not been verified using a tool or product. The goal of the WinRDBI (Windows Relational DataBase Interpreter) educational tool is to provide a mechanism by which the students can explore the formal relational query languages in an interactive environment.

WinRDBI has an intuitive graphical user interface, as shown in Figure A.1. WinRDBI has the capability to define a database schema and populate the tables. The student can than choose one of the following languages in which to pose queries: relational algebra, tuple relational calculus, domain relational calculus (including a by name version), tuple relational calculus, and SQL. The inclusion of the industry-standard query language SQL in WinRDBI increases the usability of the educational tool, providing the ability to pose SQL queries over the same database schema and instance used for exploring the formal query languages.

WinRDBI is available for educational use at the following website: winrdbi.asu.edu

## A.2 Query Languages

WinRDBI recognizes relational algebra, domain relational calculus, tuple relational calculus, and SQL. The syntax of the query languages recognized by the tool is essentially the syntax presented in the chapter coverage except for relational algebra. Since the formal syntax of relational algebra uses symbols that are not available on a computer keyword, the syntax of relational algebra recognized by WinRDBI introduces keywords in place of the symbols. This appendix provides brief coverage of any assumptions made by the WinRDBI-specific implementation of the query languages, while the WinRDBI Web page and distribution include a user guide that covers the educational tool in more detail, including the user interface.

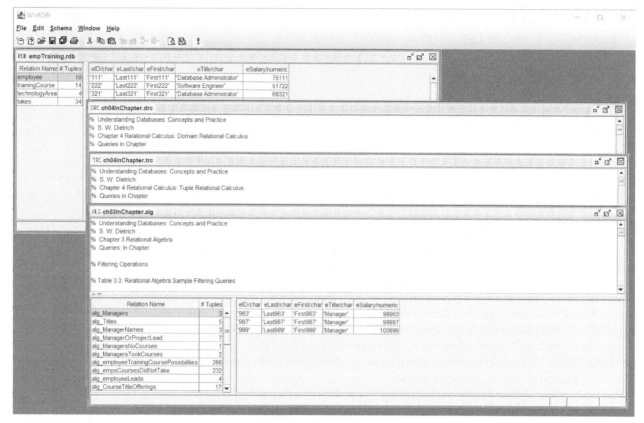

**FIGURE A.1**    WinRDBI user interface. Source: WinRDBI.

## Intermediate Tables and Renaming of Attributes

The syntax introduced for creating intermediate tables and renaming of attributes in this book is the syntax recognized by WinRDBI, where

$$\text{intermediateTable(attr1, ..., attrn) := queryExpression;}$$

assigns the result of the queryExpression to the intermediateTable, renaming the output schema of queryExpression to the schema given by the attribute list attr1, ..., attrn. If no explicit attribute list is specified, then the attribute names for the schema of intermediateTable are derived from the queryExpression.

## Relational Algebra

The mapping of the formal relational algebra symbols to the keywords in WinRDBI is shown in Table A.1 for the fundamental operators $(\sigma, \pi, \cup, -, \times)$ and Table A.2 for the additional operators $(\cap, \bowtie_\theta, \bowtie, \div)$.

The WinRDBI-specific assumptions for the relational algebra operators are summarized here:

- The union, difference, and intersect operators require that the operand relations are compatible by having identical schemas.

- The (Cartesian) product operator requires that the operand relations have disjoint attribute names.

Table A.1    **WinRDBI Summary of Fundamental Relational Algebra Operators**

| Formal relational algebra | WinRDBI relational algebra |
| --- | --- |
| $\sigma_\theta(r)$ | select $\theta$ (r) |
| $\pi_A(r)$ | project A (r) |
| $r \cup s$ | r union s |
| $r - s$ | r difference s |
| $q \times r$ | q product r |

Table A.2    **WinRDBI Summary of Additional Relational Algebra Operators**

| Formal relational algebra | WinRDBI relational algebra |
| --- | --- |
| $r \cap s$ | r intersect s |
| $r \bowtie_\theta s$ | NOT AVAILABLE |
| $r \bowtie s$ | njoin |
| $q \div r$ | NOT AVAILABLE |

- The njoin (natural join) operator does *not* require common attribute names in the operand relations. If the operand relations do not have any attribute names in common, then the natural join results in a Cartesian product.

- The theta-join and division operators are purposely not provided by the interpreter so that students investigate the equivalent definitions of these operators in terms of the fundamental relational algebra operators.

# Relational Calculus

Since there are many variations on the syntax of the relational calculus languages, the relational calculus chapters covered the syntax recognized by WinRDBI. The chapter examples, by convention, chose to limit a variable before its use in the query. Although this convention is not required theoretically (e.g. a conjunction is commutative), a variable must have a binding before its value is referenced in WinRDBI's left-to-right evaluation of a calculus expression.

## Domain Relational Calculus

As an example in DRC, consider the specification of the $Q_\sigma$ query that finds the employees who earn more than \$100,000:

{ EID, ELast, EFirst, ETitle, ESalary |
    employee(EID, ELast, EFirst, ETitle, ESalary) and ESalary > 100000 };

This specification is correct in WinRDBI since the reference to the employee table binds the variable ESalary before checking that its value is greater than 100,000.

Another assumption in DRC is the derived schema for the result of a query expression. The DRC expression denotes the schema of the resulting query expression by listing the domain variables to the left of the vertical bar (|). Since domain variables must be identifiers starting with an uppercase letter and attribute names must be identifiers starting with a lowercase letter, WinRDBI automatically converts the DRC variable into its lowercase representation for deriving the schema for a query expression. The specification of an intermediate table with an explicit schema is strongly suggested for DRC queries that will be referenced in subsequent queries.

### Tuple Relational Calculus

The only language-specific assumption for TRC is the assumed left-to-right evaluation of a TRC expression, requiring that a tuple variable is bound before referencing the value of any of its attributes. Consider the TRC specification of $Q_\sigma$

{ E | employee(E) and E.eSalary > 100000 }

where the value of the tuple variable E is bound to the employee table before checking that the value of the eSalary attribute is greater than 100,000.

# SQL

The syntax of the WinRDBI implementation of the query language of SQL corresponds to essentially SQL-92 with some additional simplifying assumptions. The most notable simplifying assumptions are the lack of support for inline views and that a nested subquery cannot involve aggregation (see discussion below). Since WinRDBI has a graphical user interface for defining and manipulating the database, the DDL and DML (insert, update, and delete) of SQL are not supported.

In addition to the basic select-from-where query expression, WinRDBI handles grouping, aggregation, having, order by, and nested subqueries. The interpreter, however, assumes that a nested subquery cannot involve aggregation. Aggregation must appear in the outermost query. This is not a severe restriction. The user needs to only break such a query into multiples queries. For example, consider a query that finds the employees earning the minimum salary over the EMPLOYEE TRAINING database.

```
select    E.eID, E.eLast, E.eFirst, E.eTitle
from      employee E
where     E.eSalary =
          (select    min(S.eSalary)
           from      employee S );
```

The above formulation uses the inherent support of aggregation in SQL to compare the salary of an employee to the minimum salary found by a nested subquery. Since the tool does not allow aggregation in a nested subquery, the following two queries find the employees having the minimum salary.

```
minimumSalary(minSalary) :=
          select    min(E.eSalary)
          from      employee E;

select    E.eID, E.eLast, E.eFirst, E.eTitle
from      employee E
where     E.eSalary = (select minSalary from minimumSalary);
```

## A.3 Implementation Overview

WinRDBI is founded on the basis of established deductive database technology that uses the Prolog logic language to query the database instance stored as logical facts and the use of the Java Swing™ API for creating graphical user interfaces (GUIs).

The WinRDBI user interface consists of one *schema* pane and any number of *query* panes. A query pane is associated with exactly one query language. The database schema and instance shown in the schema pane is stored in Prolog during execution but persists by saving the database instance to a file, having the extension .rdb, which can be opened in a later WinRDBI session. When a query pane is selected and executed, the sequence of queries specified in a query pane is translated to Prolog code and then invoked. Since the result of a query is itself a relation, the result relations for a query pane are also stored as Prolog facts and are displayed in the lower portion of the query pane. If a named intermediate table is not explicitly created for a query, WinRDBI assigns a unique name consisting of the string unnamed_ with a counter value appended to the end of the string.

## A.4 Summary

The WinRDBI educational tool provides a hands-on approach to understanding (both learning and reviewing) the capabilities of query languages for relational databases.

# BIBLIOGRAPHY

A. V. Aho, C. Beeri, and J. D. Ullman. The theory of joins in relational databases. *ACM Trans. Database Syst.*, 4(3): 297–314, September 1979. ISSN 0362-5915. doi: 10.1145/320083.320091.

R. G. G. Cattell and D. K. Barry. *The Object Data Standard: ODMG 3.0*. Morgan Kaufmann, January 2000. ISBN 1-55860-647-5.

D. D. Chamberlin, M. M. Astrahan, K. P. Eswaran, P. P. Griffiths, R. A. Lorie, J. W. Mehl, P. Reisner, and B. W. Wade. Sequel 2: A unified approach to data definition, manipulation, and control. *IBM J. Res. Dev.*, 20(6):560–575, November 1976. ISSN 0018-8646. doi: 10.1147/rd.206.0560.

D. D. Chamberlin and R. F. Boyce. Sequel: A structured English query language. In *Proceedings of the 1974 ACM SIGFIDET (Now SIGMOD) Workshop on Data Description, Access and Control*, SIGFIDET '74, pages 249–264, New York, NY, USA, 1974. ACM. doi: 10.1145/800296.811515. URL https://doi.acm.org/10.1145/800296.811515.

P. Chen. The entity-relationship model—toward a unified view of data. *ACM Trans. Database Syst.*, 1(1):9–36, March 1976. ISSN 0362-5915. doi: 10.1145/320434.320440. URL https://doi.acm.org/10.1145/320434.320440.

E. F. Codd. A relational model of data for large shared data banks. *Commun. ACM*, 13(6):377–387, 1970. ISSN 0001-0782.

E. F. Codd. Relational completeness of data base sublanguages. In *Database Systems*, pages 65–98. Prentice Hall, 1972a.

E. F. Codd. Further normalization of the data base relational model. In *Database Systems*. Prentice Hall, 1972b.

E. F. Codd. Recent investigations in relational data base systems. In *IFIP Congress*, pages 1017–1021, 1974.

S. W. Dietrich. Is LINQ in your toolbox? *ACM Inroads*, 4(1):31–33, March 2013. ISSN 2153-2184. doi: 10.1145/2432596.2432610. URL https://doi.acm.org/10.1145/2432596.2432610.

S. W. Dietrich and M. Chaudhari. LINQ ROX!: Integrating LINQ into the database curriculum. In *Proceedings of the 42nd ACM Technical Symposium on Computer Science Education*, SIGCSE '11, pages 293–298, New York, NY, USA, 2011. ACM. ISBN 978-1-4503-0500-6. doi: 10.1145/1953163.1953251. URL https://doi.acm.org/10.1145/1953163.1953251.

S. W. Dietrich and S. D. Urban. *Fundamentals of Object Databases: Object-Oriented and Object-Relational Design*. Synthesis Lectures on Data Management. Morgan & Claypool Publishers, 2010. doi: 10.2200/S00315ED1V01Y201012DTM012. URL https://doi.org/10.2200/S00315ED1V01Y201012DTM012.

A. Eisenberg and J. Melton. Advancements in SQL/XML. *SIGMOD Rec.*, 33(3):79–86, September 2004. ISSN 0163-5808. doi: 10.1145/1031570.1031588. URL https://doi.org/10.1145/1031570.1031588.

K. P. Eswaran, J. N. Gray, R. A. Lorie, and I. L. Traiger. The notions of consistency and predicate locks in a database system. *Commun. ACM*, 19(11):624–633, November 1976. ISSN 0001-0782. doi: 10.1145/360363.360369. URL https://doi.org/10.1145/360363.360369.

G. C. Everest. Basic data structure models explained with a common example. In *Proceedings of the Fifth Texas Conference on Computing Systems*, pages 39–46, Austin, TX, 1976. IEEE Computer Society Publications Office.

J. N. Gray, R. A. Lorie, and G. R. Putzolu. Granularity of locks in a shared data base. In *Proceedings of the First International Conference on Very Large Data Bases*, VLDB '75, pages 428–451, New York, NY, USA, 1975. Association for Computing Machinery. ISBN 9781450339209. doi: 10.1145/1282480.1282513. URL https://doi.org/10.1145/1282480.1282513.

J. Gray. The transaction concept: Virtues and limitations (invited paper). In *Proceedings of the Seventh International Conference on Very Large Data Bases–Volume 7*, VLDB '81, pages 144–154. VLDB Endowment, 1981.

T. Haerder and A. Reuter. Principles of transaction-oriented database recovery. *ACM Comput. Surv.*, 15(4):287–317, December 1983. ISSN 0360-0300. doi: 10.1145/289.291. URL https://doi.org/10.1145/289.291.

M. Lacroix and A. Pirotte. Domain-oriented relational languages. In *Database Systems*, pages 370–378, January 1977.

P. M. Lewis, A. Bernstein, and M. Kifer. *Databases and Transaction Processing: An Application-Oriented Approach*. Pearson, 2002. ISBN 9780321185570.

D. Maier. *Theory of Relational Databases*. Computer Science Press, New York, NY, USA, 1983. ISBN 0914894420.

M. Murray. Database security: What students need to know. *J. Inf. Technol. Educ.: Innov. Pract.*, 9, January 2010. doi: 10.28945/1132.

P. A. Ng. Further analysis of the entity-relationship approach to database design. *IEEE Trans. Softw. Eng.*, SE-7: 85–99, 1981.

Oracle. Mysql workbench, 2021. URL https://www.mysql.com/products/workbench/.

J. Ortiz, S. W. Dietrich, and M. B. Chaudhari. Learning from database performance benchmarks. *J. Comput. Sci. Coll.*, 27(4):151–158, April 2012. ISSN 1937-4771.

R. Ramakrishnan and J. Ullman. A survey of deductive database systems. *J. Logic Program.*, 23:125–149, May 1995. doi: 10.1016/0743-1066(94)00039-9.

D. P. Reed. Implementing atomic actions on decentralized data. *ACM Trans. Comput. Syst.*, 1(1):3–23, February 1983. ISSN 0734-2071. doi: 10.1145/357353.357355. URL https://doi.org/10.1145/357353.357355.

J. Rumbaugh, I. Jacobson, and G. Booch. *Unified Modeling Language Reference Manual, 2nd ed.* Pearson Higher Education, 2004. ISBN 0321245628.

T. J. Teorey, D. Yang, and J. P. Fry. A logical design methodology for relational databases using the extended entity-relationship model. *ACM Comput. Surv.*, 18(2):197–222, June 1986. ISSN 0360-0300. doi: 10.1145/7474.7475. URL https://doi.acm.org/10.1145/7474.7475.

Transaction Processing Performance Council. TPC Benchmark H, 2021. URL http://www.tpc.org/tpch/.

J. D. Ullman. *Principles of Database and Knowledge-Base Systems, Volume I.* Computer Science Press, Inc., New York, NY, USA, 1988. ISBN 0-88175-188-X.

J. D. Ullman. *Principles of Database and Knowledge-Base Systems: Volume II: The New Technologies.* W. H. Freeman & Co., New York, NY, USA, 1990. ISBN 071678162X.

P. Walmsley. *Definitive XML Schema, 2nd ed.* Pearson, Upper Saddle River, NJ, USA, 2013.

# INDEX

**A**

ACID properties, *see* transaction, ACID properties
anomaly, 249
  delete, 250
  insert, 250
  update, 249
atomicity, *see* transaction, ACID properties

**C**

call-level interface, 5, 173
candidate key
  definition, 9
  determination, 253–255
  ER diagram, 22
  functional dependencies, 253
  lossless-join, 257
  mapping ER to relations, 29–30
  normal forms (2NF), 261
  normal forms (3NF), 261–262
  relational schema, 9
  unique constraint, 14
  universal relation, 260
concurrency control, 2, 230–241
  locking, *see* locking
  timestamps, *see* timestamps
consistency, *see* transaction, ACID properties
COURSE SCHEDULE
  description, 16
  *Practice Problems
    Chapter 1, 16–17
Crow's Foot notation, 34–35

**D**

data and models, 3–6
  conceptual, 4
  hierarchical, 3–4
  JSON, 6
  network, 3–4
  object-oriented, 4
  relational, 3–4
  XML, 6

decomposition, 255–261
  definition, 255
  dependency preserving, 250, 256–257
  functional dependencies, 250, 255–256
  lossless-join, 250, 257–261
    pairwise, 257–258
    schema, 259–261
denormalization, 264
dependency preserving, *see* decomposition,
    dependency preserving
Document Type Definition (DTD),
    199–202
  external declaration, 199
  internal declaration, 199
  keywords
    ATTLIST, 200
    CDATA, 201
    DOCTYPE, 199
    ELEMENT, 199
    FIXED, 200
    ID, 201
    IDREF, 201
    IDREFS, 201
    IMPLIED, 200
    PCDATA, 199
    REQUIRED, 200
  occurrence constraints, 199–200
DRC, *see* relational calculus, DRC
durability, *see* transaction, ACID properties

**E**

EMPLOYEE TRAINING
  Crow's Foot Notation, 35
  description, 21–22
  ER diagram, 25
  ER diagram with (min, max) pairs, 27
  schema, 32
    dependency preserving, 265
    functional dependencies, 265
    lossless-join, 265

EMPLOYEE TRAINING (*contd.*)
  UML diagram, 34
  visual schema, 33
Entity-Relationship (ER) diagrams
  attribute, 22
    composite, 22
    key, 22
    multivalued, 22
  cardinality ratio, 23
  entity, 22
    strong, 24
    weak, 24
  mapping to relations, 29–33
  (min, max) pairs, 26
  participation constraint, 23
  relationship, 23
    identifying, 24
    recursive, 26
    ternary, 27–28

**F**
foreign key
  composite, 11
    example, 11
  definition, 10
  mapping ER to relations, 30
  referential integrity, 10–13
  SQL, 152–153
  visual schema, 11, 32
functional dependencies, 250–255
  attribute closure, 252–253
  candidate key, 253–255
  definition, 251
  inference rules, 251–252
  minimal set, 253
  superkey, 250–251
  trivial, 251

**G**
GRADEBOOK
  ER diagram, 40

**I**
INVESTMENT PORTFOLIO
  description, 36–37
  entity summary, 43
  ER diagram, 42
  relationship summary, 43

  schema, 43
  visual schema, 44
  *Practice Problems
    Chapter 2, 36–37
    Chapter 3, 69–70
    Chapter 4, 98–99
    Chapter 5, 136–137
    Chapter 6, 163–165
    Chapter 7, 182
    Chapter 10, 267
isolation, *see* transaction, ACID properties

**J**
Java and JDBC, 174–177
  CallableStatement, 176
  Connection, 175
  PreparedStatement, 176
  Statement, 175

**L**
locking, 233–237
  2PL, 235
    consistency, 235
    isolation, 235–236
  deadlock, 237
  exclusive (write) lock, 234
  livelock, 237
  shared (read) lock, 233, 234
  well-formed, 234
lossless-join, *see* decomposition, lossless-join

**M**
MLS
  description, 16
  *Practice Problems
    Chapter 1, 16

**N**
NEW HOME
  description, 37–38
  entity summary, 45
  ER diagram, 45
  relationship summary, 46
  schema, 46
  visual schema, 47
  *Practice Problems
    Chapter 2, 37–38
    Chapter 3, 70

Chapter 4, 99
Chapter 5, 137
Chapter 6, 165
Chapter 7, 182–183
Chapter 10, 267
normal forms, 250, 261–265
1NF, 261
2NF, 261
3NF, 261–262
BCNF, 262
normalization, 262
BCNF Decomposition, 262–264
lossless-join, 263

**O**

ONLINE RETAILER
abstract instance, 13
description, 11
referential integrity, 12
schema, 11
visual schema, 12
XML
data exchange, 212–213
structure, 212
*Practice Problems
Chapter 8, 216

**P**

persistent stored modules,
170–173
precedence graph, 231–233
primary key
composite, 11
example, 11
definition, 9
mapping ER to relations, 29–31
not null, 9
referential integrity, 10–13
SQL, 152–153
visual schema, 11, 32
Python and DB-API, 178–180
callproc, 179
connect, 178
cursor, 178
execute, 178

**Q**

query, 2

**R**

recovery control, 2, 228–229
checkpoint, 229
constrained write assumption, 229
deferred update, 229
immediate update, 229
REDO, 229
system log, 228
UNDO, 229
relational algebra
assignment (:=), 55, 61
operators
Cartesian product ($\times$), 59
difference ($-$), 57–58
division ($\div$), 60–61
intersection ($\cap$), 57–58
join ($\bowtie_\theta$), 59
natural join ($\bowtie$), 59–60
projection ($\pi$), 55–57
selection ($\sigma$), 55–57
union ($\cup$), 57–58
query optimization, 64–67
rename attributes, 55, 63
WinRDBI, A-2–A-3
relational calculus
DRC
anonymous variable (_), 88
atoms and formula, 93–94
division, 91–93
fundamental query expression, 88
quantification, 90–91
relationally complete, 94–95
variables, 88
WinRDBI, A-3–A-4
safety, 97
TRC
atoms and formula, 84–85
division, 82–84
fundamental query expression, 80
quantification, 81–82
relationally complete, 85–87
variables, 80
WinRDBI, A-4
relational data model, 7–14
candidate key, 9
constraints, 13–14
check, 14
not null, 14

relational data model (*contd.*)
    primary key, 9
    referential integrity, 9–10
    unique, 14
  foreign key, 10
  null value, 7
  primary key, 9
  referential integrity, 9–10
  schema, 7
  superkey, 9
  visual schema, 11
relationally complete, 62
  DRC, 94
  SQL, 131
  TRC, 85

**S**

safety
  relational calculus, 97
  SQL, 134
schedule, 230
  concurrent, 231
  serial, 231
  serializable, 231
serializability, 231
SQL
  aggregation, 126–128
  all, 124, 132
  alter table, 154–155
  avg, 126
  check, 153
  count, 126
    distinct, 126–127
    null values, 129
  create table, 152–153
    constraints, 153
  create view, 156
  delete, 159–160
  distinct, 114
  division, 133–134
  drop table, 153–154
    cascade, 154
    restrict, 154
  except, 124
  exists, 122
  foreign key, 153
  grant, 160–161

  group by, 127–128
  having, 128
  in, 122
  insert into, 157–158
  intersect, 124
  is, 129
  join, 120
  max, 126
  min, 126
  natural join, 120–121
  nested queries, 122–123
  null values, 129–131
  order by, 117
  outer join, 129–130
  primary key, 153
  query optimization, 123–124
  references, 153
  reflection queries, 118
  relational algebra equivalence, 114
  relationally complete, 131
  renaming attributes (as), 116, 126
  revoke, 161
  safety, 134
  sum, 126
  table aliases, 115
  TRC, 115
  union, 124
  unique, 153
  update, 158–159
  views, 124
  WinRDBI, A-4
SQL injection, 174, 176, 179
stored functions, 172–173
stored procedures, 171–172
superkey
  attribute closure, 252
  BCNF Decomposition, 262–264
  definition, 9
  functional dependencies, 250–251
  normal forms (3NF), 261–262
  normal forms (BCNF), 262

**T**

timestamp, 238
timestamps, 238–241
  basic timestamp protocol, 238
  consistency, 239

deadlock, 238
isolation, 239
livelock, 238
transaction
    ACID properties, 225
        atomicity, 225, 226
        consistency, 225, 227
        durability, 225, 228
        isolation, 225, 227
    definition, 225
transaction management
    concurrency control, *see* concurrency
        control
    recovery control, *see* recovery control
TRC, *see* relational calculus, TRC
Two-Phase Locking (2PL), *see* locking, 2PL

**U**
Unified Modeling Language (UML)
    class diagrams, 34

**W**
WAREHOUSE
    ER diagram, 39
WEB PAGE
    description, 38
    entity summary, 48
    ER diagram, 48
    relationship summary, 49
    schema, 49
    visual schema, 49
    *Practice Problems
        Chapter 2, 38
        Chapter 3, 70–71
        Chapter 4, 100
        Chapter 5, 138
        Chapter 6, 165–166
        Chapter 7, 183–184
        Chapter 10, 268
WinRDBI, A-1–A-5
    DRC, A-3
    graphical user interface, A-2
    implementation overview, A-5
    intermediate tables, A-2
    relational algebra, A-2–A-3
    SQL, A-4
    TRC, A-4

**X**
XML
    attribute, 197
    CDATA section, 201
    comment, 197
    data exchange, 211–213
    element, 197
    empty element, 197–198
    tag, 196
    valid, 198
    well-formed, 198
XML Schema, 203–211
    anonymous declarations, 204
    attribute values
        optional, 208
        required, 208
        unbounded, 207
    attributes
        base, 204–205, 208–209
        default, 208
        fixed, 208
        maxOccurs, 207
        minOccurs, 207
        name, 204
        ref, 207
        type, 204
        use, 208
    built-in types
        boolean, 204
        date, 204
        decimal, 204
        float, 204
        ID, 209
        IDREF, 209
        IDREFS, 209
        integer, 204
        nonnegativeInteger, 207
        string, 204
        time, 204
    complex types, 206–210
    elements
        annotation, 203
        appinfo, 203
        attribute, 204
        choice, 206
        complexContent, 208
        complexType, 206

XML Schema (*contd.*)
  documentation, 203
  element, 204
  enumeration, 205
  extension, 208
  fractionDigits, 205
  length, 205
  maxExclusive, 205
  maxInclusive, 204
  maxLength, 205
  minExclusive, 204
  minInclusive, 204
  minLength, 205
  pattern, 205
  restriction, 204–205
  schema, 203
  sequence, 206
  simpleContent, 207
  simpleType, 204
  totalDigits, 205
empty elements, 208–209
global declarations, 204
local declarations, 204
namespaces, 203
occurrence constraints, 207
simple types, 204–205